105 Five-Minute Plays
for Study and Performance

105 FIVE-MINUTE PLAYS
FOR STUDY AND PERFORMANCE

EDITED BY
JOHN CAPECCI AND IRENE ZIEGLER

SMITH AND KRAUS PUBLISHERS 2017

ISBN: 9781575259109

ISSN: 2016959961

Typesetting and layout by Elizabeth Monteleone

Cover by Olivia F. Monteleone

A Smith and Kraus book

177 Lyme Road, Hanover, NH 03755

Editorial 603.643.6431 To Order 1.877.668.8680

www.smithandkraus.com

Printed in the United States of America

To Bruce C. Miller, who in his forty-one years as Artistic Director of Virginia Repertory Theatre (formerly Theatre IV), inspired and launched the careers of countless theatre artists, wrote and produced hundreds of plays, musicals, and live events, and —perhaps more than any individual since 1975—enriched the cultural landscape of the city of Richmond, VA, making it destination and home to a diverse population of theatre lovers.

Contents

INTRODUCTION

Time is no match for the playwright's pen.

The popularity of the ten-minute play has proven that. From Louisville to Edinburgh to Seoul and beyond, writers of ten-minute plays have shown the enormous range of what can happen on stage in just a few minutes.

But…a five-minute play?

Is there such a thing? How short can a play be before it ceases to be a play and becomes something, well, less satisfying…such as a scene, skit or sketch?

We had those questions in mind as we set out—on publisher Eric Kraus' suggestion—to compile this collection. We asked playwrights to submit works that clocked in at five minutes or less and possessed the general features of a play: a narrative thread from beginning to end, a sense of dramatic struggle, vivid characters and emotional impact. We favored those with minimal sets and no more than five characters, expecting that a collection of five-minute plays would be particularly useful in the classroom.

What we didn't expect was more than 700 submissions. Clearly, the five-minute play is alive and ticking.

While many of the submitted works were more like scenes than plays, far more presented rich, complete worlds that were alternately lyrical, narrative, concrete and abstract. Some packed a wallop with powerful images while others used crackling dialogue to quickly establish character and motivation. Some moved at the speed of light. Others froze moments for calm meditation. An inordinate number were about digital technology and social media. Still others presented historic moments, dream states or slapstick absurdity.

We're delighted to share 105 of these gems for you to study and perform. Along with contemporary works by both new and established playwrights, we have included a few historical examples, such as those of the Italian Futurists and an early "playlet" by Thornton Wilder. (*The Marriage We Deplore* may seem long-ish, but the fact that Wilder used a "five-minute/ five-person" design may indicate how rapid-fire he intended the dialogue to fly in this drawing-room comedy.)

To get you started, here are five questions for study and five tips for performance. So set your timer: Go!

FIVE QUESTIONS FOR STUDY

1. Is the five-minute play further proof of our shrinking atten- tion spans? In the 1890s, many people wondered the same thing about another newfangled art form—the short story. The popularity of brief art forms historically has been linked to the speedy pace of contemporary life and the public's per- ceived need for a "quick fix." Valid claim? Or is it a subtle slam against short works as "common," less serious fare compared to weighty, longer works?

2. Is there something inherently radical about the five-minute play? Artists often use non-traditional forms to challenge the status quo, and short plays are no exception. The Italian Fu- turists of the early twentieth century, renounced everything old in politics and art with claims such as, "It's stupid to write one hundred pages where one would do." Brief perfor- mance art of the 1960s aimed at shocking and interrogating audiences. The Neo-Futurists, a contemporary experimental theatre company presents populist, affordable entertainment in the form of 30 plays in 60 minutes.

3. What should we call these things? Are we comfortable refer- ring to these brief acts as plays? Or would it be better to use one of the many names given to very short theatre pieces over the years: skit, scene, sketch, curtain-raiser, vaudeville, playlet, stunt, fill-in, playette, blackout, sintesi, pint-size play, flash drama, micro-drama…

4. Is this some kind of a joke? One thing was clear to us after reading more than 700 five-minute plays: the form lends itself to humor. Many of the plays read as late-night TV sketches or sitcom scenes; others employed word-play,

105 Five-Minute Plays

farce, satire, parody and gallows humor. Very many play-wrights employed the "gotcha" ending, introducing a surprise switch-up that served as a rim-shot punchline. (We've included a few masterful examples in this collection.) Fast is funny; so perhaps it's pace, not length, that makes the five-minute form good for a laugh.

5. Can five-minute plays survive? Yes, if they stick together. Like other miniatures, five-minute plays are best when they're gathered and offered en masse to bounce off or converse with one another, or make collective statements. The Italian Futurists featured their short acts in evenings of variety theatre, the Dadaists in their cabaret soireé. Today, five-minute play festivals are popping up in New York, San Francisco, Austin, London, Edinburgh and elsewhere. Apparently, it was just a matter of time.

FIVE TIPS FOR PERFORMANCE

1. Be bold. Five minutes is not long. But it'll feel like it if the first ten seconds are filled with something other than strong performance choices. If the audience senses some sort of urgency, even if subtextual, they'll hang with you from the start—even if the play's payoff doesn't come for another four minutes and thirty seconds.

2. Be active. Whether the five-minute play is conventional or abstract, your obligation as a performer remains to make active choices that answer two questions: What does my character want, and how does he or she go after it? Let those motivations inform your choices and those five-minutes will romp.

3. Raise the stakes. Many of the plays featured in this collection have deep emotional content and/or high stakes. Whenever possible, raise those stakes and challenge your characters further. Five-minute plays compress emotion and action into crystalline nuggets. It is not enough that a character wants something—he must want it so badly that even the thought of failure is unbearable. Even if the play seems less intense than this, create the challenge anyway. Strong

choices open avenues to new interpretations.

4. Stay in the now. With just 300 seconds at hand, immediacy
    is everything. Why is this story occurring right now? What
    are the characters discovering right now? How is this day
    different from any other day? What cracks open in the few
    minutes your characters are on stage? Make choices that
    show them discovering rather than informing, being rather
    than describing. In other words, show rather than tell.

5. Honor theatricality. Even if naturalistic, memorable perfor-
    mances require theatricality. It's what sets plays apart from
    other media. Plays take advantage of the "all-live" element
    unique to the genre. How is this five-minute play theatri-
    cal? How can your performance of it enhance this defining
    element? Why is seeing this live more exciting than seeing
    it on film? Identify that, and you'll share the most gloriously
    shocking, intoxicating, upsetting, invigorating or challeng-
    ing five minutes of theatre anyone can experience.

John Capecci and Irene Ziegler

Special thanks to Carol Boynton at Smith and Kraus
Publishers for so ably managing the permissions process.

THE PLAYS

Characters:
    LEX: Early thirties, wears a coat and is looking up nearby bars on her cell phone.

    COLT: Early thirties, also wears a coat, but has an umbrella that's closed at the moment.

Setting: A New York City street, sometime around 10 p.m. It's raining hard.

> ANGELA SANTILLO'S work has been performed and developed in New York City, San Francisco, Chicago, and Asheville. She has devised shows in collaboration with performers, designers, choreographers, and directors. She was a finalist for the 2015 Jerome Fellowship and is an Associate Artist at foolsFURY Theater. MFA: Sarah Lawrence College, recipient of the Lipkin Playwriting Award. angelasantillo.com

(LEX and COLT stand under an unseen scaffold. COLT holds a box of macaroons. He picks one and bites into it.)

LEX: Why didn't you tell me they were closed?

COLT: God, this is so good.

LEX: You knew they were closed.

COLT: Who knew you could make a rose-flavored anything. Who thinks of this stuff?

(He hands her the remaining half of his macaroon.)

LEX: I don't remember what flavor I tried.

COLT: And I don't remember what flavors I bought. If you eat it, I'm sure it'll count. And they remodeled Phebe's. It isn't closed.

LEX: It basically is if it's not the same as it was that night.

COLT: It's open and the décor is different. There's nothing closed about it.

(He bites into another macaroon.)

I forgot how amazing these were. Want another one?

LEX: I only ate one on our first date.

COLT: You did?

LEX: My phone was dying, we were standing here, it was pouring, and all the nearby bars were packed. You gave me one half of a macaroon, and then ate the entire box by yourself while I tried to find us a bar but I had to keep hitting the back of my cell phone, cause that was the only way it would turn on.

COLT: Your phone was dying?

LEX: Yes.

COLT: Why didn't I offer you mine?

LEX: You were focused on doing something you loved instead of noticing me. It was the beginning of a trend.

COLT: So, I have to eat all of these by myself?

LEX: Yep.

(He bites into another one.)

LEX: What does Phebe's look like now?

COLT: Gray walls, plants, white crown molding.

LEX: It was a run-down dive with wood walls last year.

COLT: You had a Guinness.

LEX: You had an IPA.

COLT: You put your hair up cause of the rain.

LEX: After you finished your macaroons, we got a cab, and I joked that I smelled like a wet dog, cause my pea coat was soaked. You agreed. I was hurt by that.

COLT: Would you like me to apologize for that, too?

LEX: That's not why I said it.

COLT: I'm sorry.

LEX: I don't want you to be sorry for that.

COLT: Well let me know; we're almost at our end. Get all your sorrys while you can.

LEX: Do you want to end it here?

COLT: No.

LEX: Cause closure isn't worth it if you're going to give me attitude all night.

COLT: You said you wanted us to end exactly how we started.

LEX: You didn't have to say yes to this.

COLT: I told you I think it's a good idea that our last date be exactly like our first. You're not the only one who needs closure.

LEX: I can't even remember what we talked about at that bar.

COLT: We shouldn't find a new place. Phebe's was renovated and hell, you can say we've been renovated.

LEX: Yeah, in a little over a year, I fell in love with you, and you fell for my editing skills.

COLT: I said I appreciated you for reading my work.

LEX: Every woman's fantasy.

COLT: Christ.

(He bites into another macaroon.)

LEX: "I appreciate you for reading my work." That's what you said when I told you I've never felt this way about anyone, which is so cliché!

COLT: I'm sorry!

LEX: You could have said you liked any little thing about me, but you made it about your work and your future.

LEX: And I never fell for your words. I fell for your arrogant conversation starters, nervous ticks, strange politics, incandescent smile, sweet tooth, arm tattoos, head bang driving, hot audacity, brick wall body, and the ease that you put into me.

COLT: And I never fell for your editing abilities. My script sold, I have to move and you won't move and you don't see me getting angry about that. I should have said something else, anything else. But this is the opportunity of a lifetime and you're not enough to make me say no to my dreams.

COLT: Let me take you to Phebe's and buy you a drink. We'll talk about something else.

LEX: What else is there to talk about?

COLT: We'll find a topic. Then I'll walk you to the subway, and we'll wait at the platform.

LEX: You'll get too close to my face.

COLT: Then we'll get on the train, I'll get off at 42nd Street while you stay in your seat. There'll be no kiss or hug or handshake. I'll watch the train pull away and worry that I blew it, and walk home wondering what it would be like if I didn't get off when I did.

LEX: At least it's raining. You can't recreate eating macaroons in the rain without the rain. You could stay on the train with me if you wanted.

COLT: I need a drink.

(He opens his umbrella and exits.)

LEX: You didn't have an umbrella the night we met.

(From offstage, he throws the umbrella towards her. She doesn't try to catch it. She follows him and exits.)

Characters:

MARIA: Louis' wife, late twenties/early thirties.

LOUIS: Maria's husband, late twenties/early thirties.

ESME: Louis and Maria's daughter, early twenties.

Setting: Louis and Maria's living room, night.

DAVID L. WILLIAMS is a graduate of the theatre department of Cornell University, where he was a four time award recipient in the Heerman's-McCalmon Playwriting contest, and recently received his MFA in playwriting from the University of Nebraska. He has written more than twenty-five plays and musicals, and his work has been produced across the United States and internationally in Italy, Canada, Denmark, Norway, and Australia. His most recent production was the world premiere of his full-length play, The Starving, at Barter Theatre. He lives in Bellefonte, PA with his wonderful wife, Kathleen and his amazing son, Samuel. playwrightdavid.com

(Lights up on a living room. ESME is there, speaking with MARIA & LOUIS.)

ESME: You need to give him to me.

MARIA: Now, slow down. Look, it's clear you're impassioned about something and probably a little confused.

LOUIS: Probably?

MARIA: And we can get you some help. I mean, that's all you're asking for, right? You want some help.

ESME: No. I want you to give him to me.

LOUIS: We're not just going to give you our child.

ESME: I'm your child, too. He'll be safe with me.

MARIA: You keep saying that.

ESME: Because it's true. I'm your daughter.

LOUIS: Our daughter is asleep in there. Our daughter is five... Nothing to say to that?

ESME: The future is different. This is what I become. And the people I'm with, they sent me back for Max.

MARIA: Is he in danger?

ESME: There's a lot of danger.

LOUIS: She's not—you're not actually buying this, are you?

ESME: I'm telling the truth.

LOUIS: Prove it.

MARIA: Yes. If you're really Esme, tell us what's written in your diary.

LOUIS: If she broke in tonight, she could've broken in last night and read—

ESME: I used my key. I still had it on my key ring, not that it would do much good where I'm from.

MARIA: What happened to our house? ...Esme?

LOUIS: That's not her name.

ESME: It's gone. This whole block is gone.

LOUIS:(*Getting out his phone.*) All right, that's enough. If you don't leave, I'm calling the police.

ESME: You read me the Little House books at night and you call me half-pint. You sing me songs from South Park with the lyrics cleaned up as lullabies. When you call Mom from work you tell her to give me a kiss on each of my fingers just from you. Ask me anything you want, I'll tell you... They sent me to get him. Bad shit's happening.

MARIA: *(Absently)* Don't swear, sweetie.

ESME: It's really good to see you both. You have no idea.

MARIA: Why? Do you not visit us much, or—?

LOUIS: So, this is like *The Terminator* or something? You're protecting your brother?

ESME: No robots, but yes, if that makes it clearer, there's a resistance and they want me to bring Max back.

MARIA: You understand this isn't easy for us.

ESME: I wouldn't believe it if I hadn't seen it myself. But this is really important. And look, I go, I come back, it'll be seconds for you guys. It'll be a while for me, but no time for you. I know it seems crazy, but—

MARIA: *I'll* go.

> *(Off ESME's reaction.)*

I'll go with you. I'll take care of Max, make sure I never let him out of my sight, and we'll come back safe and sound here.

ESME: That won't work.

LOUIS: I think that's the best solution to all of this.

ESME: It's not...Max isn't coming back, Dad.

LOUIS: Why not? If he's the solution to all of this, then why can't he come back?

ESME: He's not the solution. Max is the problem.

MARIA: He can't be. He's a sweet little baby.

ESME: He kills you. He kills you, too. He puts me in jail for three years until I escape.

LOUIS: Why would he...?

ESME: You don't understand what the future's like.

MARIA: So you want to kill him?

ESME: We have to. Or else it's all destroyed.

MARIA: What is—?

ESME: I can't stop now. I don't have time to answer all of this.

LOUIS: I thought you had all kinds of time.

MARIA: We'll talk to him, sweetie. We'll make sure he's / the best person he can be.

ESME: That's not gonna work.

MARIA: We won't yell or allow him to—

ESME: That's not gonna work, Mom!

LOUIS: You don't know that.

ESME: I know what he's done. It's not upbringing. There's something wrong with him. He kills millions of people. You hear me? Millions.

LOUIS: *(Quietly)* Oh God.

ESME: Let me take him.

LOUIS: If you have to do it, why didn't you just do it here, or take him without us knowing?

ESME: ...Because I couldn't do that to you. Or him. He's my baby brother.

> *(MARIA gets up and goes to the door to the bedrooms.)*

MARIA: This could all be a lie. This could all be a...there could be a gun to our heads twenty years from now. She could be sent under duress. Max could be the, he could be the one that'll save everybody.

ESME: I wish that were true.

MARIA: I won't let her. I don't care who she says she is. If she wants to get Max, she has to go through me.

ESME: Don't make me do it. So much depends on this.

> *(Silence.)*

Dad, help me. Please?

> *(No response.)*

I'm sorry, Mom.

(SHE pushes MARIA out of the way and exits. We hear a baby crying.)

MARIA: *(Quietly)* Please do something please.

(LOUIS doesn't move. Lights down.)

Characters:

REJ: Middle-aged man, an old boyfriend of Luz, recalls a beloved joke.

LUZ: Middle-aged woman, an old girlfriend of Rej, recalls a disdained joke.

Setting: Now. In a restaurant bar.
Props: Two chairs. A table. A bar. A water glass of chardonnay. A whisky glass of bourbon and coke.
Production Note: I have no idea of the provenance of this parrot joke. I first heard the joke in the middle eighties; it had been around awhile then, so it stands as the definition of an "old joke." This version has my own twists, but the gist and the punch-line remain another, unknown-to-me gag writer's work. I've utilized the joke as a means to reveal both symptom and diagnosis in this failed relationship.

> BYRON HARRIS is an ex-fireman, ex-banker, ex-bosun's mate on a cruise ship, ex-assignment editor at the CNN National Desk (for well over a decade), ex-teacher, and ex-bookseller. He is currently pursuing his M.F.A. in playwriting as a member of the Playwright's Lab at Hollins University. He's had various pieces (short and long) read and produced hither, thither, and thon. www.aetbyrum.com

REJ: We used to tell jokes. All of us. There used to be this national repository of jokes, which everyone somehow accessed. Something would happen in the world and by noon, there were these jokes that would float about. Like this: So Brezhnev dies and Andropov takes over. Someone asks, "Yuri, what if they don't follow you?" Andropov replies, "Then they'll follow Brezhnev." *(Beat.)* Damn, they were funny. My dad used to say there were three old bond traders in New York who would write these things on the fly morning after morning after morning....

LUZ: We used to tell jokes. Jokes about Priests and Rabbis, ducks walking into bars, cats talking to dogs. People used to arm themselves with jokes before going out to parties. One needed two or three polite, but edgy jokes to get through the evening. And a dirty joke or two helped. It was a social lubricant. Now we recycle sitcom one-liners or quote Monty Python.

(REJ rises and paces about.)

REJ: I think the internet killed the thing. If one can surf the internet, then the boredom factor lessens. Less creativity that way. Screens, screens, and more screens. Jokes as cultural markers went the way of the dodo—along with camera stores, travel agencies, booksellers.

LUZ: Jokes took weird turns. Like Helen Keller jokes. Why is it OK to tell a Helen Keller joke? Well, she can't hear them. Get it—she's deaf. Blind and deaf. Not to mention dead. *(Beat.)* It was like the racist, ethnic jokes went out, at least in proper society, but these just plain, mean jokes came in. Don't get me started on dead baby jokes. We went from evil to mean in one fell swoop.

REJ: I used to tell this joke. My parrot tale. It became my signature joke. I liked it because, well I liked telling it. And sometimes people got it and sometimes people didn't. There was always this mystery—would they get it?

LUZ: I had this boyfriend, back in college. He had this one bird
joke he just had to tell. He told it to my Mom, told it my
Dad, my friends and his, at keg parties, at dinner parties,
at the beach, in the mountains, in nightclubs and loud bars.
It was his joke. His tale. And the thing is, the damn thing
wasn't funny. Not one bit. Not at all.

*(REJ climbs on his chair, one foot on the chair and the
other on the bar. He waves his drink about as he starts
telling his joke with great enthusiasm and animation.)*

REJ: So here's how it goes. There's this guy named Lars who
really wanted a parrot. So he goes from pet shop to pet shop
looking for a parrot, any parrot. And wouldn't you know it!
Nobody has one! So he's about to give up when he spies this
ratty storefront in the last strip mall in town. And the clerk
says he's got one left, brings it out and it's a gorgeous mix
of orange and green. But this clerk he leans in and warns
him. "This is a pretty bird all right, great coloring yes. But
I need to tell you, this parrot has a bad habit. He cusses up
a storm. Terrible, foul words spew out from that beak. But I
tell you parrots are smart animals. They can learn. So you'll
need to train it up properly." Lars really wanted a parrot
remember so he goes "Fine, fine, I'll take it. This one will
do." The clerk says "Fair Enough, but you've been warned."

*(REJ mimics the clerks action as he recounts the joke.
LUZ looks over her shoulder at REJ as he starts in, as if
remembering in her mind's eye his rendition of the joke.)*

LUZ: This goof I dated, he told it over and over again. And it
kept getting longer. He inserted mild puns, invented back-
stories for the clerk and the guy buying the parrot, even
named him. I can't remember the name, but it was off-kilter.
And he kept looping in odd details.

REJ: True to the clerk's warning, every word out of this bird's
mouth was profane, mean, nasty. Like to make a sailor
blush. Lars tried and tried to adjust this bird's words. He'd
hear the cussing and cover the birdcage with a blanket. He'd
tried to speak extra polite at all times. He'd play fusion jazz,
Gary Burton on the vibraphone or Bill Chase on the trum-
pet. Lars even brought in his neighbor's parrot who liked to

---

sing Disney songs. Zippity. Doo. Dah.

(REJ drinks from his glass. LUZ looks around the audience.)

LUZ: The thing was, with that much build-up, he'd get people leaning in, ready for this killer punch line. This massive display of wit and cleverness. They waited for that big laugh.

(REJ flaps about imitating Lars and bird. LUZ sips wine, eyeballs the joker standing on the bar.)

REJ: Finally, Lars just had enough and started yelling at the parrot. Ripped him a new one. Called it every name in the book and then some. And the parrot gave it right back as good as it got. Lars shook the cage and the parrot just got madder and even more cussed. Lars, in complete and utter desperation, threw up his hands, grabbed the bird right out of that cage and threw him in the freezer. There was the expected squawking. *(Beat.)* And then dead silence. Not a sound came out.

LUZ: I think he enjoyed the power the story gave him. Elongated those pauses. People are too polite to interrupt a joke even a bad one, badly told. For two really lo-o-ong minutes, he had control over everyone. All of us, even me, melting into the carpet, looking away.

REJ: After two minutes, Lars opened the door to the freezer. The parrot calmly walked out onto Lars's arm and said "Lars, I believe I may have offended you with my nasty and ill-considered language. I'm sincerely repentant of my inappropriate actions and I fully intend to do everything I can to correct my incorrigible behavior."

(REJ takes a long swig from his glass.)

LUZ: I broke up with him for a thousand reasons. I mean ten thousand reasons. I mean a million reasons. The job at the bank, the wreck where he just had to lurch out into traffic, the broken toilet seat, that night with on the deck with the Olsen's, the toast he gave at that rehearsal dinner, running up on top of Mary's car. I could go on and on....

(Pause.)

I broke up with him for one reason, for just one reason really. I hated that joke, he knew I hated that joke. I asked him

not to tell the joke, begged him even. I couldn't decide what
was worse? That he didn't understand I really hated the joke
or that he did. He just kept on telling that joke. Everywhere.
To. Everyone.

REJ: Lars's jaw dropped at the parrot's sudden shift. But just
then, the bird leaned in and said ever so softly, "Before I
give up all I love, the one thing that gives my pathetic life
joy and purpose. Lars, can I ask you one question?" And
Lars said, "Sure."

(Pause. REJ speaks punch line in stage whisper.)

REJ: The parrot then said, "May I ask what the turkey did?"

(LUZ climbs up on her chair.)

LUZ: *(Shouting.)* May I ask what the turkey did?

REJ: *(Still a stage whisper.)* May I ask what the turkey did?

LUZ: *(Still shouting.)* May I ask what the turkey did?

*(Pause. Luz climbs down from her chair, but remains
standing. She speaks in a calm, despairing voice.)*

LUZ: Told that joke ten times a week for six months. *(Beat.)* Or
so it seemed. *(Beat.)* To me.

*(REJ climbs down from the bar/chair. Remains standing.
He no longer shouts, just snickers.)*

REJ: May I ask what the turkey did? Get it. I love that line. It's
like a litmus test for people. There are the people that get it
and laugh, and the people that don't and don't.

LUZ: So it got to the point that he'd deliver that last line and
walk away. Not even bother to see whether folks laughed or
not. It was all about him. All about him and his stupid joke.

REJ: Me, I relate to the parrot. Some folks got things to say,
things that need saying and the world just won't listen.
Blind, deaf, and dumb. I got things to say, I do. *(Beat.)* I
had this girlfriend once. She didn't get it. She'd stand there
as I started the gag. Just tried to stare me down. Willed me
to flub it or stone-faced anyone who grinned. God forbid if
somebody laughed. She was a murderer that one, a serial
joke-killer through and through.

LUZ: Whoever wrote that joke shot an arrow in the air that landed flat dab through us. Whoever told him that joke changed

his life. And mine. Whatever possessed him to keep on with the joke? Well that was that. Can you imagine spending your life in a freezer with a turkey? Not me. One day, he told his joke and did his walk-away thing and I walked away too.

(LUZ walks fast, speaks over her shoulder, exits the room saying...)

LUZ: Just another direction.

REJ: One day I broke up a room. I mean tore it down. I looked up and she was gone. Never saw her again. *(Beat.)* May I ask what the turkey did? Ha!

(REJ drains his whiskey, then slowly lumbers out of bar.)

FADE TO BLACK

Characters:
CELIA

CEDRIC

Setting: A woman sits at a table, writing primly in her diary.

> JENNIFER LE BLANC has adapted *Jane Austen's Persuasion,* which received its world premiere at San Jose Stage Company; Defoe's *Moll Flanders,* which received its world premiere at Pacific Repertory Theatre; and *We Made Bread,* which was adapted from interviews as a commission for the Arabian Shakespeare Festival. She is a frequent contributor of original short plays for Shotz SF. She is working on a new play, *Winter Storm Perpetual,* as a commission for Cerimon House. She received her MFA from the National Theatre Conservatory and her BA in English Literature from U.C. Berkeley. *A Very British Love Scene* is one of the hundreds of plays written and performed as part of SHOTZ, a "theatrical pressure cooker" that presents all-new short plays each month. jenniferleblanc.com

A man enters.

CEDRIC: Good heavens, I do apologize, I did not mean to interrupt your—

CELIA: Oh, really, I'm only too glad to have a visit from you, won't you please sit down, Mr. Fielding?

CEDRIC: Ms. Primgrass, I beg you to call me Cedric.

CELIA: Do you think it quite right?

CEDRIC: We have known one another since infancy, after all, and there are few I consider nearer, and if I may say, dearer to my heart.

CELIA: Really, Cedric, your effusiveness overwhelms me.

Silence.

CEDRIC: Capital weather, eh?

CELIA: Indubitably.

Silence.

Cedric, might I take leave to observe, if it's not too terribly impertinent, that your entrance onto the balcony seemed to indicate some, well, shall we say, urgency with regards to a possible, and I'm merely speculating, of course, topic of—if I may— conversation?

CEDRIC: Quite right. Quite right, of course. You're so delightfully and arrestingly observant, Ms. Primgrass. Right. Erm. Look, I'm crap at this; will you marry me or what?

CELIA: Good heavens, Cedric!

CEDRIC: Oh, don't good-heavens-Cedric me, Celia, damnit our parents have been plotting this for ages, and we might as well get it over with.

CELIA: Well be still my beating heart, Cedric, that was so romantic. However could I resist you?

CEDRIC: Don't tell me you want to be wooed! Bollocks. Fine. "Dearest Celia, please allow me to tell you how ardently I admire and love—"

CELIA: Bovine Scatology! Beyond the raging plagiarism, I am forced to object on the grounds of grotesque megalomania. Your fortune may be grand, Cedric, but Mr. Fitzwilliam Darcy you are not.

CEDRIC: Well what do you want? Romeo and bloody Juliet? Stupid git Tristan and his dumb as dirt Isolde? Pelleas and Flippin' Melisandre? Daft Dido—

CELIA: I confess, I never would have suspected you were capable of literary allusion. Though the rampant profanity seems right up your proverbial alley.

CEDRIC: Celia, allow me to invite you to shove it up your proverbial—

CELIA: Oh that's just grand. Leave it to you raise the level of discourse to crude euphemism and uncouth wordplay. Really, Cedric, how droll. Is there anything so insufferable as the bandying of pithy witticisms culminating in a quaint turn of phrase that, by its very brevity and dependence on the stereotypes of particular societal mores, provides humor while reinforcing outdated gender norms and ignorant pre-conceived notions about other cultures and eras that we find comically stuffy?

Beat.

Tea?

CEDRIC: Yes, please.

She rings the bell and a butler silently brings in a tea service. Butler begins to pour.

Dear Ms. Primgrass, please permit me the honor of observing how charmingly well you look. That color suits you admirably.

CELIA: Thank you, Mr. Fielding; you flatter me.

The Butler leaves.

CEDRIC: Yes, I bloody well do flatter you; you look like an overstuffed arm chair whose seams burst exposing an indecent ejaculation of lace!

CELIA: Speaking of indecent and ejaculation, how is your dear mother?

CEDRIC: If you begin with my mother, you vitriolic harpy, I shall leave at once!

He crosses to a door.

CELIA: Do spare me your flaccid histrionics, you know as well as I do that door doesn't work. It's nailed shut from the other side. Purely aesthetic.

CEDRIC: A false exit?!

CELIA: One of papa's eccentric theatrical devices.

CEDRIC: How meta.

CELIA: You should see what he did with the fourth wall.

Cedric looks at audience.

CEDRIC: Clever.

CELIA: And functional. It prevents one from shuffling off this mortal coil by leaping off the balcony. The knowledge that paying audience members would only chuck you back up on stage to make you finish out the scene.

CEDRIC: Vermin. For God's sake, don't you have your own lives?

CELIA: Peeping Toms' is what they are. Tawdry voyeurs—

CEDRIC: My dearest Celia, with your sparkling wit and devastating looks it is remarkable that you should have reached this very advanced age without attracting a husband. How is it possible that I should have the luck to find you single?

CELIA: Oh yes, dear me, whatever would I do without a husband? Who would take credit for all my success? Who would occupy my time with critical matters of procreation? And where would I find an outlet for my overwhelming urge to coddle an infantile ego?

CEDRIC: Please give leave that I may rescind my proposal of marriage.

CELIA: Leave most freely given. Thank you. I confess that swallowing lemon-soaked razor blades sounds considerably more appealing than wedded bliss with you.

CEDRIC: It would be unconscionable to prevent you from pursuing your predestined path of bitter lonely spinsterhood surrounded by mountains of romance novels, piles of bon-bon boxes and the choking stench of self-pity, knee-deep in cat hair.

CELIA: They've already announced the banns, haven't they?

CEDRIC: Yes.

CELIA: Bugger.

CEDRIC: Quite. See you on Sunday, then?

CELIA: I'll be the one in white.

> *He begins to leave.*

Thank God it's you, though. You should have seen the other poor bastards they thrust at me. It felt ungentlemanly to "engage in a battle of wits with opponents so clearly unarmed."

CEDRIC: My lady, it is an honor to meet a worthy adversary on the field of love.

> *He kisses her hand. And as a parting shot—*

Particularly when she swings such tantalizing bustle.

> *(She looks furious, until he exits through the working door. Then she smiles glowingly.)*

Characters:

CAL: Inventor, mid-40s, attractive woman

BETTE: Patent attorney, mid-40s, attractive woman

Setting: An afternoon crossing on the Staten Island Ferry–early warm autumn.

ALLAN HAVIS is professor of theatre at UC San Diego since 1988. Over three decades, his work's been produced and commissioned across the U.S. and in Europe, from South Coast Rep and American Repertory Theatre to England's Chichester Festival. Nineteen published plays by Penguin/Mentor, Theatre Communications Group, Broadway Play Publishing, Smith & Kraus, Applause Books. University of Illinois Press published his *American Political Plays.* Southern Illinois University Press published *American Political Plays, Post 9/11.* Harper/Collins published his novel *Albert the Astronomer. Cult Films: Taboo & Transgression*, published by Rowman & Littlefield. Two operas with composer Anthony Davis, *Lilith* and *Lear on the 2nd Floor.*

Recipient of Guggenheim, Rockefeller, Kennedy Center/American Express, CBS, HBO, National Endowment for the Arts Awards & Fellowships, & San Diego Theatre Critics Circle 2003 Outstanding New Play for *Nuevo California* (with Bernardo Solano). He holds a MFA from Yale. allanhavis.com

(CAL approaches BETTE by the rail of the ferry, and stares for a short time before trying to make conversation.)

CAL: When I was a young girl, I was always seasick. I was a tomboy who dressed in overalls and carried tools in my pockets. Sometimes I carried a tool belt and let things dangle. I made a lot of children toys with wood. I pretended my daddy was Geppetto.

(Pause.)

Excuse me?

BETTE: What?

CAL: Am I bothering you?

BETTE: Yes.

CAL: I don't get seasick now. Not on the ferry. I know that you're an attorney. I saw you on television a few weeks ago. On PBS. I have a patent idea.

BETTE: Better that you make an office appointment.

CAL: Please Ms. Waterbury. It is basically a small black box which can enhance the day-to-day experience like iPhone's Siri–except of course this is not a phone and one doesn't need WiFi. I could have filed my own patent with the government, but my home was broken into some months ago, and I worry that the drawings and the model were photographed.

BETTE: Highly unlikely.

CAL: But my friends told me there would be a ton of law suits, and best to start with a legal strategy. My email account was hacked. Someone knows exactly what I'm designing.

(CAL unwraps invention from a crumpled paper bag.)

BETTE: What does your invention do?

CAL: It reduces stress. For professional women only.

BETTE: How?

CAL: May I call you Bette? I hate last names. Surnames are part of the great social lie.

(Takes out box.)

BETTE: Are you bleeding?

CAL: My nose?

BETTE: Yes. Take a few tissues.

CAL: That only happens on windy days. I am so embarrassed.

> *(CAL takes out a tissue and dabs her nose carefully.)*

Of course. Medical opinion is confused about gamma rays. Whereas, I am not. What the gamma ray actually achieves is to find the decorous white lie. The small phrase that is tipped with a dollop of poison. We believe we hear these harmless remarks and shrug them off like summer house flies. But they land. They sting. They add up.

BETTE: You're saying your machine detects conversational lies?

CAL: Ninety-nine per cent, or better. The blue light shines when three or more words ring false.

BETTE: And you think this helps social life? Your box is lighting up.

CAL: It is.

BETTE: I haven't lied, Cal. I think I've seen enough. Thank you. I have to make another phone call. Who are you really?

CAL: Keep it for one week. Take it.

> *(Bette laughs artificially, still holding the box, and adopts a smug air.)*

You'll see the thing really works.

BETTE: And when my clients see the blue light?

CAL: We met before, Bette, two years ago. With Eliza, a party by the ferry landing.

BETTE: I think you're crazy.

CAL: You wore a backless black gown.

BETTE: I don't go to parties.

CAL: Do you see the flashing light?

BETTE: I don't see anything, and you should walk away now.

CAL: You were dancing with Eliza.

BETTE: Who put you up to this?

CAL: When you were a girl, you had five years of piano lessons with a very fat man from Yonkers. He was your father's cousin. You had to give a recital at a church and there was a small church fire. Your older sister Gwen has three children. You never visit Gwen. She calls you twice a year. You loved the Yankees until the city tore down Yankee Stadium. You drink scotch neat. Never alone.

BETTE: What do you want, Cal?

> *(CAL takes out something from her bag wrapped in tissue paper.)*

BETTE: What's that?

CAL: A framed photo. Of you and of me. It doesn't look like me today. I stopped taking injections. But look at my eyes in the photo.

BETTE: Who the hell are you?

CAL: I'm Capricorn. You're Gemini.

> *(Pause.)*

Neither you nor I ever had a horoscope read. We don't believe in astrology, do we?

> *(Pause.)*

We both love commuting by ferry. It's a connection that not many understand. But that's fine. Let them take the subway and bus. The ferry is for us.

> *(Pause.)*

I don't take pills. Neither do you.

> *(Pause.)*

I've only fallen in love twice in my life. Once when I was seventeen.

> *(Pause.)*

You fell in love a year or two before that. And you got pregnant.

> *(Pause.)*

Or you thought you got pregnant but had a miscarriage?

BETTE: Are you a hemophiliac?

CAL: You once recited a poem to me after we were spent. After we danced. After we kissed.

"Hope" is the thing with feathers

That perches in the soul

And sings the tune without the words

And never stops—at all

BETTE: Did I recite that?

CAL: (*Her hands on Bette's face, tenderly.*)

And sweetest in the Gale is heard

And sore must be the storm

That could abash the little Bird

That kept so many warm

BETTE: You were...I remember...you told me you could only sleep to the words of Emily Dickinson.

CAL: I did. You cried. I bled then.

BETTE: You bled.

CAL: Dark red.

BETTE: Have you been following me on the ferry these last weeks?

CAL: You said you can't do this with a woman.

BETTE: I was coming out of a divorce.

CAL: Text me, call me.

(*She tosses her stained tissues over the railing.*)

BETTE: I'm meeting someone at the landing.

(*Bette reaches for Cal's arm somewhat tenderly. Cal reaches for Bette's face and edges in for a kiss. Bette relents.*)

Characters:

KEVIN: Sales clerk at video store

STEVE: A customer

Setting: A retail store selling DVD's. A sign reads GOING OUT OF BUSINESS: ALL SALES FINAL.

> CHARLES WEST is a teacher and writer. He is the author of the novel, *The Sacred Disc*, as well as other short fiction. He has also served as a dramaturg and actor for the Woodward Shakespeare Festival. His short plays have been performed in Wisconsin, Florida, San Diego, Fresno, and San Juan Capistrano, California.

(Kevin is going through a box of DVD's with the label "S" on a table. STEVE enters, looks around, then starts looking through a box next to KEVIN.)

KEVIN: So, store's closing?

STEVE: Sadly.

KEVIN: So, why?

STEVE: Sluggish sales.

> *(Pause.)*

KEVIN: Seen any good movies?

STEVE: *Saw.*

KEVIN: Sheesh. OK, have you *saw* any good movies?

STEVE: Saw. The name of the movie is *Saw.*

KEVIN: *Saw,* you say?

STEVE: Sure.

KEVIN: Did you see *Saw?*

STEVE: Sure, I saw *Saw.*

KEVIN: Synopsis?

STEVE: Slasher, self-inflicted.

KEVIN: So, *Saw* then?

STEVE: *Saw One.*

KEVIN: My name's not Juan.

STEVE: No, the first *Saw.* Saw number one. *(Holds up single finger.)*

KEVIN: Is there a *Saw Two?*

STEVE: Certainly.

KEVIN: Did you see *Saw Two?*

STEVE: Say what?

KEVIN: *Saw Two,* number two, *Saw One* sequel?

STEVE: No, I haven't seen *Saw Two. (Pause.)* But Sue saw *Saw Two.*

KEVIN: Sue?

STEVE: My sister.

KEVIN: Your sister Sue?

STEVE: Sure, my sister Sue.

KEVIN: So, your sister Sue saw *Saw Two*, too?

STEVE: *Si.*

KEVIN: *Si?*

STEVE: Sorry, I mean yes.

KEVIN: Did Sue like *Saw Two*?

STEVE: She said "so-so."

KEVIN: Sue said "so-so?"

STEVE: So Sue said, but she's psycho?

KEVIN: Sue's psycho?

STEVE: Sadly.

KEVIN: Shame.

STEVE: Starring Alan Ladd?

KEVIN: *Shame,* not *Shane.*

STEVE: Sorry, haven't seen it.

KEVIN: Seen what?

STEVE: *Shame.*

KEVIN: No, I meant shame about Sue.

STEVE: Sue?

KEVIN: Being psycho.

STEVE: *C'est la vie.*

KEVIN: So...

STEVE: Seen *Saw Six*?

KEVIN: There's a *Saw Six*?

STEVE: Certainly.

KEVIN: Have you seen *Saw Six*?

STEVE: I'll see *Saw Six* soon.

KEVIN: Has Sue seen *Saw Six*?

STEVE: Sue's not seen *Saw Six*.

KEVIN: So...

STEVE: Sally's seen *Saw Six*.

KEVIN: Sally?

STEVE: Sally, Sue's sister

KEVIN: Sue's *sister*?

STEVE: Sure.

KEVIN: Shouldn't Sue's sister Sally, be your sister Sally as well?

STEVE: Sure.

KEVIN: So, Sally's seen *Saw Six*?

STEVE: Sally's seen all the Saws.

KEVIN: All the Saws?

STEVE: So she says.

KEVIN: Is Sally psycho like Sue?

STEVE: Shhh. Sally's sensitive.

KEVIN: *(Looks around.)* Is Sally here?

STEVE: Sally should show up soon.

KEVIN: Sally's into cinema?

STEVE: Severely.

  (Pause. They both continue looking at DVD's.)

KEVIN: Suggestions?

STEVE: *Separate Lies*.

KEVIN: Schwarzenegger.

STEVE: Susan Sarandon.

KEVIN: Sweet.

STEVE: Sharon Stone.

KEVIN: Sexy.

STEVE: Sarah Silverman.

KEVIN: Sassy.

STEVE: Stellan Skarsgård.

KEVIN: Say what?

STEVE: Swedish. Shepherd.

KEVIN: Cybill?

STEVE: Sam.

KEVIN: Spade.

STEVE: Sylvester Stallone.

KEVIN: Sissy.

STEVE: Stallone, a sissy?

KEVIN: Spacek.

STEVE: Schindler's.

KEVIN: List.

STEVE: Steven

KEVIN: Spielberg.

STEVE: Steven

KEVIN: Soderbergh.

STEVE: Steven

KEVIN: Segal.

STEVE: Seriously?

   (Pause.)

KEVIN: *Scent of a Woman.*

STEVE: *Scary Movie.*

KEVIN: *Scent of a Woman*, scary?

STEVE: *Scary Movie,* a satire of scary movies.

KEVIN: Silly.

STEVE: *Streetcar Named Desire.*

KEVIN: Stella!

STEVE: And Stanley.

KEVIN: Sure.

STEVE: *Sense and*

KEVIN: *Sensibility.*

STEVE: *Sixth*

KEVIN: *Sense* and

STEVE: *Sensibility.*

KEVIN: *Sleepless in*

STEVE: *Seattle.*

KEVIN: *Sex in the*

STEVE: *City.*

KEVIN: *Suddenly Last*

STEVE: *Summer.*

KEVIN: *Seven*

STEVE: *Samurai.*

KEVIN: *Seven Brides for*

STEVE: *Seven Brothers.*

KEVIN: *Stalag*

STEVE: *Seventeen.*

KEVIN: *Star is*

STEVE: *Born.*

KEVIN: *Star*

STEVE: *Trek.*

KEVIN: *Star*

STEVE: *Wars.*

KEVIN: *Star*

STEVE: *Ship Troopers.*

KEVIN: *Scarface.*

STEVE: "Say hello to my little..."

KEVIN: Scooby-Doo!

    (KEVIN hands DVD to STEVE. Money is exchanged.)

STEVE: *Seven, Slevin, Ocean's Eleven.*

KEVIN: So long,

STEVE: Farewell,

KEVIN: Auf Wiedersehn,

STEVE: Good night.

    (KEVIN exits. STEVE picks up one last DVD.)

STEVE: Sayonara.

(STEVE puts up CLOSED sign.)

Characters:
MIKE

CHRIS

KIMBERLY ALU is a New York-based playwright who finds her niche somewhere between comedy and drama, her plays always finding the light in an otherwise dark situation. Originally trained as an actress, she finds her performance background has given her a wonderful base as a writer and loves blurring the line between reality and myth. In addition to publication with Smith & Kraus, Kimberly has had the fortune of watching two of her other plays, *Jumper* and *Carnival Games,* produced within her first year in New York City. She spends every day writing, acting, or filming with her self-started production company Solvency Studios and falls more in love with the craft with each passing hour. solvencystudios.com/

(We open on a bare stage. After a beat, a lost-looking man, MARK, wanders onto stage. He looks around and after a few moments, speaks.)

MARK: Hello? Hello? Is..is anyone there?

(Mark wanders the stage.)

MARK: Hello? I..I think I passed out and I can't remember where I am or what happened, is anyone around? Hello?!

(After a moment, he sits, rubs his eyes and face.)

MARK: Okay, okay...I was at the bar with Joe...and then...and then what?!

(Frustrated, he turns his pockets out.)

Okay, Okay...I um..

(Finding the bar receipt.)

I went to the bar!

(Still searching, finding more)

And then to the corner store by home, alright...

(Still searching but finding nothing)

Dammit I was up the street from home! I should be home! Where the hell am I?!

(Mark tears the receipts out of frustration and sits in the middle of the stage again.

Beat.

Mark gets up and storms around. Finding no exit, he starts to panic and yells.

Beat.

Exhausted, he slumps to the ground again.)

MARK: You know, someone will come looking for me!

(Beat.)

MARK: SAY SOMETHING! YOU CAN'T JUST KEEP ME HERE AND SAY NOTHING!

(A spotlight turns on behind him to reveal a cardboard box upstage left. Mark eyes it suspiciously. After a moment, he approaches the box, taps it with his foot. He picks up the box and opens the lid.)

MARK: Oh, so you think you're funny huh?

> *(Mark reaches into the box and pulls out a small brown paper bag, a beer bottle, and a lighter from the bag.)*

MARK: Yeah, this is what I got at the corner store!

> *(Mark pulls out the receipt and examines it.)*

MARK: Look I don't know why you're doing this, but someone will come looking for me, do you hear me? DO YOU HEAR ME?!

> *(A new spotlight turns on downstage right, revealing a smaller cardboard box. Mark looks at the receipt one more time, then drops it as he slowly heads over to the box.)*

MARK: Joe, if you're doing this as some sort of prank, it's not funny man!

> *(Mark stops at the box, takes a deep breath, and leans down to open it. A loud noise echoes from down the hall.)*

MARK: Joe? Joe! Come on, man, cut it out!

> *The sound of footsteps grows louder and closer.*

MARK: Say something! What's going on?!

> *(The footsteps stop. Another man, CHRIS, early 20s, enters. He examines Mark.)*

CHRIS: Hi...I'm Chris.

> *(Mark is silent.)*

CHRIS: Did...did he tell you what's in that box?

> *(Chris gestures towards the box in Mark's hand.)*

MARK: Did who tell me? Do we know each other?

CHRIS: No, I don't think so. There was this voice, I saw these boxes in the room up the hall and he kept urging me to open them, and I wouldn't, and then I heard you yelling—

MARK: Were you abducted as well? What's the last thing you remember?

CHRIS: I was driving home with my...oh God. I had my little sister with me! SARAH! SARAH ARE YOU HERE?!

MARK: Fuck, fuck...what the fuck is going on here?!

CHRIS: What was inside that box?

(He points to the one he's already opened.)

MARK: A beer and a lighter.

CHRIS: What?

MARK: The last thing I remember buying before blacking out and ending up here.

CHRIS: Jesus.

(We hear a loud crash off stage and the lights flash brightly for a moment before returning to neutral lighting.)

MARK: What the fuck was that?!

(Chris starts breathing really heavily. He slumps to the ground. He's having a panic attack. Mark goes to him.)

MARK: Hey! Hey, it's okay, listen, it's going to be okay. We're in this together, okay?

CHRIS: Thank you, Mark.

MARK: Yes of course, listen we have to—wait...how do you know my name?

(Chris looks at him, puzzled for a moment.)

CHRIS: I..I'm not sure...I just knew your name.

(Mark backs away from him.)

MARK: Who are you?

CHRIS: What?

MARK: I never told you my name, how do you know my name?

CHRIS: I..I don't know! I don't know! I just do!

MARK: Last night, I was at a bar...and then I wake up in here, with no idea how I got here, or what happened or even who you are—

CHRIS: Mark—

MARK: And yet, you know my name despite saying you've been abducted as well? No, I don't buy it; you're working with whoever it is that has me trapped here.

CHRIS: I have no idea how I got here! You have to believe me! All I remember is driving home with my sister! We were only a couple miles from home—

MARK: I don't want to hear it—

CHRIS: —she was getting fussy. She's only five and sometimes car rides make her sleepy. I convinced mom to let me take her for a ride—

MARK: Shut up!

CHRIS: —I had gone around the block a couple times, but it wasn't enough, so I turned down a few more roads so the movement would help sooth her—

MARK: I SAID SHUT UP!

CHRIS: —we had just turned onto Chandler, only two or three blocks away-

MARK: Wait—

CHRIS: —she finally fell asleep—

MARK: —did you say Chandler?

CHRIS: Yes, Chandler Blvd.

MARK: I live over there! That's where I was!

> *(A light snaps on downstage left, revealing a very small box. Mark looks at his box, still unopened, then to Chris.)*

CHRIS: It's for me.

> *(He opens the box to reveal a child's shoe. He begins to figure it all out.)*

CHRIS: Oh, God—

> *(We hear a loud crash off stage. The lights flash brightly again before adjusting back to normal. This time, Chris is not fazed.)*

CHRIS: You didn't watch where you were going—

MARK: What?

CHRIS: —the turn was too wide, the road just wasn't big enough for both of us—

> *(The lights flash brightly again. Chris laughs. When the lights return to normal, Chris is gone, and Mark is alone again.)*

MARK: Hello? HELLO?! Chris? CHRIS! WHERE ARE YOU? HELLO?!

> *(Mark panics, then suddenly he remembers he still hasn't opened his own box. He tears the top open and looks*

inside. He chuckles. After a moment of finding pure hilarity in the contents, he pulls out a small matchbox car and rolls it across the stage. He looks around for a moment, still laughing. He laughs until eventually his humor turns to sorrow and as he begins to cry, the lights flash red.)

BLACK OUT

Characters:

AXEL: Male, twenties

ANT: Male, twenties

Setting: None. You'll need a lot of shredded paper, though.

> REINA HARDY is a playwright from Chicago. Her plays, which usually contain magic and sometimes contain science, have been seen across the country, including at Rorschach Theatre in DC, the Vortex in Austin, and the NNPN National New Play Showcase. She's been a Michener Fellow at UT Austin, winner of the KCACTF TYA Prize, finalist for the Terrence McNally Prize and the recipient of an Interact 20/20 Commission. Reina is the book writer for *Fanatical the Musical* (under development in England with the Stable), and is collaborating with Sky Candy on a devised circus show. She can make things happen with her mind. reinahardy.com

(Axel sits at the top of the belltower, holding a backpack. He reaches into it, grabs a handful of shredded paper, and throws it into the wind.)

AXEL*:* So long, Andalusia.

(He throws another handful.)

So long to all of you idiots.

(He resumes throwing. Offstage, Ant runs up the belltower, shouting desperately.)

ANT*:* Hey! Hey—wait!

(Ant enters, slows, and tries to appear calm.)

ANT*:* Hey.

AXEL: Hey, Ant. Or should I call you Mr. Antesberger?

ANT: It's cool. I heard you were up in the belltower.

AXEL: Calm down, I don't have a gun.

ANT: No, dude, I didn't think that.

AXEL: And I'm not gonna throw myself off.

ANT: I know that. I'm not like, worried or anything. So, what's in the backpack?

(Axel pulls out a handful of paper and tosses it.)

ANT*:* Oh. What is that?

AXEL: Jack shit, my friend. Jack. Fucking. Shit.

ANT: It's got writing on it.

AXEL: It's got words.

ANT: (*Reading from the paper.*) Anda...Andalusia. You finished it? Andalusia? You've been working on that thing since we were sophomores, man. It's like, 2 a.m. at the Eat n'Park, smokes, burgers, and you're telling me all this crazy shit about a dude who makes a firestorm so he can talk to some chick and I'm like—You finished it?

AXEL: I finished it completely. So, how'd you hear I was up here? (*He bends his knee and taps a technical looking plastic ankle bracelet.*) This thing have GPS tracking?

ANT: No, man, no. I mean, it beeps us when you leave the house, but it's not like, smart or whatever. Mary Jo Bang saw you go up.

AXEL: So this is official business? Where are the real cops?

ANT: They're around. But I thought if I could find you first, maybe you could just— y'know—be cool and—

AXEL: You're on the clock, bro?

ANT: I mean, I'd come look for you anyway—I—

AXEL: Jesus, Ant, take a coffee break.

(Ant sits down next to Axel.)

AXEL: On a clear day you can see I-80.

ANT: Hey, somebody's getting married. The girls look like flowers from up here, skirts blowing around. This is what I call wedding weather—girls in dresses weather.

(Axel throws another handful of paper.)

ANT: You know, with this wind, you're getting really good coverage. Some of the papers are clearing the lake.

AXEL: I'm never getting out of this town. I'm never going to see anything, or do anything. I'm going to die here and be buried in Saint Jane's and forgotten.

ANT: Don't say that.

Nobody else in our class was like—writing a book.

AXEL: Sixty thousand words. For you, Centerville. *(He tosses another handful.)*

ANT: Why do you gotta keep doing that?

AXEL: Because I'm a fuck-up, and a mediocrity, and all I ever wanted was to be heard.

ANT: Did you like, send it to that publisher and—

AXEL: I didn't send it, Ant. I read it. *I* read it, and it's...No one else is ever gonna want to read this bullshit.

ANT: I did. I wanted to read this bullshit.

AXEL: Too late now.

ANT: Only copy?

AXEL: You always were quick on the uptake, Ant.

(Ant reaches into the backpack and pulls out a handful of paper.)

ANT: You know, if I were out there on that lake, or in the wedding, or just out in front of the Eat n' Park, and I got some
shredded piece of Andalusia—it'd make today... it'd give
me something to remember.

AXEL: Yeah?

ANT: Yeah.

AXEL: Whatever.

> *(Ant throws the handful of paper. Then he grabs another
> and gets to his feet.)*

ANT: Hear me, Centerville! Hear me!

> *(He throws the paper.)*

AXEL: What the fuck?

ANT: Hear me from Saint Jane's to the Laundromat!

AXEL: You asshole—give me that.

ANT: From the sinkhole to Enrico Fermi High!

AXEL: This is so not the point.

ANT: Hear me! Hear me! Come on, Axel, bring the storm.

AXEL: Oh Jesus. *(Grabs paper.)* Listen to the rain! Let it come
down! Oh for fuck's sake. Hear us!

ANT: From Golden Links to the Eat'n Park! From the motel to
the county jail!

AXEL: From Bigs Banquet hall to the Lox Nox pavilion!

ANT: I am Anton Antesberger!

AXEL: I am Axel Wigner! Hear me!

ANT: Hear us!

AXEL: Hear us, Centerville!

ANT: Never forget us!

AXEL: Hear us brides; hear us bridesmaids! Old dudes in golf
pants, waiters, K-Mart shoppers, we too have knowledge of
your hearts and wisdom of the skies—we bring the storm!

ANT: Hear our words!

AXEL: Let them ring forever!

> *(The bag is empty.)*

ANT: That it?

AXEL: That's the end.

ANT: What do you want to do now?

AXEL: I don't know. Get high. (*Ant gives Axel a look. Axel laughs.*) Ant, is it weird that you're—like—looking after me? Since we used to be friends?

ANT: Not really. Centerville only has two parole officers, so it kinda goes with the territory. (*They stare out.*) Look at all that paper fall.

AXEL: One thing I ever did.

ANT: Nah dude, nah. It's not gonna be like that. (*They stare out again.*) Sun's setting.

AXEL: Ok. Let's go home.

   (*They watch as the lights fade out.*)

Characters

STEPHEN: A man in his forties

ANNE: A woman in her forties

Setting: A nice hotel room.

GABRIEL DAVIS is a two-time recipient of the Shubert Fellowship. MFA in Dramatic Writing from Carnegie Mellon School of Drama. Readings/Workshops at Theater for the New City, Primary Stages, Manhattan Repertory Theatre, Piney Fork Theatre, Manhattan Arts Center, Forward Theatre, Court Street Theater. Taught playwriting at Westport Country Playhouse, Joanne Woodward Apprentice Program; City Theatre Company, Young Playwrights Festival. Monologues and scenes are published in *Audition Monologues for Young Women* (Meriwether Publishing), *Best Contemporary Monologues For Kids Ages 7-15* (Applause Books). Between Beats, a screenplay, was a finalist for the Sloan Foundation Screenwriting Award and semifinalist at NY Writers Summit. gabrielbdavis.com

(Anne enters, frazzled.)

ANNE: Hi, sorry, sorry…I tried to call but it went straight to voicemail.

STEPHEN: Andrew grabbed my cell during his bath time last night…hasn't been working right—

ANNE: Wow, Stephen. Nice room.

STEPHEN: It's a suite.

ANNE: Sweet suite.

STEPHEN: Sit, I poured some bubbly for us.

ANNE: Thanks. I'm so sorry—

STEPHEN: Don't be. Let's toast. *(He hands her a glass, and raises his.)* To our anniversary.

ANNE: Anniversary?

STEPHEN: It's been one year as of today.

ANNE: Anniversaries are for married people.

STEPHEN: We're married people.

ANNE: Funny.

STEPHEN: *(Laughing.)* You to Eric, me to Ally. C'mon. Let's toast—to one year of decadent sin!

(Anne doesn't raise her glass.)

ANNE: I would have been here sooner—

STEPHEN: It's ok.

ANNE: —but Jules is scared of the new sitter.

STEPHEN: The one Ally and I recommended?

ANNE: Uh-huh. Apparently Jules found out this woman is of German descent—and you know, they're learning about the holocaust now in school and…

STEPHEN: *(Laughing.)* Your daughter thinks the sitter is a Nazi?

ANNE: It's not funny. Your son is the one who told Jules she's German.

STEPHEN: How does Andrew know that?

ANNE: I don't know, but he told Jules this, and she's freaking out, ok.

STEPHEN: Ok. We going to toast? This is a hundred dollar bottle of—

ANNE: I keep wondering why he would tell Jules that. Did he want to scare her?

STEPHEN: Do we really want to spend our time talking about our kids?

ANNE: Why? How long do we have?

STEPHEN: We're fine—Ally thinks I'm staying in DC to-night—

ANNE: Good. I mean, not good but…

STEPHEN: Yes, good. Let's celebrate. To our anniversary.

ANNE: That's kind of sick. Calling it an anniversary.

STEPHEN: Come here. Let's work some of that tension out. *(He starts rubbing her shoulders.)*

ANNE: Oh, nice. A little to the left. Oh yeah. Right there. Right…wait. *(Jules stops, pulls out her cell.)*

STEPHEN: What's wrong?

ANNE: No, I thought I felt it vibrating—I don't want to miss it if the sitter to calls—I told her she could if Jules started to freak again—

STEPHEN: She'll be fine.

ANNE: I don't know, Stephen. She's been playing this disturb-ing game at school—actually Andrew's involved too….

STEPHEN: What are you talking about?

ANNE: I guess it's because of what they're learning in school but—Andrew and Jules have been playing Holocaust at recess.

STEPHEN: What?

ANNE: It's like a game of tag—but sick. Apparently one child plays Hitler—and this child assigns people, some of the other bigger kids on the playground to be his SS officers, and they chase the other smaller kids, the "prisoners," around the playground and when they catch them, those kids have to stand and wait in an area dubbed the gas chamber.

And every time, apparently, Jules is made to play a prisoner, and the other day, Andrew was assigned as an SS officer, and he had to catch my daughter. And he did. Your son sent my daughter to the gas chamber in recess yesterday!!

STEPHEN: I'm sure he was just following orders.

ANNE: That's not funny. Stephen, she's scared of Andrew now.

STEPHEN: Scared of—those two love each other, Anne. I think I—I think I know what this is…I think Andrew tried to tell me about it.

ANNE: He did?

STEPHEN: It was about two days ago?

ANNE: Uh huh.

STEPHEN: Uh-huh. Andrew didn't tell me exactly what it was but he was upset and I could just tell something was—that he was troubled about something—so I asked and he said one of the bigger kids made him play a mean game at recess. I kinda gathered from his descriptions it was a game of tag of some kind so yes, it must be the same thing and….but he said he only played so he wouldn't get picked on himself. He felt so ashamed.

ANNE: Good.

STEPHEN: Good?

ANNE: He was victimizing other kids, Stephen.

STEPHEN: They all were it was just—it was a bad game they were all sort of trapped in. He was as much a victim.

ANNE: Oh please. He was playing an SS officer. The other children—the prisoners—were the victims.

STEPHEN: Is it that black and white to you?

ANNE: Yes.

STEPHEN: Anne, I told him, I said, he shouldn't feel ashamed. That sometimes we do things we're not proud of, because we have to, because the alternative—

ANNE: You're apologizing for his behavior?

STEPHEN: No, I'm—and they're not, they're kids—I'm just saying—a child giving in to peer pressure—from what he said, the other kids were pushing kids down, I mean, really being brutal. And some of the kids, the prisoners who were being chased, some of them were pushing each other down to escape getting tagged, hard, into the concrete, skinned knees and…I mean, for crying out loud, where were the teachers…? I mean, it sounded really brutal. And I asked him, I said, did you actually push or shove anyone? And he said—he said no, Anne. He didn't. He tagged people, as few as he could without getting noticed, and he tagged them lightly. He tried to be as gentle as he could. But what else could he do? If he didn't tag the other kids—and he did it lightly—they'd have pushed him down, injured him. So you know what. I'm glad. I'm glad he kept his head down and went along—he survived. My son's a survivor, and I don't want him to feel ashamed of that.

ANNE: I cannot believe you.

STEPHEN: And he said Jules pushed a kid down.

ANNE: What?

STEPHEN: He said your daughter, in trying to escape getting tagged, pushed other children down, and even flung other children into the aggressors. But he's the victimizer? He's the one should feel ashamed?

ANNE: Yes, he should have refused to play.

STEPHEN: That's a fairly moral stance to take.

ANNE: Yes…it is. *(Anne stands up and moves to leave.)*

STEPHEN: Where are you going? It's our anniversary.

ANNE: That's sick Stephen.

 (Ann exits. Stephen, alone in the room, raises his glass.)

STEPHEN: Happy anniversary. *(He drinks, lights fade to black.)*

Characters:

RUBY: Female – any age, any race—over-enthusiastic superfan, awaiting a book reading.

DESTINY: Female – any age, any race—over-enthusiastic superfan, awaiting a book reading.

LINDA: Female – any age, any race—bookstore owner, event host, beleaguered, cynical, exhausted.

SAVANNAH VON WOODBURNE: Female – any age, any race—self-published fantasy author, confident, diva-ish, acts more famous than she is.

Setting: A bookstore.

COLIN JOHNSON is a Bay Area-based writer, director and filmmaker. His work has been featured up and down the West Coast and elsewhere by such groups as SF Shotz, SF Olympians, Playground, Theater Pub, Awesome Theatre, Actors Ensemble of Berkeley, Bay One Acts Festival, San Francisco Fringe Festival, Empire Theater Group (Spokane, WA), Wildclaw Theater (Chicago, IL) and numerous film festivals, including the 2014 Comic-Con International Independent Film Festival, with his multi-media production entity BattleStache Studios. Recently, the Bay Area Critics Circle voted his original play, *The Night Before*, Best Script and Best Overall Production at the 2015 TAPAS Short Play Festival. Aside from theater and film, Colin also co-wrote a graphic novel entitled *Daomu* for Image Comics and Magnetic Press. He lives in Berkeley, CA. *Author Event* is one of the hundreds of plays written and performed as part of SHOTZ, a "theatrical pressure cooker" that presents all-new short plays each month. youtube.com/user/BattleStacheStudio/videos

*(Lights up on an empty podium. Opposite it are a bank
of 6-8 chairs, only 2 of which are filled. In the chairs are
RUBY and DESTINY, two super-geek superfans. They hold
several books each and can barely contain their excite-
ment.)*

RUBY: Shut up, it's about to start.

DESTINY: I didn't say anything.

RUBY: Seriously, shut up.

DESTINY: Sorry. I'm excited. Oh man. Oh no.

*(She dry heaves and then starts breathing loudly into a
paper vomit bag.)*

RUBY: Destiny, shut up!

*(LINDA approaches the podium. DESTINY and RUBY
seize up with psychotic anticipation.)*

LINDA: Okay, this seems like everybody. Hello. My name is
Linda, I own this bookstore. Today, it is my pleasure to
introduce acclaimed local author Miss Savannah Von Woodburne. Savannah has spent the last decade writing an immersive, detailed, and astoundingly robust series of fantasy
books, all of which were self-published as e-books on her
blog. Dubbed the "Adequation Neuftet" by her fan club—

RUBY: Holy crap, that's us!

LINDA: She has agreed to grant her first public appearance in
years. So, without further ado, here to read an excerpt from
her newest, and rumored final entry in the Neuftet, entitled
The Jar With a Bell in It, please join me in giving a warm,
Book Mongers welcome to Savannah Von Woodburne.

*(SAVANNAH graces the podium, owning the room.
She wears a long cloak over her shoulders and a wide-
brimmed hat with large sunglasses. Super celebrity.*

DESTINY and RUBY freak the fuck out.

*SAVANNAH basks in the praise, then has them settle
down. They're both hyperventilating. DESTINY breathes
into the vomit bag.)*

SAVANNAH: Yes. Yes! Thank you! Thank you all—two of you.
It's a pleasure and a primal exaltation to be treading these
literary boards. Yes, feel me, I am Savannah Von Wood-

burne. Let us begin.

RUBY: YOU'RE THE GREATEST!

DESTINY: BOOK SEVEN, *THE COLOR MAGENTA,* CHANGED MY LIFE!

LINDA: Yes, I love you all.

       (DESTINY passes out for a moment. SAVANNAH reads.)

SAVANNAH: *(Reading emphatically.)* "It had been seventy-three months since the last of the male species had died out in Quadrant Alpha Beta."

RUBY: Savannah! Savannah!

SAVANNAH: *(Trying to read through the commotion.)* The elders told us the extinction of the XY line would bring plentiful harvest and diplomatic harmony, but nothing could have been closer to being far away from the truth. The truth was very far away, indeed.

DESTINY: Hey Savannah!

LINDA: Please, girls, let her finish.

RUBY: Savannah!

SAVANNAH: Yes, what is it? What question couldn't wait for Narnia the She-then's backstory?

RUBY: I'm sorry, it's just—umm—we think you're—you're—oh, man, I'm shaking—

DESTINY: I named myself after the character Destiny in Book Three: *Handmaidens That Run with Foxes!*

SAVANNAH: Understandable.

RUBY: Savannah – Miss Von Woodburne—we—we wrote a play set within the Adequation Omniverse, we dedicated it to you.

LINDA: Jesus Christ.

SAVANNAH: Honestly, I'm flattered, yet still remain mildly insulted over your flagrant disregard for my emphatic reading.

DESTINY: She's mad.

RUBY: No—NOOOOO, don't be mad!

LINDA: Can we take it down a notch, please?

RUBY: We waited in line for three days!

DESTINY: We haven't eaten!

LINDA: There was no line.

RUBY: Oppressor!

LINDA: Ooookay, maybe it's time to leave.

> *(LINDA tries to escort RUBY and DESTINY off the premises. They protest, kick and scream.)*

SAVANNAH: Stop, mine Linda! They obviously hold me in high esteem, as they should. Allow them to present their arcane drama, if for nothing else than mine own amusement.

LINDA: I don't know if that's a good idea—

> *(RUBY and DESTINY immediately jump into character, starting with an elaborate, ridiculous handshake routine. RUBY rips off her clothes, revealing a shiny, skin-tight gold leotard thing. DESTINY pulls a helmet from her bag and puts it on. They both brandish crappy, homemade weapons.)*

DESTINY: 'Tis I, Velvet Salsa, the misunderstood villain from Book Five: *The Ethical Hussy*. I have returned from Space Prison to exact vengeance.

RUBY: You're no match for Keisha Thorax, protector of the harem, champion of the widows!

> *(They engage in a terribly choreographed fight, knocking over chairs, making a horrible mess, maybe while singing their own theme song. LINDA reacts accordingly. SAVANNAH remains indifferent. Ruby subdues Destiny, prepares to deliver the death blow.)*

RUBY: Your censorship and pro-patriarchy views will spell your downfall, Velvet Salsa.

DESTINY: But all I ever wanted—was to be loved.

> *(RUBY drops her weapon, stands Destiny up, and they embrace.)*

DESTINY: We can co-exist, peacefully.

> *(They stand forward and bow. There is no applause.)*

RUBY: So? What'd you think?

DESTINY: We think—umm—it would make a nice companion

---

piece for the middle sequence— books four through six—
umm—we love you.

SAVANNAH: *(Long, indifferent beat, then a happy switch.)*
Yeah, that'll work.

RUBY: REALLY?

SAVANNAH: Yes, really, mine fans. Mine children. Come.
Embrace me.

> *(They both pass out.)*

SAVANNAH: An inspired ending to a whirlpool of emotion. Am
I right, Linda?

LINDA: Get out.

> *BLACKOUT*

Characters:

AVA

MARIA

Setting: Interior; fancy restaurant—present day.

> ANNE FLANAGAN'S plays include *Lineage, Artifice, First Chill, Skirts,* and *Death, Sex & Elves.* Flanagan's work has been produced and/or developed at the Bloomington Playwrights Project, Strange Sun Theater, Ohio Wesleyan University, The Blank Theatre, Ensemble Studio Theater LA, Georgetown Theater Co, Rogue Machine, Dayton Playhouse, Hobo Junction, and Crack the Glass among other venues. Publications include *Artifice* (Dramatic), *Best Women's Stage Monologues* (Smith & Kraus), *Best Contemporary Monologues* (Applause), and *Monologues From The Heart; Vol. II* (JAC.) Anne has worked as an actor, inner city school teacher, private investigator and nude model - none of which were as exciting as one might think. anneflanagan.net newplayexchange.org/users/2115/ anne-flanagan

(AVA sits at a table. MARIA enters. They hug enthusiastically.)

MARIA: Ava! *Finally*, we meet for lunch!

AVA: Maria! I know, I've been so crazy busy!

MARIA: Please, I barely have time to breathe!

AVA: Girl, I could die of asphyxiation right here.

> *(They sit. Ava plucks a bottle of wine from the table and pours.)*

MARIA: When did I last see you? Celine's party?

AVA: Ugh— Celine— she's so competitive.

MARIA: Right?! Très annoying. Friendship is *not* a competition.

AVA: Exactly! Thanks to gals like Celine, people think women can't be friends. That we're always trying to out-do each other.

MARIA: Ridiculous.

AVA: Totally. That whole evening, Celine was like ME ME ME ME. And of course we had to hear her 'kidney story.' *Again.* I mean, she donated a kidney, great but—

MARIA: Who hasn't, right?

AVA: You've donated a kidney?

MARIA: Of course! Haven't you?

AVA: Yes! Both, in fact.

MARIA: I gave mine to a soldier in Iraq.

AVA: Mine went to orphans in New Orleans.

MARIA: I was in New Orleans when Hurricane Katrina hit!

AVA: Me too! I rescued two families in the French Quarter.

MARIA: I rescued thirty nuns in the lower Nine. And sixty kittens.

> *(They each take a sip of wine. Then a bigger sip. Then they both CHUG what's left, simultaneously slamming their empty goblets on the table with a BANG.)*
>
> *(Beat.)*

AVA: *(Refilling wine glasses.)* I think Celine's so competitive because she's insecure.

MARIA: Agreed. I feel quite sorry for her.

AVA: I feel horribly. I think I'll take her to lunch.

MARIA: I think I'll take her to the ballet.

AVA: I think I'll take her to Europe.

> *(They lift their wine and freeze, glasses held aloft. Like a gun fighter's "Mexican standoff," they each slowly take a drink and then just as slowly replace their glasses on the table.)*

MARIA: Be careful in Europe. I was in France during those awful terrorist attacks—

AVA: Me too— I was in Paris. IN the concert hall!

MARIA: Reminds me of Boston. I was running the marathon when that bomb exploded. To this day— nightmares!

AVA: Do tell! I still have nightmares about Dallas and the grassy knoll.

MARIA: You were there when Kennedy was shot?

AVA: Shh. It's classified.

MARIA: I feel you. I was in Haiti when that quake struck. Seven point oh!

AVA: Pfft. San Francisco in 1906? That was a seven point eight! I barely made it out alive.

MARIA: At least there wasn't a volcano! In Pompeii? I survived the quake but came thiiiis close to eating it when Vesuvius erupted.

AVA: At least lava is warm. Try nearly freezing to death in the ocean! Hubby was like "Oh, the Titanic sounds fun" and then, pow, hit an iceberg and I'm clinging to a slab of wood for dear life.

MARIA: Don't mention oceans! It brings back Pearl Harbor flashbacks.

AVA: You think you've got flashbacks?! I close my eyes, I'm right back in Hiroshima— oh, the humanity!

MARIA: That's what I said when the Hindenburg when down!

AVA: Who cares about a blimp? I saw *both* the Columbia and the Challenger blow up.

MARIA: Me too! I saw it first hand at NASA.

AVA: I saw it from Mars. And then I went up in a spaceship and there was this black monolith and a bunch of monkeys and I had a murderous computer named Hal.

MARIA: Lucky! Could've used a computer when I helped Schindler make his list. Or when I had to tally casualties after the Black Plague—

AVA: Black Plague— ha! I had to count the dead after the Crusades! Recording four hundred years' worth of torture and—

MARIA: Recording torture? Try seeing it first-hand! When they nailed my man J's hands to the cross, I about lost it—

AVA: No, I about lost it when that crazy MoFo walked out of the cave three days later. Mary Mags and I were both like What. The. Hell?!

MARIA: What the Hell? What the Hell was up with that meteor?! Like one minute I'm dodging a T-Rex and then BAM! The dinosaurs're GONE.

AVA: I witnessed the first fish grow legs and crawl outta the ocean. L'il critter crawled right over my toes. I was like Evolution— DAAAYM!

MARIA: No surprise to me— when God and I sat down to design the Universe, He told me that—

AVA: Yeah, yeah, old news. Who do you think combined matter and energy to make a Big Bang in the first place?!

(Raising her glass.)

All so that billions of years later, I could break bread with a dear friend. To Friendship.

MARIA: *(Raising her glass.)* To friendship. It's not about winning or losing.

AVA: It's not about one-upmanship.

MARIA: Never!

AVA: It's about support.

MARIA: Hear! Hear!

AVA: It's about sisterhood.

MARIA: Hallelujah!

(They each drink; happy and relaxed. Beat.)

AVA: *(Sotto voce.)* But I won.

Characters:

THE YOUTH

THE WOMAN

Setting: Idiotic interior of an elegant youth's bachelor apartment—prints on the walls, a very low divan, several vases of flowers, as in all bachelor apartments. A newly-acquired painting is in front of the divan on an easel.

> UMBERTO BOCCIONI (1882 - 1916) was an influential Italian painter and sculptor who helped shape the revolutionary aesthetic of the Futurism movement. Published in 1915 as part of the manifesto *The Futurist Synthetic Theatre*, *Bachelor Apartment* demonstrates the Futurist aesthetic of speed and compression.

THE YOUTH (*listening eagerly near the door*): Here we are! (*Opens it.*) Good morning!... How are you?

THE WOMAN (*advancing, with a certain reserve*): Good morning. (*Looking around her.*) It's nice in here…

THE YOUTH (*with fervor*): How beautiful you are! Very elegant! Thank you for coming... I doubted…

THE WOMAN: Why? Where is the painting? I came to see it.

THE YOUTH: It Is this one. (*He takes her by the hand and conducts her in front of the painting. While THE WOMAN looks at it squinting, THE YOUTH takes her in his arms and kisses the nape of her neck.*)

THE WOMAN (*struggling energetically*): Sir! What are you thinking of? These are really cowardly…

THE YOUTH: Excuse me. (*He grasps her again forcefully and speaks close to her mouth.*) You are very beautiful! You are mine! You must be mine!

THE WOMAN (*struggling in a way that makes her seem serious*): Sir! Leave me alone!... I'll call for someone! I am a respectable woman!... Leave me alone!

THE YOUTH (*mortified, letting her go*): You are right. I ask your pardon... I don't know what I am doing... I will leave you.

THE WOMAN: Open the door for me! I want to get out of here!

THE YOUTH (*going to open the door*): Go!

(*With this word, THE WOMAN lets her fur coat fall, and appears in black silk panties, with her bosom, shoulders, and arms nude. With coquetry and modesty, she runs to crouch on the divan.*)

THE WOMAN: You are timid, after all... Turn that painting, and come here! . .

Characters:

> SERGEANT BARTHOLOMEW "BAGS" MALONE, a world-weary cop one week shy of retirement.

> OFFICER GABRIELA GOMEZ, a young go-getter, looking to make a name for herself on the force.

Setting: Just outside the entrance to some nondescript building. The present.

> LIAM KUHN is a writer and television executive. His plays have been performed in New York, New Jersey, California, Vermont, New Hampshire, Oregon, Ireland and England. His first play, Absolving Buckner, was published in *New Playwrights: Best New Plays of 2002*, by Smith & Kraus. He's also written for various magazines and other publications, and his children's fiction has appeared in an anthology from Dutton Children's Books.

> A graduate of Dartmouth College and the National University of Ireland—Galway, Liam now lives in New Jersey with his wife, daughters, and dog, Madigan.

Two cops, SERGEANT "BAGS" MALONE, a slovenly fuck-up, and OFFICER GABRIELA GOMEZ, an over-achieving rookie, flank a door upstage center, ready (more or less) for action.

MALONE: You're sure this is the place?

GOMEZ: Affirmative. You think they saw us approach?

MALONE: Nah, we're good. Call it in.

GOMEZ takes out a walkie-talkie and quietly speaks into it.

GOMEZ: This is Officer Gabriela Gomez and Sergeant Bartholomew—

MALONE: Bags.

GOMEZ: Sergeant "Bags" Malone. 10-97. We are in position, at the target site, ready to proceed.

A garbled, incomprehensible response comes over the walkie-talkie.

GOMEZ: They don't want us to move in until backup arrives.

MALONE: Fucking pussies. No offense.

GOMEZ: Why would I—wait, because I *have* a pussy, or you think I *am* a pussy?

MALONE: No offense. It's just something you say. You say something, then you say "no offense." It's a, whaddayacallit, figure of speech. "Achoo." "God bless you." Doesn't mean anything.

GOMEZ: It's supposed to. It's supposed to negate the awful thing you just said.

MALONE: Look, kid, you wanna argue schematics, or you wanna get in there and crack skulls?

GOMEZ: If our intel's right, they're gonna be unarmed. Not expecting anything. The boss man and two underlings. We go in there, we could take 'em ourselves, have 'em booked and processed before backup even gets here.

MALONE: I hope, man. No offense. I need a collar like this.

GOMEZ: *We* need a collar like this. But you're right: we put this guy away, we stop half the flow of crack in the city. Think of the lives we'll save.

105 Five-Minute Plays

MALONE: Yeah, that, too. Not what I was thinking.

GOMEZ: You looking to make Lieutenant?

MALONE: I'm looking to do one thing right before I retire.

GOMEZ: You got time.

MALONE: I'm retiring tomorrow.

GOMEZ: What!? Nobody tells me anything.

MALONE: Yeah. Pension kicks in. Nobody's shot me yet, so, why tempt fate?

GOMEZ: That's fucked up.

MALONE: What, you're gonna miss me, Gomey?

GOMEZ: No. Jesus. It means this bust. Something's gonna go wrong.

MALONE: Why would you say that?

GOMEZ: Whenever a cop goes out on "one last case," something always goes south. Haven't you seen literally any movie ever?

MALONE: Come on. A straight shooter like you believes that Hollywood hooey?

GOMEZ: Ah, this is fucked. I'm going in.

MALONE: Precinct said wait for backup.

GOMEZ: Yeah, and you called 'em pussies. I'm going in.

MALONE: I'm up for cracking skulls as much as the next man, no offense. But if we do this, I'm going in first.

GOMEZ: Oh, hell no!

MALONE: Hate to pull rank on you, kid, but if I get a medal of valor, pension kicks up a grade.

GOMEZ: This is *my* case. I did all the legwork. I tracked him here. Confirmed the shipment. Plus I'm a better shot, if it comes down to it.

MALONE: You'll get your chance. Not today.

    SHOTS ring out from behind the door. Both officers freak out.

MALONE: Uh, ladies first.

GOMEZ: After you, I insist.

MALONE: Hey, you're the better shot.

GOMEZ: (*Into the walkie talkie.*) Officer Gomez, reporting shots fired. I repeat, 10-57. Shots fired, 10-57. Sergeant Bags is moving in.

MALONE: You slick sonuvabitch. Well, you gotta die of something.

> *MALONE draws, does a sign of the cross, kicks open the door, exits through it.*

MALONE: (*Off-stage.*) Freeze, motherfuckers! This is a raid! Get your hands in the air or I'll blow your fucking face off your fucking shoulders and wipe your fucking ass with it! No offense!

> *After a beat, MALONE returns, red-faced.*

MALONE: Yeah. We should go.

GOMEZ: Wait. What?

MALONE: Let's just go. Let's get out here.

GOMEZ: It wasn't the guy?

MALONE: It's a, um, toddler's birthday party. A little crippled kid.

GOMEZ: But the gun shots?

MALONE: They had a balloon artist.

GOMEZ: Balloon artist. Huh.

MALONE: Imagine that.

GOMEZ: Imagine that. Did they have cake?

MALONE: Yeah. It wasn't good. You wanna grab a beer?

GOMEZ: Yeah. I could grab a beer.

> *LIGHTS down.*

Characters:

NANCY: Female, any age; professionally adept at pleasantly saying "I'm sorry."

ALEX WILSON: Male, twenties to thirties; Ray's son; assertive, manipulative.

RAY WILSON: Male, fifties to sixties; Alex's father, grief-stricken.

Setting: Baggage Claim, Mitchell International Airport, Milwaukee, WI. The present.

Notes: Stage directions are suggestions. Abandon at will. Diversity casting is encouraged. Inspired by an actual event.

LAURA ARWOOD began writing plays in 2014. Her work includes *Misanthrope Under The Mistletoe* (produced by Hobo Junction, Chicago IL), *When Jill Was Away* (produced by South Baldwin Community Theatre, Gulf Shore AL), *Baggage Claim* (Playwrights Roundtable, Carrboro NC) and *Defender Of The Dead* (Burning Coal, Raleigh NC). *Mistletoe* and *Baggage Claim* reached the finals in the Chicago and Carrboro festival competitions. She serves on The Cary Playwrights Forum Board of Directors. Laura Arwood holds a Ph.D. in Genetics and was a college professor for twenty-five years. She currently resides in Raleigh, NC.

*A podium is DOWNSTAGE CENTER with a sign saying
"NNW AIRLINES." NANCY is behind the podium wearing
a badge that says "NANCY, Customer Service Representative." ALEX is in front of the podium.*

ALEX: Let me get this straight. My dad's luggage is here but my dad is not.

NANCY: I'm sorry sir. Your father's connecting flight to Detroit was late.

ALEX: That doesn't explain how his luggage made it.

NANCY: Our baggage handlers have the highest efficiency rating in the industry.

ALEX: Then maybe you should just fly baggage.

NANCY: I'm sorry sir. Please accept this coupon for a complementary non-alcoholic beverage for your next flight aboard North by Northwest Airlines.

> *NANCY tries to hand ALEX a coupon.*

ALEX: Aren't drinks free on your flights?

NANCY: I'm sorry sir. Please accept two coupons.

> *NANCY picks up another coupon. ALEX waives them away.*

ALEX: Forget the coupons. When will my dad get here?

NANCY: Promptly at 5:06 pm. Tomorrow.

ALEX: What? We have to be somewhere tomorrow at two.

NANCY: I'm sorry sir. Please accept this complementary coupon—

ALEX: Forget the coupon. I'll pick him up. Just give me his suitcase.

NANCY: I'm sorry sir. Releasing luggage to non-passengers is against company policy. Please accept—

ALEX: Don't tell me. A complementary coupon. Look...

> *ALEX glances at NANCY's name tag.*

ALEX: *(cont'd)* Nancy. Tomorrow's going to be tough on my dad and I'm facing a ten-hour round trip from Milwaukee to Detroit. Can't you forget 'company policy' just this once?

NANCY: I'm sorry sir. Company policy forbids—

ALEX: I really need your help...

ALEX glances at NANCY's name tag again.

ALEX: *(cont'd)* Nancy. I wouldn't ask if it wasn't important.

NANCY: I'm sorry sir—

ALEX: Come on...

ALEX glances at NANCY's name tag a third time.

ALEX: *(cont'd)* Nancy. I know there's a rebel inside you just itching to break company policy.

NANCY: I'm probably going to regret this, but all right. I'll need some identification.

ALEX hands over his wallet. NANCY types into her computer. She hands back the wallet then gives ALEX the suitcase from behind the podium.

ALEX: You're an angel. Thank you.

NANCY: You're welcome.

ALEX exits STAGE RIGHT with the suitcase. NANCY calls after him.

NANCY: *(cont'd)* Have a nice day and remember "Why run? Fly North By Northwest."

NANCY resumes working on the computer. RAY rushes in from STAGE LEFT.

NANCY: *(cont'd)* How may I help you, sir?

RAY hands NANCY his ticket.

RAY: I'd like to pick up my bag. It came in on Flight 2310 from Detroit.

NANCY examines the ticket.

NANCY: Ray Wilson? I thought you missed your connection.

RAY: I got a flight on another airline.

NANCY: I'm sorry sir. Your bag isn't here. Please accept this coupon—

RAY: What? But that bag had my suit! I'm attending a funeral tomorrow! I have to have that suit! And you lost my bag?

NANCY: Oh no, sir. Our baggage handlers have the highest efficiency rating in the industry. Your son has your bag.

RAY: Are you trying to be cruel? My son is dead.

NANCY: But he was just here. Big as life.

> *RAY gasps at her insensitive remark. NANCY gasps at her faux pas.*

NANCY: *(cont'd)* I'm sorry, sir! But that man knew your flight information! His driver's license said Alex Wilson!

RAY: Now I don't have a suit to wear to my son's funeral.

NANCY: *(aside)* No good ever comes from breaking company policy.

> *NANCY pulls out a form and begins to fill it out.*

NANCY: *(cont'd)* You can buy a new suit and we'll mail you a reimbursement check.

RAY: But I maxed out my credit cards to pay for the funeral! I don't have enough to pay for a new suit.

> *RAY sobs. NANCY pulls out her checkbook and begins filling out a check.*

NANCY: I'll write you a personal check for two hundred—

> *RAY sobs louder.*

NANCy: *(cont'd)* Four hundred—

> *RAY sobs louder.*

NANCY: *(cont'd)* Eight hundred dollars.

> *NANCY tries to hand RAY the check.*

RAY: I can't take your money.

NANCY: Yes you can.

> *RAY shakes his head.*

RAY: It wouldn't be right.

NANCY: I won't feel right unless you do.

RAY: Really, I can't.

NANCY: I insist.

> *RAY takes the check from NANCY.*

RAY: You're an angel. Thank you.

NANCY: You're welcome. (*Pause.*) Yes...well...I should report to my supervisor.

NANCY begins to exit UPSTAGE CENTER then turns back.

NANCY: *(cont'd)* I am sorry, sir.

NANCY exits. RAY continues to sob. He glances to make sure NANCY is gone then looks STAGE RIGHT.

RAY: Wait up Alex! We've got a check to cash!

LIGHTS OUT

Characters:

ALICE: black journalist, fifties

ETHEL: black journalist, late forties

LOUIS: black journalist, late fifties

Setting: January 25, 1961. The White House correspondents' press room.

Inspired by Alice Dunnigan, Ethel Payne and Louis Lautier.

> LOLLY WARD grew up in Bethesda, MD, moving west to attend Stanford University, where she received her bachelor's and master's in English and Creative Writing. As a member of The Actors' Gang theater, she took on many roles, winning an LA Weekly Award for Masha in *The Seagull*. After opening Tim Robbins's *Embedded* Los Angeles, she toured with it to London and New York, where Robbins directed a film version at the Public Theater. Transitioning to writing, she won Stanford Magazine's fiction contest with her short story, *How to Change Someone's Life, Not Your Own*. Her plays include *72 Objects*, (semifinalist, O'Neill National Playwrights Conference; finalist, IATI Cimientos), *Theory of Nothing, Gone*, (finalist, Portland Civic Theatre Guild), and *Mate*, workshopped with Eric Tucker and The Actors' Gang. She was a member of the LA-based Antaeus Playwrights Lab and the Playwrights Union before moving to Oregon, where she joined the board of the Portland Area Theatre Alliance. lollyward.com

Alice and Ethel enter quickly.

ALICE: No, I do not need to sit down! We've been sitting down. I am going to stand up!

ETHEL: He called on you, Alice!

ALICE: Don't I know it.

ETHEL: Jack Kennedy.

ALICE: President John F. Kennedy. Times they are a-changing.

ETHEL: Right away, first thing. He points to you and says, "Yes, ma'am." Just like that.

ALICE: Good thing I had a question ready! I hadn't needed one.

ETHEL: Long time coming.

ALICE: Three years! That Eisenhower.

ETHEL: Did you have to go and say his name?

ALICE: Dwight D. Eisenhower, and don't let anyone forget it. We showed up for work on time. Scraping together money for a meal, putting on the same worn-out shoes year after year. Calling out, "Mr. President! Mr. President!" To cover his press conferences. To hear what he had to say. And he never wanted to hear what we had to say. Refused to hear.

ETHEL: Three years. That's an awfully long time to sit down on the job.

ALICE: Goodbye, Ike! Mr. *Former* President Ike, I hope your next three years are spent trying to talk while people ignore you. While they talk over you. While they look past you.

Louis walks past.

LOUIS: You ladies had to go stirring up trouble again.

ALICE: Excuse me, Louis. Was that directed at us?

He stops.

LOUIS: Can't leave well enough alone. Just like with Ike, you had to push him on the questions.

ALICE: Well, we are members of the press. It's in our job description.

LOUIS: To get information. To relay that information. Not to alienate the President of the United States.

ETHEL: We ask the questions our readers want to hear.

LOUIS: You started it, Ethel. You got us into hot water at that press conference a few years ago when you set off Eisenhower. Demanding to ask about segregation.

ETHEL: People should be able to travel between states without being segregated.

LOUIS: Smoke came out of his ears.

ETHEL: Between states, it's pathetic! It was 1954 and still backward as ever.

ALICE: I'd like to segregate him. Keep him away from his family and friends because his hair is gray or his eyes are blue or whatever.

ETHEL: All the black suits get to go on this nice train, but the brown suits have to go on that one!

ALICE: Anyone whose first name starts with the letters "A" and "E" is ignorant, but anyone whose first name starts with "D" is brilliant and gets to sit at the front of the bus.

ETHEL: That's convenient for "*Dwight*." But old "Alice" and "Ethel" have to sit in the back. Not to mention you, "*Louis*." Where do you fit in? Pretending to be one of them.

LOUIS: I don't like segregation any more than you do.

ETHEL: Oh well, rules is rules. Nothing personal, of course.

ALICE: Nah, it's nothing personal; it's just our lives. Our dignity. It comes down from God, don't you know! A and E and L names are bad, and D names are good!

ETHEL: You can't judge a book by its cover, but you sure can judge a person that way.

LOUIS: You all don't know how to go along to get along.

ALICE: And where's that gotten you?

LOUIS: First Negro member of the National Press Club.

ALICE: I wouldn't be so proud of that.

LOUIS: I'm damn proud.

ETHEL: You're a card-carrying Republican.

LOUIS: Damn straight.

ETHEL: You don't even know how much they use you. How much they hate you.

LOUIS: You better watch it! You're wrong. They voted me in.

ETHEL: Barely!

LOUIS: They hate *you* because you won't play along. Because you cause trouble any chance you get.

ALICE: Ahh, so this segregation issue across the United States is just Ethel and me causing trouble?

LOUIS: Play by the rules. Work with the system. You'll be surprised how far you'll get.

ALICE: With all due respect, Louis—

LOUIS: Yes?

ALICE: Never! That system is a cage, and you're locked up inside it.

LOUIS: You're the ones locked up! Stuck in the old way. Full of hatred.

ETHEL: I've had enough humiliation to last a lifetime.

ALICE: At one press conference with Eisenhower, I stood up fifteen times to ask a question. Fifteen. Every light face around me got called on, but my brown face faded into the background. The President's advisor even asked me to submit my questions in advance, and then publicly denied that he had done that. You think anyone else had to have their questions vetted ahead of time? Anyone else would have stood for that?

ETHEL: No, ma'am.

ALICE: Anyone else called uppity and a liar?

ETHEL: Just us.

ALICE: And then today—Jack Kennedy. First thing in office, he calls on me. Wants to hear what I have to say. And I got a lot to say.

ETHEL: Amen.

ALICE: I'm going to type up my question and Kennedy's answer and send it to the press. Not the Black press, not the White press — the whole press. Because everybody needs to know that change has come. It's here.

ETHEL: We're here. We're still here.

ALICE: And we're not going anywhere.

ETHEL: Except to lunch, right? I'm starving. This day took it out of me.

Louis starts to walk away.

ALICE: What do you think, Louis? You coming with us?

LOUIS: With you?

ALICE: That's right. With us.

LOUIS: No. Ma'am. Thank you kindly. I have a meeting with the Republican National Committee. They asked me to write a column for the Black press.

ALICE: That's where they keep you.

LOUIS: That's where I want to be.

ETHEL: Come on, Alice. Let's go celebrate. We got our voices back.

ALICE: So long, Louis. Ethel and I are stepping out. I'm filing this story and then I'll meet you there, Ethel. Story first. The story always comes first.

Lights out on the old era.

Characters:

IZZY KUTSCHER: forties - late fifties, the patient. She is waiting to take an angiogram.

ABBY BROWN: forties - late fifties, Izzy's life-long friend, come to keep her company.

HOSPITAL LIAISON: (Voice)— lets patients and families know where to go and how things are.

Setting: New York City hospital, outpatient waiting room filled with both patients and families. Couches, hanging televisions with the news. Maybe a newspaper on a coffee table. Now.

> D. LEE MILLER is the author of a several plays including *The Moon From Mars, The Quickening, When The Dodgers Left Brooklyn* and *The Beulah Ballantine Contest.* Among her list of honors is Critics' Choice at the Double Image/Samuel French Short Play Festival and finalist at Actors Theatre of Louisville and Ensemble Studio Theatre. Among other theatres, her plays have been presented at Emerging Artists Theatre New Works Series, 13th Street Repertory Theatre, Ensemble Studio Theatre, West Bank Cafe, CAP 21, Alice's Fourth Floor, LaMaMa, ETC, the Vital Theatre and the Shenandoah Valley International Playwrights Retreat. Lee is proud to have participated in the first two years of the 365 Women a Year: A Playwriting Project with *Beatrix In The Shadows* at the Sheen Center and *Taro and Capa* at the Theater for the New City. Her play *Origami Tears* is published in the anthology *Facing Forward* by Broadway Play Publishing.

(Izzy sits on a couch, paper and pen in hand. Her arm is already prepped for an IV and her hospital ID is on her wrist. Her iPhone is by her side. She spies her friend entering.)

ABBY: Sorry— Traffic is a nightmare. Oh, you don't look good, honey. How do you feel?

IZZY: I've been better. Thanks for coming.

ABBY: Can I get you something to eat?

IZZY: I can't eat or drink for three hours before the test. I never had breakfast.

ABBY: Me, neither. And I missed dinner last night. So why did the cardiologist—

(Bing—text message on Izzy's phone. Izzy ignores it; Abby reads:)

'What the fuck are they waiting for? Tell them to take you now! Keep us posted!' Sweet.

IZZY: The office. Every half hour like clockwork.

(Shows her paper.)

Can you help me with this?

ABBY: You don't need that. —Why did the cardiologist send you here?

IZZY: The EKG lines turned upside down.

ABBY: You've been sitting out here for hours!

IZZY: I'm an add-on. They said if the pain gets worse I should go downstairs to the ER.

ABBY: So go downstairs!

IZZY: I'm okay so long as I'm sitting. The echo showed tachycardia. Remember Old Man Chamberlain? I feel like he looked. The angiogram will let us know if there's a blockage or if I'm doing it to myself.

ABBY: You mean practically giving yourself a heart attack? That's ridiculous.

IZZY: The name it translates to is 'Broken Heart Syndrome'.

ABBY: Puh-lease: You're not even going out with anyone. Haven't in years!

(Izzy checks newspaper on table.)

One of the buyers at work has vagina.

IZZY: Angina.

ABBY: Right. Oh, I got you a coloring book and pencils. It's supposed to help you relax.

IZZY: Oh, that's great cause I can't seem to focus on much. ...Y'know, I haven't been overly stressed—I've been really on top of things—getting stuff done.

ABBY: Get real! You're a single mother of a teenager and you work 50 plus hours a week— Where is she?

IZZY: Staying with a friend.

ABBY: Oh, your mother called—trying to find you. You didn't tell her?

IZZY: She has a bad heart. She's eighty-seven. Today. Happy Birthday, Mom!

ABBY: I sang to her on the phone. Didn't your Dad die on her birthday? And her sister?

IZZY: Can we talk about something else?

(Bing.)

I know it's a lot to ask— but I'm keeping this very easy—no organ donations—just do everything possible to keep me alive.

(Bing.)

What did you tell Mom? About where I was.

ABBY: I told her you were stuck on the F train. That you texted.

(Izzy starts to color.)

Why can't they just call your sister? She loves to sign things.

IZZY: She's out of the country. Abby, the chances of actually needing the health proxy is, like, nil.

ABBY: Legal stuff is not my thing. —You still color outside the lines!

IZZY: What?

LIAISON (VOICE): The Chin family?

ABBY: You should've called 911. And now I've lied to your mother.

IZZY: I didn't tell you to lie to her. Why did you? —Because you care.

ABBY: So?

IZZY: Just take a walk, would you? Get some lunch.

ABBY: I had lunch. I missed breakfast. —This is so like you. You always have to handle everything yourself. You never let anyone do anything!

IZZY: Because no one 'gets' me. I want peace. So shut up about coloring out of the lines, or lying to my mother, or how I should've gone to the ER—

ABBY: Izzy, you called me.

IZZY: No one else was available! —Abby, I'm— I'm—

ABBY: I know. You're in pain, you don't know what you're saying. You were always hot and cold: friends for a couple of years and then you'd disappear.

IZZY: Or maybe you got a boyfriend and dropped all your female friends. Tommy, Ben—

LIAISON: Isabelle Kutscher?

ABBY: How can you bring that up when this is life and death. This. If you're old enough for this, then I am, too.

> *(Beep.)*

You're too young for this. I'm too young for this! I hate your office! I hate being older!

IZZY: Sure beats the alternative. You're fine, Abs.

LIAISON: Isabelle?

IZZY: Here!

> *(To Abby.)*

You'll be here when I'm done? You won't pick up a doctor or orderly or anything?

ABBY: Puh-lease: your mother would never forgive me! You're like a sister to me.

> *(Takes a moment, and signs health proxy.)*

Characters:

ACTOR 1

ACTOR 2

Setting: A bus stop.

CHERYL FARE is a performing arts professional and educator residing in Richmond VA, actively engaged in juggling projects as a producer, director, playwright, singer/songwriter, actor and teacher. Cheryl is CEO of Free Jambalaya, a Richmond non-profit production company dedicated to the development of original works for the stage. Cheryl served as the Producer for Richmond Shakespeare for several seasons, successfully guiding the company through its merger with Henley Street Theatre (now Quill Theatre), and earning the company the Richmond Theatre Critics Circle Best Play award for *Comedy of Errors* in 2013. Cheryl is the author of dozens of short plays on metaphysical themes, and is a published songwriter and recording artist with 3 single releases and international radio play from her 2009 release, *Springfield.* Cheryl holds BA degrees in Drama and Sociology from the University of Mary Washington, and an MFA in Stage Management & Arts Administration from VA Tech. facebook.com/Cheryl-Fare-SingerSongwriter

(Actors come to center stage, and face the audience. They are waiting for a bus. Pause.)

1: I think the bus is late. I always hate it when the bus is late.

2: I think it's hot out. I always hate it when it's hot out.

1: When the bus is late, then I am late, and it ruins my whole day. Nothing to be done.

2: When I start feeling hot, my cheeks turn red, I get light-headed, and I can't think all day. As you say, not a thing to be done.

1: For some reason today, it crossed my mind to wonder if it really matters. Imagine that.

2: Really? Curious. Very curious, indeed.

(Pause.)

1: Did you hear about what happened with the lady with the big you-know-what?

2: No. I must know all about that. Do tell.

1: Well, if you must know…it fell off.

2: No! I didn't know that was possible.

1: There you have it. You spend your time looking back to keep an eye out, as they say you should, and then looking ahead to be sure, as they also say you should, and then it happens. After all that time being there, it falls off, and that's bad.

2: Yes, bad. So they say, very bad.

1: But I wonder, if it happened to me, would it be all bad?

2: What a thought! They always said it would be bad.

1: Yes, but I wonder.

2: *(Dubious.)* Well, that seems worth considering, at least.

(Pause.)

1: Every day I come and wait. I did it yesterday, and I expect I will do it tomorrow.

2: I made a mistake once, and now it happens over and over again.

1: One day I did not come, just to see what would happen.

2: Really! So, what happened?

105 Five-Minute Plays

1: I didn't know how to act, so I thought it was a mistake.

2: No matter what I do, I still make a mistake. It happened yesterday, so now I'm just waiting for it to happen today.

1: There's an expert on TV. He says that the best predictor of future behavior is past behavior. So, there you have it. Nothing to be done.

2: Well, if he said it on TV, we know it must be true.

1: Just so. Nothing to be done.

2: Just so. Not a thing to be done. (*Pause.*) Do you ever wonder what words mean? I mean, once you say something over and over again, do you forget what it means, or wonder if it really means what you think it means?

1: Um, maybe. Pardon?

2: If there is nothing to be done, must that be a bad thing?

1: It always has been before.

2: But what if it is not a bad thing? What if it means something else?

1: Really? But what else could it mean?

2: Perhaps, just perhaps, it means that we need do nothing.

1: Do nothing? But what are we if we do nothing?

2: We just are. I am, you are, and everything is in order.

1: Radical. Brilliant, really, for you to think such a thing.

2: Oh, I don't think I thought of that myself. Perhaps it just is.

1: What an idea. But then, what about being late?

2: Perhaps you need do nothing.

1: Huh. And what about being hot?

2: Perhaps I don't mind.

1: Maybe.

2: Maybe.

Characters:

COMMUTER: A woman in her late forties, arm in a cast.

COACHMAN: A man in his late forties, smoking a cigarette.

HORSE: Shiny chestnut coat, bandage on his head.

RUBEN CARBAJAL's award-winning plays have been performed across the country, with published works that include *The Gifted Program, Portland*, and the collection *Hold & Other Short Plays*. rubencarbajal.net

Stage is dark. Sound of a galloping horse. Traffic horns. A neigh. Tires screech. A collision. Then, a slide of a contemporary photo showing a carriage and car collision.

Another slide, a title card:

HORSE: *(Reads caption for photo and context of the crash.)*

Pool of light on a COMMUTER, seated in a folding chair.

COMMUTER: I hate driving in the city. I always worried I was going to kill one of those bike messengers. But this?

Lights out on COMMUTER, pool of light on COACH-MAN, also seated in a folding chair.

COACHMAN: It was a horn, I think. Spooked him. After that, I mean, it was all over for us.

Lights out on COACHMAN. Pool of light on HORSE.

HORSE: I don't remember much. I think they sedated me. But I've seen the pictures. The wires picked it up. Made a couple of front pages. Even went viral, I'm told.

Lights out on HORSE. From this point on, single pool of light on whomever is speaking.

COMMUTER: To be honest, I think it would've been better for everyone if I had hit a bike messenger. I know that sounds really shitty, but it's true.

COACHMAN: The press has been crazy. Before, we'd get a few of the PETA people on us, you know, protesters? They'd harass the tourists as we'd take them through the park. Placards, and whatnot. You get called every name in the book. But this? It's just out of control.

HORSE: I'm not going to comment on the whole animal rights issue. I've accepted my lot in life. It's not easy. The asphalt gets hot. There's the carriage, which is no picnic. I drag around mostly Midwesterners who, let's face it, aren't exactly anorexic supermodels. On the other hand, there are countries where horsemeat is a delicacy. I have a cousin who works at a petting zoo. Sounds like a good gig, right? But the guy rides in a perfect circle all day. That's no life. I get to see all kinds of things. I like listening to the conversations. The oohs and ahhhs. You know, guys trying to impress dates. I'm a sucker for that kind of stuff.

COMMUTER: I know it sounds cold, but do you know if I would've hit a messenger, this wouldn't have made the second to last page of the Daily News? A couple hundred of those poor bastards get squashed like bugs every year; you think anyone gives a crap? Hit a horse, and suddenly I'm one notch above a child pornographer. I've been getting honest-to-god death threats. I mean, the horse ran into me.

COACHMAN: There was a strange moment there when he freaked out... All day, every day, that horse goes where I say he goes. You take it for granted. Suddenly, I'm at his mercy. Where will he take me? Where will my life go from here? Will I die?

HORSE: I was scared. I remember that. The papers said I got spooked by a car horn. Maybe.

Initially, perhaps. But I think what really freaked me out was the realization that I was in control. The reigns were loose. I'd been handed the power over my own fate. Was this what I had hoped for all along? My whole life I've been told where to go, when to turn, how fast, how slow. Now, here I am in the middle of 5th Avenue, the storefronts illuminating rain-soaked streets...the master of my own destiny. Where will I go from here? Where will I take my life? Will I die?

COMMUTER: My husband took me on a carriage ride once. It was Valentine's Day. Snow everywhere. Traveling at that speed, the world slows down. The hoof-beats transform you to a rhythm New Yorkers aren't accustomed to. Like a heartbeat. You take notice. The bare branches carrying all that snow in their arms. Wrapped in a wool blanket, next to the man you settled for. The same view you might see a hundred years ago. Longer, even. You think about time. And the way we conduct our lives now. And it's so quiet. You feel like you're in one of those snow globes, like the world is covered in glass. About halfway through, you get a little unsettled. You know, just over the walls of the park, the city is moving. You're separated. From those going to their jobs. Making decisions. Participating in life. By the end of it, you're full on anxious. You want the ride to end. You want to get back to your apartment. Your life. New Yorkers are in New York because we don't like to ruminate. We don't want time to phi-losophize or listen to our souls. It's just too damn terrifying.

Why do you think we've plugged ourselves into machines 24-7? Anything, we'll take any damn distraction to stave off an empty moment of contemplation.

COACHMAN: I don't know. It's basically over for me. The whole business. Good riddance, I guess. It's just not worth it any more. Too much controversy. Too much bullshit. Someone's always got a problem with something. There used to be certain things that were always New York. Egg Creams. A decent strip club. Smoking a joint on the street without being hassled. Not anymore. I got cited. Bad publicity. Company fired me. Not sure what I'll do. My cousin has a pedicab business he started a few years ago. He says I'll have to start at the bottom, work my way up. Whatever. Maybe it'll get me back into shape.

HORSE: Well, the carriage company retired me. Some upstate hippie couple agreed to take me in. I'll get some needed time off. Some of my earliest memories are of the sky. A horizon unimpeded by buildings. It'll be good to return to that. I think I'll miss the city, though. When I look at that photo, I have to admit, I'm overcome with this strange feeling of pride. I think to myself, this is a metaphor for something.

Lights out. Curtain.

Characters:

MR. LOVEWORTH: The owner of a dating agency. Age open.

LESLIE: A woman looking to date again. Age open.

Setting: The Happy Endings Dating Agency. The present.

ANDREW BISS is playwright and author whose works have been produced in New York, London, Los Angeles, and many other cities across North America, Europe and Australia. His plays have won awards on both coasts of the U.S., critical acclaim in the U.K., and quickly became an Off-Off-Broadway mainstay. He is published by Smith & Kraus, Inc., Bedford/St. Martin's, Pioneer Drama Service, and Meriwether Publishing Ltd. He is a graduate of the University of the Arts London, and a member of the Dramatists Guild of America, Inc. andrewbiss.com andrewbiss.blogspot.com

(At rise: MR. LOVEWORTH is found seated behind his desk, scribbling notes in a book. Presently, there is a knock at the door. Upon opening it he discovers LESLIE.)

MR. LOVEWORTH: You must be Leslie.

LESLIE: Yes. And you must be Mr. Loveworth.

MR. LOVEWORTH: Right again.

LESLIE: Sorry?

MR. LOVEWORTH: Do come in.

LESLIE: Thank you.

MR. LOVEWORTH: Firstly, let me say welcome to the Happy Endings Dating Agency—where love isn't just a dream, it's a calculated decision.

LESLIE: Thank you.

MR. LOVEWORTH: Do take a seat.

LESLIE: You're a little different than I imagined.

MR. LOVEWORTH: How so?

LESLIE: I don't know. Something about your voice—I imagined you taller.

MR. LOVEWORTH: I have a tall voice?

LESLIE: Well, no, I…

MR. LOVEWORTH: So, what brings you to our humble, and some might say, old-fashioned little establishment?

LESLIE: Well, boredom, I suppose. Boredom with my non-existent love life. It's like there's a void inside of me that needs filling. I admit I did try a few of the online agencies first, but it all felt so anonymous and…well, cold, really.

MR. LOVEWORTH: You don't have to explain to me, Leslie. We here at Happy Endings are quite aware that when it comes to love, there's no substitute for the personal touch. Now, there's absolutely no reason to lose heart. You simply need to pay a little mind to how others perceive you.

LESLIE: But…I don't know how to be anything other than who I am.

MR. LOVEWORTH: And therein lies the problem.

LESLIE: But this is it—this is me.

MR. LOVEWORTH: But it's not enough. It's not enough to just *be* in this day and age.

LESLIE: Why ever not?

MR. LOVEWORTH: Look, Leslie, I'm only trying to help you achieve your goals, but if I'm to do so, you're going to have to confront some uncomfortable truths. Now, in Prehistoric times, things were much more straightforward. You could simply wrap yourself in a pelt, grunt a few times at your heart's desire and live happily ever after. These days things are a little more complicated. Every aspect of your being has to be cultivated and contrived. Nothing can be left to chance. The way you dress, the way you walk, the way you smile, the way you talk, all of it has to be manufactured with absolute precision in order to create the *real* you —— the one that closes the deal. Then and only then will you have become something truly viable in today's fickle and uncertain market.

> *(Pause.)*

LESLIE: Can't someone just love me for who I am?

MR. LOVEWORTH: But if you don't know who you are —— what's to love?

> *(Beat.)*

LESLIE: The question marks?

MR. LOVEWORTH: Let me put it this way. Let's say I send you out to meet with a very nice gentleman who you find yourself very attracted to, and the next evening you anxiously await his call. He, meanwhile, that very same evening, is enjoying cocktails with friends who are all eager to hear the outcome of his first date, and to whom he relays any one of the following: "She redefined the word dull." "From the way she dressed I assumed she was manic depressive." "Her hair kept reminding me of my grandmother." "She was nice enough, but God, that annoying laugh!" Or perhaps, "In a million years I could *never* get used to that nose."

> *(Beat.)*

Do you see what I mean?

LESLIE: *(Overwhelmed.)* I…it's…it's all too much. I…can't do it.

MR. LOVEWORTH: Incidentally, *your* nose—have you considered surgery?

LESLIE: Oh, that's it. That is it! I've had it!

MR. LOVEWORTH: I was only going to suggest a slight—

LESLIE: This is ridiculous!

(Standing.)

I'm sorry, I've had enough.

MR. LOVEWORTH: I'm sorry?

LESLIE: I've had enough.

MR. LOVEWORTH: Look, let's not overreact. I'm here to help.

LESLIE: Yes…and you have. You really have.

MR. LOVEWORTH: Good. Now sit down and let's—

LESLIE: I'm leaving.

MR. LOVEWORTH: Now?

LESLIE: I should never have come.

MR. LOVEWORTH: What about love?

LESLIE: I've gone off it.

MR. LOVEWORTH: But you need it. Everyone does.

LESLIE: It's too much trouble.

MR. LOVEWORTH: But your boredom? Your void?

LESLIE: I'll fill it with something else.

MR. LOVEWORTH: A cat?

LESLIE: A catechism. I'll take the vows.

MR. LOVEWORTH: A nun?

LESLIE: I hear a calling.

MR. LOVEWORTH: I hear nothing.

LESLIE: Thanks for everything.

MR. LOVEWORTH: But don't you want—

LESLIE: Goodbye.

(LESLIE exits.)

MR. LOVEWORTH: …a happy ending?

(BLACKOUT)

THE BALLAD OF CESS POOL AND LIL TINA
(A SHORT PLAY IN THE POETIC STYLE OF A SESTINA)
Dara Silverman

Characters:

    CESS POOL

    LIL TINA

Setting: Night.

> DARA SILVERMAN is an artist and educator, living and working in the Bay Area. She received her Bachelor's Degree in film from New York University, and her Master's Degree from San Francisco State University in playwriting. She has used her skills as an educator at The Academy of Art University, The Palo Alto Children's Theater and The Alameda County Juvenile Detention Hall. A true dabbler at heart, Dara has worked in theater in a variety of capacities, including constructing sets for the Virus Theater in Silver City, NM and designing props for SF Playhouse in San Francisco, CA. She has made several short films, which screened nationwide at festivals, and has written several plays, including *Lost*, *Almost* and *Purple Beastly.*

(A thick, rolling fog over fields of tall grass, silver-streaked in the moonlight. An old beat up car, hopefully a Studebaker. Cess Pool gets out of the driver's seat. He lives up to his name, but in a sexy way.)

CESS POOL: Can't barely see my own hand right in front of my face in this woolly mist.

(He waves his hand in front of his face, stretches his arms, struts a bit.)

CESS POOL: But I can see the moon all right, clear as if she were showing me her secret things that weren't allowed.

(Pause.)

Makes me wanna get down on my knees and pray.

He gets down on his knees.

CESS POOL*:* Oh sultry stewardess of the night sky, tonight you've blessed us with a stealthy peace. The fog gives us our solitude while your silvery streaks light the way for me to behold my Lil Tina, my fine and fresh maid.

LIL TINA: *(From the car.)* Cess Pool, if you're dead set on beholdin', you're just gonna have to wait.

(Cess Pool jumps up, rushes to the passenger door and opens it.)

CESS POOL: I'll die from doing the wait.

LIL TINA: If you croaked out here, it'd be days before you'd go missed.

CESS POOL: Grant me but a leg, so sturdy and well made.

LIL TINA: Fair enough. But that's all that you're allowed.

(She extends her long leg from the passenger seat. A stiletto, obviously.)

CESS POOL: Oh, the moon's got nothing on your gorgeous gam, true giver of peace.

LIL TINA: Get on your knees boy, let me see how you pray.

(Cess Pool gets down on his knees and kisses the leg up and down.)

LIL TINA: Cess Pool, you make me feel as though you were a lion and I were your prey.

CESS POOL: Let me see your face now Lil Tina, streaked wet with fog, and please don't make me wait.

(Carefully, Lil Tina steps out of the car. She is not little.)

LIL TINA: Careful now, these shoes ain't made for this scrappy land, this pulpy piece.

(Lil Tina surveys the scene, the land, the sky. She breathes in the air.)

LIL TINA: Nothing moister with moisturizer than the dewy nighttime mist. I'da sold it over the counter if I thought Mother Nature would have allowed.

CESS POOL: They'da sold it right back once they realize ain't nuthin in this world coulda made them resemble you Lil Tina, my dazzling and delicate maid.

(Lil Tina rolls her eyes.)

LIL TINA: Well let's make to doin' cause the doing needs getting made. May the good moon turn her back to our sins, her hands clasped 'gainst her darkened back side to pray.

CESS POOL: The good moon has seen more lovers than stars in the sky, she knows what is and what ain't allowed.

(Cess Pool goes to the trunk of the car and opens it. He pulls at a lifeless body, wrapped in a tarp and secured with rope.)

CESS POOL: Come here Lil Tina; help me shoulder the weight.

LIL TINA: But Cess Pool, I can't see nuthin' in this hairy mist.

CESS POOL: Don't mean you can't carry your piece.

LIL TINA: Only if you stop your naggin' and give me some peace.

(Lil Tina begrudgingly helps Cess Pool take the body out of the trunk.)

CESS POOL: Peace ain't something that's given, peace is something that's made.

LIL TINA: Well we one step closer to makin' it, here in this dingy mist.

(They drag the body to the ground. Cess Pool takes out two shovels and tries to hand one to Lil Tina.)

CESS POOL: Wrap your pretty paws round this shovel Lil Tina like you're learnin' to pray.

> *(Lil Tina takes the shovel, resentfully.)*

CESS POOL: Now put your foot on the blade and lean in with all your weight.

LIL TINA: If my husband coulda seen me, shovelin' in these pricey pumps he woulda laughed aloud.

CESS POOL: But your husband can't never see you again, thanks to all the heaven's have allowed.

LIL TINA: May he rest in peace.

CESS POOL: Well until we finish diggin' this here hole, his peace is just gonna have to wait.

> *(They dig.)*

LIL TINA: Oh no, my little cotton shift is all covered in dirt 'cause of this darn mess you made.

CESS POOL: I'd quit complainin' if I were you, if I wanted to get outta here in one piece!

> *(Lil Tina stops digging.)*

LIL TINA: Don't you think for a second your innuendo was missed!

> *(Cess Pool stops digging.)*

CESS POOL: How have I allowed myself to lie upon this bitter bed that I have made?

LIL TINA: You've made your peace, you're stuck with me, my tender prey.

CESS POOL: I suppose we belong to each other now, under the weight of our own consciences, here in the everlasting darkness, here in the dirt and dampening mist.

> *(They look at one another. Uh oh.)*

Characters: 8 Performers

DAVID KODESKI is the creator of *David Kodeski's True Life Tales,* a series of solo performances based on found diaries, letters, photographs, scrapbooks, and other thrift store ephemera. He lives in Chicago. *Christmas in June* is one of the thousands of plays written and performed by cast members of the experimental theatre company, The Neo-Futurists, in their show, *Too Much Light Makes The Baby Go Blind,* an "ever-changing attempt to perform 30 plays in 60 minutes." truelifetales.com

(Everyone excepting David is in winter gear—Christmas caroling. David is center. Behind him, standing on chairs, are John and Phil, with hole punches and white paper making "snow." Marjorie is off stage right.)

DAVID: I call my Dad. Hi it's me. What's going on?

DIANA: It's hot there he says.

DAVID: Here too I tell him.

MARJORIE: *(Carries a sign: "Niagara Falls 500 miles.")* He lives 500 miles away. *(She joins the carolers.)*

DAVID: To the east. He usually gets today's weather tomorrow so I'm not surprised when he tells me.

DIANA: It's hot there he says.

DAVID: And he tells me he's hung some hanging plants and worked a bit on the rock garden.

DIANA: The baskets were a buck ninety-nine, he says.

DAVID: He tells me he's going to buy an air conditioner for her when she comes home. My mother has been in hospital since December. It was snowing then.

ANITA: Skarenhe's in the nursing home now he says.

NOELLE: The staff is overworked. Her regular doctor isn't part of the HMO.

ANITA: They say he couldn't take her hospital gowns home to be washed anymore.

NOEL: Streptococcus my-rah-strep-toh-whatever…

ANITA: He said he went down to the laundry room of the nursing home and they were all backed up.

MARJORIE: He said he caused a scene.

DAVID: My father has a temper. Slow to burn but explosive. When I was a boy, I would have dreams, and this is how my father would sound:

PHIL: RAAHH. RAAAAARRRR. GAAAAARRRRRR RRRRRRAAAAAAAARRRRR!!!!!!!!

MARJORIE: He said he caused a scene.

DAVID I can imagine.

PHIL: She has been in the hospital since December.

MARJORIE: Diabetic shock.

PHIL: Pneumonia.

MARJORIE: Did she have a heart attack?

DAVID: Did she or didn't she?

JOHN: Gall stones.

LUSIA: Ulcers.

JOHN: Rheumatoid arthritis.

LUSIA: She can stand for about a minute.

JOHN: She can take a few steps on her own.

LUSIA: She tried the walker and made a couple of steps.

JOHN: There are good days.

LUSIA: There are bad days.

DIANA: She won't eat.

PHIL: She threw up.

DIANA: High protein diet and dialysis.

PHIL: He got mad and told her: If you don't eat you're going to
    go on those supplements and then the IV.

DAVID: PT.

DIANA: Physical Therapy.

DAVID: PT he calls it. She had her PT.

    In my father's house, there are hanging plants for a buck
    ninety-nine on the back patio. He's going to buy an air con-
    ditioner for when she gets home.

PHIL: She has to take 10 steps on her own.

DAVID: In my father's house, the Christmas tree still stands.
    (It's artificial, of course, I mean I'm talking about my
    parents here… wouldn't all of this be 10 times more sad and
    pathetic if it were real tree?)

ALL: Fa la la la la la la la la

DAVID: The Christmas tree still stands with all the presents un-
    derneath—unopened—waiting for the day when my mother
    gets home. I got a beautiful photo album for my sister Carol

so that she could put pictures of her new baby in it—and for her wedding pictures which will take place in October—if my mother gets out of the hospital in time. I haven't seen her since January. In the darkest times I worry that I will never look her in the eye again. I have my mother's eyes.

Characters:

MIRANDA: A woman in her early twenties. Insecure.

JORDY: Another woman in her early twenties. Charismatic and self-confident.

Setting: Pizza place. Lunchtime.

CAROLYN GAGE is a playwright, performer, director, and activist. The author of nine books on lesbian theatre and seventy-five plays, musicals, and one-woman shows, she specializes in non-traditional roles for women, especially those reclaiming famous lesbians whose stories have been distorted or erased from history. Her work is widely produced, and in 2014 she was one of six featured playwrights at UNESCO's World Theater Day in Rome. She has won the national Lambda Literary Award in Drama and her play, *Ugly Ducklings* was nominated by the American Theatre Critics Association for the prestigious ATCA/ Steinberg New Play Award, an award given annually for the best new play produced outside New York. She has also been awarded numerous grants and fellowships. Her papers are archived at the Sophia Smith Collection at Smith College.

carolyngage.com

(Two young women are sitting at a pizza restaurant. They have ordered a double-cheese pizza, and it has just arrived. MIRANDA is a young woman in her early 20's. She is insecure about her looks and she wears conservative, professional clothes. JORDY, a young woman in her early 20's, is self-confident and wears very trendy "hipster" clothing. JORDY serves the slices for both of them.)

MIRANDA: Oh, my god… It's really cheesy.

JORDY: Double cheese… Here… *(She cuts and passes her the slice on a plate. The cheese hangs down in long strings.)*

MIRANDA: *(With concern.)* That's a lot of calories.

JORDY: *(With enthusiasm.)* Yeah it is! *(MIRANDA lifts up the piece. It's hotter than she anticipated, and the cheese slides down her face. She starts laughing.)*

MIRANDA: Ooooo… Napkin! Napkin…! *(JORDY has taken out her phone and is taking a picture.)* No! Jordy, don't you dare!

JORDY: There! *(She hands MIRANDA the napkins and then looks at the photo and starts laughing.)*

MIRANDA: Let me see! *(She grabs the phone.)* Oh, my god! *(JORDY grabs it back.)* You delete that!

JORDY: Hell no. It's going on Facebook.

MIRANDA: You wouldn't!

JORDY: Wanna bet?

MIRANDA: Don't! *(JORDY is fiddling with the phone.)* Oh, my god, you're serious. Jordy! No! What if Michael sees it?

JORDY: *(Focused on the phone.)* That's the whole point.

MIRANDA: No! Jordy! Don't!

JORDY: *(A realization.)* He's never seen you eat pizza…has he? *(MIRANDA doesn't say anything.)* Your fiancé has *never* seen you eat pizza!

MIRANDA: Delete it! Please, Jordy…

JORDY: What? Were you going to wait until after you're married to eat pizza with him?

MIRANDA: Give it here…

JORDY: Isn't that some kind of fraud or entrapment or something. You're the law school student.

MIRANDA: *(Desperate.)* Come on, Jordy…I'll pay for dessert!

JORDY: *What?* Now you want to *bribe* me?

MIRANDA: *(Serious.)* I just really want you to delete that picture. *(JORDY looks at her for a moment and then deletes it. She shows the phone to MIRANDA to prove it.)* Thank you. *(MIRANDA unrolls the knife and fork that are in the napkin. JORDY just watches her. MIRANDA ignores her.)*

JORDY: Do you let him see you without makeup? *(MIRANDA pretends not to hear. She begins to cut the pizza into pieces with the knife.)* Do you fart in front of him?

MIRANDA: I don't think that's any of your business. *(JORDY picks up her pizza.)* Do *you* eat pizza in front of your girlfriends?

JORDY: *(With her mouth full.)* Apparently.

MIRANDA: I mean your girlfriend-girlfriends. The ones you date.

JORDY: Yeah.

MIRANDA: *(Rationalizing.)* Well, it's different between women.

JORDY: Duh.

MIRANDA: *(Setting down the knife and fork.)* You know, Jordy, this isn't fair.

JORDY: What?

MIRANDA: You judging me. You're all cute and sassy and your family has a ton of money and you're all why-aren't-you-like-me-all-spontaneous-and-authentic, but there's actually a lot of privilege behind your free-to-be crap. *(JORDY is digesting this.)* What?

JORDY: *(Defensive.)* I'm *thinking.*

MIRANDA: Well…?

JORDY: Well, that's probably true. *(MIRANDA waits. A beat.)* Objection sustained. *(They eat pizza in silence for a moment.)* But what if it's like the glass slipper?

MIRANDA: What?

JORDY: The pizza thing. It's like Cinderella and the glass slipper. It's the test. Maybe you eat pizza in front of all kinds of people, and maybe most of them who see you with food on your face think it's disgusting, but then there's going to be somebody someday who sees you with double cheese on your chin and thinks it's absolutely charming.

MIRANDA: Nobody's going to think that.

JORDY: I do. *(MIRANDA goes quickly back to her pizza. JORDY watches her.)* Ouch…

MIRANDA: *(Defensive.)* I'm not lesbian.

JORDY: Didn't say you were. Just said I enjoy watching you eat pizza.

MIRANDA: *(Putting down the fork.)* I'm sorry, Jordy. If I was a lesbian, I'd go for you in a heartbeat.

JORDY: Actually, I don't think you would. I think you'd be all weird with me like you are with Michael, because you're afraid of intimacy. Yeah. If you can just pretend to be someone you're not, then it's kind of like a buffer. You can slip away anytime and then console yourself with the fact they never saw the real you anyway. You know what? I'm closer to you as a friend than you would ever let me get as a lover.

MIRANDA: *(Awkward pause. MIRANDA is at the end of her skill set for communicating. She tries to make a joke.)* Yeah. Way to ruin a pizza, Jordy.

JORDY: Sorry. *(MIRANDA goes back to eating.)* Not. *(A beat.)* You know what, Miranda? I think we're done. *(JORDY turns away with her phone and begins to check messages. MIRANDA, alarmed, watches her, but JORDY is completely absorbed with her phone.)*

MIRANDA: *(Frightened and desperate, she picks up a slice of pizza and places it cheese-side-down on her head. JORDY is lost in her cell phone and does not notice. MIRANDA takes a photo of herself with her phone. She sends it to JORDY. JORDY sees it and does a take. She turns quickly to MI-RANDA.)*

JORDY: *(Stunned.)* I can't believe you did that.

MIRANDA: And I'm going to Facebook it… *(She sends the photo to Facebook.)*

JORDY: Michael's going to see it…

MIRANDA: Well, if he doesn't love me as much as you, then maybe I should rethink my options.

JORDY: Maybe you should. *(The women share a smile and a pizza.)*

Blackout

Characters:

MAN

WOMAN

Setting: The bar. Late. This couple has been there a while.

ALLAN STAPLES is a New York-based playwright and screenwriter whose work has been developed at the Kennedy Center, Playwrights' Center and the Jungle Theater. His work has been produced by the Minnesota Fringe Festival, Thirst Theatre, Short+Sweet Singapore, Bloomington Playwrights Project and the Brick Theatre among others. His one-act, *Why Actors Can't Love* won the American Theatre Coop Award and his original pilot, *The Experimentalist*, was awarded first place in the 1st TV Script Writing Competition. He's also been a finalist in the New Works of Merit Playwriting Contest, Denver Film Festival screenplay competition, West Field Screenwriting Awards and the American Gem Short Script contest. Allan received his MFA in Playwriting from the New School for Drama and is a member of Actors' Equity Association. allanstaples.com

WOMAN: So. Out of curiosity. When you say those words…

MAN: Yeah...

WOMAN: What, exactly, do they mean to you?

MAN: What? No, c'mon. We're not going to do this, *please*...

WOMAN: Do what?

MAN: I think we should go...

WOMAN: Why? I'm curious is all. Curious to know what the phrase means to you. Like if I said, 'God, I love this meal' it is because the process of combining the ingredients, the preparation and the cooking of said ingredients, has been done expertly and that gives me pleasure.

MAN: So what?

WOMAN: So if you say you love me, what, exactly, does that mean to you?

MAN: I don't understand this.

WOMAN: You're intelligent, somewhat. You should understand.

MAN: Hey, why are you attacking me? I thought saying that was a good thing.

WOMAN: In my experience, it can be, or it can't be.

MAN: That's everything. You've just explained everything.

WOMAN: I'm trying to...understand is all...

MAN: By asking unfair questions? Because saying, 'I love you,' is nothing like saying, 'I loved that quesadilla.'

WOMAN: Fine! So tell me what it is like.

MAN: Don't say quesadilla, but what does it mean to you?

WOMAN: It means that on the list of people I've talked with and the list of people I've had sex with, your cumulative score ranks you the highest. *(Beat.)* Currently.

MAN: Now that? That's not romantic.

WOMAN: I was going for accuracy, not romance. So it's your turn now.

MAN: It's a...feeling I have, I don't know-

WOMAN: Oh! A feeling? Like nausea?

MAN: No, the opposite of nausea.

WOMAN: That's romantic.

MAN: Do you feel neglected? Do you feel unloved?

WOMAN: No.

MAN: So there you go.

WOMAN: There I go?

MAN: There you go.

WOMAN: So my not feeling the opposite of what I'd like to feel-

MAN: ...means you feel that way, yes.

WOMAN: So by not hating someone, does that mean you love them?

MAN: No-

WOMAN: So what you said was wrong?

MAN: Perhaps.

WOMAN: Would you kill someone for me?

MAN: Would I kill someone for you...? Ah, who?

WOMAN: Anyone. *(Beat.)* A person.

MAN: What person?

WOMAN: A random person.

MAN: Ahmmm, Hitler yes, my mother no.

WOMAN: A neutral person.

MAN: People aren't neutral.

WOMAN: The Swiss.

MAN: The Swiss government is neutral. The citizens are... assholes.

WOMAN: Would you lie for me?

MAN: For what reason?

WOMAN: To save my life...

MAN: From who?

WOMAN: The Government.

MAN: Sure.

WOMAN: Would you steal for me?

MAN: Bread yes, diamonds no.

WOMAN: Money. For an operation.

MAN: Cancer treatment yes, breast enhancement no.

WOMAN: Would you fall on a grenade for me?

MAN: To save your life? Yes. To amuse you? No.

WOMAN: Wait, what's wrong with my boobs?

MAN: Nothing!

WOMAN: You are a weird man.

MAN: Oh, I'm weird? But you're not?

WOMAN: I'm weird because instead of sitting quietly and not understanding the depth of what you say you feel towards me, I ask questions in an attempt to understand it.

MAN: Well fine.

WOMAN: What—?

MAN: When phrased like that—

WOMAN: That's what it is!

MAN: I think you're just trying to be…difficult.

WOMAN: Difficult—?

MAN: Yeah—

WOMAN: Difficult like Susan B Anthony-

MAN: Oh c'mon—

WOMAN: What—?

MAN: It's not exactly Women's Suffrage—

WOMAN: Not *per se-*

MAN: Not at all. *(Beat.)* I don't think the Socratic Method works for all subjects.

WOMAN: Fine.

MAN: Are you mad? *(Beat.)* You're mad.

WOMAN: You're treating something that— while not super vitally important— is somewhat important to me and you dismiss it like it's ridiculous.

MAN: I'm sorry. But it is ridiculous.

WOMAN: And that's why I'm mad.

MAN: So you are mad.

WOMAN: I wasn't before—

MAN: A second ago—

WOMAN: And now I am. It's called change.

   (A moment.)

MAN: Do you love me enough to let me watch sports in my underwear?

WOMAN: Yes.

MAN: In your underwear?

WOMAN: I mean, sure.

MAN: In a third party's underwear?

WOMAN: Okay, listen.

MAN: If you were a virtuoso violinist, would you give it up for me? If you had to not drink orange juice ever again to save my life...from lions, would you? Could you tickle someone to death for me? Are those things you'd be willing to do?

WOMAN: Those are random questions, they aren't tethered to anything meaningful.

MAN: I'm trying to understand the depth of your feeling towards me by asking ridiculous questions that have no basis in actually assessing anything, much less your feelings towards me…

WOMAN: Are you saying my methodology is flawed?

MAN: I'm saying, I think they wanna close and we should go.

WOMAN: One last question.

MAN: What?

WOMAN: When you say, 'I love you,' what does that mean to you? Because I'm not leaving here until—

MAN: It means I love you. I love you. Period.

WOMAN: But what kind?

MAN: I don't know, the real kind?

WOMAN: But if it were the...fake kind you wouldn't tell me, would you?

MAN: No, absolutely not, no...

WOMAN: So how do I know if it's the real kind?

(A moment.)

MAN: Well. That's the hard part, I guess.

(A sad moment.)

WOMAN: We should go.

(She begins to gather her things.)

MAN: Hey.

WOMAN: What?

MAN: You know, there's nothing else I can say. I can only promise you that I mean it, and you either believe it or not...

(She nods.)

WOMAN: I know. *(Beat.)* And that's why it kinda sucks.

The lights fade.

Characters:

    HORTENSE: A wealthy, middle-aged woman.

    CHAUNCEY: A wealthy, middle-aged man, Hortense's husband.

    MARIGOLD: An exotic cheese dealer.

Setting: A coatroom. The recent past.

> AMANDA PETEFISH-SCHRAG is an Assistant Professor of Theatre at Iowa State University. Her professional credits include work as a director, playwright, and puppeteer. Her plays have been produced at theaters and festivals across the country. Amanda is a member of the Dramatists Guild.
> dramatistsguild.com/memberdirectory/getmembership.aspx?cid=39558

(HORTENSE enters sneakily. She waits. CHAUNCEY enters sneakily. Both assume they are alone. They see each other—)

CHAUNCEY: Ahhh!

HORTENSE: Ahhh! I mean, ah, Chauncey, what a pleasant surprise.

CHAUNCEY: *(Trying to appear casual.)* Indeed. Imagine meeting you here.

HORTENSE: Were you looking for something?

CHAUNCEY: Me? No. I was just— just— well, yes, I was looking for something. I needed to check my coat for a cigarette.

HORTENSE: You don't smoke, dear.

CHAUNCEY: Indeed. A very fine observation. But, of course, I wasn't looking for a cigarette to smoke, I was checking to be sure that no one had put cigarettes in my coat. You know how I despise tobacco products.

(He finds his coat, checks the pocket.)

No. No cigarettes here, thank goodness.

(Beat.)

So, what brings you to this coatroom, my dear?

HORTENSE: Me? Oh, of course. You see, I thought this was the ladies lavatory. Obviously I was mistaken. Ha, ha. Seems rather ridiculous now.

CHAUNCEY: Indeed.

HORTENSE: Of course, now that you've checked your coat, I imagine you'll be getting back to the party.

CHAUNCEY: Yes. Yes I will. I just wanted to take a bit of a "breather" first. Of course, you'll be wanting to get to the ladies lavatory.

HORTENSE: Absolutely. I was simply admiring the architecture of this...closet. So rare to see such workmanship in this day and age. Quite remarkable.

CHAUNCEY: Indeed. But, hadn't you better be going dear? Nature waits for no woman, and you know how you get when you haven't...well...you know.

HORTENSE: No, I'm quite sure I don't know. I find your crude implications offensive. You've wounded my feelings deeply, Chauncey.

(She turns away from him.)

I really need to be alone now. Go.

(She waves him away.)

Just go.

CHAUNCEY: Dear Hortense, you know I'm only looking out for your best interests. There, there. Oh, look. Your mascara's run all over your face. You should really go clean yourself up a bit. You do look a fright.

(He starts to take her toward the door.)

HORTENSE: *(Burying her face in his shoulder.)* Oh my love, I'm so sorry. I know your intentions are nothing if not pure.

(She lifts her head.)

Oh, dear. Look at that. I've made quite a mess on your collar. Best you should go tidy that up before the stain sets in.

(She tries to move him toward the door.)

CHAUNCEY: My appearance means nothing if you're not happy, dear. Here, take this–

(He hands her some cash.)

And go buy yourself a nice gin and tonic at the bar.

HORTENSE: *(Stumbling a bit)* Oh, dear. I do seem to be a bit dehydrated. I feel rather dizzy. Could you go fetch that drink for me, love?

CHAUNCEY: It is awfully stuffy in here. Best step out there—

(He opens the coatroom door.)

—and get a breath of fresh air.

HORTENSE: *(Tossing the cash out the door)* Oh my, look what I've done! Could you go get that for me, dear?

CHAUNCEY: *(Looking out the door)* Egads! Hortense, there are poor people trying to take our money. Quick! Stop them!

(CHAUNCEY lifts HORTENSE and carries her toward the door.)

HORTENSE: *(Putting out her legs to stop him from removing her from the coatroom.)* Those poor people are too terrifying! Please, go fight them off! Protect me, love of my life!

CHAUNCEY: *(Still trying to force HORTENSE from the room.)* Best to face one's fears head on, dear heart.

HORTENSE: Good advice, Sweetums. Best to take fear by its balls!

> *(HORTENSE grabs CHAUNCEY's crotch and squeezes. CHAUNCEY collapses in pain, dropping HORTENSE on her derriere. Both sit, collapsed on the floor of the coatroom.)*

Perhaps some ice from the bar would help your injury, Schnookums.

CHAUNCEY: Shut up, Hortense.

HORTENSE: My, my. Someone needs to take a time out. As in, out of here.

CHAUNCEY: All right. Confess. Why are you in here?

HORTENSE: I ought to ask you the same question. In fact, I will. Why are you in here?

CHAUNCEY: I'll tell when you do.

HORTENSE: *(Crawling over toward him.)* Tell me!

> *(She grabs his crotch again.)*

Tell!

> *(CHAUNCEY grabs her hair and pulls her down.)*

CHAUNCEY: You tell!

> *(MARIGOLD enters.)*

MARIGOLD: I'm here, love –

> *(She sees them both on the floor and stops. HORTENSE sits up and straightens her hair and dress. CHAUNCEY tries to act casual.)*

CHAUNCEY and HORTENSE: *(Overlapping.)* This is not— I'm not— I was just— what it looks like is—

> *(They both glare at each other.)*

CHAUNCEY: Marigold, this is not what it looks li—

HORTENSE: Wait just a moment! You know Marigold? *(Beat.)* Are you? With her?!

CHAUNCEY: Certainly not! I am— Wait just a moment! How do you know her? *(Beat.)* Are you? With her?!

(CHAUNCEY and HORTENSE begin to argue about who may or may not be having relations with Marigold.)

MARIGOLD: Would you two keep it down! This is a disaster. I told you— no unnecessary attention.

(Both CHAUNCEY and HORTENSE explain at the same time that they both followed her directions for their secret meeting. As they explain, they both realize the other has come to the room for the same reason.)

HORTENSE: Wait. So you're not having an affair with her?

CHAUNCEY: Goodness no. Why you know you are the only woman for me my love. *(Beat.)* So you're not—

HORTENSE: With Marigold? I should think not. Tribadism may be fine for those that like it, but I prefer the masculine attentions of my one and only.

CHAUNCEY: My love—

HORTENSE: Dear heart—

MARIGOLD Are we going to do this, or what?

(She opens her coat and reveals a wide selection of exotic cheeses. Both CHAUNCEY and HORTENSE are immediately distracted by the sight and odor. They lean in toward MARIGOLD, then each notice the other.)

HORTENSE: Wait. Are you? Are you here to—

CHAUNCEY: Buy exotic contraband cheeses? Yes!

HORTENSE: You mean you also—

CHAUNCEY: Have a mad passion for French Stinking Bishop and Idaho Goatster?

HORTENSE: Yes!

CHAUNCEY: Yes!

HORTENSE: But I had no idea! Had I known we could have—

CHAUNCEY: Shared our exotic cheese passion and ripped away the veil of secrecy that has thus far masked the fullness of our true congruity.

(They kiss passionately.)

MARIGOLD: So are you two going to buy some of this or not? People are starting to get suspicious. I can only pretend to have terrible B.O. for so long.

CHAUNCEY: We'll take it all!

MARIGOLD: The Rhino Horn Quartirolo Lombardo is going to cost you.

CHAUNCEY: Nothing is too much for my love boodle.

(CHAUNCEY and HORTENSE rub noses. MARIGOLD takes several brown packages from her coat and hands them to the couple. She waits for payment.)

MARIGOLD: Excuse me?

(CHAUNCEY and MARIGOLD point to the money they have thrown out the door. MARIGOLD sees it, shrugs, and exits. The couple breaks away from each other, stands, opens the brown packages from MARIGOLD.)

CHAUNCEY: After you, my dear.

HORTENSE: Oh, no. After you, love.

(HORTENSE feeds her cheese to CHAUNCEY. He eats it. CHAUNCY feeds his cheese to HORTENSE. She eats it. They look at each other. Beat. They throw themselves at each other, kissing passionately amidst the cheese as the lights fade.)

Characters:
  TWO PEOPLE

MICHAEL FRAYN was born in London in 1933 and began his career as a journalist on the Guardian and the Observer. His novels include *Towards the End of the Morning*, *The Trick of It* and *Landing on the Sun*. *Headlong* (1999) was shortlisted for the Booker Prize, while his most recent novel, *Spies* (2002), won the Whitbread Novel Award. His fifteen plays range from *Noises Off* to *Copenhagen* and, most recently, *Afterlife*. *Cold Calling* is from *Matchbox Theatre: Thirty Short Entertainments* (2015).

— *Congratulations! You have won the...* And he's hung up.

— Again? That's the third time!

— He doesn't even wait till I've got to the end of the sentence! I don't get any further than *'Congratulations! You have won the...'* —and wham! Already the phone's back on the hook. What's happened to the world? People used to be so excited when you rang to tell them! They thought it was a real honour!

— Honour? These people don't know what the word means. Money, money, money—that's all they think about these days.

— Yes, then there's the money. You'd think they'd be pleased about the money.

— What—the odd few million kronor? They look in the paper, and there are bankers taking home ten times as much for wrecking the economy! Which one was that? Peace? So he's a politician? Naturally, then. Coining it already. Pay-offs, backhanders. Then off to work for a bank himself. Forget Peace.

But what if he doesn't ever realise he's won?

— Then we're several million kronor to the good. Try one of the others. What's the next one on the computer? Medicine. Try Medicine.

— Medicine? Big Pharma? On a royalty from some billion-dollar drug that's killing everyone in Africa?

— Maybe. Or maybe not. Maybe a humble doctor. A saint. Runs an obesity clinic in the jungle. Doesn't want a single krona for himself. But now, thanks to us, he can install flush toilets and flat-screen TVs. He'll be all over you!

— Yes, you can joke about it. You haven't got to do it.

— Come on! I'm dialing it for you.

— It's not nice, you know, being hung up on all the time. You feel rejected. You feel everyone hates you.

— Don't take it so personally.

— I can't help taking it personally! It's something about my voice, isn't it. As soon as they hear it...wham!

— Right, you're through. He sounds charming, this one. Modest, hopeful. I don't think this one's going to hang up on you. Off you go.

— They all sound hopeful when they pick up the phone. Then...

— Get going. He's waiting.

— He's going to be the same as all the others... *Congratulations! You have...*

— And the phone's back on the hook already. Quickest yet. Look, I don't think I can go on with this job. The stress is really getting to me.

— OK, let's think. Maybe it *is* something about your voice. A bit *too* positive, perhaps, a little *too* encouraging. They think you're trying to sell them something.

— How else can you say 'congratulations'?

— So maybe *don't* say 'congratulations'.

— *Don't* say 'congratulations'? What are you talking about? It's in the script they give you!

— Forget the script. Get straight to the money. Where are we? Literature. Perfect. He's, what, a poet or something?

— She. Some woman in Lithuania.

Wonderful. She really needs the money. Economic collapse. Husband left her. Kids to support...OK, I'm dialling... Suddenly there's going to be this voice on the phone: 'Our records show that you may be entitled to a substantial payment...' Something along those lines... I'm through... Oh my God! She sounds desperate! Away you—

— *Hello! Our records show...* And wham. I can feel chest pains.

— OK, let's come at it a bit more obliquely. Work up their anticipation... What's the next one on the computer? Physics... I'm getting it for you... Just give your chest a rub— you'll be fine... It's ringing... He's a scientist, so start with something scientific. Catch his interest. The computer. Start with the computer. Something about his name coming up on the computer. He'll be intrigued.

— The computer... ? *Hi there! Your name has come up on our computer and...* I told you.

— Never mind. His loss, not ours. We're about twenty million kronor up. Three more to go. Where have we got to? Biology?

— I think I'm going to take early retirement...

— Now, with Biology we'll try something completely different. Something a bit more streetwise. You remember the old advertising maxim? 'Don't sell the steak, sell the sizzle'? So you're not going to tell this Biology guy anything about a prize. You're going to tell him about the trip to collect it! Yes? OK, I'm dialling... He's in Bangalore. It's hot and dusty. The air conditioning in the laboratory's broken down. He's dreaming of cold and snow. A call from Scandinavia, and already his tongue's hanging out. So then you tell him about the free champagne. The five-star hotels. The world-class gourmet cuisine. The beautiful blonde hostesses... Here you go...

— This is the very last one I'm going to try...*Hi there! You have won an exciting free trip to Stockholm...*And already he's... No! He hasn't! He's still there!

— What did your wise old Uncle Sven tell you? Quick—'free champagne, free champagne...'!

— *Enjoy beautiful free champagne... world-class blondes... five-star hostesses...* Now he's hung up... No, he hasn't! I don't believe this...! *Hello? You're still...? Oh, thank you! Thank you, thank you, thank you!* 'Thank you for holding! Thank you for listening! You don't know how much this means to me! So, yes, world-class free hostesses... What? Where do I want to go? Where do I want to go...? Nowhere! Not me—you! You're coming here! Yes? To Stockholm! The fantastic fairy-tale city often known as the Athens of the North! Wait, wait. I'll read you the official citation...* Where's my piece of paper...? What a sweetheart! He's hanging on every word...! *Right You're really still there...? Wonderful. I'll take it from the top. The—whole script Is that all right? You've got a moment? You won't suddenly...? No, OK, here we go, then... Congratulations! You have won the Nobel Prize for Biology...! Oh...Oh, I see. I'm so sorry...*

— Even this one?

— Wrong number. Minicab firm in Malmo...

Characters:

THE MOTHER

THE FATHER

THE BROTHER

THE SISTER

Setting: The inside of a living room or parlor. There are two chairs, standing side by side—facing the audience—at center, downstage.

> JOHN LADD is currently living with his two favorite pets, Bunny and Roma, in a small town in upstate New York where he is working on a number of projects. His work has been produced at Manhattan Repertory Theatre, The Short Play Lab, ActSense Theatre Company, the Bad Theater Festival, NYC Equity Library/Piney Fork Press Theater, The Puzzle, and other venues. He is a Resident Playwright at the Manhattan Repertory Theatre.

(Enter THE MOTHER and THE FATHER.)

THE FATHER: *(Looks out the window.)* Okay, okay— Susan just pulled up—

(he pauses to watch, then quickly)

—and there's Teddy. He just pulled in behind her— and they're getting out.

THE MOTHER: Perfect— right on time. I'm going to the kitchen to make sure everything is set for lunch.

THE FATHER: I'll join you. I don't want them to think that we have nothing better to do than stand around and wait for them.

(THE MOTHER and THE FATHER exit. THE BROTHER and THE SISTER enter, look around in a nostalgic way.)

THE BROTHER: Well, it still looks the same.

THE SISTER: It does, it does—though it does feel a little strange.

THE BROTHER: What—being back here?

THE SISTER: Being back here under these circumstances.

THE BROTHER: Listen, listen—hey, I'm sorry that your marriage broke up.

THE SISTER: (Well, what can you do— at least there weren't any kids.

THE BROTHER: Yeah, that's a good thing.

(Pause.)

Did you see it coming? You know, Ken leaving and all?

THE SISTER: Not anymore than you saw your job leaving for some Third World country.

THE BROTHER: And, so, here we are— back at home.

THE SISTER: I am— and I'm sure that you are— very grateful that Mom and Dad were gracious enough to take us back in.

(Pause.)

I mean, what would we have done—

(Enter THE MOTHER and THE FATHER.)

THE FATHER: *(With open arms.)* Susan.

THE MOTHER: *(With open arms.)* Teddy.

THE BROTHER: Mom.

THE SISTER: Daddy.

THE FATHER: Please, sit— both of you.

(THE BROTHER and THE SISTER sit down. To the end of the play, both parents hover as THE BROTHER and THE SIS-TER slowly regress to more and more infantile behaviors and mannerisms.)

THE MOTHER: Who would have thought?

THE FATHER: This is terrible— the worst. Both of us are totally— *totally*— disappointed in both of you.

THE BROTHER: But, Dad—

THE FATHER: But nothing! Tell me— tell us— both of you— where did you go wrong?

THE MOTHER: Or was it us? Were we too easy on you? Slack? Not demanding enough when you were growing up? Maybe we were too indulgent— even maybe too understanding?

THE SISTER: It wasn't anybody— things just happened.

THE FATHER: Oh? Kenny leaving you for another woman just happened?

THE MOTHER: You never listened to me— I don't know what you saw in him.

THE BROTHER: Mom, that's not fair.

THE FATHER: Not fair? You're right! It's not fair! It's not fair that I paid for you going to college so that you could get a job that you would— *and did*— lose!

THE MOTHER: *(To THE SISTER.)* And, you, too! I gave you the best years of my life- I sacrificed for you- and what? Now you're putting us through this?

THE SISTER: But you said—

THE BROTHER: You said that it would be all right to come home until we can get back on our feet.

THE SISTER: We have nowhere else to go. How can you talk to us like this?

THE MOTHER: Oh! Listen to this! You know what? I don't deserve this! You ungrateful bitch! You're not the same sweet child I remember!

THE FATHER: You asked for this and now you bad-mouth your mother?

THE BROTHER: Do you want us to go?

THE FATHER: Where? Where would you go?

THE MOTHER: Out on the street? Live in your cars? Bounce from friend to friend?

THE FATHER: And while you were doing any of those things, everyone would be watching you! And you know what they would see? They would see you bringing shame on this family!

THE MOTHER: Oh, no— not while I'm still alive!

THE FATHER: No, you're not going anywhere. You can stay— but there will be rules—

THE MOTHER: and chores! Things need to be done around here. You know, your father's not getting any younger.

THE FATHER: And you're going to have to do your own wash. You can't leave it for your mother to do. It's too much for her. You can't become a burden!

(THE BROTHER and THE SISTER fall off their chairs and slowly assume fetal positions on the floor.)

THE MOTHER: Why are you lying on the floor like that? I wish I'd never had kids! Look at the two of you! Is it too much to ask for the two of you to sit in your chairs like the adults you're *supposed* to be?

THE FATHER: All right, already! Get up! Get up and go to your rooms!

(THE BROTHER AND THE SISTER manage— with dif-ficulty— to exit stage-right.)

THE MOTHER: And keep the music down!

THE FATHER: And, if you know what's good for you, don't let me hear any doors slamming!

THE MOTHER: They're pathetic— they're nothing like us.

THE FATHER: Not now, they're not, but now that we've got them— here under our roof— we'll whip them into shape, however long it takes— *trust me.*

BLACKOUT

Characters:

SHE

HER

Setting: A table.

JACOB MARX RICE has had his plays produced at Actors Theatre of Louisville, La MaMa ETC, Nuyorican Poets Café, Soho Playhouse, Atlantic Theatre Stage 2, and others. His play, *Chemistry* won the 2015 Producer's Pick at the Cincinnati Fringe Festival and the 2014 Excellence in Playwriting Award at the New York International Fringe Festival. Jacob is the winner of the 2012 Seymour Brick Memorial Prize for Playwriting and a finalist for the 2015 Eugene O'Neill Theatre Center National Playwrights Conference. Education: Columbia University newplayexchange.org/users/6221/jacob-marx-rice

(SHE and HER sit at a table. SHE is eating Oreos. SHE twists off the top of the Oreo, eats the cream and then eats the cookie. HER watches, a look of deep concern and need in HER eyes.

SHE picks up another cookie and turns, acknowledging HER for the first time.)

SHE: Wanna cookie?

(HER face lights up. The best news all day.)

HER: Yes.

(SHE gets up and gives HER a cookie. HER nibbles the cookie around the edges like a gopher. SHE twists off another Oreo top, eats the cream and then eats the cookie. They both finish their Oreos.)

SHE: Wanna drink?

(More great news.)

HER: Yes.

(SHE walks out of the room and returns with a cup. SHE hands it to HER, who drinks with both hands. HER chugs the entire thing like someone lost in the desert. HER finishes drinking and wipes HER mouth. SHE watches HER now.)

SHE: Wanna wet willy?

(HER does not want a wet willy.)

HER: Yes.

(SHE gets up and walks over to HER. She sucks on SHE's pinkie finger and then gives HER a long, luscious wet willy. It's horrible for HER. SHE sits back down.)

SHE: Want another cookie?

(Relief. Relief and cookies for HER.)

HER: Yes.

(SHE gets up and gives HER a cookie. HER eats the cookie the same gopherish way. SHE does not eat a cookie. She just watches HER. HER finishes HER cookie.)

SHE: Wanna kiss me?

(HER looks questioningly at SHE but SHE stares back dominantly.)

HER: Yes.

(HER walks over and kisses SHE on the cheek. HER returns to HER chair. SHE watches HER, clearly not pleased. Pause.)

SHE: Wanna kiss me on the lips?

(More confusion for HER. More futile resistance giving way to resignation.)

HER: Yes.

(HER stands, goes over to SHE. HER kisses SHE on the lips, a very light peck. HER goes back to HER seat. SHE stares at HER for a long time.)

SHE: Wanna bleed?

(A panic. Fear and questions lance across HER face.)

HER: Yes.

(SHE stands and exits. SHE returns with a knife and hands it to HER. HER takes it and slowly draws it across HER arm in a long wavy pattern. HER blood is apple red. SHE watches HER.)

SHE: Wanna third cookie?

(Suspicion. A dangerous question, and yet also an opportunity for a cookie.)

HER: Yes.

(SHE gets up and gives HER a cookie. HER eats the cookie the same gopherish way. SHE also eats a cookie, removing the top and eating the cream first. They both finish the cookies.

HER watches SHE. She does not look back. Then, SHE turns to HER.)

SHE: Wanna die?

(A long, long pause. HER begs SHE to reconsider. Asks for mercy. Tries to resist. SHE stares back at HER, refusing to budge.)

HER: Yes.

(Blackout.)

Characters:
ROBERT

DENISE

DANIEL GUYTON has won numerous writing awards for his stage plays and screenplays, including the Best Horror Screenplay Award from the Los Angeles Film & Script Festival, two playwriting awards from the Kennedy Center/ACTF Festival, and many others. His stage plays have been produced over 300 times around the world, and he has received over 40 publications. He is a theatre professor at Georgia State University, and is a member of both the Dramatists Guild and the Writers Guild of America East. danguyton.com

(DENISE stares at a piece of paper in her hand. Her husband ROBERT stares at her proudly.)

ROBERT: Well, what do you think?

DENISE: I… don't know what to say.

ROBERT: Are you surprised?

DENISE: Of course!

ROBERT: Happy Valentine's Day, sweetheart.

(He kisses her on the forehead.)

DENISE: Well, it's just… you know. I was kinda hoping for flowers, or… candy. But a funeral arrangement?

ROBERT: Well, sure. Don't you want to know that your future is secured? Our future? *(He shows her the pamphlet.)* Look honey, we'll be buried right next to each other. In the lover's plot. The gravestone will be a large heart, with both of our names engraved upon it, with the words, "For they so loved each other, that true love will never die."

DENISE: But that's a little creepy, don't you think?

ROBERT: No, I think it's romantic.

DENISE: And what if we don't die together? What if… you know, you die first and I remarry? Or I die first and you remarry? What if…?

ROBERT: Would you want to remarry? Because I don't. You… you're the only woman I've ever loved.

DENISE: Aw, that's sweet, sweetheart. But… statistically speaking, men do die earlier than women and…

ROBERT: And?

DENISE: And I'm not sure that I want to die alone.

ROBERT: Oh.

DENISE: I'm sorry. But…it's just…

ROBERT: No. No that totally makes sense. I…guess I never really thought of it that way. I just…thought… "Until death do us part" and…

DENISE: And what?

ROBERT: And I hadn't really considered what would come after that. I…I guess it makes sense that you would move on.

---

105 Five-Minute Plays

DENISE: Don't take it like that, honey. I just… it's not like I *want* that to happen, it's just… I'm being realistic. *(ROBERT turns away sadly.)* Well listen, what about you? What will you do?

ROBERT: *(Dejected.)* Well, statistically speaking, I'll probably be dead.

DENISE: This is true. But…if you weren't? If I died first, would you…?

ROBERT: I don't know. I…guess. If you wouldn't be upset about it?

(She takes his hand.)

DENISE: Of course not, Robert. I would want you to be happy. Always.

ROBERT: *(Starting to get excited.)* Well… ok then. Yes! In that case, I think I would. In fact, there's this one lady at work I've been talking to…

DENISE: Whoa, whoa, whoa. Excuse me?

ROBERT: Oh no, no! I'm not… I mean… we were talking about *her* situation. I'm not… No, no, she lost her husband a few years ago. And now she's remarried. And so we were talking about what that's like. And… and it never occurred to me to think like… you know… about *us*. But now that you bring it up, she… does seem really happy. I mean, like, really, *really* happy. I've never seen her this hap–

DENISE: *(Getting nervous.)* Ok, let's not get ahead of ourselves here.

ROBERT: I mean, not happi*ER*, per se, just… happy. For the first time in a long time, I think. And… the more she and I talk about it, the more I realize that… maybe there *can* be life after one of the partners dies.

DENISE: That's right. I'm… I'm glad you see it that way, Robert. I'm…

ROBERT: *(Lost in a distant daydream.)* Tell me again about these statistics?

DENISE: What?

ROBERT: Well, you said, you know, "statistically speaking, I'll probably be dead." But… you know, are we talking *long* odds, or…?

DENISE: Ok, listen. Just…listen. Whatever you do, just…
please make sure she's not *prettier* than me. Ok? I don't…
think I could handle that.

ROBERT: But you'll be dead, sweetheart.

DENISE: Yes, but…I will haunt you from the grave. Seriously.
You have my permission to remarry, but the woman *must* be
a troll.

ROBERT: Oh. Um. Ok. *(He considers this.)* What about your
sister?

DENISE: What?!

ROBERT: I mean, she's single. She's not…

DENISE: No no! Oh no, you will not touch Christine. You will
not *date* Christine. You will not even fantasize about Christine, or so help me, I will rise up like a phoenix from the
ashes and I will cut your balls off. Understand? *(She holds
up the paper.)* You will be lying in this coffin next to me so
fast, it'll make your head spin.

ROBERT: Whoa. Jesus. I just… figured she was biologically
similar to…

DENISE: Don't even finish that sentence.

ROBERT: All right. I'm… fine. Christine is off the table. I…
(Beat) I'm just trying to think of women I know that…

DENISE: Robert! You are not supposed to plan this in advance!
I don't have any guys in my mind! I just… know that if something ever happened to you, I'd want to marry again. Not
right away. Not even in the next five years! Just… someday.
So I don't have to be alone. That's all. And besides, this is
all purely hypothetical anyway. We're both probably gonna
die together in some horrible plane crash or something. So…
there's no need to even talk about this.

ROBERT: But I'm afraid of heights, so…

DENISE: As well you should be! Since that's the way we're both
gonna die. *(Small pause.)* Eventually. *(Small pause.)* Way off
into the future. *(Small pause.)* Robert, listen. I love you very,
very much. And you're very thoughtful, in… in your own
way, to get me this. *(She holds up the paper.)* But I wish you
had talked with me first about it, that's all.

ROBERT: It was supposed to be a Valentine's Day surprise.

DENISE: And it was. Believe me, I was *completely* surprised. *(She stands and looks at him.)* But if it makes you feel any better, I will accept this gift. Ok? And if we die together, then yes. I would love nothing more than to be buried next to you for all eternity. *(She drapes her arms around him, seductively.)* But if you die first, then I am outta here. I'm selling my half of this plot to the next highest bidder, and I am moving on. *(Beat)* I just hope the person I sell it to is not a snorer.

ROBERT: Right. Or more beautiful than you.

(She pulls away.)

DENISE: Bitch, ain't no one more beautiful than me.

(He laughs and pulls her in again.)

ROBERT: All right, all right. That's true. Well, listen, if you die first, then I will promise you this, ok? I will go out and find a woman who is…uglier than you. Not *too* much uglier, but…slightly. And I will move on down the road as well. Do you have any restrictions on how well they can cook?

DENISE: No.

ROBERT: Good. So…kinda ugly, but…excellent chef. Got it.

DENISE: Hmm…that sounds kinda like *you.*

(She plays with his nose. ROBERT laughs.)

ROBERT: Well, I guess there's only one solution then.

DENISE: What's that?

ROBERT: We're both gonna have to live forever.

(She smiles seductively.)

DENISE: I like the sound of that.

(They kiss.)

Characters:
    TWO PEOPLE

> MICHELLE HAUSER is an award-winning freelance writer and humorist. Her work includes contributions to CBC Radio, McSweeney's, Writer's Digest, The Globe and Mail and numerous lifestyle magazines and newspapers. Michelle's weekly humour column *Laugh Lines* is syndicated by Postmedia, Canada's largest newspaper chain. She and her husband Mark live in a small town near Toronto (Napanee) with their son Joseph and Grandma Harriet. michellehauser.ca

1: So a Jew, a Christian and a Muslim walk into a bar…

2: Stop, stop, stop!

1: What?

2: That's not funny.

1: But I haven't even done the joke yet.

2: Yeah, but it won't be funny. There's nothing funny about Jews and Christians and Muslims going places together, especially bars. Try something else.

1: OK… a lesbian and a tattooed millennial walk into a bar…

2: No, no, no!

1: What's wrong with a lesbian and a tattooed millennial? You don't even know where I'm going with this.

2: I don't need to know where you're going. If there's a lesbian it won't be funny — lesbians have never been funny. And millennials are super sensitive about their tattoos. Anyway you need to stop writing jokes about people in bars. Bar jokes are done. They're just not funny anymore.

1: But all kinds of people go to bars. It's a great place to put people from different backgrounds.

2: In real life, maybe, but not in jokes. Just put the joke someplace other than a bar.

1: OK… two guys are sitting on a park bench.

2: Much better!

1: And the one guy says to the other guy…

2: Wait a minute — are they gay or straight?

1: They're straight.

2: Good. Are they Christians or Jews or what?

1: They're atheists.

2: Even better. This is going to be so funny now. I can feel it. OK, go ahead and make the joke.

1: Two straight atheists are sitting on a park bench…

2: Wait, it's not a playground park is it?

1: What does it matter?

2: Two straight guys in a playground? Are you nuts? People might get the wrong idea; they could be pedophiles or something and there's NOTHING funny about pedophiles.

1: Alright, alright… two straight atheists are sitting on a park bench near a winding path with no children in sight…

2: Good, good, go on…

1: …and the one guy says to the other guy…

2: Oh my God!

1: What?

2: I forgot to check, are the guys black or white?

1: They're white, OK? Two blindingly white guys who only like women and don't believe in God who've never even thought about messing with a kid, or going anywhere near a playground, are sitting on a park bench trying to make a fucking joke…

2: Whoa! You can't say fuck anymore. Fuck's not funny.

1: Since when?

2: Since last year, I think. It's misogynistic or something. Just don't say it.

1: …

2: What? What are you waiting for? Go on, make the joke.

1: No, I lost it.

2: Ah, don't do that. You're getting all stiff and tight — just loosen up and make the joke. Don't over think it.

1: OK, here's a different one, though. A bone-head comedian meets a politically correct asshole for a cup of coffee…

2: Now that's a good set-up. You're really getting the hang of it now!

1: You think?

2: Of course! Assholes are the funniest people alive!

Characters:

BOB: Twenties. An office worker in the Chicago Loop. Average looking, leaning toward nerdish. Has a crush on TRACI.

TRACI: Twenties. Smart. Conscientious. Driven. Works with BOB.

ANNOUNCER (O.S.) Crackly PA Voice

Setting: A northbound Chicago El platform. The near future. Shortly before midnight.

TREY NICHOLS is a playwright, actor, and teacher based in Los Angeles. His plays include *Fathers at a Game, The Night Gwen Stacy Died, Todd's Hollywood Tours, The Meadows, PCH, Impact,* and *From Beyond* (adapted from the story by H.P. Lovecraft). His holiday solo show, *A Lesson in Proper Bow-Fluffing Technique* received an LA Stage Alliance Ovation nomination for Best Solo Show. Trey is a longtime-member of Moving Arts, a theatre company dedicated to developing and producing new plays. For the last few years, Trey has been active with Moving Arts' acclaimed, immersive theatrical phenomenon *The Car Plays*, with performances at The WoW Festival at the La Jolla Playhouse and The Off Center Festival at Segerstrom Center for the Arts in Costa Mesa. Trey is a proud member of the Dramatists Guild and The Alliance of Los Angeles Playwrights. He holds a B.S. in Theatre from Northwestern University. Trey also moderates a popular playwriting workshop held in a secret lair in West Los Angeles. treynichols.net

(TRACI stands at center, wielding a baseball bat dripping with blood and bits of skin and skull. She's a wreck. SHE looks around cautiously, then leans forward, gazing off stage left for the next train.)

CRACKLY ANNOUNCEMENT: Attention all passengers. Due to the current state of emergency, southbound train service to The Loop has been suspended indefinitely. The last northbound service tonight will be a Purple Line train to the Howard Station, which has been designated a safe zone.

(SOUND of GLASS BREAKING.)

Oh my god! No! They got in!

(LOUD GUTTURAL SOUNDS, MOANING, CHEWING.)

Get off me! NO! AAAAHHHHHH!!!

(THE RADIO CRACKLES. Then SILENCE. TRACI takes it all in. She grips the bat harder. BOB appears from stage right, inching cautiously toward TRACI. He wears a surgical mask.)

BOB: H-hello?

TRACI: Ah!

(She turns toward him, ready to strike.)

BOB: Hey, hey, it's okay, I'm not one of those things, I'm just waiting for the train like you.

TRACI: You shouldn't go sneaking up on people like that! I almost bashed your head in.

BOB: Traci?

TRACI: Oh my god. Bob?

BOB: Wow. It's really you. It's so good to see you.

(He goes in for an awkward hug.)

TRACI: It's good to see anyone. You know, you don't have to wear that mask. The virus isn't airborne.

BOB: How do you know?

TRACI: It was on Twitter.

BOB: Was it legit?

TRACI: Did you see the National Guard troops on Halsted?

BOB: Yeah.

TRACI: Were *they* wearing masks?

BOB: I didn't notice. There was too much shooting.

> *(BOB removes the surgical mask.)*

TRACI: How did you even get up here?

BOB: I distracted the walkers with a White Sox pennant from the newsstand. That got them really riled up! Thank God for undead Cubs fans. That's loyalty!

TRACI: Did you just say "walkers?"

BOB: Yeah, why?

TRACI: They're not "walkers." They're zombies. *Zombies.* It drives me crazy that TV shows like *The Walking Dead* apparently take place in some alternate universe where zombies don't exist, so everyone comes up with clever names for them like walkers or roamers or, or, what's that other one, biters! It's like, get a clue people! They're fucking *zombies*! Now that the shit's real, can we finally start getting it right?!

> *(Small pause.)*

BOB: Well, zombies or not, you look great.

TRACI: Thanks, I guess. Sorry, I don't mean to take it out on you.

> *(Emotional.)*

Oh, Bob.

BOB: *(Misinterpreting; moves closer to her.)* Oh, Traci...

TRACI: I've done something horrible.

BOB: I'm sure it's not that—

TRACI: I killed Josh.

BOB: Josh. You mean "Josh" Josh?

TRACI: Yes, Josh. Joshy. I killed him with this bat. His brains are splattered all over our apartment.

BOB: I didn't even know you two were still dating?

TRACI: We weren't and then we were. It's complicated—it *was* complicated—in the way of all office romances. And now he's dead.

BOB: What happened?

TRACI: He brought home a pizza after work. We were having dinner watching the news reports of all the chaos in the streets. Then he started leaning toward me. He'd just gotten a text alert that Butler shot a three-pointer against the Cavaliers, so I thought he was moving in for a sloppy victory kiss. Then I noticed his eyes. Dead. Vacant. Sauce dribbling down his chin....I got away just before he tried to eat my face. But he just kept coming at me. So I grabbed the bat. I had no choice. Fucking Giordano's!

  (Beat.)

BOB: To tell the truth, I never thought Josh was that good for you.

TRACI: Like it matters now.

BOB: He treated you like shit, pardon my French. Maybe other people around the office didn't notice, but I did. You're a good person, Traci. You deserve better.

TRACI: That's sweet. Maybe you're right. Maybe that pizza was a blessing.

BOB: What do you mean?

TRACI: That's what killed him. They're saying the virus started with tainted mozzarella. It's like mad cow disease that jumped the species barrier, infecting humans.

BOB: Really? Then how come you—?

TRACI: Josh ate the pizza; I had salad.

BOB: Oh. Then you're not infected. So...there's only one thing that makes sense now.

TRACI: What's that?

BOB: You and me. Repopulating the planet.

TRACI: Um, you're a nice guy, Bob. But we're not the last two people on Earth.

BOB: Then let's take it slowly. Why don't you let me help clean up Josh's brains over a bottle of wine?

TRACI: I'm not going back to the apartment. I'm taking the Purple Line to Howard. It's safe there.

BOB: Okay fine. Just let me go with you. Cuz if this is the

zombie apocalypse, I can't think of anyone else I'd rather spend it with. I'll protect you. And be there for you. And we can just...

(HE goes in for a sweet but lingering kiss. A moment. TRACI's demeanor changes, sad but resolved. He's oblivious.)

TRACI: Oh Bob.

BOB: Oh Traci.

(SOUND of an EL TRAIN APPROACHING. HE turns to look. SHE raises the bat toward BOB.)

BOB: *(CONT.)* Here it comes! We're gonna make it!

(Notices the raised bat.)

Hey, what are you doing?

TRACI: Your breath. It's. Cheesy.

(She starts advancing on him.)

BOB: Okay hold on, I had one slice of pizza for lunch on a meal deal combo but look at me I'm fine I'm totally fine and they're gonna find a cure for this thing, it's not the end of the world, Traci. Traci!

(He cowers. She raises the baseball bat to strike. The TRAIN SCREECHES in to the station.)

BLACKOUT

Characters:
MAYA

JESS

Setting: A household bathroom.

REBECCA ROBINSON has a Master's Degree in Advanced Theatre Practice from the Royal Central School of Speech and Drama. She is an alum of the Royal Court Writers Program and studied acting at Rose Bruford College. Her work has been performed across the UK and in the US. Shorts: *Pro* (Above the Arts, Blue Elephant Theatre, Bread and Roses Theatre, Lincoln Arts Centre, Little Black Box Theatre, Horse and Stables), *Fractured* (Bridewell Theatre), *Hard Shadows* (Tricycle Theatre), *Choice* (The Bugaloo, Haggerston, Lincoln Arts Centre), *Poison* (Take Courage Theatre). Extracts of: *Jackal* (Bath TheatreLab, All you read is Love), *Doe* (Unheard Festival, Bread and Roses Theatre, Clear Line Festival, Khaos Company Theater). Full Length: *Doe* (Bread and Roses Theatre - London, Kings Arms Salford, Temple Bar Manchester). Devised Full Length: *#waterloobridge* (Above the Arts, Rag Factory, Little Angel, Tobacco Factory), *Here We Come Together, Here We Fall Apart* (Camden People's Theatre). ebeccarobinsonplaywright.com foxbloomtheatre.com/

(There is a toilet, a sink with a mirror above and a bathtub, with a toweling bath mat on the floor beside it. The sink area is cluttered with make-up, and there are other items around the room pointing to female occupiers of the house. The room is brightly lit, clinically so. MAYA sits on the floor of the bathroom, back against the bathtub. She wears no make-up and looks somewhat disheveled. JESS is heard entering from what we assume, but cannot see, to be the front door. Calls out to no response. JESS enters the bathroom.)

JESS: What are you doing?

MAYA: Sitting.

JESS: Yeah I can see that. *(Beat.)* Why are you sitting in here on the floor?

MAYA: I'm just thinking.

JESS: Maya?

MAYA: No, I'm alright, I'm just thinking.

JESS: Think in the living room.

MAYA: No, I was just thinking, like, this is like a home to us.

JESS: Well, yeah.

MAYA: No, like the bathroom. Like women.

JESS: Maya, what are you on about?

MAYA: Honestly, listen. Women. In bathrooms. So much happens here

JESS: Maya.

MAYA: Listen, seriously. Like women, we're, we're what? We're like destined? We spend so much of our lives here. So many significant things.

JESS: Like what?

MAYA: Well women. We're women. Where do you grow up? Become a woman? Bathroom. First period. First moment we realise what we're supposed to be. Mothers. But we're just kids right?

JESS: I guess.

MAYA: Of course we are. We're kids. Able to mother kids. Suddenly. We're. We don't know. So unsure. So not ready.

JESS: Yeah.

MAYA: But it happens.

JESS: Of course.

MAYA: And kids. Having kids. In toilets. They don't even know.

JESS: Maya.

MAYA: No, I'm fine, I promise. I just got to thinking.

JESS: Come in the living room. Let's sit down. Have a chat.

MAYA: Jess. I'm fine. I'm really fine. Just thinking is all. *(Beat.)* Like we grow up. And this weird little room, this room that we're supposed to excrete in. We're supposed to get rid of all that shit we don't need. But for us. For women. It becomes this big thing. This important place. *(Beat.)* We go in packs to the place, for fucks sake. It becomes this weird, physical, intrinsic part of you. It's inseparable. We judge each other there. You notice? All the time. Does she wash her hands, is she thin enough, does her arse look big in that dress, is she too thin? Slag. *(Beat.)* Do we like her? Are we friends? Would we be? How she looks. Does she pass? Does she fit into a suitable little box that we want her in? Skinny professional. Rock Chick. Movie-star beauty? Frump. Who is she? *(Beat.)* We make these judgements automatically. And sure, we make them everywhere, But in the bathroom, all bets are off. We're like fucking lionesses. Prowling. Ready for the kill. Do you think we all think that?

JESS: Maya. *(Pause.)* No. *(Beat.)* I don't know.

MAYA: We are. We don't mean to be but we are. We all preach about equality and we all want it, for women's sake, but cut to the throat of it and we're just animals, hoping to out-do the others. *(Pause.)* These tiny rooms. They hold so much.

   (Pause.)

JESS: You know once? When I was struggling to find a place to live here. I had to crash on a whole load of friend's sofas. *(Beat.)* It was hard. I had to hope. And rely on their good grace, that they liked me enough to help me out. And you know what? I got super lucky. 'Cause I did have some good friends. Some golden friends who really helped me out. This one girl, Kay, she would always be there for me. Didn't seem to matter when I contacted her, a couple of hours

105 Five-Minute Plays

before even. She'd always help me out. Thing was though, she was, well, she was having a baby. *(Beat.)* Pregnant. Still helping me out, but had so many bigger things to worry about! And anyway, one night I got to her place. And her boyfriend, good guy, and their housemate, well they had this thing. So's not to disturb her they'd only have a drink at night if it was in the bathroom. Bathroom parties they called them. So there I was, initiated into my first bathroom party. It was surreal. Awesome, but surreal. So basically we just drank in a bathroom, no difference to any ordinary drinking sessions, except we were in a bathroom, and if we needed to pee, the others turned away and that was how it went. But I know what you mean. Like, personal. Something about that whole night. It was personal. And I shared things there I never had before. I don't know. Weird. *(Pause.)* I'm sorry. Not the subject. Maya, listen—

MAYA: Do you remember? Where we first met?

JESS: Don't!

MAYA: You know though! Like *(Beat.)* Destiny? I don't know. Nic's Party. And she was wasted.

JESS: We all were.

MAYA: Yeah.

JESS: And, oh my god, Josh?

MAYA: Yes! And we all let it happen because we knew!

JESS: And it was crazy.

MAYA: Shit, I wouldn't't've wanted to be her the next morning!

JESS: No way! *(Beat.)* But I guess you're right. It was the bathroom. *(Beat.)* You and me.

    (Pause.)

MAYA: I'm not okay. I'm just not *(Beat)* okay. *(Beat.)* Coping. Or whatever.

JESS: I know.

MAYA: I'm trying.

JESS: It's bound to take time. I know. I know it's hard.

    (JESS puts her arms around MAYA, tries to comfort her.)

MAYA: I'm not talking about the baby.

JESS: What do you mean?

MAYA: This isn't about the baby.

JESS: Maya?

MAYA: Alright. It's not just about the baby. But.

> *(MAYA covers her face with her hands and exhales. Her knuckles are red and swollen. Sits like this for a moment.)*

JESS: Show me your hands.

MAYA: What?

JESS: Show me your fucking hands.

MAYA: Why?

JESS: You fucking know why. Show me.

MAYA: Jess.

JESS: MAYA. We're supposed to be trying again. *(Pause.)* What the fuck are you thinking.

> *(MAYA tries to stand up.)*

MAYA: I can't do this.

JESS: Sit down.

MAYA: Jess I'm sorry. It's too much. *(Beat.)* It's too much all at once. I'm sorry.

> *(Pause.)*

I want to move. I don't want to be here anymore. Too many bad memories. Okay? *(Beat.)* I want to talk about moving. I'll be alright if we move. *(Beat.)* Force of habit you know, this room.

JESS: We're supposed to be trying again.

MAYA: We will. But let's talk about moving okay? Fresh start.

> *(MAYA exits.)*

Inspired by "Youth and Art" by Robert Browning.

Characters:
FOUR YOUNG ARTISTS

> MONICA FLORY is a playwright, director, and teacher. Recent works include *Americans in Breshkistan* (Edinburgh Fringe Festival), *Viper Fairy* (Acting Manitou), *Leaving IKEA* (with Dano Madden and The Artful Conspirators at Brooklyn Lyceum), *The Secret Garden* (Philly P.A.C.K.), *The Adventures of Peter Rabbit and Friends* (Youth Theatre Northwest), *Last Summer* (Poly Prep CDS), *Afterlight* (NYC Fringe), *Briar Rose* (Philly P.A.C.K.) and *Third Wheel* (Manhattan Comedy Collective). Her adaptation of *The Jungle Book* and her TYA play *Once Upon A Pandora's Box* (both published by Playscripts) have been produced internationally. Her plays are published by Playscripts, Smith & Kraus, Indie Theater Now, Tree Press, and Brooklyn Publishers. She lives in Philadelphia with her husband and children. monicaflory.com

ONE: I saw you. You had your violin case on the subway. There was a sticker on the case, with a red word on it. I wasn't close enough to read what it said.

TWO: I saw you. You had your abstract work up in Chelsea. I follow your work, and I knew it was you, standing there, watching the people watch your painting. I wanted to tell you that of all your paintings, that one is my favorite.

THREE: I saw you. We were in the same improv class, different semesters. You laughed when I did that monologue about my cat. I don't really have a cat. I was funny that night. You laughed so hard.

FOUR: I saw you dance, and I knew immediately that I wanted to screw you.

ONE: I saw your fingers moving.

TWO: You tried to look like you weren't looking at them, but you wanted to see their faces.

THREE: Sometimes I hear your laugh, even though you never came to one of my shows again.

FOUR: When I saw you, I didn't know you were with him.

ONE: I saw you, but I'm not sure you saw me.

ALL: Did you see me?

THREE: I was working on a song about the sky, about how the sky is so expansive it encompasses every emotion. My guitar was in my lap every minute I wasn't in school. I still have the callouses.

TWO: I was working on a documentary about the disappearance of honeybees. I had to suit up to get the footage I needed.

FOUR: I was working on...this thing? It was kind of a multi-media, site-specific, performance art installation piece?

ONE: I was working on a portrait of you. Because I found a picture of you online. I gave you plaid hair. It's not like you were ever going to see it.

ALL: I was working on...

(Pause.)

You were working on...

(Pause.)

FOUR: I wanted you so bad. "Do that turn thing," I wanted to tell you. "Do that turn thing in my lap."

ONE: It was something about your fingers in your hair.

THREE: I would do anything to make you laugh again.

TWO: Your eyes were like a sparrow, darting from their faces to your phone to their faces. Wanting but not wanting to seem like you wanted. Anyway, I got stung. I got stung too many times, and I gave up caring about honeybees.

FOUR: It never really materialized. I had this vision, this grand idea. But I couldn't find a space that worked.

THREE: It never sounded how I wanted it to sound. My fingers hurt.

ONE: I finished your portrait. The paint was still wet when I threw it in a dumpster.

FOUR: You painted me.

ONE: It wasn't you.

FOUR: Pretend it was me.

ONE: I saw you. I painted you.

FOUR: You gave me plaid hair.

ONE: You weren't supposed to see it.

FOUR: I see you.

ONE: It's not really done.

FOUR: I see you.

ONE: It's not really my best work.

FOUR: I see you.

ONE: I think I'm going to take up sculpting instead.

(FOUR and ONE kiss.)

FOUR: Art is better than love is better than art, right?

ONE: Yeah, I get that.

FOUR: This could have happened once.

ONE: We missed it, right?

FOUR: Yeah. It's gone.

(Curtain.)

Characters:
MAGGIE

BILLY

Scene: A corn field in Middle America. Midnight.

DAVID LEE WHITE has worked with Passage Theatre, McCarter Theatre, Dreamcatcher Rep, Writers Theatre of NJ, Rider Univ. and Drexel Univ. He was commissioned by NJPAC's Stage Exchange Program to create the play *Sanism*. His play *Blood: A Comedy* was produced at Passage (2009) and Dreamcatcher Rep (2012). His play *Slippery as Sin* also received its world premiere at Passage in 2011. The one-act play *White Baby* was produced at Emerging Artists Theatre in NY. His newest play *Real True Crime* was developed at the Hive Exposed series in NY in March of 2015, and his solo show *Panther Hollow* has been seen at Dreamcatcher Rep, Drexel University, The Arcade Comedy Theatre and the United Solo Festival in NY. Since 2005, he has been creating oral-history based plays with Trenton area teens including *If I Could in my Hood I Would*, *Fire Girls* and *Urban*. He created "Stoop Theatre" with Trenton High students, which was the subject of a Regional Emmy nominated episode of PCK Media's *State of the Arts*. davidleewhite.net

(MAGGIE is running through the field pulling BILLY by the hand.)

BILLY: Where are you taking me?

MAGGIE: Come on! I gotta show you something.

BILLY: What is it?

MAGGIE: Look. Up there. *(Points to the sky.)* Beautiful, isn't it?

BILLY: Yeah.

MAGGIE: You know, they say that it takes so long for the light from those stars to reach us, that they may have actually died out years ago and we just don't know it yet. Our own sun could go out completely and we wouldn't know it for about eight minutes. Kind of makes you feel small doesn't it?

BILLY: Eight minutes.

MAGGIE: Billy…we've known each other since we were kids, right? Well, I gotta tell you something—

BILLY: Whoa. Is that true?

MAGGIE: Is what true?

BILLY: That the stars might be dead? Where did you hear that?

MAGGIE: I read it. Somewhere. Anyway, this thing I wanted to tell you—

BILLY: Oh, man…this is freaking me out.

MAGGIE: Yeah, I know it's weird but I've felt this way about you for a long time—

BILLY: So, seriously…some of those stars may be completely dead? But it's just the light we're seeing?

MAGGIE: Uh…yeah.

BILLY: That's effed up. I mean that is…effed. Up.

MAGGIE: Okayyyy…

BILLY: And like…the sun could go out and we wouldn't know for eight minutes? Did you make that up?

MAGGIE: No. It's science.

BILLY: That is…*(Puts hands on head.)* Aaaaaa…I'm just…how would we know, then? If the sun went out?

MAGGIE: We wouldn't. We wouldn't know for eight minutes.

BILLY: Then how would we get someplace safe in time?

MAGGIE: There wouldn't be…there's no…it's the sun. There would be no safe place.

BILLY: What? Wait…WHAT?

MAGGIE: Could we talk about something else?

BILLY: Hold on. We would just have to go someplace warm, right? Where there's heat. I mean it would be dark and everything…

MAGGIE: No…without the sun, we'd all, you know, die.

BILLY: Holy Shit. Hooooo! Holy Shit. This is really upsetting. I mean this is really upsetting.

MAGGIE: I didn't mean to—

BILLY: It's like we'd just freeze to death, right? Is that what you're saying? That we'd all freeze to death?

MAGGIE: Pretty much right away.

BILLY: Goddamn. I'm sorry. I don't know what's…can't… breathe…

MAGGIE: Are you hyperventilating?

BILLY: Can't…catch…breath…

MAGGIE: Put your head between your knees.

BILLY: We'd freeze? Jesus…why did you tell me that?

MAGGIE: I don't know. I was just being poetic.

BILLY: Freezing to death because the sun is gone? That's poetic???

MAGGIE: Well…because we're all gonna die someday.

BILLY: OH MY GOD! I mean, I know…but OH MY GOD! Have you ever thought about that? Like what if it's just nothing? And you fall asleep and you don't wake up? And you don't know what it's like to experience nothingness because you can't experience something that's nothing. CHRIST! I gotta sit down. I feel nauseous. Why do you think about this stuff?

MAGGIE: I don't know. I just said it. I was looking for a way to tell you—

BILLY: Is this what a heart attack feels like? Am I having a heart attack?

MAGGIE: I don't think so.

BILLY: I think I smell toast. Do you smell toast? I mean is someone making toast somewhere because I shouldn't be smelling toast. That means a stroke, right?

MAGGIE: I don't—

BILLY: Feel my arm. Is it tingly?

MAGGIE: I don't think I'd be able to feel –

BILLY: Because I definitely feel like there might be a tingle. HEEEEEEEE! It's like there's blood in my brain! I can hear my own blood! *(Puts his hands over his ears.)* Yayayaya I can hear myself yayayaya…

MAGGIE: Look, I'm sorry I brought it up. Can I get you some water?

BILLY: No. Don't touch me! Just sit there and don't move. Am I breathing? Can you see me breathing?

MAGGIE: You're definitely breathing.

BILLY: Am I breathing too much? Sometimes I over-breathe and hyper-oxygenate. What does my face look like?

MAGGIE: It looks like…I don't know…your face.

BILLY: *(Playing with face.)* Is this my face? Can I feel my face?

MAGGIE: I want to go home.

BILLY: Well don't just leave me here to stare at the dead stars, for crying out loud.

MAGGIE: You'll be okay.

BILLY: Okay…I'm fine…I'm fine… *(Pause.)* I guess they are kind of pretty. I mean…as long as you don't think about the fact that they might be dead. *(Pause.)* What did you want to tell me?

MAGGIE: Huh?

BILLY: You wanted to tell me something.

MAGGIE: Oh! Uh…nothing. Nothing.

Characters:

MAN: A man in his twenties to thirties.

WOMAN: A young woman in her twenties.

Setting: Office-building elevator.

> KEVIN SCOTT CHESS, while watching TV as a child, realized the value of truth, justice and the American Way. Years later, working as an investigator and regularly dealing with people of varying degrees of sanity, dependency, instability and hidden agendas, Kevin began to write as a systematic refuge (translate: "outlet") in order to alleviate stress and anxieties addressed in his occupation. Being an investigator has trained Kevin in the practice of observation of human interaction and speech, realizing a good way to observe human behavior is to fade into the background and not bring attention to himself.

(At rise, WOMAN is standing in the elevator, tense, nervous. She is dressed semi-professionally. She carries a purse.

A voice from off-stage as we hear running.)

MAN (O.S.): Hold the elevator! Please hold the elevator!

WOMAN leans forward and frantically presses a button over and over, in a staccato machine-gun rhythm.

(MAN enters, carrying in both hands a heavy box at least the size of a banker's file box. He enters the elevator. As he leans in and presses a button—)

MAN (CONT'D): Thank you! *(Loud sigh.)* I heard you hitting the button. Thank you.

(WOMAN looks hesitant, looks down. She slowly backs to the far corner from where MAN is standing. Holding her purse in one hand, she eases her other hand into her purse.)

You know, you just can't be too careful nowadays...

(The SOUND of the elevator rising. As it rises, both characters react, bending their knees slightly.

A few seconds later, we hear the SOUND of the elevator suddenly stopping; the LIGHTS in the elevator dim, then rise. Both characters react to the unexpected stop. We hear the SOUND of two alarm rings, brief siren sound.

Both characters are puzzled. MAN leans in and presses a couple of buttons, hands still holding the box.

WOMAN nervously taps her foot, looks around as if for an escape route. She leans in and presses the alarm button in the elevator.)

WOMAN: Oh my gosh! The alarm button is out! *(Frantic now.)* Oh no, no we can't be stuck here—why did the elevator stop?

(WOMAN pulls out her phone, begins to dial, looks again at the screen. Surprised—)

No signal! What?!

(She is suddenly as if in a cage, and more frantic. Her eyes, afraid.)

MAN: You know, they'll—

WOMAN: No, stop!

> *(MAN tilts his head, unsure of the reason for her sudden behavior.)*

MAN: Do you need a bathroom?

WOMAN: Shut up, you hear! Stay away from me! I'm warning you—!

> *(MAN looks grim, slowly bends and puts down the box. As he stands—)*

MAN: Whew! *(Softer.)* That was heavy.

> *(MAN smiles and approaches with opens hands, the way somebody approaches a strange dog.)*

Look, I...

WOMAN: Youuu STOP! I have mace!

MAN: Hey, wait, look—

WOMAN: NO! My therapist warned me about men like you! Situations like this! You—you probably followed me into the elevator! You creep! STAY AWAY! STAY BACK!

MAN: Ma'am, really, look—

WOMAN: No, SHUT UP! It's a man's world and you all think we, we women are at your beck and call, that we are here for YOU and YOUR SEXUAL PLEASURE; YOUR PER-VERTED PLEASURE!!

> *(She takes his picture with her phone.)*

Well, not anymore. I took your PICTURE! You SCUM!

> *(WOMAN stashes her phone in her purse, pulls out mace, sprays in his direction.*
>
> *MAN reacts, coughs, covers his eyes, bends over. He is freaked, attempts to physically recover.)*

Make a move and I will SPRAY MORE! I would shoot you, if...I WILL shoot you! I have a gun! My therapist is waiting, and will come looking for me!!

> *(Breathing heavily, MAN puts up an arm in defense.)*

You. You are suspicious and creepy— I REFUSE TO BE A VICTIM AGAIN, YOU HEAR! I was hitting the door-close button when I heard you run for the elevator, YOU CREEP!

I didn't want you NEAR ME!

MAN: Okay, okay! I'm not doing anything! OKAY! Look, I am getting low, crouching to the floor... I am turning, so you can see my hands. Watch my hands. Nothing doing. Just! Don't. Don't spray. Calm. Don't spray, I am not gonna plan on raping you. You are safe.

(WOMAN reacts, arm jerky on the mace.)

NO— no. Don't think it. You are safe. Be calm. All is calm.

WOMAN: Stay where you are!!

MAN: I understand. You have been victimized. You don't want it to happen again.

(She is tense, points the mace.)

Sounds like you need a good man, a good person, to protect you, help you feel secure.

(MAN slowly stands.)

It's okay. I know people who have been victims. I know how you feel—

(ELEVATOR LIGHTS brighten, elevator jerks to life, SOUND of elevator rising.

WOMAN stands with the spray poised. Her floor. We hear "DING!" as the doors open.

WOMAN backs out, spray poised, eyes wild, then runs offstage.

MAN stands, exhausted, sighs, bends to pick up the box, then drops it and kicks it, so the audience can see inside.

The box is empty.)

Characters:

BUS DRIVER: Any age or race.

BOY: Any age or race.

WOMAN: Any age or race.

FEMALE VOICEOVER: The voice of the bus.

Setting: A metropolitan bus.

> IRENE ZIEGLER is an actor, author, playwright, and excellent parallel parker. She is the recipient of the Mary Roberts Rinehart Award in Drama for *Rules of the Lake*, which was also tapped by the New York Public Library as a Best Book. Her full-length plays include *Full Plate Collection, Rules of the Lake*, and *The Little Lion* (adapted from the novel by Nancy Wright Beasley). Her short plays have been produced internationally. As an actor, Irene has appeared in numerous stage plays, films, and television series (see imdb.com.) She lives in Richmond, VA where she is a voice talent and part time teacher of acting and playwriting at The University of Richmond. Ireneziegler.com   Irene-zieglervoiceovers.com

*(AT RISE: BUS DRIVER comes to the end of the line,
parks the bus. He notices a BOY sitting by himself.)*

DRIVER: Are you lost?

BOY: No, sir.

DRIVER: Is this your stop?

BOY: No, sir.

DRIVER: You realize we've reached the end of the line.

BOY: Yes, sir.

DRIVER: I don't start up again for another few minutes.

BOY: Yes, sir.

DRIVER: And then I just go back the way we came.

BOY: Yes, sir.

DRIVER: You're just going to sit here, then?

BOY: Yes, sir. If that's okay.

DRIVER: Okay by me.

BOY: Thank you.

DRIVER: I just saw you back here and wanted to make sure you
were, you know…

BOY: I'm not lost.

DRIVER: Okay. Just checking.

(A WOMAN gets on the bus.)

DRIVER: You're welcome to sit, ma'am, but we don't get to
moving for another few minutes yet.

WOMAN: Oh, I see. Can you turn the air on?

DRIVER: No, ma'am, I'm sorry. I gotta keep everything cut off
until I'm back on line.

WOMAN: Oh, I see.

DRIVER: Yes, ma'am.

WOMAN: I'll just wait then.

DRIVER: Suit yourself.

(SHE sits. DRIVER addresses BOY.)

DRIVER: You gonna be all right, then?

BOY: Yes, thank you.

DRIVER: Okay. I'm right outside if you need me.

BOY: Um, there is one thing, actually.

DRIVER: What's that, son?

BOY: Can you make the bus talk?

DRIVER: Talk?

BOY: Yeah, you know.

DRIVER: Oh, you mean the GPS voice?

BOY: I don't know what you call it. The voice that says what the next street is.

DRIVER: Yeah, yeah. The GPS voice.

BOY: Can you play it?

DRIVER: Well, I have to switch the motor on to do that.

>   *(BOY stares.)*

I'm sorry, son.

BOY: Okay.

DRIVER: Like I told this lady, I can't run the air either, so…

BOY: Okay. I'll just wait.

DRIVER: Awright. We'll be leaving here in a few minutes.

>   *(DRIVER leaves the bus. WOMAN turns to the boy.)*

WOMAN: I like the bus lady voice, too.

BOY: Yes, ma'am.

WOMAN: I don't see so good, so I like it she announces the next stop.

BOY: Yes, ma'am.

>   *(SHE unwraps a piece of gum.)*

WOMAN: Would you like a piece of gum?

BOY: No thank you.

WOMAN: I have more than one.

BOY: No thank you.

>   *(WOMAN busies herself with gum, purse, belongings.)*

WOMAN: Which one is your stop?

BOY: None.

WOMAN: None?

BOY: No, ma'am. I don't live on the bus route.

WOMAN: You don't?

BOY: Nuh uh.

WOMAN: Then why do you ride the bus?

BOY: Because it talks.

WOMAN: Ooooh, you like that it talks.

BOY: Yes ma'am. I like the voice.

WOMAN: It's nice, isn't it?

BOY: Yes, ma'am. It's my mother.

WOMAN: What's your mother, dear?

BOY: The voice.

WOMAN: You mean it sounds like your mother?

BOY: No ma'am. It's my mother.

WOMAN: The bus is your mother?

BOY: No ma'am. Just the voice.

WOMAN: Oh, I see.

BOY: She's dead.

WOMAN: Who's dead, dear?

BOY: My mother.

> *(A beat.)*

WOMAN: I see. So you—

BOY: Ride the bus. Yes ma'am.

> *(The driver gets on the bus.)*

DRIVER: Okie dokie. Back the way we came.

> *(HE starts up the bus.)*

FEMALE VO: Welcome to the Greater Metro Transit System. Please have your Go Pass ready.

WOMAN: That's your mother?

BOY: She's not finished.

FEMALE VO: I love you, Reggie.

> *(The BOY smiles at the bewildered woman. The bus pulls away.)*

Characters:

CAMERON: Female or Male, thirties - fifties

NICK: Male, thirties - fifties

Setting: A small, elegant restaurant. The present.

Author's note: This meal happens within two time frames: "real time," meaning the last 5 minutes of the meal, and "compressed time," meaning the last 5 years of their relationship.

TOM SMITH is a playwright and director. His plays are published by Samuel French, Playscripts, and Youth-PLAYS, among others. Monologues from his plays appear in five collections of works, and his short plays have been produced internationally. His work has been enjoyed by audiences in cities across the U.S., including Seattle, Kansas City, San Francisco, and Chicago, as well as in Australia, Belgium, Canada, Germany, Ireland, Latvia, Netherlands, New Zealand, Romania, Sweden, Switzerland, and the United Kingdom. Tom is also the author of The Other Blocking: Teaching and Performing Improvisation (Kendall Hunt) and articles and reviews for Theatre Journal, Theatre Topics, The Players Journal, and several resource books. Tom graduated from Whitman College with a BA in Dramatic Arts and Secondary Education certification, and earned his MFA in Directing from University of Missouri-Kansas City. He is a proud member of the Dramatist's Guild and Stage Directors and Choreographers Society. tomsmithplaywright.com

(CAMERON and NICK have just finished an elaborate meal.)

CAMERON: That was astonishing!

NICK: I haven't eaten like that in—

CAMERON: And the wine—

NICK: Buttery. And so much—

CAMERON: Phenomenal! Especially for a local wine—

NICK: Why we don't—

CAMERON: We can hardly afford—

NICK: I know. But still…we deserve this!

CAMERON: We really do.

> *(Beat.)*

NICK: I'm giddy! I'm actually—

CAMERON: Every single course was so—

NICK: The perfect meal!

CAMERON: *(Gazing appreciatively.)* Thank you.

NICK: For what? For this?

CAMERON: For tonight. For everything.

NICK: I need coffee.

CAMERON: Get dessert, too. Treat yourself! I'm perfectly at peace. I could stay like this forever…

NICK: I didn't get the gym today, but I'd really like something…sweet.

> *(CAMERON stares at NICK's tie, confused.)*

What?

CAMERON: Your tie.

NICK: I've had it for years.

CAMERON: It doesn't look that old.

NICK: Ok. Are you sure you don't want dessert? They have a tiramisu that's—

CAMERON: It's not really you.

NICK: The tie?

CAMERON: That too.

> *(Beat.)*

How long have we been coming here?

NICK: I don't know. A few months?

CAMERON: Months?

NICK: Right?

CAMERON: Five years. Years. Do you honestly have no sense of time? Of history?

NICK: What's with you tonight? You're acting—

CAMERON: I'm just trying to—

NICK: We were enjoying this incredible meal together. And now…this?

CAMERON: Now this.

NICK: Where's our waiter?

> *(Beat.)*

Do you think someone gave me this tie? Is that why you're— We should be talking about something. Some thing. Not…

CAMERON: It's only conversation.

NICK: It's accusation.

> *(Long look. NICK takes off his tie.)*

Do you want to smell it?

CAMERON: You can't do that here! There's a—

NICK: That way you can tell if there's some trace of deception.

CAMERON: I didn't say a word!

NICK: I want dessert!

> *(HE throws his tie on the table. Pause.)*

CAMERON: Five years!

> *(Pause.)*

NICK: Is this how you ended your last relationship?

CAMERON: What?

NICK: I'm just asking.

CAMERON: Is this how I ended my last relationship?

NICK: Well…?

> *(Beat.)*

CAMERON: You should take yoga with me. You're getting doughy.

NICK: No, I'm not!

CAMERON: You shouldn't miss a work-out. You need structure, routine.

NICK: I missed one day!

CAMERON: One day is a lot! One day is everything. But, go on: order dessert! Since you must!

NICK: Yoga is trendy. It's for sissies.

CAMERON: Order two desserts. Hell, you "deserve" it!

NICK: It's for people who get their news from one paragraph stories on the internet.

CAMERON: Your father was overweight. Too many "sweets."

NICK: You're not skinny, you know. We're both just fit.

> *(Pause.)*

Let's get the check…

CAMERON: Just let me sit here a moment.

NICK: Stewing?

CAMERON: Staring.

NICK: And what do you see?

CAMERON: I don't know.

NICK: Oh, c'mon… You know everything.

CAMERON: You tell me. What do I see?

> *(Long, uncomfortable stare. NICK's guilt flashes to the surface for a fleeting moment.)*

NICK: We should go…

CAMERON: …I need to…digest.

> *(Pause.)*

NICK: *(Grabbing CAMERON'S hand.)* I was wrong. I don't

want anything else. I'm sated.

(NICK looks at CAMERON, hopeful. HE slowly puts his tie back on. CAMERON reaches over and straightens it up.)

What?

CAMERON: It…wasn't right.

(Slowly rises and exits, leaving NICK alone at the table.)

Characters:

Any age, any gender, any shape. We are all stardust, right?

AARON

GRIFF

DANA SCHWARTZ is a playwright working in Los Angeles. Her work has been produced in theaters around the country. Other works include the full length plays *Space* and *The Poppy Party,* one act plays *Condolences* and *PTA,* and the late night hit, *Your Momma.*

AARON: Do I know you?

GRIFF: Yes.

AARON: I do, don't I?

GRIFF: Yes, you do.

AARON: You're here because of the…

GRIFF: Yes. I'm afraid so.

AARON: (*Pause.*) How did you find me?

GRIFF: It wasn't easy.

AARON: Well. Good. I'm glad it wasn't… I'm glad it was difficult.

GRIFF: I'm sure.

AARON: Wouldn't you be?

GRIFF: Naturally.

AARON: But you found me none the less.

GRIFF: Well, it is my job.

AARON: Of course. Of course it is. And you are quite…well, your reputation does precede you.

GRIFF: Thank you?

AARON: It was meant as a compliment. To you. I mean, it's a good thing. That you have a reputation. And that it…precedes you. That's good for…well, for business. Right?

GRIFF: Right.

AARON: It's not great for ME, but it must be nice for you. To have achieved that level. Of success. In your…career? Do you call it a career?

GRIFF: I don't really call it anything actually. But yes, I suppose it's a career. Of sorts. Not like YOURS. Of course.

AARON: Don't you judge me.

GRIFF: No. I don't judge. I just carry out the…

AARON: Oh that's clever. I didn't realize you were so witty! Just my luck, a final bit of comedy. I suppose I should be grateful you aren't a mime.

GRIFF: I feel like you are being sarcastic. It's not an attractive quality. In a person. Especially, you know, now.

AARON: Why "now"?

GRIFF: No, forget it.

AARON: Please!

GRIFF: You sure?

AARON: By all means.

GRIFF: Well, I wanted to…I was going to ask. Ok well lately, I have sort of been keeping…track. Record. Of people's last…of a person's last…you know. Words.

AARON: Oh? Like a…souvenir?

GRIFF: No! More like an…added service really. I feel like those final thoughts are…of value. And since I, as you mentioned, have a bit of a reputation now and have been doing so well, plus honestly I do quite enjoy the work, I thought it would be nice to… give back. A little something. So I decided, if the person was interested of course, I could record their last…well, you know. And pass them along.

AARON: Pass them along?

GRIFF: Via courier, or email. Tweet. Along those lines.

AARON: That's…that's really nice actually.

GRIFF: Thank you! I was quite pleased with the idea myself. And it has really been lovely, I have to say. People have responded rather well. There's a look you get. When you know. How you want to be…remembered. It's beautiful.

AARON: I can imagine!

GRIFF: So? Are you? Interested?

AARON: Of course! Of course I am. So is there, like, a…limit or anything? Length or time or number of characters or anything like that?

GRIFF: You know, at first I didn't have any parameters on it at all. Stream of consciousness, what have you. But then, and I'm not saying that you would do this, but some people started, well, taking advantage. Drawing it out. Buying time, so to speak. So now I'm afraid that yes, you are limited to three lines. I find that to be an adequate length. Brevity is the soul of…well, you know.

AARON: 3 lines.

GRIFF: You'll find it remarkably easy I think. Most people seem to do their best work under a dead line. (*Chuckles.*) Get it?

AARON: Deadline. Yes, witty.

GRIFF: Sorry.

AARON: Don't be. Ok, let me think…

GRIFF: Don't over…

AARON: Please!

GRIFF: Fine. (*Fidgets.*) Got it?

AARON: Not…

GRIFF: First thing that pops in there, usually the best. In my experience.

AARON: Rosebud?

GRIFF: See, that's funny!

AARON: Thanks.

GRIFF: But no.

AARON: Oh wait.

GRIFF: Yes??

AARON: Oh I think…

GRIFF: You've got it??

AARON: I think…oh this is perfect!

GRIFF: Write it down!

AARON: You don't want to hear it?

GRIFF: I don't want to get it wrong. You had the look. (*Griff hands Aaron a small notebook and pencil.*)

AARON: (*Writing fiendishly.*) …of man. There.

GRIFF: May I?

AARON: Please!

GRIFF: (*Reading.*) …of man. (*Looks up at Aaron.*) Oh. Oh my.

AARON: Right?

GRIFF: My compliments.

AARON: Really?

GRIFF: Sincerely. It's poetry. You missed your calling.

AARON: Thank you.

GRIFF: Thank YOU. (*Carefully tears out paper, folds it lovingly and tucks it into a pocket.*)

AARON: I think I'm ready.

GRIFF: Agreed. It's been a pleasure.

AARON: Really?

GRIFF: Really. I have enjoyed these moments.

AARON: Enough to….?

GRIFF: Oh no. No, that's not up to me. Nothing to be done there. But it has been a pleasure. I look forward to sharing your thoughts.

AARON: You really are good at your job.

GRIFF: I know. (*Griff reaches out to Aaron, lights fade out.*)

Characters:

TRISTA

CHLOE

Setting: A café.

CRISTINA LUZÁRRAGA hails from Short Hills, New Jersey. She graduated from Princeton University with a B.A. in Comparative Literature. Subsequently, she moved to Chicago where she studied improv and sketch writing at iO Theater and The Second City Conservatory and performed stand-up around town. Her full-length play *Due Unto Others* was produced by Princeton's Lewis Center for the Arts. Readings of her short plays *Hippo Woman* and *Baker's Three* were conducted at Greenhouse Theater in Chicago. Cristina tends to write dark comedies in which people tell inappropriate jokes and do things that are generally frowned upon. She is currently pursuing an MFA in Playwriting at Ohio University.

(A cafe. TRISTA sits with a coffee. CHLOE enters, hair is in a French braid.)

TRISTA: Hey! Chloe!

CHLOE: Hi, oh my goodness!

(They hug awkwardly.)

CHLOE: It's been—how many years?

TRISTA: Almost fifteen.

CHLOE: Gosh!

TRISTA: I'm so happy I found you on Facebook. Can you believe we've been living close by all these years, and we're just now...

CHLOE: It's crazy.

TRISTA: So I saw you got married! And had a baby!

CHLOE: Yep!

TRISTA: That's...wow. Congrats.

CHLOE: Thanks...

TRISTA: Anyway, I invited you here because there's something I want to ask you.

(Beat.)

Will you be my maid of honor?

(Uncomfortably long silence.)

CHLOE: Um...I'm gonna get a coffee. Do you want coffee?

TRISTA: *(Holding up her coffee and revealing a second one.)* All set. And I got one for you too.

(Beat.)

Look, don't worry! I'm not going to be a—whaddya call it?—King-Kong-Bride or anything. It's going to be a low-key affair. We'll skip the bridal shower since those are for sorority bitches. But I'm thinking a spring wedding at, like, a bookstore or...a space observatory. (I'm not religious and church weddings are stupid.) But I'm definitely open to suggestions. I love the pics from your wedding even if it was in a church.

CHLOE: Yeah...Trista, I'm flattered. I just—don't you have,

like, a girl cousin? Or maybe an old college roommate? Or a co-worker who might be a better choice? I mean, I haven't even met the groom, right? I feel like I at least need to know about him, about you guys.

TRISTA: His name's Devin. He's from New Hampshire. We can totally set up a meeting so you guys can get acquainted. He keeps hounding me, like: Trista, I want meet your friends! He's got all these buddies he wants to be groomsmen, and I'm, like: Woah, pump the breaks! Let's keep this thing small.

CHLOE: So you've told him about me?

TRISTA: Of course! I was, like, Chloe and I were BFFs in eighth grade. And I told him how you could French braid like no one's business. Remember I used to ask you: Where do you keep your third hand? And is it baby size or normal?

CHLOE: What?

TRISTA: Because you were so good at French braiding it was like you had an extra hand! Get it?

CHLOE: It wasn't really funny though because my brother has a baby hand.

TRISTA: How is Jeremy?

CHLOE: He's good. Look, I just don't think—

TRISTA: —and remember I used to call you ChloChlo the Dodo?

CHLOE: Because I got put in the slow track for math. Yeah, I remember.

TRISTA: You couldn't do long division until you were fourteen!

CHLOE: I used to call you Trista the Mista because of your hairy lip.

TRISTA: *(Suddenly angry.)* My mom wouldn't let me wax my face! You knew that!

    (Beat)

We were just kids though. No harm, no foul.

CHLOE: This is probably going to sound kind of offensive, and I'm sorry. But, I have to ask: Do you have other friends? Because I just feel like I must be really low on the list if you do.

TRISTA: Yes! God! I have lots of friends!

CHLOE: Okay! Great! I just—it's awesome that you're getting married. Devin sounds really nice.

TRISTA: He is. He's very social...And just so you know, I could have asked other people. There's my bunk-mate Greta from camp. But she lives in Singapore now. And there's Theresa from my office. But she's technically my boss, so it seems weird to put her in that position. And Mario, my gay neighbor would probably be into it. But I don't want to make a political statement with a male maid of honor because my grandparents would flip. So I have friends!

CHLOE: Cool...

TRISTA: You'll meet them at the wedding.

> *(Pause.)*

CHLOE: Trista, I just want to say how impressed I am by how you've been able to overcome certain obstacles. It can't be easy moving through life with Asperger's Syndrome, and it seems like—

TRISTA: —what? I don't have Asperger's!

CHLOE: Oh. Well, I meant that as a compliment! I mean, you're so good with numbers and—

TRISTA: —fuck you, I'm not retarded!

CHLOE: Autistic.

TRISTA: Autistic! Whatever! Jesus!

CHLOE: Okay, shh! People are staring.

TRISTA: I will have you know that I'm officially neurotypical with social anxiety and eccentric tendencies!

CHLOE: All right, I'm sorry! What I meant was: You've always been...kooky, which is why I liked you in eighth grade. And, to be honest, why I didn't really like you after eighth grade. And, you know, you hear stuff through the rumor mill. Like, a few years ago, people were saying that you got kicked out of a sorority because someone saw you eating your toenails.

TRISTA: Who told you that? It just wasn't a good fit. Which, yes, okay, has been something of a pattern. And why I feel so fortunate to have found Devin...and you. Remember in school when I used to speak English backwards sometimes, just for kicks, and everyone was saying that I was possessed by the devil? And you were like: Hey, she's not possessed by the devil...That means a lot.

CHLOE: I'm sorry I made fun of your hairy lip.

TRISTA: I've had laser hair removal since then. I know a guy if you're interested. He can totally help with...

> *(Pointing at CHLOE's face.)*

CHLOE: Okay, that! Do you see that? You just insulted me---again! I like my eyebrows, thank you very much. And I don't appreciate you calling me stupid—and whatever that was about baby hands.

TRISTA: I didn't mean to offend you. I don't mean to offend anyone. It just happens. A lot...I bet you're pretty good at long division now.

CHLOE: Is that joke?

TRISTA: Um, yes...? (I don't know.) I'm not good with jokes. Oh, but I do have one! A joke, that is. I told it to Devin yesterday.

> *(Collecting herself to tell a joke.)*

You know how tabloids employ so-called "body language experts" to determine if, like, Brangelina's cheating or Miley Cyrus is a goblin or whatever. Well, I think I'd make a really good body language expert. Here are my qualifications: I'm not autistic.

> *(Beat.)*

End of list.

> *(Very long beat.)*

Get it? Because body-language experts are full of shit but also I'm pretty bad at reading social cues.

> *(CHLOE is baffled but titters in spite of herself.)*

CHLOE: That's kinda fucked up. Pardon my French.

TRISTA: I know.

CHLOE: And Devin liked the joke?

TRISTA: Loved it.

(CHLOE takes a deep breath.)

CHLOE: What do you want me to say in the wedding toast?

(Blackout.)

Characters:
TWO PEOPLE

MICHAEL FRAYN was born in London in 1933 and began his career as a journalist on the Guardian and the Observer. His novels include *Towards the End of the Morning, The Trick of It* and *Landing on the Sun. Headlong* (1999) was shortlisted for the Booker Prize, while his most recent novel, *Spies* (2002), won the Whitbread Novel Award. His fifteen plays range from *Noises Off* to *Copenhagen* and, most recently, *Afterlife. Finishing Touches* is from *Matchbox Theatre: Thirty Short Entertainments* (2015).

Darling, you know how much I appreciate the way you're always...well...

—...helping you, yes, but don't be silly, darling—I love helping you.

...always helping me, particularly when I'm saying something, and I...you know...

—...hesitate.

...hesitate for a ...

—...moment...

...a moment, yes, and at once...

—...It's usually only for a fraction of a second, darling.

Exactly. And at once you very kindly try to...

—...finish the sentence for you.

...finish the sentence for me. Because you're so much...

—...I'm not cleverer than you, darling!

...not just cleverer, but because you think so much...

—...I do think faster, it's true.

...faster. And you know how...well...how...

—...to finish sentences.

...how...

—...how to speak Italian? How to make apple strudel?

...how grateful I am. And you're very good at it because you...

...usually know what I'm going to say. And because, well, it simply...

—...saves so much time.

...so much time. Or it would...

—...if you didn't insist on going on and saying it all over again.

...if I didn't...Exactly!

—...Which is a pity, darling, because we could spend the time we saved doing something else, and since you've brought the subject up, I can't help noticing that sometimes when you go on and finish the sentence I've already finished you do it in a way that sounds just a tiny bit impatient.

No, no, it's just that I feel I would very occasionally like to...
well...like to…

—...get to the end of a sentence yourself…

...the end of a sentence myself. Just to see what it was...you
know...what it was...well, what it was…

—...like.

Yes, and then also there are times when you…

—...get it wrong. Of course.

...get it wrong, and you make me…

—...say things that you *weren't* going to say, that's true, and I'm
sorry, but then sometimes I'm right, and you *were* going to
say them, only you change your mind just because I've said
them for you.

Possibly, though by the time I say what I'm going to say…

—...the conversation has usually moved on.

...moved on, and you don't notice me saying what I *am* actually
saying, and so you go on thinking I've said…

—...what I thought you were going to say, I know, but, darling,
if what I thought you were going to say was what you *were*
going to say, and you only *didn't* say it because I said it for
you, then what I *remember* you saying is what you actually
would have said if I hadn't said it for you, so it's truer to
your intentions for me to remember it that way, and believe,
me, I don't *enjoy* finishing your sentences for you--I only do
it because…

...because otherwise we'd be here till midnight before I get to
the end of even this sentence--and here you might take note,
incidentally, that I *can* sometimes finish sentences perfectly
quickly…

—...if they're someone else's sentences.

...if they're someone else's sentences.

—...Though I notice you never finish other people's sentences,
only mine.

Only yours, very possibly--but if so that's because I always
know...*I* always know…

—...you always *think* you know…

...what you're going to say...

—...Only you *don't*, as it happens.

Let's put it to the test then. I know exactly...I know precisely...

—...what I'm going to say next.

...what I'm going to say next.' You've said it. Precisely. Exactly.

—...One of these days, you know, darling, I'm going to...

...strangle me. Yes, unless I get in first, and...

—...strangle *me*? Is that what you're trying to say? You'd strangle *me*?

I shouldn't need to, darling, because if I *tried* to strangle you, you'd interrupt me, as usual, and...

—...strangle *myself*, perhaps?

...strangle *yourself*--or else get it wrong, as you so often do, and strangle some other poor fellow altogether. Either way it will somehow turn out to be...

—...Your fault. Well, of course, it *would* be.

Of course, and I shall end up getting...

—...as angry as usual.

...fifteen years. Though at least that's a sentence I might be able to finish in peace.

Characters:

JOSHUA: Male, twenties.

JUNE: Female, twenties.

Setting: An empty room with a single chair.

> REINA HARDY is a playwright from Chicago. Her plays, which usually contain magic and sometimes contain science, have been seen across the country, including at Rorschach Theatre in DC, the Vortex in Austin, and the NNPN National New Play Showcase. She's been a Michener Fellow at UT Austin, winner of the KCACTF TYA Prize, finalist for the Terrence McNally Prize and the recipient of an Interact 20/20 Commission. Reina is the book writer for *Fanatical the Musical* (under development in England with the Stable), and is collaborating with Sky Candy on a devised circus show. She can make things happen with her mind. reinahardy.com

(JOSHUA, a young man, enters a room. JUNE, a young woman, is sitting in a single chair.)

JOSHUA: Oh, it's you.

JUNE: Weren't expecting me, were you? (*She gets up, offers him the chair.*) Come on, sit down.

JOSHUA: I was going to call you, but—

JUNE: Don't worry. I just came here to tell you that I took care of it. You can go.

(JOSHUA and JUNE step forward, face the audience, speak swiftly without inflection.)

JOSHUA: I was born in Orlando, Florida. Seriously. A place where all roads lead to Disneyland. It's the end of the exodus, ultimate retirement. If you're born in Florida there's only one place left to go.

JUNE: I'm a friend to the Jews. That is, I desire access to Jewish cock. Which is pretty friendly. In college I signed up for Hillel, in order to score a free promotional squeezable Star of David. After I discovered the fringe benefits there was no going back.

JOSHUA: I am 23 years old and extremely fond of holiday-themed marshmallows.

JUNE: I'm frightened of pumping gas.

JOSHUA: I was raised with the help of my grandmother. She wanted a grandson. My mom was 36 and single. One day she just showed up in Orlando and said, here! Here's the baby! Here!

JUNE: All of my early sexual experiences were highly questionable, and involved being harassed by perverts on the internet. Now there are so many sexual professionals on the internet that I have to harass the perverts.

JOSHUA: I once ate an entire sweet potato pie.

JUNE: My AP geometry score was five. My AP biology score was five. My AP literature score was five.

JOSHUA: I have always felt a longing to be part of something larger than myself.

JUNE: My AP history score was 4. Assholes.

JOSHUA: Shopping at Ikea with someone else gives me great contentment. There are rugs, mirrors, desks, dinner tables, cutlery, frames, lights, everything in the world you need, all reasonable and flat.

JOSHUA and JUNE: I want to make a life—

JOSHUA: —that's extraordinary.

JUNE: Maybe in one of those model rooms.

JOSHUA: I had a crush on Britney Spears when she was a Mouseketeer.

JUNE: I had my first orgasm while thinking about David Bowie in the movie Labyrinth. I don't think he's Jewish.

JOSHUA: When I got back from Orlando, that weekend, all of the furniture was gone. Every stick that we bought together. But she left the one chair that she found in the alley. That's how I knew she took me seriously.

JUNE: In college, I joined an Anglican choir.

JOSHUA: This was the first song I learned.

JOSHUA and JUNE: WHO'S THE LEADER OF THE CLUB THAT'S MADE FOR YOU AND ME

JOSHUA: M I C KEY M O U SE

HEY THERE HI THERE HO THERE YOU'RE AS WEL-COME AS CAN BE

M I C K E Y M O U S E

MICKEY MOUSE!

MICKEY MOUSE!

FOREVER LET US HOLD OUR BANNER HIGH!

JUNE: *My soul doth magnify the Lord: and my spirit hath rejoiced in God my Saviour.*

For he hath regarded: the lowliness of his handmaiden.

For behold, from henceforth: all generations shall call me blessed.

JUNE: I wasn't raised with any kind of religion. My grandmother sent me a children's Bible as a present and I thought it was a storybook. It is a storybook.

JOSHUA: Was it because she wasn't brave enough? Was it because she loved this place that much? Is that why I'll never have a father?

JUNE: It's a storybook.

JOSHUA: I have to believe in something.

JUNE: It's a storybook. I think I could turn Wolf Blitzer straight. Oh. He's not gay.

JOSHUA: I believe that everybody has to believe in something.

JUNE: I'm thinking of Anderson Cooper.

JOSHUA: The first time I touched her I got hard like that. Like she was flipping a switch.

JUNE: I'm not really big on politics but I never got the whole Israel thing. Why does anybody want to live there? It's dry and unpleasant, and it explodes all the time. Isn't the promised land in Manhattan? Or Boca Raton?

JOSHUA: It's terrible to not know who you are.

JOSHUA and JUNE: If I had a daughter, I would name her Josephine/Beatrice.

JUNE: My mother would prefer not to have grandchildren. She doesn't want to be old.

JOSHUA: I never believed she loved me, so it was an unpleasant surprise when I found out she did.

JUNE: When the thought first crossed my mind, I felt betrayed. When you think that something's not going to happen, it means you've also thought it will. Wanted it.

JOSHUA: The first thing that I ever got from my father was a newspaper clipping about a cafe bomber. I remember it had his address.

JUNE: He's not going to marry me.

JOSHUA: I was twelve.

JUNE: He's not going to marry me.

JOSHUA: Old enough to start thinking about it.

JUNE: He's not going to marry me.

JOSHUA: If there's any time to go it's now. When I don't have anything holding me back. I don't even have furniture.

JUNE: I regret leaving even that chair. It was *my* chair.

JOSHUA: WE'LL DO THINGS

    AND WE'LL GO PLACES

    ALL AROUND THE WORLD

    M I C K E Y M O U S E

JUNE: (*overlapping with the last line of JOSHUA's song*) The name of that song is the magnificat.

JOSHUA: MICKEY MOUSE!

JUNE: Or song of Mary.

JOSHUA: MICKEY MOUSE

JUNE: It's Anglican.

They re-enter the scene, repeat exactly as before.

JOSHUA: Oh, it's you.

JUNE: Weren't expecting me, were you? Come on, sit down.

JOSHUA: I don't have much time. I was going to call you, but—

JUNE: Don't worry. I just came here to tell you that I took care of it. You can go.

Characters:
  EBENEEZER SCROOGE
  GHOST

ARTHUR M. JOLLY is a two-time Joining Sword and Pen winner and finalist for the Woodward/Newman Drama Award. He has penned over 50 produced plays, with productions across the US and in Canada, Europe, Africa, Asia, and South America. Published plays include *A Gulag Mouse, Trash, Past Curfew, Long Joan Silver, The Christmas Princess, The Four Senses of Love, How Blue is My Crocodile, Snakes in a Lunchbox, What the Well Dressed Girl is Wearing, The Bricklayer*, and two short play collections, *Thin Lines* and *Guilty Moments*. Jolly is a member of the WGA, The Alliance of Los Angeles Playwrights, and The Dramatists Guild, and is repped by The Brant Rose Agency. arthurjolly.com

(AT RISE: EBENEEZER SCROOGE, in a void.)

EBENEEZER: Good Spirit—assure me that I yet may change these shadows you have shown me! I will honour Christmas in my heart, and try to keep it all the year. I will live in the Past, the Present, and the Future. Oh, tell me I may sponge away the writing on this stone!

(The GHOST OF CHRISTMASES YET TO BE, YET TO BE appears.)

GHOST: I am the Ghost of Christmases Yet to Be, Yet to Be! The fourth ghost!

EBENEEZER: I was told three spirits—

GHOST: I didn't think I was gonna make it, but my schedule opened up at the last -

(His phone chimes.)

Hold on.

(Texting.)

Chill. b-r-b.

(To Ebeneezer.)

Sorry. Where were we?

EBENEEZER: Spirit— I have seen my future— my own grave-stone, a miser's death...

GHOST: That's short term. I get to show you what happened after that.

(The Ghost takes Ebeneezer's hand.)

EBENEEZER: What is this place?

GHOST: It's called a mall.

EBENEEZER: That sorry figure with the squalling child upon its knee—

GHOST: Fake beard and pit-stains? The rest of the year, he works a checkout counter. His boss made him do this 'cause he's morbidly obese. Type two diabetes— so now, when he'd rather be home with his wife and the puppy they adopted because they can't afford a kid on minimum wage— he's here till eleven, every night. Sat on by little brats. Flu-ridden, half of them unvaccinated. Some of them pee on his—

EBENEEZER: Spirit— why depress me with such awful sights?!

GHOST: The puppy's sick too. Canine cancer, it's gonna die in a few—

EBENEEZER: Stop it! Why do you torment me! I have resolved to change my ways! I want to bring joy and good to all, throughout the year. I want Tiny Tim to walk and live, I want to pay Bob Cratchit a wage that will allow him to put clothes on the lad's back and warm food in his belly— to keep Christmas in my heart all the year long!

GHOST: Christmas sucks. I just hate it. The whole Christmas— winter...

(Beat.)

I suffer from Seasonal Affective Disorder...Self-diagnosed.

(Beat.)

Oh wait— I have to show you this kid!

EBENEEZER: Not another vision, I beg you spirit—

GHOST: This one's funny—there's this kid in North Dakota who is allergic to the artificial spray-flocking they put on trees. That fake snow aerosol? I mean, talk about specific—but he goes into anaphylactic shock, head swells up like a melon...

EBENEEZER: I know not of this air-soll of which you speak—

GHOST: That's not the funny bit! Guess what they have on the fake tree in the ER? All over it!

EBENEEZER: No more! Show me no more visions! Tell me how I should keep Christmas. The other spirits told me with joy, and openness, the whole year long.

GHOST: Oh, no. No, no— Look, we spend more on freakin' *wrapping paper* every year than we spend on food aid to starving children.

EBENEEZER: I thought, maybe my experience might serve as a warning to others, to turn them from the path of selfish concerns, to open their hearts to all mankind.

GHOST: Not so much.

EBENEEZER: Nothing changes? The poorhouses—are they still in operation?

GHOST: We got better: for-profit prisons.

EBENEEZER: The union workhouses?

GHOST: Union's a bad word in the future. Less child labor—
I'll give you that. At least in this country— not any less in
an absolute how-many-six-year-olds-are-working-today
numbers.

> *(Beat.)*

Let's start simply...does it have to be the biggest goose in
the shop? What about a nice vegan nut-loaf.

EBENEEZER: What on God's green earth is a—

GHOST: I like that you give Bob a raise— I mean, that's tangi-
ble. That makes a difference...but how? You're a loan shark.

EBENEEZER: A money lender.

GHOST: What's your interest rate? Prime plus I'll-break-your-
legs? So, you give Bob a raise, at the expense of some suffering widow who can't make her payments as it is.

EBENEEZER: I will forgive her debts...

GHOST: And the next one and the one after? You'd be broke in a
month. You don't have any marketable skills beyond owning
money and lending it at usurious interest. Like Sallie Mae.

EBENEEZER: How about at not-usurious interest?

GHOST: Prime plus I'll-only-break-one-leg?

EBENEEZER: Maybe no legs at all. A finger or two.

GHOST: Now you're getting it.

> *(His phone chimes again.)*

Hold on—

> *(He checks it— texts back:)*

On my way.

> *(To Ebeneezer.)*

There's a part of you— a legitimate part— that recognizes
that shunning mankind is a way of protecting yourself; but
nonetheless at a psychological cost. Hence, the whole...
let's get real, Christmas ghosts? Jungian counter-projection
if you ask me. I imagine you're somewhere on the autism

spectrum, to be honest— but we can save the analysis for
the next visitation.

EBENEEZER: The next?

GHOST: Easter, too much chocolate— you get the spirits of
moderation, sugar-shock and bad acne— whatever. Let me
sum up: None of it helps. You're Scrooge, *the Scrooge..*
you're *a* scrooge. An adjective. But there are concrete steps
you can take—we can all take... maybe it's about compas-
sion, or something...it's just not goddamn Christmas, okay?
I friggin' hate it.

   (Beat.)

Bye.

   (The Ghost VANISHES into the gloom.

   *Ebeneezer wakes as if from a dream, and runs to the
window.)*

EBENEEZER: *(Calling down.)* You there! Boy! Do you know
the poulterer's, in the next street but one, at the corner? The
one with the prize turkey hanging in the window—as big
as you are, my boy! Here's a shiny sixpence— run there,
as quick as you can, and ask if they do a vegan nut-loaf! If
not, get a moderately priced turkey— nothing ridiculous.
Try and get some kale, too —broccoli, something with some
vitamins. As quick as you can, boy, and you shall have a
gold sovereign—a half-crown— a shilling... you shall have
another shiny sixpence. Which is a perfectly good wage, but
should not contribute to inequitable distribution or escalate
the rate of inflation. And Merry Christmas, if you choose
to celebrate it, without presupposing judgment if you have
another faith or indeed no faith at all! Seasonal greetings,
every one!

   LIGHTS OUT

Characters:

PAUL: Thirty-five, male; a marine biologist.

JOEY: Childlike, any gender; a Great White shark.

CREW: (3-5), any age; marine researchers and crew members onboard.

Setting: Morning, a boat on the ocean off the coast of South Africa

> This play was inspired by: Benchley, Peter. "Great White, Deep Trouble." *National Geographic* 197, no. 4 (2000): 2-29.
>
> SARA LYONS is a young theatre artist and dramatist with a passion for history and storytelling. She uses her skills in playwriting, directing, dramaturgy, acting and producing to bring the stories around her to life, both past and present. She plans on creating a theatre company that specializes in immersive and experimental theatre based on forgotten historical narratives and our natural world. Sara is a graduate of SUNY New Paltz, with degrees in Theatre Arts and History. She is a proud alumni member of Alpha Psi Omega, the National Theatre Honor Society, Kappa Lambda chapter. www.saralyons.net

(Lights up on stage. PAUL and the CREW enter on one side in a boat. JOEY enters from the other side.)

PAUL: *(to CREW)* Hold on, do you see that? In the water there!

JOEY: What IS that?

PAUL: *(to CREW)* It's a little one, where's its mom?

JOEY: I've never seen anything like that before...

PAUL: *(to CREW)* Of course it has a mom, these babies travel in groups.

JOEY: Is it a fish?

PAUL: *(to CREW)* No really, they're delicate creatures, they're nothing like Jaws...

JOEY: Maybe it knows where my mom went!

PAUL: You are gorgeous, little buddy!

JOEY: Why is it growling, is it going to hurt me?

PAUL: *(to a CREW MEMBER)* Bill, cut the motor, we don't want to scare it.

> *(Bill cuts the motor. Beat.)*

JOEY: Maybe not!

PAUL: Poor thing must be lonely. Come on, bud, don't be shy!

JOEY: Maybe it's nice!

PAUL (*Simultaneous.*) Poor thing needs a—

JOEY (*Simultaneous.*) Maybe he'll be a—

BOTH: Friend!

PAUL slowly extends an arm, open handed, towards JOEY.

> *(Beat.)*

PAUL: Here buddy, come here...

JOEY: What's it doing?

PAUL: Just a little closer...

JOEY: Maybe if I...

> *(JOEY inches forward, slowly, and then places their chin in PAUL's hand. PAUL gives JOEY chin scratches. It's heaven. JOEY swoons from the overstimulation.)*

105 Five-Minute Plays

JOEY: OH MY GOD.

PAUL: Whoa there, friend, easy! *(to CREW)* See, Great White Sharks have tons of electro-receptors on their snouts. We're not sure why, but this always seems to have the same effect.

JOEY: What was that? Mom never did THAT before! But then again, Mom doesn't have those…

    (JOEY looks down at extended fins, wondering what on earth fingers are.)

PAUL: *(to CREW)* Let's check the next sector.

    (The boat starts to leave.)

JOEY: Wait, I don't even know your name!

PAUL: *(to CREW)* Oh don't worry, he'll be right as rain in no time.

    (JOEY follows.)

JOEY: But I'm scared, please stay!

PAUL: No, buddy, you can't come with us, not where we're going.

JOEY: Please, I'm lost, and you're so nice!

PAUL: Buddy, you're already lost! We can't lead you further away, you need to find your family!

JOEY: *(Simultaneous.)* I thought we were—

PAUL: *(Simultaneous.)* Don't you miss your—

BOTH: Friends?

PAUL: *(to CREW)* Maybe we should stay a bit longer, just to be sure...

JOEY: …My mom's gonna flip a fin when I tell her about you!

PAUL: *(to CREW)* Maybe Mom is one of the sharks we tagged last year.

JOEY: She said the last time she saw anything like this, they have her the cool blinky thing on her back. She says it makes her feel silly, but I think it's cool.

PAUL: *(to CREW)* Should we tag this one? I think I'd like to see it growing up...

JOEY: Maybe I can get a cool blinky thing!

PAUL: Grab one out of the box, I'm sure we can find a way to justify this in the budget.

> (*A CREW MEMBER grabs a tag, which PAUL takes and stretches towards JOEY.*)

JOEY: Wait, what is that?

PAUL: Okay, here buddy, come a little closer

JOEY: Oooooh boy oh boy oh boy oh boy!!

> (*JOEY inches to PAUL, who slowly places the tag on the young shark, tenderly.*)

PAUL: Aaaaand— there!

JOEY: Wow, really?!

PAUL: There we go, bud! And it looks like your family found you!

JOEY: *(to offstage)* Mom? Mom! You're back! Look what I have— we match!

PAUL: I guess we better leave you to it. Hey—

> (*PAUL extends a hand, JOEY looks at it, and then at PAUL. JOEY cracks a grin, and rushes over to put a chin in PAUL's hand. PAUL gives a tiny scratch, and JOEY melts.*)

PAUL: Hang tight, little buddy!

JOEY: Bye! Be safe!

BOTH: I'll see you soon…Friend!

> (*Both smile, finally understanding one another. JOEY departs first, swimming along to see Mom. PAUL watches, and then exits with the CREW as the boat takes off for the next sector.*)

FIN.

Characters:

WOMAN

CRITIC

ARTIST

Setting: An artist's studio.

> UMBERTO BOCCIONI (1882 - 1916) was an influen-
> tial Italian painter and sculptor who helped shape the revo-
> lutionary aesthetic of the Futurism movement. Published
> in 1915 as part of the manifesto, *The Futurist Synthetic
> Theatre*, *Genius and Culture* demonstrates the Futurist aes-
> thetic of parody, irony, speed and compression.

*In the centre a costly dressing table with a mirror in front
of which a very elegant WOMAN, already dressed to leave
finishes putting on rouge. At the right a CRITIC, an ambigu-
ous being neither dirty nor clean, neither old nor young,
neutral, is sitting at a table overburdened with books and
papers on which shines a large paper knife, neither modern
nor antique. He turns his shoulder to the dressing table. At
left the ARTIST, an elegant youth, searches in a large file
sitting on thick cushions on the floor.*

THE ARTIST *(leaving the file and with his head between his
hands)*: It's terrible! *(Pause.)* I must get out of here! To be
renewed! *(He gets up tearing the abstract designs from the
file with convulsive hands.)* Liberation!! These empty forms,
worn out. Everything is fragmentary, weak! Oh! Art!...who,
who will help me!? *(He looks around; continues to tear up
the designs with sorrowful and convulsive motions.)*

    *(THE WOMAN is very near him but doesn't hear him. The
CRITIC becomes annoyed, but not very and going near
her, takes a book with a yellow jacket.)*

THE CRITIC *(half-asking the WOMAN, and half-talking to
himself)*: But what's the matter with that clown that he acts
and shouts that way?

THE WOMAN *(without looking)*: Oh well, he is an artist... he
wants to renew himself, and he hasn't a cent!

THE CRITIC *(bewildered)*: Strange! An artist! Impossible!
For twenty years I have profoundly studied this marvelous phenomenon, but I can't recognize it. *(Obviously, with
archeological curiosity.)* That one is crazy! Or a protester!
He wants to change! But creation is a serene thing. A work
of art is done naturally, in silence, and in recollection, like
a nightingale sings... Spirit, in the sense that Hegel means
spirit...

THE WOMAN *(intrigued)*: And if you know how it is done,
why don't you tell him? Poor thing! He is distressed...

THE CRITIC *(strutting)*: For centuries, the critic has told the
artist how to make a work of art...Since ethics and aesthetics
are functions of the spirit...

THE WOMAN: But you, you've never made any?

THE CRITIC *(nonplused)*: Me?...Not me!

THE WOMAN *(laughing with malice)*: Well, then, you know how to do it, but you don't do it. You are neutral. How boring you must be in bed! *(She continues putting on her rouge.)*

THE ARTIST *(always walking back and forth, sorrowfully wringing his hands)*: Glory! Ah! Glory! *(Tightening his fists.)* I am strong! I am young! I can face anything! Oh! Divine electric lights...sun...To electrify the crowds...Burn them! Dominate them!

THE WOMAN *(looking at him with sympathy and compulsion)*: Poor thing! Without any money...

THE ARTIST *(struck)*: Ah! I am wounded! I can't resist any longer! *(Toward the WOMAN, who doesn't hear him.)* Oh! A woman! *(Toward the CRITIC, who has already taken and returned a good many books, and who leafs through them and cuts them.)* You! You, sir, who are a man, listen... Help me!

THE CRITIC: Calm down...let's realize the differences. I am not a man, I am a critic. I am a man of culture. The artist is a man, a slave, a baby, therefore, he makes mistakes. I don't see myself as being like him. In him, nature is chaos. The critic and history are between nature and the artist. History is history, in other words, subjective fact, that is to say fact, in other words, history. Anyway, it is itself objective.

(At these words the ARTIST, who has listened in a stupor falls on the cushions as if struck by lightning. The CRITIC, unaware of this turns and goes slowly to the table to consult his books.)

THE WOMAN *(getting up dumbfounded)*: My God! That poor youth is dying! *(She kneels in front of the ARTIST and caresses him kindly.)*

THE ARTIST *(reviving)*: Oh! Signora! Thank you! Oh! Love... maybe love...*(Revives more and more.)* How beautiful you are! Listen...Listen to me... If you know what a terrible thing the struggle is without love! I want to love, understand?

THE WOMAN *(pulling away from him)*: My friend, I understand you...but now I haven't time. I must go out...I am expected by my friend. It is dangerous...He is a man...that is to say, he has a secure position...

THE CRITIC *(very embarrassed)*: What's going on? I don't understand anything...

THE WOMAN *(irritated)*: Shut up, idiot! You don't understand anything...Come! Help me to lift him! We must cut this knot that is choking his throat!

THE CRITIC *(very embarrassed)*: Just a minute...

> *(He carefully lays down the books and puts the others aside on the chair.)*

Hegel...Kant...Hartmann...Spinoza.

THE WOMAN *(goes near the youth, crying irritably)*: Run!... come here, help me to unfasten it.

THE CRITIC *(nonplused)*: What are you saying?

THE WOMAN: Come over here! Are you afraid! Hurry...back here there is an artist who is dying because of an ideal.

THE CRITIC *(coming closer with extreme prudence)*: But one never knows! An impulse...a passion...without control... without culture...in short, I prefer him dead. The artist must be...*(He stumbles, and falls clumsily on the ARTIST, stabbing his neck with the paper knife.)*

THE WOMAN *(screaming and getting up)*: Idiot! Assassin! You have killed him. You are red with blood!

THE CRITIC *(getting up, still more clumsily)*: I, Signora? How?! I don't understand... Red? Red? Yours is a case of color blindness.

THE WOMAN: Enough! Enough! *(Returns to her dressing table.)* It is late. I must go! *(Leaving.)* Poor youth! He was different and likable! *(Exits.)*

THE CRITIC: I can't find my bearings! *(Looks attentively and long at the dead ARTIST.)* Oh my God! He is dead! *(Going over to look at him.)* The artist is really dead! Ah...he is breathing. I will make a monograph. *(He goes slowly to his table. From a case, he takes a beard a meter long and applies it to his chin. He puts on his glasses, takes paper and pencil, then looks among his books without finding anything. He is irritated for the first time and pounds his fists, shouting.)* Aesthetics! Aesthetics! Where is Aesthetics? *(Finding it, he passionately holds a large volume to his chest.)* Ah!

Here it is! *(Skipping, he goes to crouch like a raven near the dead ARTIST. He looks at the body, and writes, talking in a loud voice.)* Toward 1915, a marvelous artist blossomed... *(He takes a tape measure from his pocket, and measures the body.)* Like all the great ones, he was 1.68 meters tall, and his width... *(While he talks, the curtain falls)*

Characters:

LISA

ALEX

Setting: A boxing ring.

KATI FRAZIER is a playwright, dramaturg, and theater administrator from North Carolina, now based in New York City. She has a deep artistic interest in magical realism, non-linear timelines, and queerness in every sense of the word. Her plays include: *Virtue Of Fools, The Last Year, 15 Feet: A Story Told From A Distance, The Couch, a sex thing (or, a bunch of liberals getting uptight about the sociopolitical implications of their desires)*, and *Patronage*. Her plays have been produced at Brooklyn's The Brick, Random Access Theatre, Rabbithole Studios, City Arts, Open Space Cafe Theatre, Winston Salem Theatre Alliance, and The Greensboro Fringe Festival. katifrazier.alturl.com

(AT RISE: A boxing ring. LISA and ALEX enter. Both women wear boxing gloves, sports bras, athletic shorts. LISA beats her head with her gloves, rolls it around her shoulders. ALEX is more subdued, gloves at her sides. Bolded lines are where a character is definitely making a move or punch, But they needn't be the only times. Let the action affect speech.)

ALEX: I know you hate these conversations.

(DING DING! LISA jumps into a boxing stance, she floats like a butterfly. ALEX shuffles, avoiding her.)

ALEX: We have to talk about it, though. I mean. Things have changed.

LISA: Let's just get Chinese for dinner.

(LISA throws a punch, ALEX dodges, shaken.)

ALEX: You know that isn't what this is about.

LISA: Fine, what about pizza!

(LISA goes for the head. She hits ALEX in the jaw. ALEX fumbles back.)

ALEX: Lisa, come on. Listen to me.

(LISA fakes ALEX out. ALEX holds her gloves up now, trying to emulate the boxing stance.)

LISA: If you're going to dump me—

ALEX: Jesus, every time I want to have an actual conversation.

(LISA throws a punch, ALEX dodges, then hits LISA with a light body shot.)

LISA: Ah! Don't get testy.

ALEX: Just listen to me, for fucking once.

LISA: Fine, fine, talk!

(A full-on fight begins, punches, shuffling feet, the whole deal.)

ALEX: We've made a lot of promises, but they were all under different circumstances.

LISA: What do you mean?

ALEX: Fuck, you know what I mean.

LISA: If you're going to talk then—

ALEX: I'm talking about marriage.

> *(ALEX lands a mean right hook.)*

LISA: Fuck!

> *(LISA stumbles back, then dives back in.)*

ALEX: Don't act so surprised.

LISA: That's a low blow, Alex.

ALEX: What?

LISA: Metaphorically—

ALEX: Oh.

LISA: Don't act hurt.

ALEX: I didn't know commitment was suddenly a taboo subject.

LISA: I don't mean it like that.

ALEX: Oh yeah? How do you mean it?

LISA: Do we have to have this conversation?

ALEX: Why can't we?!

LISA: We don't need to rush into this.

ALEX: Who's saying we need to rush?

LISA: Well if you aren't pushing for it, then why—

ALEX: I'm saying we already talked about it. You already asked me to marry you.

> *(Silence. LISA retreats, ALEX throws a few punches that fail to land. LISA rallies.)*

LISA: That was different.

> *(LISA throws a punch, hits ALEX in the side. ALEX is winded for a minute.)*

ALEX: What, because it wasn't possible?

LISA: Yes! I wasn't on one knee! I just...threw the question out. It was all hypothetical.

ALEX: You didn't think it would ever happen—

LISA: We both agreed that going to Boston to get married, and coming back to where it wouldn't be recognized—

ALEX: And you really thought—

LISA: Yes. I didn't think it would happen.

ALEX: That's bullshit!

(ALEX's vigor renews. She begins pummeling LISA.)

ALEX: So you pretended you were ready? You pretended you wanted to marry me? You faked it all for what? So I'd stay with you? So I'd move in and start a life? That is a lie and you know it. I can't believe, no I refuse to believe that you would be that conniving. That you, of all people, would use an impossible marriage for a strategic effect.

(LISA shuffles away, dodging her around the ring, regaining her bearings.)

LISA: I wasn't trying to manipulate you!

ALEX: Then what?

LISA: I love you.

ALEX: That's such a cop out, you fucking—

LISA: I do! And I thought...I thought that by the time we could get married I'd be ready to get married.

ALEX: What are you saying?

(LISA dives back in on the offensive.)

LISA: Are you deaf? I'm not *(punch)* fucking *(punch)* ready *(punch)*

(ALEX staggers back, LISA lets her have the space for a moment.)

ALEX: Lisa...

LISA: I'm sorry. I'm

ALEX: You marched with me. We went...we went with all those other women to apply for marriage licenses. We got arrested.

LISA: I know.

(ALEX moves back in, tired.)

ALEX: That's not fair...you could have said. *(Punch.)*

(Their hits get lazy, they are exhausted.)

LISA: I wish I was ready. *(punch)*

ALEX: It all feels so pointless. Why did we fight so hard

(Punch, punch.)

LISA: Are you serious. Do you mean...

> *(She is panting now.)*

that you wouldn't have fought if you didn't want to marry someone?

ALEX: It's different...

> *(She is also exhausted, ALEX hits LISA lazily on the side
> of the head. LISA barely reacts.)*

I would have fought, but...

LISA: Personal.

ALEX: What?

LISA: It wouldn't have been quite as personal.

ALEX: Well, it was personal for me.

> *(They rest their boxing gloves on each other's shoulders,
> doing that thing that happens toward the end of the match
> where they are so tired they are hugging, while occasion-
> ally tapping the other with a weak punch.)*

LISA: Don't say that.

ALEX: You fucking pretended it mattered—

LISA: It mattered. Alex. I want to be able to marry you.

ALEX: But you don't know if you want to marry me?

> *(Silence. They breathe heavily)*

LISA: I just...I don't know. I've never...I've never been allowed
to actually think about it. Fantasies are great but...they're
fantasies.

ALEX: I didn't fantasize. I planned.

LISA: I...I didn't plan.

> *(ALEX hits her head against LISA's, one of the last violent
> act's she can muster.)*

LISA: I love you.

ALEX: I know. I know...but...what if you're never ready?

> *(They rest their heads against each other, swaying.)*

LISA: Then we stay like this

ALEX: I can't sit in stasis. I have to keep moving.

LISA: But I...I'm not...

ALEX: You might not be.

LISA: But I've— I'm not...If I'm not.

ALEX: I thought you were

LISA: But I might not be...

ALEX: Then.

LISA: Then what do we do?

> (Silence. DING DING. The match is over. They lift their heads and look at each other.)

Characters:

SADIE: About eighty, but a woman never tells her age.

BESS: The same.

Setting: The common room in a home for seniors

LOJO SIMON's plays include *Adoration of Dora* (KOLT Run Creations, Idiom Theatre, KCACTF/ATHE David Mark Cohen National Playwriting Award), *Nice & Slow* (Noorda Theatre Center for Children and Youth 2017 School Tour), *Love All* (OC-Centric New Play Festival), *Moscow* (Sam French OOB Festival, City Theatre, KCACTF Ten Minute Play Award, Tribal Humor Festival, Best of Tribal Humor), and *Ginger America* (WWU British Theatre Tour, Ensemble Theatre of Chattanooga, T. Schreiber Theatre, Badass Theatre). Plays with Anita Simons include *J'oy Vey* (Florida Rep PlayLab) and *Heartland* (Dayton Playhouse FutureFest, published by Sense). These and other plays have been presented in Arizona, California, Connecticut, DC, Florida, Idaho, Montana, New York, Ohio, Oregon, Utah, Tennessee, Washington and Wisconsin. Lojo also is a dramaturg, working on new play development and production dramaturgy in southern California.lojosimon.com

SADIE: Thank you all for coming and goodnight. That's what he said, just like that. Not even a peck on the cheek.

BESS: Men!

SADIE: I don't understand why he said *all*—thank you *all* for coming. What did he mean *all?*

BESS: Maybe he needs his glasses adjusted.

SADIE: Thank you all for coming and goodnight. Who does he think he is? Milton Berle?

BESS: He didn't kiss you goodnight?

> *Sadie gestures: Maybe he kissed her but if he did, it wasn't very impressive.*

No kiss? He must not have liked you. I heard he favors Kate, in 3B.

SADIE: Thank you all for coming—what could it mean?

BESS: Egh, he's old! You expect him to make sense? Forget it! There's plenty more fish in the sea.

SADIE: I want to make love again.

BESS: You didn't even get a kiss.

SADIE: Never mind him. I want someone handsome, debonair, romantic. To hold me in his arms, dance me across the floor—

BESS: No wheelchair, no walker? That eliminates most of 'em in this place.

SADIE: You know, Bess. Like before.

BESS: We were young then. I'm not sure I could dance anymore, with my arthritis.

SADIE: Try me. Come on. Stand up. What can it hurt? Listen for the music.

> *They hold each other, formally at first, and begin to waltz. Music comes up, and they relax into it.*

There, that's nice, isn't it?

BESS: Feels good.

SADIE: Yes.

BESS: What is love, anyway? A peck on the cheek and you're doin' their laundry.

SADIE: I loved my husband very much, God rest his soul.

BESS: At our age, who needs it?

SADIE: Dancing with you feels like love.

Music stops. Sadie and Bess let go but still stand close.

BESS: When I was a girl, the headmistress of my school was a nun, and all the girls made fun of her because she had a mustache. I prayed before bed each night that I wouldn't get old and become a spinster with a mustache like her. Now, I wish I had said a different prayer.

SADIE: I went with Sam to feel less alone. But it didn't help.

BESS: He didn't even kiss you goodnight. Rotten fella!

SADIE: I heard from Rose that the new one downstairs— Ira— is a good kisser.

BESS: Oh, my! She said that?

SADIE: During canasta. Now all the girls know.

BESS: Well…he has no teeth.

SADIE: Bess, would you mind dancing with me again? If it's not too hard on your knees.

Sadie and Bess embrace formally, ready to dance. In silence, they slowly begin.

BESS: I can't hear. Is there music?

SADIE: Yes, Bess. Yes, there is.

Lights fade.

GIVE ME BACK MY SCRUNCHY, BITCH!

A SHORT PLAY ABOUT LOVE, BETRAYAL, AND BRITNEY SPEARS

Tommy Jamerson

Characters:

> STEFFIE: Sorority sister, loves her sexy best friend slash roommate Bettie, obsessed with Britney Spears.

> BETTIE: Sorority sister, also loves her sexy best friend slash roommate Steffie, not as obsessed, but still in-love with, Britney Spears.

Setting: Steffie and Bettie's dorm room. Present day.

> TOMMY JAMERSON was born in North Carolina and raised in Northwest Indiana. He graduated from Indiana State University with a concentration in playwriting and directing. While there, he was presented with the Angel of the Year: Humanitarian Scholarship, wrote for Indiana's Gender Hate and Violence Conference, and served as a judge for the Midwest High School Playwriting Competition. His children's plays, *The Big Bad Bullysaurs, Princess Pigface, Choose Your Own Oz,* and *Alice the Brave & Other tales From Wonderland* have all received numerous productions around the country. His one-act campy comedy, *Rags to Bitches: A Battle of Wits & Wigs*, recently won Best Short Play at the 14th Annual Downtown Urban Theatre Festival in New York City. Tommy holds an MFA in Playwriting from the University of New Orleans and resides in Caldwell (NJ) with his husband, Mark, and their dog, Darby. Tommy is a proud member of the Dramatist Guild. tommyjamersonplays.com/

> *(STEFFIE walks into her dorm room, as her roommate
> BETTIE watches television.)*

STEFFIE: Hey, Bitch!

BETTIE: Hey, Slut!

STEFFIE: I had the suckiest suck day ever! My math teacher, Mr. Toushit, promised me that if I slept with him, I would totally get an A on my test.

BETTIE: And?

> *(STEFFIE holds up the paper. It has a large "F" on it.)*

Omigod! He totally drew your "A" wrong. So, are you like totally excited for Rush tonight?!

STEFFIE: Um *Yeah*! I got *the* cutest outfit ever!

> *(She proudly opens her closet door, revealing a tiny pink
> strapless dress, a pink boa, and matching pink and white
> polka dot shoes.)*

It's totally me, right? Christian Dior dress— $3,900 Pink and White Prada shoes—$2,900, a Wal-Mart boa— 99 cents.

BETTIE: Aw, cheap things are funny!

STEFFIE: And to top it off, my one-of-a-kind, all-time favorite pink with white polka dot scrunchy that Britney Spears herself gave to me at her OOPS! THIS TIME I'VE RE-ALLY DONE IT AGAIN COMEBACK TOUR— Need I say, Priceless?

> *(Beat.)*

…wait a minute! Something's missing…wait! My— where's my scrunchy?

BETTIE: What?

STEFFIE: My scrunchy, it's gone!

BETTIE: *Shut-The-Front-Door-Mary Kate-And-Ashley-Olson!* Are you serious!?!

STEFFIE: *(Rummaging through her things.)* As herpes! That scrunchy means everything to me – if I don't find it I'll get depressed and shop at HOT TOPIC!

BETTIE: Ew, don't say that! Maybe it's like in your bed or

something? That's where you keep everything else, books, socks, boyfriends…

STEFFIE: Wait! What…*is that?*

 (STEFFIE pulls BETTIE'S hair by her ponytail.)

BETTIE: Ouch, that's my hair!

STEFFIE: *(Yanking the scrunchy from BETTIE'S HAIR)* No, I mean this— right here! Is that *my* scrunchy?

BETTIE: *(Snatching it away from her.)* What? No! It's mine! Besides it looks nothing like yours— it's white with pink polka dots, not pink with white polka dots.

STEFFIE: Bettie, I am not a retarded wheelchair person, okay! I know what my one-of-a-kind oh-so-important pink with white polka dot Britney Spears scrunchy looks like, and you have it! I know you've always been jealous that I was the one that Britney gave her scrunchy too, but I never expected you to try and steal it! Now give it back!

 (STEFFIE lunges for it, as BETTIE pulls back.)

BETTIE: Steffie, stop!

STEFFIE: I will not! You're always doing things to hurt me! Remember the time you forgot to wake me from the tanning bed and I went to formal all burned and bloated?

BETTIE: It wasn't that bad.

STEFFIE: I looked like the girl from PRECIOUS!

BETTIE: *(Through fits of laugher.)* Yeah you did— I mean, c'mon; it was an accident!

STEFFIE: Accident, huh? What about the time we got drunk and decided to get matching Kendal and Kylee Jenner tattoos on our hoo-haas? As soon as I got mine, you chickened out! Now Kendal doesn't have a Kylie! Was that a mistake too, Bettie? Hmmm?

BETTIE: I was sober by then! Besides if I had Kelly Rippa's face tattooed on my hee-haw I would've look like a total clam smacker! Steffie, I am your sorority sister slash super-hot best friend, and I would never try and hurt you on purpose!

STEFFIE: No?

BETTIE: Never!

STEFFIE: Okay, alright, one last thing then; if it was never your intention to hurt me, then why, when we were dating those identical football players, Drex and Rex, did you go behind my boney back and SLEEP WITH MY BOYFRIEND*!?*

BETTIE: *(Gasping!)* Who told you that!

STEFFIE: Rex – my ex! But it doesn't matter because to get you back, I had SEX…with DREX!

BETTIE: But, I totally didn't mean to have sex with *your ex*, Rex, I thought he was *my ex*, Drex! I can't believe you would do that!

STEFFIE: Well I can't believe you would steal my scrunchy!

BETTIE: For the last time, I didn't do it! I am sorry that I haven't been the best friend in the world, but if you're going to let little things like accidentally burning you to crisp, or allowing your ex-boyfriend glazing my donut behind your back ruin our sexy and fabulous friendship, then fine! Whatever!

STEFFIE: That's right, "Whatever!" "Whatever" on our sexy friendship, and "Whatever" on you!

BETTIE: Fine with me!

STEFFIE: Good!

BETTIE: Good!

STEFFIE: *(Grabbing her things.)* I'm going to go grab my usual lunch of a gluten free tick tack and a pineapple and penicillin smoothie— all to keep my body lookin' feelin' right and lookin' tight—and when I get back you'd better be gone! There's just one thing I need to do first.

BETTIE: Take some Kaopectate to keep all that bullshit from coming out of your mouth?

STEFFIE: No. Make you…give me…back my…SCRUNCHY, BITCH!

> *(STEFFIE lunges at BETTIE, as the two engage in some comedic fisticuffs. During their scuffle, the covers are pulled off of STEFFIE'S bed, revealing, what else…a pink scrunchy with white polka dots.)*

Oh shoot, my scrunchy! So shut up, you didn't steal it after all. You were telling the truth the entire…time. Gee, I guess I should like apologize or something. Sorry.

(BETTIE turns away from STEFFIE.)

Come on Bettie, you can't seriously still be mad at me. I'm like really, truly totally-super-duper, "I love you like the father of your unborn babies" sorry.

BETTIE: What. Ever.

STEFFIE: Poop stains. Well, I guess I had that coming.

BETTIE: I guess you did.

(STEFFIE looks down at the scrunchy in her hand, then up at BETTIE. She takes a deep breath, sighs, and walks over to her one-time friend. She knows what she has to do.)

STEFFIE: Fine. Here…I wanna trade.

BETTIE: What?

STEFFIE: I wanna trade. I want you to have my Britney Spears pink with the white polka dot scrunchy, and I'll take your plain old white with the pink polka dot scrunchy.

BETTIE: But why?

STEFFIE: Because I'd rather have a boring scrunchy and you as my sexy best friend, than my super-hot Britney Spears scrunchy, and us not being friends at all.

BETTIE: You really mean that?

STEFFIE: Surprisingly, yes.

BETTIE: Oh Steffie, you old slut!

STEFFIE: Bettie, you stupid bitch!

(The two hug.)

Let's never fight again!

BETTIE: Never ever!

(The two switch scrunchies, and hug each other once again as a pop song plays and the lights fade. Blackout. Silence.)

Inspired by *A Brave New World* by Aldous Huxley

Characters:

SAM

JORDAN

CASEY

TAYLOR

ROBIN

Setting: An American publishing office, distributor of the Gospel of Huxley (i.e. an edited *Brave New World)*. The not-so-distant future, with a retro-1960s vibe.

LAURA PITTENGER is a playwright and director whose plays have been seen at FringeNYC (The HVAC Plays, publisher: ITN), The Gallery Players (Brooklyn), Last Frontier Theater Conference (AK), GI60 One-Minute Play Festival (Brooklyn), The Playwrights' Center, the Kennedy Center American College Theater Festival and Ball State University (BSU). In New York, she has directed at the Sheen Center, Project Y (Parity Plays), The Tank, The Producers Club and BSU. Literary manager of Turn to Flesh Productions, curating works with "modern themes, classical styles." BSU graduate. Member: Dramatists Guild, NPX. laurapittenger.com

*SCENE: Lights up on a publishing office. Four employ-
ees are seated at desks performing repetitive tasks. All
four are dressed in suits and ties, with hats, decidedly
masculine. They all look like men at first glance, but the
two in the middle are women (SAM and JORDAN) while
the other two are men (CASEY and TAYLOR). None of
them should wear makeup or hint at any femininity. Their
female boss ROBIN, also dressed as a male, supervises,
hawk-like, over her subordinates.*

*The rhythm of their work is undercut by music. SAM stops
her work momentarily and touches her stomach. She
presses a bell in front of her, to request a break. ROBIN
impatiently nods her away. JORDAN watches SAM leave.
ROBIN goes to JORDAN.*

ROBIN: Jordan.

JORDAN: Yes, Mr. Robin.

ROBIN: You are slack, as of late.

JORDAN: I know, Mr. Robin.

ROBIN: You know. Then why not fix it?

JORDAN: Yes, Mr. Robin. I will.

> (*ROBIN goes back to skulking. JORDAN sweats, begins to
> work faster. SAM reenters and returns to her work. Jordan
> whispers to SAM)* I covered for you.

SAM: Thanks. I'm sorry. I seem to have a bug.

JORDAN: Yes. A virus?

SAM: Perhaps.

JORDAN: You might be due for a Cleansing.

SAM: Yes.

ROBIN: SILENCE. Please stand and recite the Equality Pledge.

(All rise and put hands over their stomachs.)

ALL: I pledge allegiance to Equality in the United Free Nations, and to the ideals of Fordism, one world under the prophet Huxley, indivisible, with sameness and justice for all. Your biology is my biology, and mine is yours, forever.

ROBIN: You may now take your three-minute break.

(ALL rise and rummage for their lunches or pull out phones, and quickly exit. JORDAN takes SAM aside.)

JORDAN: Are you sure everything is all right?

SAM: Of course. Why wouldn't it be?

JORDAN: Because I think you have the signs.

(SAM does not answer.)

You run to the washroom and come back, looking green. You eat frequently and are sluggish in your work. Your feet have swelled. I don't see how it could be possible, but I've... researched the Pre-Equality Era, and it all adds up. You're my best mate, Sam. Tell me what's going on.

SAM: I don't know what you're talking about.

JORDAN: Did you escape the Equalization?

SAM: Of course not.

JORDAN: Your eggs were harvested, eradicated, just like everyone else's?

SAM: Yes.

JORDAN: Then explain. I know what I've seen, and I can help you, if you just...explain.

SAM: ...There's a possibility that the Equalization may have failed.

JORDAN: How? There's a one-in-a-million chance—

SAM: I know, but...can you swear to Huxley that you will never tell anyone?

JORDAN: I swear on Huxley's gospel.

105 Five-Minute Plays

SAM: There was a raid, during my Equalization. Some of the rebels entered the facility and we all had to flee. There wasn't time to complete the operation. And I...I didn't want them to.

JORDAN: Why not?

SAM: Back in my days at the Archival Office, I found a box. There was classified material inside but it wasn't marked, it must have slipped through the censors somehow. And in the box there was a picture of a woman, in the old garb, colored fabric, circling the waist but not enclosing the leg, and she was holding...what looked like, to me...her own offspring.

JORDAN: Sam! Did you turn it in to the Classified Bureau?

SAM: Keep your voice down. No, I just stood there, looking at the picture, and...she wasn't screaming. She looked happy.

JORDAN: That photograph was doctored, to be sure.

SAM: No, she looked happy, with that thing in her hands. Like she wanted it there. It was peaceful. I couldn't believe it either, but the more I looked at it the more real it felt.

JORDAN: So what did you do with it?

    (SAM doesn't answer.)

Sam, I am warning you, this—if they knew you were even holding that kind of documentation they'd have you let go, or worse. And whose sperm is it? It can't have just happened—no one is allowed to disregard the safety protocol.

    (SAM eyes her cautiously.)

I'm only trying to help.

SAM: You could be one of them, for all I know.

JORDAN: I'm your mate. I would never sell you out, I swear it. And even if I was one of them, you'd already be doomed, wouldn't you? Because I know your secret. Please. Trust me.

SAM: Does it really matter whose sperm it was?

JORDAN: No. I guess not.

ROBIN: *(From the back.)* One minute remaining!

JORDAN: So what are you going to do?

SAM: Nothing.

JORDAN: Nothing? Sam, that's impossible.

SAM: Is it? What could they possibly do to me?

The woman in the photograph looked happy.

JORDAN: Sam—

SAM: Happy. Now how could that be a lie?

Maybe it's not a fake.

JORDAN: If you alert them now, and tell them you've been infected, they might be merciful. But you can't let this go on, not knowingly. You won't stand a chance.

SAM: I have nothing to lose.

JORDAN: You have everything to lose. Look.

JORDAN loosens her tie, untucks her shirt, and shows SAM her stomach. There is a large incision, an old wound, some raised marks all along the scar. SAM winces, then realizes.

SAM: I need to think.

JORDAN: Don't think. Just do. You can't afford to test them.

SAM: I said, I need to think.

ROBIN: Time's up! Return to your stations. The next break will occur in four and one half hours.

> *(ALL return to their positions and begin to work. The rhythm of the work resumes. JORDAN eventually stops. She begins to shake. Then she puts her head down and begins to cry uncontrollably.*
>
> *ROBIN puts her hand down on JORDAN's shoulder and nods to CASEY and THOMAS. They grab her roughly and though she struggles, they carry her from the room, as ROBIN follows closely behind. We hear a series of slaps and then screaming.*
>
> *SAM sits alone in the room. She stops working. She stares straight ahead, not saying a word. The music overwhelms all other sounds as the lights black out.)*

Characters:
   PATIENT

   MOTHER

   DOCTOR

   THE STAGE DIRECTOR

Setting: *Community room: ordinary.*

> BRUNO CORRA (1892-1976) and EMILIO SET-
> TIMELI (1891-1954) published the manifesto, *The
> Futurist Synthetic Theatre*, with Filippo Tommaso
> Marinetti in 1915. *Gray + Red + Violet + Orange* is
> one of the seven sketches included that demonstrate the
> Italian Futurists' aesthetic of very brief scenes, often
> absurd acts, and breaking the "fourth wall."

(A PATIENT with bandages on his right arm and leg, sitting in the chair, speaks to his old MOTHER, a humble housewife. The young PATIENT is 30 years old but has long hair and is plentifully bearded.)

PATIENT: Mama! What pain…What torture!…If I think that for two more months I must stay riveted to this chair, I am seized with agony…an agony…But then, Mama, will I be able to save this arm? I feel I will remain hampered all my life…My leg is better…But my arm!

MOTHER (*Staying lovingly close to him*): But don't think these horrible thoughts! It's bad for you. You must look for distractions…

PATIENT: I can't, Mama…

SERVANT (*entering*): Here's the doctor.

MOTHER: Let him come in.

PATIENT: Oh! Thank goodness you came early!

(The old DOCTOR enters gravely.)

DOCTOR (*To the* MOTHER): Good morning…

MOTHER (*Going up to him and shaking hands*): Doctor…

DOCTOR (*To the* PATIENT): Good morning…How are you?

PATIENT: Ah! My arm hurts terribly...and also my leg...

DOCTOR (*Putting on his glasses*): Well! Let's take a look…

PATIENT Ahi!…Ahi!…Ahi!…Oh!!

MOTHER: Holy Madonna...

DOCTOR: Hand me the water basin with the sublimate, and also give me a little cotton…

(MOTHER goes to do this.)

DOCTOR (*Looking at the wound*): Not bad! Not bad…Courage…It is healing…

MOTHER: And the leg?

DOCTOR: It's better not to touch it today… We shall look at it tomorrow. (*To the* PATIENT.) I recommend not moving… Stay absolutely still…the smallest movement can destroy everything good that was done in a week of absolute rest…

(After bandaging the wound again, he goes, with his hands

stretched out in front of him to wash himself.)

MOTHER (*Carrying another washbasin*): Here, Doctor....

DOCTOR: Thank you. (*The* DOCTOR *washes himself.*)

MOTHER: Well?

DOCTOR: He will recover...He will recover...

MOTHER: Nothing will remain to hamper him?

DOCTOR: Oh Lord, Signora! It's not easy to tell...It is certain, however, that the arm will not be able to stretch or move...

> *(The PATIENT, who has looked fixedly at the the spectator in the first row of the orchestra, at this point springs out of his chair with the savage leap and, pointing at the particular spectator, yells at the top of his voice.)*

PATIENT: Ah! It's him... It's him... He is the murderer of my brother! Seize him... don't let him escape! There... First row... seat number eight.

> *(He starts to jump down from the apron.)*

> *(The actors who play the parts of the MOTHER and the DOCTOR grasp him, other actors, stagehands, and firemen enter from the wings.)*

EVERYONE (*Pulling him.*): Stop! Stop it!...What is it?...Stop it!...For pity's sake...Hold him...Stop it!...Come away!...

THE STAGE DIRECTOR (*Runs in*): Lower it, lower the curtain!! Lower it!

> *(The curtain falls while the recovered PATIENT is carried away by force. Pause. The footlights are relit as the cured PATIENT comes out sweetly, humiliated, with a loutish air and without a beard, and makes a gesture to speak.)*

HEALED PATIENT: No! Don't inconvenience yourselves, ladies and gentlemen! Forget it! Now I remember, the murderer of my brother had one eye less...The gentleman has both of his...Excuse me...We shall begin the performance immediately. (*With a sigh.*) Ah! It was really a regrettable misunderstanding...

Characters:

JANNA: Clerk

MAURICE: Manager

MAN: Intruder

Setting: A pizza place. The present.

THOMAS W. STEPHENS—playwright, director, educator—founded the Department of Theatre at Randolph-Macon Woman's College (now Randolph College) in Lynchburg, Virginia. His plays have been produced or developed at numerous venues, including the National Playwrights Conference of the Eugene O'Neill Theater Center; Berkeley Stage Co.; Source Theatre; Pittsburgh New Play Festival; D.C.'s Capital Fringe and One-Minute Play Festivals; Dallas Theater Center; American Conservatory Theatre; Audrey Skirball Kennis Theatre; Barter Theatre; the Kennedy Center's Page to Stage Festival; Ashland New Plays Festival; Baltimore Playwrights Festival; and Great Plains Theatre Conference. Honors include Actors Contemporary Ensemble Playwriting Award; Wheaton College Playwriting Competition Award; Doorway Arts Playwriting Award; Carol Weinberg Best Play Award; and the Charles M. Getchell New Play Award of the Southeastern Theatre Conference. A member of The Dramatists Guild, Tom lives and writes in Washington, DC TomStephensPlaywright.com

(JANNA and MAURICE in uniforms and paper caps. MAURICE sweeps the floor. JANNA, behind counter, talks on phone and writes on pad.)

JANNA: Yeah, right. Right, got it.

(Reading back.)

Mushrooms, reg. Peppers, olives, double cheese. Anchovies, reg. Banana chips, uh-huh.

(Pause.)

Just kidding.

(MAN enters, a ski mask covering his head and face. His shoes are wrapped in duct tape, and his hands are thrust deeply into his jacket pockets.)

MAN: Hands up.

MAURICE: *(Sweeping, he glances up).* You're late.

JANNA: (*Still on phone.)* Banana chips was a joke, man. Ha-ha. How about plantains instead?

MAN: Hands up!

JANNA: *(On phone.)* Get light, buddy.

MAURICE. You were supposed to be here over an hour ago, Larry.

JANNA: *(On phone.)* Yeah, yeah—same to you.

MAN: Give me the money. All of it.

JANNA: We'll have it there for you in twenty-five minutes, world don't end meantime. Ha-ha.

(JANNA hangs up the phone; MAURICE stops sweeping.)

MAURICE: Put your uniform on, Larry, and move it. We got orders stacked up like pyramids.

MAN: Give me the goddamn money, I said!

JANNA: Hey—whassup, Larry?

MAN: *(Approaching the counter and banging on it.)* I ain't Larry! And I want all the money—so scoop it out of the cash register! Now! And open that freaking safe! Now, I said! Go!

JANNA: *(Laughing.)* Yeah, yeah. Like somebody here knows

---

the combination. Right.

MAURICE: Larry, you ain't on the clock till you take off that stupid mask and get into uniform.

MAN: *(Whipping out a handgun and waving it about.)* I'm armed! I'm dangerous! I'm gonna pump you full of lead! And I ain't no Larry!

JANNA: *(Grinning, she throws her hands into the air.)* Hands up! Hands up! You got me! Oh, go ahead and shoot, Larry— my chest is made of steel.

MAURICE: *(Also grinning.)* That's what you got there, girl? Whoa, *whoa*—Janna, babe!

(His hips in gear.)

Magnet time!

JANNA: *(Dancing and prancing.)* Yo, Maurice!

MAN: I mean it! I mean business! I am a serious criminal!

(Out of patience, MAURICE whacks MAN with the broom. The gun flies out of his hand as MAN falls to the floor, arm raised to protect his head from the broom action. JANNA retrieves the handgun. MAURICE stops beating MAN and pulls off the ski mask.)

MAURICE: You —Larry!—are a serious asshole. Now take that duct tape shit off your shoes. Leave all the footprints you can. Just get to work.

MAN: *(On the floor, he sits up and begins pulling duct tape off his shoes.)*

Aw, crap...

(MAURICE resumes sweeping; JANNA, grinning, gangster struts and waves the handgun about.)

JANNA: Hands up. Hands up. Serious woman of steel, here—

(JANNA inadvertently pulls the trigger; the gun goes off. The explosion of sound is deafening. ALL freeze. JANNA trembles violently, then grows still. She slowly, grimly turns to MAN.)

JANNA *(cont'd.)* Fucker. Oh, dirty fucker. You weren't kidding. Were you.

Stephen Kaplan

Characters:

MARTHA GRAHAM: A dancer/choreographer

HELEN KELLER: A deaf and blind woman

POLLY THOMSON: Helen's interpreter and companion

Note: While the women would realistically have been in their 60s and 70s in 1954, accuracy in age-casting is not necessary and the actors can be any age.

Setting: Martha Graham's Dance Studio. 1954.

STEPHEN KAPLAN wrote his first play, *And Jack Came Tumbling After* when he was 15. Selected other plays include: *Community* (finalist: Seven Devils; semi-finalist: Premiere Stages); *Exquisite Potential* (NJ Playwrights Contest, Dezart Performs, finalist: Woodward/Newman, semi-finalist: Seven Devils); *A Real Boy* (This Is Water Theatre and semi-finalist: Play-Penn, Ashland New Play Festival, Dayton Playhouse FutureFest and MTWorks' Newborn Festival); *Una Casa/A Home* (finalist: Landing Theatre's New American Voices Reading Series, Route 66 Theatre's New Play Development Program); *For Unto Us* (Barrington Stage Company, Luna Stage, QueerShorts, Onstage Atlanta); *In Mrs. Baker's Room* (Commission: Abingdon Theatre Company, Father Hamblin Award, Theatre Southwest); *The Seventh Son* (semi-finalist: Ronald M Ruble New Play Festival). He is the New Jersey Regional Representative for the Dramatists Guild. bystephenkaplan.com newplayexchange.org/users/255/stephen-kaplan

(MARTHA GRAHAM'S dance studio. 1954. MARTHA, HELEN KELLER and HELEN'S companion/interpreter POLLY THOMSON sit beside a table set for tea.

Throughout the scene, POLLY interprets what MARTHA is saying by signing into HELEN'S hand. POLLY repeats everything HELEN says as HELEN's speech is not the clearest.)

MARTHA: Excuse me?

HELEN: Maybe you did not understand me.

POLLY: Maybe you did not understand me.

MARTHA: No, I think I understand you perfectly.

HELEN: What I was trying to say was simply / that I had some ideas.

MARTHA: I understand what you were trying to say.

HELEN: This was not meant to be presumptuous.

POLLY: This was not meant to be pre—

MARTHA: (*Sharp.*) Miss Thomson. Thank you.

POLLY: (*Beat.*) I beg your pardon?

MARTHA: I can understand her. You don't have to keep repeating for her. (*POLLY signs for HELEN.*) No. That comment was addressed to you, Miss Thomson, not to Miss Keller.

POLLY: We are the same. I am her voice.

MARTHA: I think she has quite a strong voice of her own.

POLLY: I am also her ears to communicate what others are saying.

MARTHA: And are you also her eyes telling her *your* thoughts and interpretations of things about which you know very little? (*POLLY signs for HELEN.*) No, you don't need to—

HELEN: These are my own thoughts.

POLLY: These are my own thoughts.

HELEN: Perhaps I did not express them clearly enough.

POLLY: Perhaps I did not—

MARTHA: No. You were very clear.

HELEN: I did enjoy the piece very much.

POLLY: I did –

MARTHA: But you have…notes…that's the word you used, yes? Things that you did not like about the dance piece.

HELEN: Things that could make it better.

POLLY: Things that—

MARTHA: Better?

HELEN: We have always been open with each other.

POLLY: We—

MARTHA: Yes, but Helen—

HELEN: You once said that you valued my thoughts.

POLLY: You once said—

MARTHA: Thank you. Miss Thomson.

POLLY: I really need to finish her—

MARTHA: No. You don't.

POLLY: Miss Graham, it's incredibly disrespectful for you to not / fully hear her out.

MARTHA: Miss Thomson, I believe that Miss Keller wants to be treated as an equal, isn't that correct, Helen?

HELEN: That is correct.

POLLY: That is—

MARTHA: So I would appreciate it if you would let me treat Miss Keller as I would anyone else. (*Beat.*) Thank you. (*To HELEN.*) Helen, you are my friend and I respect that you *think* you have an opinion—

HELEN: I do not think I have an opinion. I have an opinion.

POLLY: I do not think I have—

HELEN: I know that I have a habit of putting my foot in my mouth sometimes. Which is quite a triumph for someone who cannot even see her feet. (*Beat.*) That was a joke.

POLLY: I know that I have—

MARTHA: Helen, you can understand my reluctance to fully engage in a conversation about this.

HELEN: I am not a child.

POLLY: I am not—

MARTHA: I never said you were.

HELEN: You are treating me like a child.

POLLY: You are treating me—

MARTHA: Miss Thomson! That's enough! (*POLLY signs this to HELEN.*) Helen, could you please communicate to Miss Thomson that you are being fully clear. If you are not, then I will tell you and will then welcome her assistance. Now, in regard to your notes, *I* would not be bold enough to venture offering *my* opinion on matters like…hearing aids or… something in which I am woefully ignorant.

> (*HELEN signs to POLLY.*)

POLLY: If you do not wish to hear what I have to say then our conversation is finished.

> (*HELEN and POLLY rise.*)

MARTHA: What's going on?

> (*HELEN signs to POLLY.*)

POLLY: I thank you for your time and for the tea. I hope I shall be able to visit you again the next time I am in New York.

> (*HELEN and POLLY head to the door.*)

MARTHA: Are you giving me the silent treatment? (*MARTHA watches as POLLY signs for HELEN. HELEN keeps walking.*) You are. (*POLLY interprets for HELEN. HELEN keeps walking. MARTHA moves to stand in front of them to block their progress. THEY stop.*) You know that it's not polite to pretend you can't hear somebody just because you're deaf.

> (*Beat.*)

HELEN: I am not woefully ignorant.

POLLY: I am not woefully ignorant.

HELEN: And it is only by communicating that we can go beyond ignorance and blindness. You taught me how to feel the vibrations. The way the air moves when your dancers soar past me. I can *feel* it. I may not be able to see it with my eyes or hear it with my ears but I can *feel* it in my heart and my soul. And is that not where art is meant to be. Or am I so woefully ignorant about that as well?

(Silence. Then—)

POLLY: And it is only by communicating that we—

(MARTHA holds up her hand to stop POLLY.)

MARTHA: No. You are…most totally correct. It is I who…it is I who has been blind in this situation. *(SHE sits.)* Please. Tell me what you didn't feel during the dance.

(POLLY signs. Beat. HELEN sits.)

HOLDING

Brynne Frauenhoffer

Characters:

RYLIE: Thirties. Female. Any ethnicity.

BRIGID: Twenties. Female. Any ethnicity.

Setting: A sparse bedroom

> BRYNNE FRAUENHOFFER, after graduating from The University of Oklahoma with her B.F.A., moved to Chicago to pursue a career in writing and performing. She is currently developing two full-length works, *Bury Me* and *Synchronicity*. She has also assisted playwrights Dana Lynn Formby, Laura Jacqmin, and Elaine Romero on world premiere productions of their plays. brynnefrau.com

(Lights up on a sparse bedroom where Brigid is reading on her bed. RYLIE enters.)

RYLIE: You up? I've got Jell-O!

BRIGID: *(Startled.)* Oh my God! You're not supposed to be in here!

RYLIE: I'm sneaky. They all fell asleep watching Dateline.

BRIGID: They shouldn't have that on here.

RYLIE: I don't mind as long as it keeps 'em snoozing.

BRIGID: You scared me. I thought you might be Kevin.

RYLIE: Kevin scares you?

BRIGID: He's so big. I can never tell what he's gonna do.

RYLIE: He's nice, when you talk to him.

BRIGID: Only you can't get him to *stop* talking.

RYLIE: They'll probably move him up to 13 soon if he doesn't calm down. It's stricter upstairs. So, you want some Jell-O or what? I've been stashing it behind my toilet.

BRIGID: Ew.

RYLIE: C'mon, it's packaged.

BRIGID: I'm fine.

RYLIE: It's cherry. Not that lime slime. You told me you like cherry. And it's brand name, see?

BRIGID: Dinner was really heavy. I got the steak.

RYLIE: Ooh, rookie mistake. Do you have a food thing? Is that part of your deal? 'Cause Jell-O is super low in calories. Fat-free.

BRIGID: No. You saw me eat that pie yesterday.

RYLIE: They stuck me back on Abilify so I try to be careful. Makes me crazy fat. Ha-ha! Like--yeah. I have a cookie, too, if you want it?

BRIGID: *(Laughing.)* Do you have secret pockets or something? You should probably go. I don't know what happens if they find you in here.

RYLIE: Worst case scenario? They move us up to 13. But they like me. And at least we'd be together. Can I sit here?

BRIGID: Sure.

RYLIE: Do you like having a private room?

BRIGID: It's nice.

RYLIE: I'd be afraid, to be by myself.

BRIGID: I like that it's quiet. I feel calmer.

RYLIE: Sorry I'm messing with your Zen.

BRIGID: No, you can stay, it's...I just don't want to break the rules. I'm leaving soon.

RYLIE: Really? Who's your doc?

BRIGID: Zhang. He said tomorrow, maybe.

RYLIE: That's optimistic.

BRIGID: I admitted myself.

RYLIE: That doesn't matter. They get to decide when you leave.

BRIGID: I feel better. So.

RYLIE: Do you? I mean...you look scared. You don't talk in sessions. You *listen* better than anybody. Today, when I was... you were the only one looking at me. That helped me. That was sweet. But you don't say anything, to anybody, unless they're getting vitals.

BRIGID: I talk to you.

RYLIE: But you still seem scared. Are you scared of me? Or of all of us?

BRIGID: I'm scared we'll get in trouble…

RYLIE: I don't think that's it.

BRIGID: I don't want them to make me stay longer!

RYLIE: Then why did you commit yourself?

BRIGID: I'm better now! I thought this would help, and it didn't much, but I'm okay enough—

RYLE: Really? 'Cause—

BRIGID: I'm ready to go, I don't belong here.

RYLIE: Not like me. Not like Kevin, or Aileen, or Bald Man, or any of the rest of us fuck-ups.

BRIGID: I'm just a different...thing. I don't think this place can

105 Five-Minute Plays

help me. It's a holding area. It's not fixing anything, I just have even more time to THINK and FEEL and eat too many mashed potatoes and watch depressing garbage like Dateline. Seriously, Dateline?!

RYLIE: Okay, okay, yeah. You're right, it's a holding area. For all of us. It's not like I feel all better after I show off my cut-up wrists in session. You're not different.

> *(Beat.)*

BRIGID: You said it's cherry Jell-O?

RYLIE: Yeah. The real thing, no generic B.S.

BRIGID: Do you have a spoon?

RYLIE: You gotta drink it.

> *(BRIGID does.)*

RYLIE: It can be kinda like a vacation, if you think about it.

BRIGID: What?

RYLIE: People making your food, cleaning your room, hosting group yoga. I mean it's on linoleum but whatever, free yoga. I'm still sad as fuck, but I like you, so I think you should stick around, enjoy the stay.

BRIGID: I like you too.

RYLIE: Yeah? I thought I was bugging you.

BRIGID: I like that you let Kevin talk to you, and you visit me, and you save me Jell-O, even though you want to die.

RYLIE: If I have to be alive, might as well try to live, right?

Characters:

DAD: Late forties

SON: About twenties

Setting: A suburban living room. Evening.

ALEKS MERILO is a Portland-based playwright and drama teacher. Merilo's scripts include *The Widow of Tom's Hill* (A winner of the Julie Harris Playwriting Competition, and produced off-Broadway at 59E59 Theaters in NYC), *Exit 27*, (Winner of the Coho Productions New by Northwest Playwriting Contest, performed at multiple theaters, including the Landing Theatre in Houston, Texas, and The Sanguine Theatre Company in New York City) and *Little Moscow*, (Winner of Dubuque Playwriting Contest, performed at the Labute New Play Festival, and at the Arundel Festival in the UK). Originally from Palo Alto, CA, he holds a BA in Theater, and an MFA in playwriting from The UCLA School of Theater, Film, and Television. aleksmeriloplaywright.com

(Evening, a suburban living room. DAD sits forward on the couch, looking straight out to the audience. He is watching TV. He is in his late 40's, a corporate worker at the end of the day, watching a football game. He still wears his work clothes, but his tie is undone and his shirt unbuttoned at the collar. Enter SON, about 20. In jeans and a T-shirt, he could be an all-American kid, but he looks just a little nervous, presently.)

SON: So, the Niners' winning?

DAD: *(Not looking away from TV.)* Ungh…

SON: *(Pause. He leans in the door frame.)* So, who is playing?

DAD: You're interested in sports all of a sudden?

SON: I was just wondering who—

DAD: Shhh! *(Hushing his son with a raised hand, Dad leans into the TV.)* Damn it. Offsides...
(Pause.)

SON: So, I'm taking an art history course next quarter. Looks pretty cool.

DAD: *(Still watching TV.)* You're really into that now, aren't you…

SON: Yeah.

DAD: Hmmm…

SON: Yeah. The class is Romanesque stuff. Well, it was either that or—

DAD: Son, this is a playoff game.

SON: Oh, yeah. Sorry. *(Silence. Son slowly works his way over to the couch.)* Hey, uh, Dad?

DAD: Hmmm?

SON: Um...*(Sits down on chair near the couch.)* I just wanted to tell you...um...I wanted to tell you that...I like you.

(Dad breaks eye-contact with the screen and looks at his Son, confused.)

DAD: What?

SON: I just wanted to tell you that I like you.

(Pause. Dad turns off the TV. He takes his feet off the chair

DAD: What the fuck happened?

SON: Huh?

DAD: What's the story?

SON: What do you mean?

DAD: What's this all about? *(Rising.)* Did you crash my car
again?

SON: Huh? Um...No...

DAD: Where is it?!

SON: Right out the window...I haven't touched it. It's fine...

DAD: Look me in the eyes. Are you lying to me again?

SON: I don't even drive the thing!

DAD: Why should I trust you?

SON: *(Disgusted)* Dad, it's a Geo!

DAD: Well. Sit down. *(They sit.)* Now. Talk to me. Lay it on
the table. Like in they said in your mother's therapy, "What
pieces do we have to work with?"

SON: Pieces? None! I mean, Christ, this is a joke, right?

DAD: Quit stalling. Talk.

SON: *(Speechlessly chuckles.)* Geez...I—um...

DAD: Why are you laughing? Are you on drugs again?

(Silence. A nerve has been hit.)

SON: Dad. I haven't even smoked a cigarette since I was like
fifteen.

DAD: Speed again?

SON: I don't do anything like that anymore! I'm totally clean!

DAD: Sure. And how do you explain the beer bottles all around
your apartment?

SON: I collect them! And, Christ, I'm twenty-one!

DAD: Oh, how convenient. Come on. It's gonna be easier on all
of us if you just come on out with it!

SON: Dad, come on...This is not easy for me to say...

DAD: You knocked someone up.

SON: Dad, I don't even have a girlfriend.

DAD: Maybe you should have thought about that before you became a philosophy major!

SON: Hey, If I knocked-up some girl I barely knew, I'd just be mimicking my old man, right?!

DAD: Oh is that right? Well, at least your mom and I can admit that you were an accident and an effeminate, community college, twenty-one year-old, pot smoking virgin!

SON: I don't smoke pot!

DAD: Listen, *(Taking out his wallet.)* here's $150 bucks. If you need to pay bail again, it's all I got. I'm not going to ask any more questions. It's your life. Fuck it up all you want, just leave me out of it.

> *(Neither of them move.)*

You're still here.

SON: Bit and pieces, yeah.

DAD: Son, sit down. *(They take their seats across from each other.)* If I've taught you nothing else, just remember this: When people make mistakes, it's okay, as long as they deal with the consequences. No matter how ugly those consequences may be... Like when you were born, for example. At least your mother and I were responsible about it. Maybe we didn't want to get married, but damn it, we did! So why don't you get this big secret off your chest. And then we'll see what we can do about it. If you have another tattoo that you need removed, I'm sure we can work something out. *(Pause.)* So what do you need to tell me?

> *(They sit opposite each other, leaning in. The son takes a deep breath.)*

SON: Dad...I just wanted to tell you that...I like you, Dad.

DAD: *(Pause. Confused.)* But?

SON: But what? But nothing. I just wanted to tell you that I like you.

DAD: *(Pause.)* There's nothing else?

SON: Not that I can think of. No.

DAD: That's all there is?

SON: Yeah. That's all there is.

DAD: And...The car?

SON: The car's fine, Dad.

>*(Silence. They stare at each other.)*

DAD: Oh. Well. I like you too.

SON: Hey, thanks.

>*(Pause.)*

DAD: You're a bit of a pussy every now and then...But...That doesn't mean I don't like you. Okay?

SON: *(Nodding)* Okay.

>*(They sit in silence for a moment. Slowly, Dad takes the remote in his hand, and turns the TV back on. They resume watching the game.)*
>*Blackout*

Characters:
SHE

HE

STEVE MCMAHON is a Scottish actor and writer based in New York City. He studied at the American Academy of Dramatic Arts (AADA), where he graduated in February, 2016 with the Lawrence Langner Award for Voice & Speech. He has since performed with the Adirondack Shakespeare Company and Hudson Shakespeare Company, and his writing has been performed in New York by Nylon Fusion and Take Ten Festival, Secret Theatre, Manhattan Rep, and in Scotland at the Traverse Theatre and Strangetown. stevemcmahon.org

> *SHE and HE, at a distance, looking at each other, per-*
> *fectly still.*

SHE: Is it you?

HE: Where am I?

> *A shift. SHE is alone.*

SHE: Are you there? Where did you go?

> *A shift. SHE and HE, at a distance, looking at each other,*
> *perfectly still.*

SHE: Is it you?

HE: It's me.

> *HE moves closer.*

SHE: No. Not yet.

> *HE stops, waves.*

HE: It's me. See?

SHE: I can't see you.

HE: Can you hear me?

SHE: I hear you.

HE: Can I come closer?

SHE: Hmm. I don't know.

HE: Why not baby?

SHE: No, no. Don't call me that.

HE: Okay, okay.

SHE: Come closer.

> *HE moves closer.*

Not that close.

HE: Okay. Just let me know when you're ready.

SHE: Why did you come back?

> *A shift.*

HE: I don't know.

> *A shift.*

SHE: Why did you come back?

HE: Where am I?

> *A shift.*

SHE: Why did you come back?

HE: I didn't.

> *A shift.*

SHE: Why did you come back?

HE: I…missed you.

SHE: You did?

HE: I think so.

SHE: You did. You did.

HE: Okay.

SHE: You missed me and you had to come back to me even though you didn't know how to get here and you're here. You're here with me.

> *A shift. HE is alone.*

HE: I don't know where I am anymore. I don't know where I'm going.

> *A shift. SHE and HE, at a distance, looking at each other, perfectly still.*

SHE: I didn't think I'd see you again.

HE: I'm sorry.

SHE: I didn't think I'd hear your voice.

HE: I'm here now.

SHE: Is that enough?

HE: That's for you to decide.

SHE: I don't know.

HE: You don't know?

SHE: I don't know if that's enough.

HE: There's no rush. Take all the time you need.

SHE: Come a little closer. Just a little.

> *HE moves a little closer.*

HE: Here okay?

SHE: Yeah.

HE: Can you see me yet?

SHE: No.

HE: Oh.

SHE: I can smell you though. You need a shower.

> *HE laughs.*

HE: Okay.

SHE: Come closer.

> *HE does.*

SHE: Closer.

> *HE does.*

SHE: Closer.

> *HE does. They are very close now, looking at each other, perfectly still.*

SHE: Oh. It's you.

HE: It's me.

> *A shift. SHE and HE, close to each other.*

SHE: Where have you been? What happened to you?

HE: I'm fine, I'm fine!

SHE: I was so worried!

HE: You didn't have to be.

SHE: I was terrified!

HE: Why were you –

SHE: Because I love you alright? I love you and you're here and I feel like I can finally breathe again and this horrible lump at the back of my throat has been swallowed and the tears threatening to leave their ducts can finally flow and flow as happy tears not sad tears and I can look at you at your actual face in person right here not in chunky pixels on a phone or computer screen and I can touch your skin the soft bits and hard bits and the smooth bits and the bits with hair and

105 Five-Minute Plays

and and all the other things that you can do when you have the person you love in front of you I won't go into details you must be exhausted do you want to sit or have a bath or sleep or are you hungry do you want something to eat I can I can I can rustle something it'll be ready in no time don't you worry oh god I'm rambling stop talking stop talking I physically can't make my mouth stop moving can you help me plea—

HE puts his hand over SHE's mouth.

(Muffled under the hand.)

Thank you.

HE waits to see if SHE will be quiet. SHE nods. HE removes the hand.

HE: It's good to see you too.

They smile at each other.

Characters:

SHE: Clerk. Female.

HE: Clerk. Male.

APPLICANT: Either gender.

Setting: An office. Two desks face each other from opposite sides of the stage. Downstage is a chair or a line of chairs. There is a door upstage.

> MAX GUTMANN's plays have been performed in New York City, Orlando, Santa Barbara, and throughout the San Francisco Bay Area. The Orlando Sentinel greeted his play *The Legacy* with an above-the-masthead headline announcing "The Legacy thrills with every deft twist." maxgutmann.com

At rise: HE and SHE are seated at the desks, each intently rifling through a thick book, pausing occasionally as though to make mental notes, then continuing their rapid search. APPLICANT enters from the side (not the upstage door), waits to be noticed, then finally speaks.

APPLICANT: Excuse me, I have an interview with Mr. —

SHE: *(Pleasantly, as she will address the APPLICANT through-out the play.)* Yes. He's expecting you. Please have a seat.

APPLICANT: Thank you.

(APPLICANT sits. Pause. HE and SHE rifle through their volumes. Eventually, HE looks up, keeping a finger on his place, and speaks to SHE, who pauses to listen.)

HE: Flat-nosed, scum-slurping troglodyte!

(APPLICANT, thinking she has been addressed, turns. HE and SHE go back to flipping pages.)

SHE: *(From book, like the previous line.)* Verminous git!

HE: *(From book.)* Sheep-molester!

SHE: *(From book.)* Half-wit!

HE: *(After a longer pause, from book.)* Lice-ridden, prognathous arthropod!

SHE: Prognathous?

HE: Yes.

SHE: You have "prognathous"?

HE: Of course, I have.

(Pause. SHE considers.)

SHE: *(Rising, starting toward him.)* Let me see. Show me.

HE: Oh, very well, I withdraw it.

SHE: Cheat!

HE: *(Mimicking.)* You have "cheat"? Show me. Let me see.

(SHE glares, then dashes to her desk, flips pages furi-ously.)

SHE: *(From book.)* Contemptible, two-faced double-dealer!

(APPLICANT stands and waits a moment as HE and SHE

continue flipping pages. THEY stop when APPLICANT speaks.)

APPLICANT: Pardon me. Are you certain Mr.—

SHE: Yes. I'm terribly sorry for the delay. He'll be with you momentarily.

APPLICANT: Thank you.

>   *(APPLICANT sits.)*

HE: *(From book.)* Undesirable, festering puss bag!

SHE: *(From book.)* Flatulent toad-sucker!

HE: *(From book.)* Harridan!

SHE: *(From book.)* Innocuous, inarticulate, self-important amoeba!

>   *(HE pauses in his rifling, looks at SHE.)*

HE: You're using a dictionary.

SHE: I'm not.

HE: You are.

>   *(HE crosses to her, examines her book.)*
>   This is a dictionary.

SHE: So?

HE: It's against the rules.

SHE: It's not.

HE: It is.

SHE: Not.

HE: Is.

SHE: Not.

HE: Fine. Shall I ask then?

SHE: You don't have the nerve.

HE: Don't I?

>   *(HE crosses toward the upstage door.)*
>   I'm asking.

SHE: Do.

HE: *(At the door.)* I'm about to knock.

    (SHE makes no move.)

Last chance.

    (Slowly HE raises his fist as if to knock.)

SHE: Oh, very well. Have it your way.

    (SHE tosses the dictionary aside, removes another book from her desk.)

HE: *(Back at his desk, from book)* Impecunious mastodon!

SHE: *(From book)* Odorous, sick-making vomitus.

    (Buzzer rings.)

He's ready to see you now.

APPLICANT: *(rising)* Ah. Thank you.

    (SHE crosses to door, pauses.)

SHE: Have a nice day.

    BLACKOUT

Characters:

> REBECCA: Late forties. She looks very much like the underpaid office worker that she has been for twenty-four years.

> ANDREW: Late twenties. His charm is intellectual rather than physical.

Setting: The rooftop of a twelve-story building in an unnamed American city. Sunrise. Sunday morning. Autumn.

> DAVID-MATTHEW BARNES is the author of more than 40 stage plays that have been performed in three languages in eight countries. He is a member of the Dramatists Guild. He has been an educator for more than a decade. He lives in Denver. pinwheelplays.com davidmatthewbarnes.com

(When the play begins, ANDREW is standing in the center of the roof. He is looking down at a black shoe: a man's leather loafer. He kneels to the ground to pick the shoe up. He moves slowly, emotionally wounded.

A second before his hand makes contact with the shoe, he freezes at the sound of a voice. REBECCA has entered the roof from the dark and spoken.

Andrew picks up the shoe and holds it close to him.)

REBECCA: Is that it?

ANDREW: *(He does not look at her.)* It's just a shoe.

REBECCA: That's all that's left?

ANDREW: All that's left?

REBECCA: Of him?

ANDREW: You're not a cop?

REBECCA: No. They're all gone now.

ANDREW: And the reporters?

REBECCA: Scattered away. *(Beat.)* One of them told me about the shoe. She said it was left behind. I can't imagine how the police could forget about it.

ANDREW: Why would they need it?

REBECCA: Evidence, perhaps.

ANDREW: It wasn't a murder.

REBECCA: *(She moves closer to him but their eyes have not met yet.)* Are you planning to keep the shoe?

ANDREW: That depends. Would you prefer to have it?

REBECCA: They were his favorite pair.

ANDREW: Black loafers. I used to have a pair when I was a kid. Catholic school. I used to put pennies in them. Wish for things.

REBECCA: Do you know who I am?

ANDREW: *(He turns and looks at her. When their eyes meet, the moment is emotional for both of them.)* Yes.

REBECCA: How long did you know my husband?

ANDREW: Five years.

REBECCA: That long?

ANDREW: I'm Andrew. *(He offers his hand. She does not shake it.)*

REBECCA: He never mentioned you.

ANDREW: No?

REBECCA: Not once. *(Beat.)* There seems to be a lot I didn't know about my husband.

ANDREW: Me, too.

REBECCA: Details. A lot of complicated details. People I've never met.

ANDREW: He was a good man.

REBECCA: So I've been told.

ANDREW: I didn't know he was married.

REBECCA: How could you not? If you knew him for five years, I mean. He never mentioned me? No casual conversation like, "My wife and I had a great weekend." Or "I need to call my wife to let her know I'll be out late…that I won't be coming home tonight." We never had you over for dinner. Maybe that was my fault. I'm not much of a cook. *(Beat.)* The reporter who told me about the shoe…she said you were his best friend. She said it like I was supposed to know you. She said, "Andrew is still here." I must have looked confused because she said, "Your husband's best friend." Is that how you introduced yourself to the police when you got here? Were you Paul's best friend?

ANDREW: Believe me, he never mentioned that he was married. *(Beat.)* I don't even know your name. One of the police said they had to find you. They called you next of kin. I'm not sure what that makes me.

REBECCA: I was his wife for twenty-four years.

ANDREW: You must have loved him very much.

REBECCA: I did. And I believed that my husband loved me, too.

ANDREW: You don't anymore?

REBECCA: *(After a breath.)* The moment I saw you – .

ANDREW: I believed that your husband loved me, too.

REBECCA: Don't say that.

ANDREW: I'm sorry.

REBECCA: *(She explodes.)* My husband had to be scraped off of the sidewalk. An open casket is not an option, Andrew.

ANDREW: I shouldn't have said anything.

REBECCA: No, but he should have.

ANDREW: I had no idea. If I would have known that he was married—.

REBECCA: What would you have done? Sent him back home to me? My God…I'm probably the reason why he jumped.

ANDREW: We both were.

REBECCA: I knew that you existed. But I thought you were blonde. One of his students maybe. A *woman*.

ANDREW: I was. One of his students. I met him my first year of grad school.

REBECCA: Let me guess. The two of you shared a mutual love of literature.

ANDREW: Emily Dickinson.

REBECCA: Well, I prefer Nora Roberts. Another mark against me. I was never smart enough for Paul.

ANDREW: Do you want the shoe?

REBECCA: Throw it over the edge for all I care.

ANDREW: I was thinking of doing that. *(Beat.)* The shoe…me.

REBECCA: Don't let me stop you.

ANDREW: He left a note.

REBECCA: What? Where is it?

ANDREW: He wanted us to go together…he and I. To jump. He called me and left me a message to meet him. By the time I got the message and rushed over here, he had already jumped. If he would have waited…impatient, I guess.

REBECCA: The note he wrote…it was for you?

ANDREW: He mentioned you in the P.S. He wrote, "Tell my wife that I am sorry." They found the note in the front pocket of his shirt. It had my name on it. The ink was still wet. It smeared when I touched it. *(He holds up his fingertips to show her the black ink.)* I think he jumped because of the guilt he must have felt. Paul was terrified that someone would find out.

REBECCA: Someone like me?

ANDREW: It makes sense now.

REBECCA: How can it?

ANDREW: He didn't like who he was.

REBECCA: You knew him well enough to know that?

ANDREW: I want to keep the shoe.

REBECCA: Why, Andrew? What purpose could a shoe possibly serve?

ANDREW: It's all I have left of him.

REBECCA: You don't have any pictures? No scrapbook of the two of you being madly in love. God, all of those ridiculous conferences I thought he was going to. I was so dumb. Obviously, he was with you.

ANDREW: I tried to make Paul very happy.

REBECCA: *(She peers over the edge of the building.)* Yeah, well, obviously you didn't do a very good job at it.

> *(Andrew suddenly leaps on to the ledge. He looks down to the street below. He almost loses his balance, starts to slip.*
>
> *Rebecca reaches out and grabs the back of his jacket to steady him. In his struggle to keep his balance, Andrew drops the shoe. It hits the ground near Rebecca's feet.)*

ANDREW: *(Yelling below; as if to Paul:)* You didn't think I was really going to jump, did you?!

> *(Rebecca bends down and picks up the shoe. She holds it in her hand. She looks at it, looks at Andrew who is standing with his back to her.)*

REBECCA: Who knows? People in love do crazy things, right?

ANDREW: Only if the love is true.

> *(On impulse, Rebecca steps forward and shoves Andrew off of the ledge of the building. She clutches the shoe as the world around her seems frighteningly quiet. She is desperate for a sign of life but she is now completely alone on the roof.*
>
> *Her emotional state crumbles quickly. The reality of what she has just done creeps in.*
>
> *She disappears, back into the dark from which she came, taking her tears and her dead husband's shoe with her.*
>
> *(Lights fade to black.)*

Characters:
DOUG

EMILY

MARTIN

BILLY MANTON spent most of the 20th century non existent, and will most likely spend more of the 22nd century dead. He is a New York-based playwright who dabbles in stoner comedy and high Sci-Fi. Other works include *Do Onto Others, You Don't Have The Balls,* and *Red Planet (or One Way Ticket).*
facebook.com/BillyManton/

DOUG: Username: WingKing.

EMILY: PradaEmpanada.

MARTIN: PadTaiBigGuy. Age: 24

DOUG: 23.

EMILY: Don't ask a lady her age. Hobbies: Bad Horror Movies.

MARTIN: Web Comics.

DOUG: Such a foodie.

MARTIN: Moody foodie, must watch Bob's Burgers—

EMILY: Must watch Arrested Development—

ALL: Must have a Netflix account.

MARTIN: Must appreciate jazz—

EMILY: Be a lover, not a fighter.

DOUG: Gotta love bad puns!

MARTIN: Interested in: Men.

EMILY: Men.

DOUG: Men. And Women.

*Emily and Doug turn in towards each other and begin
their first date.*

EMILY: I can't believe you've never been here before!

DOUG: Yea, I must've passed by it, like, a million times.

EMILY: Trust me, the empanadas, out of this world—

DOUG: So THAT'S where the name is from!

Emily gestures to her shoes.

EMILY: PradaEmpanada loves Empanada Mama!

DOUG: Oh god, too much rhyming.

EMILY: What happened to Mr. "Must make bad puns"?

DOUG: That's not really a bad pun, just a mouthful of word.
    Word attack, bad mouth feel!

EMILY: You know what has a good mouth feel? The ceviche—

DOUG: Oh god, don't even get me started, my ex-boyfriend made the best—

EMILY: Ex...boyfriend?

DOUG: Yea, his name was Todd, he made it with—

EMILY: No no no, hold up, you said ex... boyfriend?

DOUG: ...yea?

EMILY: Oh...

> *She turns away from Doug. Doug makes a 180-degree turn over to Martin.*

MARTIN: Hey, it's really great to finally meet you!

DOUG: PadTaiBigGuy? I expected someone a little...

MARTIN: Bigger?

DOUG: I was gunna say less twinky, but yea, kinda.

MARTIN: I get that a lot.

DOUG: But god, this place is amazing!

MARTIN: Yes, one of those little secret gems, you know!

DOUG: How did you even find this place?

MARTIN: Just, know the right people.

DOUG: You must really get around the food scene, this place is sooooo much nicer than where my last date took me, it's a nice change of pace.

MARTIN: Why? Were they a McDonald's kind of guy?

DOUG: No, she took me to this little place downtown, Empanada Mama. I mean, it was delicious but—

MARTIN: She?

> *Doug turns back around to Emily. She's on her phone.*

DOUG: Oh my god, those empanadas were AMAZING!

EMILY: Yea...

DOUG: I don't get how you had just two of those flavor pockets. They were so good!

EMILY: Eh, I've had better.

DOUG: But, I thought you said this was like, your favorite place.

EMILY: Yea, I don't know, just, not feeling it...

Doug turns back to Martin. Martin stares at his phone.

DOUG: Oh, you know who's the worst? Guy Fieri! With his frosted tips and everything, bastardized the Food Network.

MARTIN: ...what?

DOUG: Nah just, ya know, you go from cooking greats to that ass clown, being like, "I'm Guy Fieri here, eating out of a dumpster."

Perhaps some forced laughter?

DOUG: Get it, cause, he's like a little, food gremlin...

MARTIN: Yea...

Doug turns back to Emily.

EMILY: So listen, I don't think this is going to work out...

Doug turns back too Martin.

MARTIN: You seem like a really nice guy...

Back to Emily.

EMILY: I don't really know how to say this...

Back to Martin.

MARTIN: I know this is a little blunt but...

Doug turns out to the audience.

MARTIN and EMILY: I don't date Bi guys.

Martin and Emily leave Doug alone. A moment of recognition.

LAST TREE, EASTER ISLAND

Michael Erickson

Characters:

    ONE: A young Rapanui (Easter Islander).

    TWO: A young Rapanui (Easter Islander).

Setting: Easter Island, South Pacific. Mid-17th century.

> *"I have often asked myself, 'What did the Easter Islander who cut down the last palm tree say while he was doing it?'"*
>
> *From: Collapse: How societies choose to fail or succeed, by Jared Diamond*

MICHAEL ERICKSON is the author of *Alien Hand Syndrome, Honor Student* and several other award-winning, produced plays. He teaches playwriting at Webster University and is an MFA graduate of the University of California, San Diego. ericksonwrites.com

At rise: projection of a large moai (giant stone statue of a head) on a grassy hillside. Two Rapanui (Easter Islanders) stand in front of a scrawny palm tree. One raises an ax.

ONE: Whoa, whoa, whoa, it's the last tree!

TWO: I know, but the new chief wants to have a feast—

ONE: And the last pig, too?

TWO: He says we need to have a feast before we start carving the next Maoi.

They look at the giant head behind them.

ONE: Haven't we got enough big heads on the island?

TWO: New chief: new big head.

ONE: I feel like I'm being watched all the time.

TWO: I don't make policy.

Prepares to swing ax.

ONE: Why's it always a head? You know? A torso would be nice. Legs. Arms. Wait!

TWO: What?

ONE: Come on, it's the last tree on the island.

TWO: How we gonna cook the pig for the feast without a fire?

ONE: Think about it, man. If we cut down all the trees—

TWO: What?

ONE: Some people are saying it could be bad.

TWO: Oh, "some people." The same kooks who're always predicting the end of civilization.

ONE: Yeah, but still—

TWO: Are you questioning the chief?

ONE: No—

TWO: I think he knows a lot more about this than we do.

ONE: I guess.

TWO: He is descended from the sun god.

ONE: Enh...so he says.

TWO: You're doubting the chief?

ONE: It's a good story, but come on.

TWO: I'm not having this conversation. My job is to cut down this tree for the feast. If I don't, my head gets chopped off.

ONE: Okay, okay. Sorry.

Two swings at the tree.

ONE (CONT): But wait a second.

TWO: What?!

ONE: There used to be a lot of trees on the island. Right?

TWO: So?

ONE: We used 'em for shelter, cooking, rolling the big heads—

TWO: And your point is?

ONE: The birds are gone. The pigs are gone. Our crops are failing.

TWO: Yeah?

ONE: I don't know. Seems like maybe there is a connection—

TWO: No. No. No way. Weren't you at the meeting?

ONE: What meeting?

TWO: Where the high priest explained it all.

ONE: No—

TWO: So, here's the shaman's analysis, which I happen to agree with: We sacrifice the last tree and the last pig to honor the gods. Carve another big head. The gods will be so pleased the trees and pigs will come back.

ONE: Really?

TWO: He did a whole big presentation. Cut open a bunch of lizards and looked at their guts. Showed them to us. I gotta tell you, very impressive. Very scientific.

ONE: Wow.

TWO: It's right there in the entrails. Cut down the last tree. Eat the last pig. Carve a Maoi. Trees come back. Pigs come back. Birds come back. Soil comes back so we can farm again.

105 Five-Minute Plays

ONE: Well, all right. That makes sense. Lemme give you a hand with that.

They chop the tree.

ONE (CONT): Wait a second.

They stop.

TWO: What?

ONE: What if it doesn't work?

TWO: It'll work. Lizard guts don't lie, my friend.

ONE: Okay, but just for the sake of argument—

TWO: What if it doesn't work?

ONE: Uh huh—

TWO: Trees don't come back? Pigs don't come back?

ONE: Yeah.

They think for a minute.

TWO: Well, we...sail to another island. One with trees and pigs.

ONE: Aw, of course.

TWO: Better trees and pigs!

ONE: Why didn't I think of that?

TWO: You worry too much. It's good to be skeptical, but you can overdo it.

ONE: You're right. You're right. Sorry.

TWO: Okay. Back to work.

They resume work. ONE stops.

ONE: What a relief.

We build boats.

We build...

We build ...

Beat.

Wait a second...

BLACKOUT

Characters:

GREEN LEAF 1: Sassy, pop-culture savvy, wise-cracking, something of a bully.

GREEN LEAF 2: Earnest, anxious to keep the peace, not the brightest leaf on the tree.

ORANGE LEAF: Older, funny, lots of personality.

Setting: A backyard, late afternoon. Three leaves are attached to the same tree. Two green leaves are near each other, on the same branch. The third leaf is orange, attached to another nearby branch. The third leaf "blows" in and out of the conversation.

We suggest the green leaves are attached to a "branch" by their feet, swaying and moving in a leaf-like fashion. They could stand on a bench. The orange leaf could sit on a tall stool, and stand when she "blows" into the conversation. The garden gnome is DSC. Perhaps some twittering bird sound effects at the top of the scene?

> CYNTHIA UHRICH is the owner and acting instructor of IN THE MOMENT Studio in St. Paul, Minnesota. She has been a guest teacher at St. Cloud University, Minneapolis Media Institute, and served on the faculty of Minneapolis Community Technical College in the Cinema Division. She has cast 50+ short films. A working actress and filmmaker, in 2012 she created the non-profit IN THE MOMENT FILMS with the mission of employing women in the field and developing original stories. She just completed the short film *Robert in the Bedroom* on the topic of Alzheimer's. She wrote, produced and directed the film. Two of her monologues (from a memoir she's writing) were published in *Dirty Girls Come Clean: The Anthology Vol. I* (Freshwater Press.) She garnered 3rd Place in the Wisconsin Writers Association's Jade Ring Competition in Adult Fiction for her story *Gathering Beauty*. Currently, she is writing a short film titled *Code Green* to be produced by her

non-profit on the topic of anorexia. www.InTheMomentStudio.biz

JEN TUDER holds a Ph.D. in speech communication with an emphasis in performance studies from Southern Illinois University. She is an Associate Professor in the Department of Communication Studies and the Department of Theatre and Film Studies at St. Cloud State University. She has presented her solo shows, *Sex Across the Curriculum* and *Sex Across the Catechism*, at the Minnesota Fringe Festival. Currently she is touring *Suicide Punchline*, her solo show about surviving suicide loss, to stages across the country. jtuder2002@yahoo.com

*GREEN 2 is snoozing in the warm sunshine. GREEN 1
leans over and shouts into her ear:*

GREEN 1: Whooo! "I'm a leaf on the wind!"

GREEN 2: (*startled out of her nap*) Is it time? Are we falling?

GREEN 1: Nah, I'm just messing with you.

GREEN 2: Why would you do that? That's mean.

GREEN 1: It's cool—I saw it on the TV, through the window.

GREEN 2: No, it was cool when the man on the TV said it.
When you say it, it makes me shake. (*She shudders.*)

GREEN 1: Like a leaf?

(GREEN 2 shoots a look at GREEN 1. She is not amused.)

GREEN 2: Okay, look. Let's just sit here and photosynthesize
quietly. (*She looks toward the gnome.*) I don't want the
Great and Terrible Guardian to come over here? Do you?

GREEN 1: Who? Mr. Action-pants? He hasn't moved all summer. He never moves.

GREEN 2: As far as you know.

GREEN 1: You're such a sap. Why don't you make like a tree
and leave!

*(A wind comes up, blowing the GREEN LEAVES. OR-
ANGE blows into the conversation, laughing.)*

ORANGE: Nice comic re-leaf!

(GREEN 1 and 2 just stare at ORANGE.)

ORANGE: Get it? Re-leaf? No? Tough branch.

(G2 giggles a little. G1 elbows her.)

GREEN 2: Ow! What? She's funny.

ORANGE: What kind of tree can fit into your hand? A palm
tree!

(G2 laughs a little louder.)

ORANGE: Why did the pine tree get into trouble? Because it
was being knotty!

(G2 guffaws.)

ORANGE: How can you tell that a tree is a dogwood tree?

105 Five-Minute Plays

ORANGE & GREEN 2: By its bark!

ORANGE: Thanks, folks, I'll be at the Palms all week!

GREEN 1: What are you even doing over here?

> *(G2 nudges G1, who is being rude.)*

GREEN 2: Can we help you?

ORANGE: I want some delicious sunshine from this side of the tree.

GREEN 2: Generations of leaves before us have enjoyed this sunshine.

GREEN 1: This *has* always been *our* sunshine.

ORANGE: I see. *(remains decidedly in place.)*

> *(GREEN 1 & 2 blow aside for a private conversation.)*

GREEN 1: Can you believe her?

GREEN 2: *(laughing.)* Good one!

GREEN 1: Seriously, she needs to leave.

GREEN 2: *(Laughs, trailing off as G1 just looks at her.)* Oh. I thought we were still doing the thing.

GREEN 1: She doesn't belong here.

GREEN 2: That's not nice.

GREEN 1: But she's *orange*!

ORANGE: You know I can hear you.

GREEN 2: I'm so sorry. It's not that we're *leafist*…

ORANGE: Let me stop you there.

GREEN 1: This isn't about us, this is about you.

ORANGE: You think I'm not good enough to enjoy the sunshine.

GREEN 2: Of course you want some of our sunshine. But we worked hard to make this branch what it is.

GREEN 1: You can't just blow over here, expecting us to just give you our sunshine.

ORANGE: *Your* sunshine? I suppose next you will be saying

that the Guardian is *green.*

GREEN 1: The Guardian *is* green!

GREEN 2: Let's calm down. Let's just close our eyes, take some deep breaths, and remember: we all photosynthesize.

ORANGE: That's the first sensible thing I've heard—

GREEN 2: —We all have our own places to do that, so maybe you should—

GREEN 1: —Blow off!

ORANGE: I beg your pardon?

GREEN 1: You heard me. This is the problem with you leaves…

ORANGE: "You leaves?" What does *that* mean?

GREEN 1: You leaves barge in, take what you want, and complain when someone says something.

ORANGE: I haven't complained, and you don't own the sun. Or the rain. Or the wind.

GREEN 2: Enough. Both of you, shake stems, and let this go.

(GREEN 1 looks up and down ORANGE.)

GREEN 1: Okay, but wash it, first.

ORANGE: That. Is. It.

GREEN 2: Uh-oh.

ORANGE: I've been calm. I've been reasonable. I've tried to talking to you. But I have had enough.

GREEN 1: Yeah? What're you gonna do about it?

(She leans in menacingly towards ORANGE. G2 tries to pull her away.)

ORANGE: Take you down a branch.

(ORANGE leans in as well.)

GREEN 2: Leaves, please!! We are all part of the same tree!

GREEN 1: I'm a leaf on the wind. I'M A LEAF ON THE WIND!!!

(GREEN 1 shoves ORANGE. ORANGE shoves back, knocking GREEN 1 into GREEN 2. GREEN 2 is almost

105 Five-Minute Plays

knocked off the branch. ORANGE sees this and tries to help GREEN 2. GREEN 1 mistakes that for another hostile move and shoves ORANGE right off the branch. She blows away, squealing and tossed this way and that by the wind until she rolls off-stage.

BOTH GREEN 1 & GREEN 2 stare in shocked silence for a beat.).

GREEN 2: What did you do?

GREEN 1: I did what I had to do. She was going to hurt you.

GREEN 2: She was going to help me.

GREEN 1: Those leaves are only out for themselves. You saw her. She was out of control.

GREEN 2: No. You were.

(G2 leans away from G1, she sags.)

GREEN 1: Whose side are you on?

GREEN 2: It's not about sides. This was wrong. She just wanted some sun.

GREEN 1: What?

GREEN 2: You were wrong. You just kept yelling and pushing and then you…

GREEN 1: I saved you. I saved all of us.

GREEN 2: From what? From an orange leaf?

(We suggest a slow fade, something like the sunset, so that the last line is spoken in twilight.)

GREEN 1: From ALL the orange leaves. We have to stick together. Someone has to protect us.

GREEN 2: But I wonder who's going to protect us from you.

Characters:

A MAN, LIKE A FRIEND

A WOMAN LOOKING FOR A FRIEND

Setting: The scene takes place in a coffee place or wherever people might go for a date.

LIOR ZALMANSON is an Israeli-born writer, new media artist, curator and researcher, whose works mostly focus on the information society and experiences of digital culture. His first full length play *Yingale*, won the Haifa Fringe Festival in 2009, ran for more than four years on the Israeli stage and received a local production in Belgrade by the former Serbian minister of culture, Bratislav Petković. He created *Listening To The Enemy*, a collaborative audio play featuring strangers from the internet which was commissioned by the Israel Museum (co-created with Eran Hadas) as well as *Swipe Me Right*, a neo-cabaret on Kabbalah and Tinder commissioned by LABA theater New York. His latest work, a screenplay for the film *Operator,* which tells the story of a single-mom-killer-drone-operator, has been chosen for the competition of the 2016 Tribeca Film Festival. Lior pays rent in New York City where he researches online behavior at New York University and the Metropolitan Museum Media Lab. lior-zalmanson.com

WOMAN LOOKING FOR A FRIEND: I'm sorry. First dates are always so embarrassing to me.

LIKE A FRIEND: I really do understand what you're saying. But you know it's like that for everyone, don't you? There's really no reason to feel uncomfortable.

WOMAN LOOKING FOR A FRIEND: You mean you feel the same way?

LIKE A FRIEND: Maybe I did once, but I'm used to situations like this by now. You know what I mean?

WOMAN LOOKING FOR A FRIEND: You must be one of those people who goes out all the time. Everything seems to go so smoothly with them. All you do is sit down and the words start flowing...

LIKE A FRIEND: It's not always that easy, but based on my experience, all you gotta do is find a good topic of conversation. That always helps to break the ice. So, what do you want to talk about?

WOMAN LOOKING FOR A FRIEND: Whoa! I don't like it when I have to choose. Like I said, it makes me all nervous. I'm sorry. I must sound like the most pathetic thing you ever met.

LIKE A FRIEND: Absolutely not! I think you're adorable!

WOMAN LOOKING FOR A FRIEND: Thank you. So are you, to tell you the truth.

LIKE A FRIEND: Thanks.

(He smiles. Pause.)

WOMAN LOOKING FOR A FRIEND: Okay, then. So, what do you want to talk about?

LIKE A FRIEND: I'd love to talk about anything you want.

WOMAN LOOKING FOR A FRIEND: Then let's talk about shopping. I've never been out with a guy who wanted to talk about shopping.

LIKE A FRIEND: Hold on. I just want to make one thing perfectly clear. I mean, if you'd rather call it going out...

(He makes quotation marks in the air.....)

---

then I'll go with it, if that's what you want. But right now, that's not what we're doing.

WOMAN LOOKING FOR A FRIEND: I'd just feel more comfortable calling it that. Why? What would you call it?

LIKE A FRIEND: I'd say we're talking, like friends.

WOMAN LOOKING FOR A FRIEND: Friends.

LIKE A FRIEND: Not like "friends" friends. Like friends. That's actually the name of our service too: "Like Friends."

WOMAN LOOKING FOR A FRIEND: I didn't know that. I mean, my mother set this whole thing up between us. She told me that she found a guy who seemed nice.

LIKE A FRIEND: Sally, that's right. Your mother is very sweet, and she really loves you too. That's why she bought you a coupon. So, here I am with you, and I can talk to you about anything you want. Okay, then. Shopping it is.

   (Pause.)

Well, to tell you the truth, I don't really like shopping.

WOMAN LOOKING FOR A FRIEND: But would you mind pretending you do?

LIKE A FRIEND: I could, but I just want you to know that it won't be very convincing. Let's say you start getting excited about something you bought. I can nod and smile, sure, but I won't have a lot to add to the conversation. Would that still work for you?

WOMAN LOOKING FOR A FRIEND: It doesn't sound that exciting when you put it like that.

LIKE A FRIEND: I'm sorry, but honesty really is the most important thing for us. It takes a second for our clients to tell that we're faking it, and then we get really negative feedback.

WOMAN LOOKING FOR A FRIEND: Would you mind not calling me a client? I really do want to get to know you. It's very important to me that we become friends.

LIKE A FRIEND: Then let's become friends. Do you want me to recommend a topic for conversation?

WOMAN LOOKING FOR A FRIEND: Sure, but come up with something interesting.

LIKE A FRIEND: Well, we could talk about what it takes to find happiness.

WOMAN LOOKING FOR A FRIEND: Happiness? As in being happy?

LIKE A FRIEND: Yeah, I just think there's something about happiness that money can't buy.

WOMAN LOOKING FOR A FRIEND: You're right. That's so true.

LIKE A FRIEND: By the way, if you want to add time to our conversation, all you have to do is give me your credit card info. It will charge it automatically.

WOMAN LOOKING FOR A FRIEND: No, I'm fine with us just talking for now.

LIKE A FRIEND: Happiness then?

WOMAN LOOKING FOR A FRIEND: Happiness. The state of mind.

LIKE A FRIEND: Research shows that friends are a very important component of happiness. Actually, quality time with a friend could really boost your self-esteem, your *joie de vivre*. It can even increase your lifespan. What do you think?

WOMAN LOOKING FOR A FRIEND: I dunno.

A FRIEND: Did you ever have a really close girlfriend that you were always glad to be around?

WOMAN LOOKING FOR A FRIEND: Sure.

LIKE A FRIEND: And did she make you feel good about yourself?

WOMAN LOOKING FOR A FRIEND: Yeah, until she ran off with my fiancé. She hasn't been a friend since then, or even "like a friend," for that matter.

LIKE A FRIEND: That's the whole idea. We set up "Like Friends" because we believe you can have all the advantages of having a friend without all the bother. We'll never sleep with your boyfriend, we'll never betray your trust, we'll never insult you, and we'll never say anything you don't want to hear. We'll just…

WOMAN LOOKING FOR A FRIEND: Love me?

(Pause)

LIKE A FRIEND: We'll respect you and spend time with you… I mean as much time as your subscription allows.

WOMAN LOOKING FOR A FRIEND: And how much time do I have left in my subscription?

LIKE A FRIEND: Five minutes.

(She stares at him, not sure what to say next.)

END

Characters:

ARLENE: eighties, Female.

MAX: sixteen, Male.

ARLENE and MAX should be different ethnicities.
SETTING: The viewing room of a small funeral parlor. The present.

JESSICA LUCK is a Brooklyn-based actor and playwright. She is a graduate of Yale College and is currently a Louise Rockwell Scholar at ESPA/ Primary Stages. She is a proud member of the Beehive Playwrights Collective and The Playground Experiment. She regularly performs in the rock band My Dear Mycroft and the improv team The Jessicas. JessicaLuck.com

(The viewing room of a small funeral parlor. The coffin is downstage center. ARLENE is sitting off to the side. MAX enters holding an expensive bouquet. MAX looks around furtively, but doesn't see ARLENE. He stops halfway up the aisle to the coffin, and stands dumbfounded, unsure what to do with the flowers.

Long pause as MAX stands awkwardly.)

ARLENE: How did you know her?

MAX: Oh!

ARLENE: Didn't mean to startle you.

MAX: No! I just—

ARLENE: Must've given you a fright!

MAX: I didn't realize you were—there was anyone there…

> *Pause.*

> I thought they were closed.

ARLENE: Oh, Phil lets me stay until 7. He's always here late doing paperwork, anyway.

> *Pause.*

> How did you know her?

> *No answer.*

> School?

> *He nods.*

> You were on the paper? *(off his blank look)* With Angela?

MAX: …No. I just—I wanted to drop these *(Indicates flowers)*… I don't want to interrupt.

> *Turns to exit.*

ARLENE: You can give them to her.

MAX: Oh… I, um… I can just put them here or…

ARLENE: Lilies.

MAX: Um, I guess…

ARLENE: She loved lilies.

> *Pause.*

ARLENE: Were you on the Student Council with her?

> *No response.*

The Food Bank?

> *MAX shakes his head.*

Go ahead. They did a beautiful job *(indicating the casket)*.

MAX: Oh… it's just. I've never—we don't—I've never seen a—

ARLENE: It's ok. There's nothing to be afraid of. They did a beautiful job.

> *Pause. MAX awkwardly approaches the coffin.*

Gorgeous, isn't she?

> *Nods again.*

Luminous.

> *Pause.*

It's not right.

> *Pause.*

You're not supposed to outlive your grandchildren. Disrupts the natural order of things.

> *He stands at the coffin.*

It's not right.

MAX: No, ma'am.

ARLENE: She had such a sweet voice. Have you heard her sing? At Church?

> *No answer.*

Oh, that's right. You said you're not…

> *He shakes his head.*

She was an angel. Like her name!

> *Pause.*

Didn't they do a good job? They weren't sure they could do an open coffin with the—but they were able to do the top. You can't really tell, but she's wearing her prom dress. It came in the mail right after the—… She looks so lifelike I half expect her to sit up! Don't you?

MAX: Yeah…I guess…

ARLENE: She's in a better place. That's what we believe. Do your people believe that too?

MAX: Well, um…I guess. They might, but I'm not—I don't believe, really. I'm not… a believer. *(Beat)* But I'm sure she is….Angela…It's pretty messed up here.

ARLENE: *(shaking her head)* Ain't that the truth.

I should give you a minute. Do you want some privacy?

MAX: Um, no… I should…

ARLENE: Take your time.

He does. Long pause. MAX turns to ARLENE.

MAX: I'm sorry.

ARLENE: Thank you.

MAX: No—I'm…. I'm *sorry…*

ARLENE: Of course. It was good of you to come.

MAX: She should have… She was so much better.

ARLENE tries to stand with her cane, but MAX kneels before her and embraces her about the waist.

MAX: I'm so sorry.

ARLENE: I know.

Pause as they embrace. MAX gets up and starts to exit.

ARLENE: Will you sign the book?

MAX: Oh… Um… I…

ARLENE: Please, Max.

MAX is taken aback that ARLENE recognizes him. He walks to the book and stands there awkwardly for a while coming up with something to write. He finally does and quickly exits.

ARLENE reads what he writes, walks up to the coffin, kisses Angela, and closes the lid.

"Two can be as bad as one— it's the loneliest number since the number one." -Harry Nilsson

Characters:

WENDY: thirties.

JOHN: Her husband, thirties.

KEVIN: Her coworker, thirties.

Setting: WENDY and JOHN's house. Evening. The end of dinner.

LIZZIE VIEH is a playwright and actor. Her full-length plays include *The Loneliest Number*, *Backwater Rising*, *Barrier Islands*, and *Wisconsin Death Trip*. Her work has been performed at the Samuel French Off-Off Broadway Festival, The Wild Project, Daryl Roth Theater, MTC Studios, The Kraine and The Brown/Trinity Graduate Program. MFA Brown/Trinity, BA Brown University. www.lizzievieh.com

Around 9 pm at JOHN and WENDY's house. They've invited KEVIN over for dinner. Dessert is almost over. KEVIN is in the bathroom.

JOHN: He's not into it.

WENDY: You don't know.

JOHN: He's so quiet.

WENDY: I've worked with him for almost a year. He's always quiet. It's how he is.

JOHN: He's not into it.

WENDY: I don't know what we're gonna do if he says no. I don't have a backup. August is a long month.

JOHN: We'll be fine.

WENDY: Just the two of us?

JOHN: He's coming back.

KEVIN comes back from the bathroom.

KEVIN: Guys, thanks so much for dinner. This was great.

WENDY: Come back, sit down….

KEVIN: You know, it's a Wednesday—

JOHN: Wendy has a thing she wants to say.

KEVIN: Oh. Okay.

KEVIN sits. Pause.

WENDY: I was talking about the number three?

KEVIN: Yeah?

WENDY: It's a very powerful number.

KEVIN: Uh huh.

WENDY: One is—it's just one. And two is unstable. But three— there's power in three.

KEVIN: My lucky number is seventeen.

WENDY: Ours is three.

KEVIN: Cool.

Pause.

JOHN: Your move, Wendy.

WENDY: It's not that we don't love each other. It's just…two is…

JOHN: It's hard.

WENDY: Think of a stool. Can it stand on two legs?

JOHN: No.

WENDY: It wobbles.

JOHN: It falls over.

WENDY: It needs three legs. We've been married…five and a half—?

JOHN: Five years, eight months.

WENDY: I know what he's going to say before he says it.

JOHN: I avoid certain topics so she won't tell the same story again.

WENDY: If we go to a party, we talk *to each other*.

JOHN: God. We do.

WENDY: Why? Why do we do that?

JOHN: It's a vortex. We try to get away…and yet there we are… gravitational pull…talking to each other, about…

WENDY: Groceries.

JOHN: Our day.

WENDY: The toilet.

> *WENDY and JOHN are lost for a moment, staring at each other.*

JOHN: It can get claustrophobic.

WENDY: So we started having thirds.

JOHN: Every month we get a new third.

WENDY: Kevin. Will you be our third?

> *Longish pause.*

KEVIN: Do I get paid?

> *JOHN laughs.*

WENDY: No. No.

KEVIN: That's okay. I'll do it.

JOHN: Great! Great. You want another beer?

KEVIN: Okay.

    JOHN leaves to grab beers.

WENDY: You know Kevin, we see each other every day at work, but we don't really talk. You're so quiet. I wonder, "What's going on in his head?"

KEVIN: You do?

WENDY: Oh yeah. And since you don't say much, I just keep talking and talking…do you get that a lot?

KEVIN: People confide in me.

WENDY: You must have one of those faces.

KEVIN: I love you.

WENDY: What?

KEVIN: It's very painful.

    JOHN comes back with two beers.

WENDY: I do like baseball, which is unusual for a Libra. We're very feminine. We like clothes, jewelry, perfume.

KEVIN: You have a very distinct perfume. I think I smell it all the time. Everything in me lifts, but it's never you. You guys wanna talk about loneliness?

JOHN: What?

KEVIN: It's worse with two? You can be lonely by yourself, but it's worse in a pair. Cause you're not supposed to feel that way. But you do.

JOHN: I wouldn't say that's necessarily our problem…

KEVIN: It's the human condition. One consciousness per body.

WENDY: But there are other people…

KEVIN: False. One is the only real number. Three is three separate ones. We're alone.

JOHN: Well Kev. That doesn't sound like a great attitude for the newest member of our three.

KEVIN: Maybe not.

JOHN: Then why did you agree to join us?

KEVIN: Cause when I see your wife I feel like my heart's been
ripped out of my chest and if I don't do something about it I
might kill myself.

Longish pause.

JOHN: Nice choice, Wendy.

KEVIN: Wendy—

WENDY: I'm sorry. I wouldn't have asked. This isn't what I
expected. I thought…I'm not worth this.

*KEVIN stares at WENDY. Then shotguns the rest of his
beer in several large gulps. Then leaves.*

JOHN: Maybe we should just have a kid.

Characters:

JERRY: A gay African American man in his thirties.

MRS. WILKINSON: A feisty Senior Citizen.

Setting: Bookstore—Day.

> ANNIE WOOD is a Hollywood native, lifelong actress, writer, optimistic realist and an enthusiasm enthusiast. She's an award-winning playwright with a web-series that she created, wrote and starred in: *Karma's a B*tch.* Her books can be found on Amazon. She's into yoga, zen, dogs and contemplating stuff. anniewood.com DoGoodStuff.org

JERRY works at the information desk. He is working on the computer. MRS. WILKINSON approaches.

MRS. WILKINSON: Excuse me, I'm looking for a book.

JERRY doesn't look up from his laptop.

JERRY: Well, seeing that this is a bookstore, You're in luck.

MRS. WILKINSON: I was hoping you might help me find a specific book.

JERRY: There's a computer over there for our customers. It will answer all of your questions.

MRS. WILKINSON: I remember when human beings answered questions.

JERRY: The computer can tell you what books we have in stock, which editions, the price and the aisle location. And it could have done that ten times over in the time it took us to have this little chat.

MRS. WILKINSON: *(under her breath)* Not exactly 'service with a smile.'

JERRY: Oh, fine. What book?

MRS. WILKINSON: First tell me your name.

JERRY: Why?

MRS. WILKINSON: I like to know whom I am doing business with.

JERRY: Jerry. What book?

MRS. WILKINSON: Now ask me my name.

JERRY: Must I?

MRS. WILKINSON: I insist.

JERRY: *(reluctantly)* What's your name?

She puts out her hand for him to kiss.

MRS. WILKINSON: Mrs. Wilkinson. Pleasure to meet you, Jerry.

JERRY: Charmed, I'm sure.

He kisses her hand.

MRS. WILKINSON: See now, a computer can't do that, can it?

Jerry rolls his eyes as Mrs. Wilkinson takes out a piece of paper.

MRS. WILKINSON *(CONT'D)*: Okay, I need a coffee table book on the artist, Jackson Pollack. Have you heard of him?

Jerry looks up the book on his computer.

JERRY: *(reads)* American Abstract Expressionist Painter, born in 1912, died in 1956. He was the husband of artist Lee Krasner and studied under Thomas Hart Benton. Ed Harris directed and starred in the film 'Pollack' in 2000. *(stops reading)* Good movie.

He turns the computer towards her.

JERRY *(CONT'D)*: Is that the one you are looking for?

MRS. WILKINSON: Oh, yeah. That's the one.

JERRY: You're an art lover?

MRS. WILKINSON: Me? No, it's for my daughter. She's trying to impress a snobby artsy-type in her building.

She's looking at the computer screen.

MRS. WILKINSON: I had a guy paint my kitchen last year. The floors looked just like that when he was done.

JERRY: *(offended)*: Well, then your kitchen painter was a genius!

MRS. WILKINSON: He was an idiot who overcharged.

Jerry makes one more click on his laptop.

JERRY: Your book is waiting for you up front. Thank you for shopping with Books For You.

She doesn't want to go.

MRS. WILKINSON: I also liked the movie.

JERRY: Excuse me?

MRS. WILKINSON: Pollack. With Ed Harris. I also liked it.

JERRY: You saw the movie?

MRS. WILKINSON: I especially enjoyed the complex, love-hate relationship Pollack had with Lee Krasner. Didn't you?

JERRY: It was very intense.

MRS. WILKINSON: Yes. And the brooding. I have such a weakness for brooding men.

Jerry smiles.

JERRY: I know. Same here.

They smile at one another for a moment.

JERRY *(CONT'D)*: I'll bet you have some interesting stories to tell.

MRS. WILKINSON: Why? Because I'm old or because I'm ballsy?

JERRY: Both.

Mrs. Wilkinson leans and whispers, mischievously.

MRS. WILKINSON: You're not wrong.

Jerry laughs.

MRS. WILKINSON *(CONT'D)*: You see, isn't it nice to look up from that screen of yours every now and again?

JERRY: Yeah, I guess this wasn't so terrible.

MRS. WILKINSON: Good. Well... I guess I'm going to go get a fancy shmancy latte of some sort on the top floor. Do you like fancy shmancy lattes?

JERRY: The fancier the better.

MRS WILKINSON: You're on break!

Mrs. Wilkinson closes Jerry's laptop for him.

JERRY: But, my boss..

Mrs. Wilkinson looks over to the left.

MRS. WILKINSON: She hasn't looked up from her phone once.

Jerry smiles and takes off with Mrs. Wilkinson.
BLACKOUT

Characters:

EVA: An aristocrat, fifty

CHARLES: Her second husband

JULIA: Eva's daughter, twenty-five

GEORGE: Eva's son, Julia's brother

PHYLLIS: George's wife

Setting: Living room of Mrs. Eva Hibbert-Havens, Boston.

The works of novelist and playwright THORNTON WILDER (1897-1975) explore the connection between the commonplace and the cosmic dimensions of human experience. He won the Pulitzer Prize for his novel *The Bridge of San Luis Rey*, and two additional Pulitzers for his plays *Our Town* and *The Skin of Our Teeth*. For more information about Thornton Wilder, please consult thorntonwilder.com

"This play, appearing here for the first time, is dated June 10 1917, in the author's hand, when Wilder was a Yale sophomore. In his drama, Wilder always worked most comfortably within self-imposed parameters of idea and structure. Here he plays with drawing room comedy, class structure and a 'five-minute/five-person' design. The first two themes reoccur many times throughout his career, notably in *The Matchmaker* (1954), and in his last novel *Theophilus North* (1973).
"   From: *The Collected Short Plays of Thornton Wilder, Volume II.*

At the rise of the curtain Eva Hibbert-Havens is seated, dressed for dinner, in a beautiful chair from which she does not rise until the close of the play. She is a stout aristocratic lady, assertive but illogical. In short, a Boston grande dame. She calls to her second husband who passes in the hall:

EVA*:* Charles! Come in, please.

CHARLES (*Offstage, reluctantly*): I could wait in the den, dear, until they come.

EVA (*Firmly*): Well, please sit down just for a minute.

> *(Charles Havens comes in. He is an absentminded, slightly apologetic man in a tuxedo.)*

I haven't told Daughter yet just who the guests are. I told her to dress for dinner quietly and she'd find out later who they were.

CHARLES (*Indifferently*): Surely it wouldn't hurt her to say that her brother is coming to dinner.

EVA (*Severely*): Her brother, and her brother's wife.

CHARLES (*Mildly*): Yes, her brother's wife. Her sister, so to speak.

EVA: Well, if I had told Daughter that! —And I want her to look especially well tonight. (*Forcefully*) To contrast with the rouge and tinsel of her "sister."

CHARLES (*In surprised protest*): But George's wife won't wear rouge and tinsel.

EVA: How do we know what George's wife won't wear? Where did he find her, I'd like to know? In a station lunchroom, very likely. In a prize shooting gallery.

CHARLES (*Amusedly*): In a circus, perhaps.

EVA (*With indignation*): I mean that my son, George Hibbert *Junior*, of the Boston Hibberts, married miles beneath him.

CHARLES (*Absentmindedly*): Was that her name?

EVA: As you say, he may have married a trapeze artiste.

GEORGE (*Prosaically*)*:* Dear, you're always reminding me that you married beneath you when you married me. Why blame George for doing what you have found fairly satisfactory?

EVA: I blame George because he is a young man with still some prestige to make. When I married you I have been for eight years the widow of the most distinguished citizen of Boston. I could've married someone much lower than my husband's assistant manager, and still faced the world.

CHARLES (*Gently*): My dear, I was not your husband's assistant manager. I was his foreman.

EVA: Foreman, never. I used to see you sign his checks for him. I married my husband's sub-manager; George has married his landlady's furnace-shaker.

CHARLES (*Shaking his head*): He has dragged the name of Hibbert in the cold bin.

> *(Enter Daughter in her evening dress. A beautiful girl of twenty-five is Julia Hibbert-Havens. She's strong-minded and so has naturally found with such a mother that concealment is the best policy. We know her to be excitingly tricky, so we are able to appreciate that her demureness in the presence of her mother is a trifle exaggerated.)*

JULIA: Well, mother, who are these secret guests were having tonight?

EVA: Who, indeed!

CHARLES: It's your brother George.

JULIA: And his bride?

EVA: Yes, his acquirement. He holds an indignation meeting against me for two years because I married your present father, and then he marries a Nobody and breaks the silence by inviting himself to dinner.

JULIA: Who was she?

EVA: No one seems to know; a boarding house girl; someone says, a waitress in a station lunchroom–

CHARLES:—You said so yourself.

EVA: Perhaps the proprietress of a shooting gallery–

CHARLES:—That was your guess.

EVA: Don't interrupt! And Charles heard that she was from the circus.

CHARLES: I didn't hear, I guessed.

EVA: Well, take your choice. Those are the rumors. George has married beneath him. It's a wonder the church allows it. Every debutante marries her chauffeur; her brother marries her ladies maid. It is a national danger. If everybody married beneath them where should we be, I'd like to know. It is the peril that lurks for democratic nations. It shows the nationwide admiration for the lower classes that is deplorable. That's what George said in his terrible letter after I had married a second time. Such names he called me! It was like Forbes-Robertson talking to his mother in *Hamlet.**

CHARLES (*Vaguely*): Ah… is there a situation like that in *Hamlet*? (*He wanders to the bookcase*)

EVA (*With alarm*): No, there is not… Not the slightest.

JULIA: What does it matter?

EVA (*Anxiously*): Do let us be frank with one another. You don't realize how difficult this is for me. What are you doing, Charles? You're not listening to me.

CHARLES: Oh, yes I was. I was seeing if I could find *Hamlet*.

EVA: Julia, I want you to burn every copy of *Hamlet* there is in the house.

JULIA: It'll spoil the sets, mother.

EVA: There are more important things than preserving sets.

JULIA: Not in Boston.

EVA: What was I saying, Charles?

CHARLES: You wanted us to be frank with one another. My dear, I've been frank. I understand perfectly that your son was angry with you when you married me. I wrote him that I did not pretend to be more than a plain ordinary man.

JULIA: Mother, it's you that are not being frank.

EVA (*Crying*): Haven't I told you that she was a station restaurant waitress?

CHARLES (*Pained*): dear me! What an affliction!

JULIA: All the better. Then he's in a glass house; and won't dare throw stones at you anymore.

EVA: It's not that I mind. I'd like to give him a good talking to, myself. It's because I'm in a glass house.

CHARLES (*Gently*): My dear, seeing that this doesn't concern me, may I retire to my den until your son arrives? (*He is unnoticed*)

JULIA: Now there'll be peace in the family. No more mutual recrimination; everybody wears muzzles in fact, they've married muzzles.

CHARLES: I daresay he's timorous about coming to see you now.

EVA (*Sharply*): Not at all! There's always you as a precedent.

CHARLES (*Cowed*): Dear me! So there is, so there is. There's the doorbell now.

EVA: Now don't anyone be tactless.

JULIA: Don't anyone mention boarding houses or glass houses, or anything that might cause self-consciousness.

CHARLES: Am I to stay in the room all the time?

EVA: Yes; they are not to think I have any regrets.– I shall soon find out which rumor was correct.

> (*Enter George and his wife. George is a obstinate young man; Phyllis is an extraordinarily pretty young girl with large blue eyes. Her hair is arranged to resemble Billy Burkes; she's exquisitely dressed and has charming manners. It is the most difficult moment in her life.*)

GEORGE (*Kissing his mother*): How are you, mother? Mother, and this is my wife.

EVA (*Offering her cheek*): You may, my dear. (*After Phyllis has kissed her*) We meet at last, so to speak.

PHYLLIS (*Blushing*): Better late than never, as they say.

GEORGE (*to Charles, shaking hands stiffly*): How do you do, Mr. Havens. Phyllis, this is my father.

PHYLLIS (*Faintly*): I'm very happy to know you.

EVA: George, why don't you introduce your wife to daughter?

JULIA: Oh, we have met, mother.

EVA (*In astonishment*): When was that?

JULIA: I have called on them several times.

EVA (*With evident displeasure*): So that's how you spend your time in Atlantic City. And never say a word about it to me!

JULIA: I was saving it as a pleasant surprise.

EVA: You misjudged!– Were you ever in Boston before, Phyllis?

PHYLLIS: Unfortunately not. I have been kept pretty regularly to Atlantic City.

EVA (*Marveling*): And yet Boston is so close!

PHYLLIS: I have occasionally run up to New York for shopping.

EVA (*Urgently*): Charles! My smelling salts– in the hall. But naturally from your position in the station you were able to see the trains depart for Boston.

PHYLLIS (*Agreeably*): Oh, yes. There are trains.

EVA (*Nodding her head and neck enigmatically*): Hmmm – yes... Yes. Did you find it monotonous?– Standing over the counter, long hours...?

PHYLLIS (*At sea*): You mean, did we come by boat?

JULIA: No, dear, mother means: did you find the trip longer than you expected?

PHYLLIS (*To her*): I like traveling.

EVA: I see! Naturally. How fortunate. There must be long waits while the tents are being nailed down.– Then there's the long, hot parade.

PHYLLIS (*to George*): I'm afraid– I do not understand...

GEORGE: You mean, mother–?

JULIA (*To the rescue*): By parade, mother means the boardwalk at Atlantic City we all hear so much about.

PHYLLIS (*To Eva, brightly*): Oh, no. It's a pleasure, I assure you. And on the hottest days there are the awnings –that's what you meant by "tents."

EVA: Yes, yes. But no doubt there are tents, too. Fortune tellers, and—

PHYLLIS:—a very few.—

EVA:– And among them, the shooting gallery.

PHYLLIS (*Seeking light*): *The* shooting gallery?

EVA (*Boldly*): The one you were interested in.

(At last Phyllis is completely perplexed.)

PHYLLIS (*In a pretty confusion*): I'm afraid I'm very dull. But I've heard of the subtlety—the wit—of Boston conversation. I have always lived quietly with my mother in our little home on the North Shore. I've had little experience–

JULIA:– Don't apologize, Phyllis. Mother has a playful way you'll understand when you get to know her better.

EVA: I was not aware of it.

CHARLES (*Soothingly*): Now Eva! You know you're famous for your wit.

GEORGE: It has developed then in the last year – amazingly.

EVA (*Reporting*): Think of what I had to bear.

GEORGE: I warned you in a good time.

(Fortunately, dinner is announced at this point.)

EVA (*Rising and repeating a formula used by all Boston hostesses at informal dinners to relatives*): We live very simply, but of such as it is we try to obtain the best, and to that you are always welcome. (*She leads the way out with Charles*)

PHYLLIS (*Turning, at the front of the stage; plaintively*): I don't understand your mother at all, George—(*She sees Julia and runs to her*) When are you to be married, Julia?

JULIA (*Smiling down at her happily*): On Saturday afternoon at four o'clock.

PHYLLIS: Why at four?

JULIA: Because they don't let the dear boy out of the factory until three; and he says he *must* brush his hair.

(They go on into dinner.)

*(Sir Johnston Forbes-Roberson was a British actor whose daughter and son-in-law, Dinah and Vincent Sheehan were Wilder's close friends.)

Characters:

YVONNE: Middle-aged married black woman.

STANLEY: Middle-aged married black man.

AURIN SQUIRE is playwright, multimedia artist, and independent journalist. He's a resident playwright at New Dramatists and has been in residence at The Dramatists Guild, National Black Theatre, Brooklyn Arts Exchange, Ars Nova, and The Eugene O'Neill Center. Squire graduated from The Juilliard School, was a Lila Acheson Wallace Playwriting Fellow, and holds degrees from New School University and Northwestern. He's worked as a reporter for publications like Talking Points Memo, The New Republic, American Theater Magazine, Take Part, and Fusion.
sixperfections.blogspot.com

DAY ONE
(Yvonne and Stanley read phones.)

STANLEY: Riots! It just keeps going on and on. In our own city.

YVONNE: Nothing changes.

STANLEY: I wouldn't say nothing. But it's too slow.

YVONNE: You remember that Nina Simone song ... "Mississippi Goddamn?"

STANLEY: What about it?

YVONNE: That's the chorus: too slow! Washing the window! Too slow! Picking the cotton! Too slow. You're just plain rotten! Too slow. Too damn lazy. Too slow. Thinking crazy!

STANLEY: I prefer Sam Cooke: "A Change is Gonna Come."

YVONNE: 'Too slow.' I wonder if that old record player works. Maybe we could throw something on.

STANLEY: Why?

YVONNE: To ease the pain.

STANLEY: Maybe it shouldn't be eased.

DAY TWO

YVONNE: We were boycotting a lunch counter that wouldn't serve blacks in Daytona Beach.

STANLEY: Did we know each other by then?

YVONNE: Yes, but I didn't want to invite you. You were too angry and this was a non-violent gathering. So I was in German class when we got the news that Kennedy had been shot. We went out the next day and this guy drives by in a pick-up truck grinning, and he screams at us... "they killed your president."

STANLEY: So?

YVONNE: They killed 'your' president. As if he wasn't his as well. As if...we weren't citizens in the same country, fighting for the same rights. Kennedy was the black man's president so it's cool to smile, laugh, and be happy cause the black man's president is dead.

STANLEY: What does that have to do with this?

YVONNE: Whenever there's another Rodney King or Trayvon Martin, or Ferguson, Missouri...I remember that voice. Our tragedy isn't theirs.

STANLEY: It's not as bad as the 60s.

YVONNE: Too slow.

DAY THREE
>*(Yvonne enters from work.)*

YVONNE: What's with all the junk in the living room?

STANLEY: As a surprise, I was trying to fix the record player.

YVONNE: Stan, what kind of foolishness is this?

STANLEY: Well since we're listening to a broken record on the news, I figured we might as well listen to a few old ones, too.

YVONNE: But I thought you said we shouldn't be listening to music at a time like this?

STANLEY: I want to cope. And deal with it.

YVONNE: You were the one who said maybe pain shouldn't be eased. That we have to take active measures, not sit around.

STANLEY: You were the one who wanted to be happy and listen to music!

YVONNE: Don't belittle me. I wasn't just wanting to listen to silly records and be happy.

STANLEY: Okay, just calm down!

YVONNE: You calm down!

DAY FOUR
>*(Yvonne is reading on her phone.)*

YVONNE: Why doesn't the governor do something?!?

STANLEY: Are we still fighting?

YVONNE: How much more does it take? The whole world is watching. And we are failing.

STANLEY: So I'm guessing we're only going to communicate in news soundbites now?

YVONNE: The autopsy says through the top of the head.

STANLEY: The funeral is tomorrow. What if we went?

YVONNE: Went to the funeral? But we don't know them.

STANLEY: We know about loss. We know about having kids and hoping for the best and fearing the worst. Let's go and pay our respect. As parents.

YVONNE: You're just saying that to appease me.

STANLEY: I'm saying it because I want there to be less anger, less shouting, less rage. And more honor, more thoughtfulness, more...of something that is missing.

DAY FIVE
(They return from the funeral.)

YVONNE: ...beautiful service. I feel like there's some closure. Stan?

STANLEY: I don't know where to put this. Seeing them made it real. The casket. The mother and father. It wasn't news. It was searing. *(He exits.)* I need better words.

YVONNE: Where are you going?

(Stanley puts on a "Mississippi Goddamn" record. He re-enters.)

YVONNE: I guess he fixed it. My goodness: "Mississippi Goddamn."

It's the 21st century. And the record sounds like it could have been cut yesterday...too slow.

STANLEY: Nina Simone said she wrote this song after Medgar Evars was shot down and those four little girls were killed in a church bomb. She was sitting at her kitchen table trying to assemble a makeshift gun so she could go and shoot the first white person she saw. But the barrel kept falling apart so she sat down and tried to write a song that was like a gun.

YVONNE: St. Louis. Missouri. Midwest. America...

(Nina Simone pounds on the piano and sings in the background.)
BLACKOUT

Mistletoe #1

Matthew A. Everett

Characters:

RICCO: Male, age twenties to fifties.

SHARON: Female, age twenties to fifties.

Race, disability, age – all completely open. In fact, if you want to change the name and gender and make it two women or two men, I'm OK with that, too. (My preference would be, in any case where a woman is involved in the mix, that she be in Sharon's position of power. But if you can make a case to play it the opposite way, go for it.) If they're young, it means one thing. If they're older, it means something else. Have at it.

MATTHEW A. EVERETT is the recipient of a Drama-Logue Award for Outstanding Writing for the Theater (*Heaven and Home*), and a three-time recipient of support from the Minnesota State Arts Board: 2007 (for *Love's Prick*), 2002 (for *The Hopes and Fears of All The Years*), and 1999 (for *Leave [or, The Surface of the World]*). He recently served as Playwright-In-Residence at Workhouse Theatre Company and moderator of their Greenhouse Project monthly new play reading series (2012-2016). Excerpts of his work are also published in three volumes of the *Audition Arsenal* series, *We Just Clicked*, and *The Playwrights' Center's Monologues for Men*. He is a member of the Dramatists Guild and a compulsive blogger about the Minnesota Fringe Festival in particular, and theater in the Twin Cities in general. He holds an MFA in stage management from the Yale School of Drama. matthewaeverett.com lulu.com/spotlight/matthewaeverett

(RICCO enters. He's wearing some form of headgear with mistletoe prominently attached to it. Could be a baseball cap. Could be a more elaborate holiday hat. Could be just a refashioned wire hanger contraption to comfortably be worn on one's head.)

(SHARON enters.)

(They look at one another a moment.)

(Then she focuses on the headgear.)

SHARON: That seems a little desperate.

RICCO: It's a joke.

SHARON: A joke.

RICCO: A holiday-related party joke.

SHARON: So you're not expecting people to kiss you?

RICCO: I'm not expecting it, no. If I should be kissed, however, I will not be surprised.

SHARON: Oh, so this is an easy out.

RICCO: What?

SHARON: For any people who might be inclined to kiss you. They can just blame it on the mistletoe.

RICCO: Oh. Yeah. I guess.

SHARON: You had something else in mind?

RICCO: More of an ice-breaker kind of thing.

SHARON: So, you're talking to someone, you're getting along –

RICCO: Maybe they're wondering, "Should I kiss the guy?"

SHARON: You're wondering "Should I kiss the woman?"

RICCO: We can reference the mistletoe. And it's the holidays. And it's a party.

SHARON: So it's an easy out.

RICCO: I was thinking of it more as bringing people together.

SHARON: As a joke.

RICCO: Good natured holiday fun.

SHARON: With saliva.

105 Five-Minute Plays

RICCO: You're framing it as a way to keep your distance.

SHARON: Can you blame me?

RICCO: No.

SHARON: Don't get me wrong. I'm glad you're here. It's nice that Cheryl invited you.

RICCO: She warned you, right?

SHARON: Of course.

RICCO: I asked her to warn you.

SHARON: She did. Not necessary, but polite of you both.

RICCO: Some friends just refuse to be in the custody of one side or the other in a breakup.

SHARON: Cheryl's stubborn that way.

RICCO: "Just because you guys couldn't make it work—"

SHARON and RICCO (cont'd): "—doesn't mean I should have to lose a friend, too."

RICCO (cont'd): You're looking good.

SHARON: Thanks. You, too.

RICCO: Life treating you well?

SHARON: It is.

RICCO: Anyone special?

SHARON: Not tonight.

RICCO: I'm kind of taking a break, too.

SHARON: Probably wise.

RICCO: 'Til you figure out what mistake you made, it's hard to keep yourself from repeating it.

SHARON: This is true.

RICCO: Merry Christmas, Sharon.

(SHARON leans in and kisses RICCO on the cheek.)

SHARON: Merry Christmas, Ricco.

(RICCO looks at SHARON, unsure.)

SHARON (cont'd): Mistletoe.

(She leaves.)

(He watches her go.)

105 Five-Minute Plays

Characters:

LILY: Female, age twenties to fifties

CLAIRE: Female, age twenties to fifties

Race, disability, age – all completely open. If they're young, it means one thing. If they're older, it means something else. Have at it.

MATTHEW A. EVERETT is the recipient of a Drama-Logue Award for Outstanding Writing for the Theater (*Heaven and Home*), and a three-time recipient of support from the Minnesota State Arts Board: 2007 (for *Love's Prick*), 2002 (for *The Hopes and Fears of All The Years*), and 1999 (for *Leave [or, The Surface of the World]*). He recently served as Playwright-In-Residence at Workhouse Theatre Company and moderator of their Greenhouse Project monthly new play reading series (2012-2016). Excerpts of his work are also published in three volumes of the *Audition Arsenal* series, *We Just Clicked*, and *The Playwrights' Center's Monologues for Men*. He is a member of the Dramatists Guild and a compulsive blogger about the Minnesota Fringe Festival in particular, and theater in the Twin Cities in general. He holds an MFA in stage management from the Yale School of Drama. matthewaeverett.com lulu.com/spotlight/matthewaeverett

(LILY enters from one side of the stage. CLAIRE enters from the other.)

(They see one another.)

(They both produce mistletoe and wave it enticingly over their own heads.)

CLAIRE: Hey, Lily.

LILY: Hey, Claire.

(They slowly approach one another.)

(They each move their mistletoe above the other person's head.)

(They kiss.)

(They enjoy it for a bit.)

(They part, sigh.)

LILY: I miss college.

CLAIRE: Me, too.

LILY: I love holiday parties.

CLAIRE: Me, too.

LILY: You drunk?

CLAIRE: Stone cold sober, lady.

LILY: Good to hear.

CLAIRE: Darling, if I wasn't into you, there wouldn't be enough eggnog in the continental United States to make that kind of magic happen.

LILY: See you New Year's Eve?

CLAIRE: Absolutely.

LILY: I should get back to my date.

CLAIRE: Me, too.

(LILY and CLAIRE head back off in the directions from which they appeared, calling out for their dates in the crowd.)

LILY: Dan?

CLAIRE: Roger?

(They exit.)

Based on the life of Ernest Just, a pioneering African-American biologist of the early- to mid- twentieth century.

Characters:

ERNEST JUST

BENITO MUSSOLINI

Setting: Rome, 1933.

STEVE GOLD is a New York-based playwright and the author of the full-length plays *Smash the State, Women and Guns* and *Wyatt Earp's Jewish Adventure.*

(Lights up on a bare stage that is dimly and spookily lit. A ghostly atmosphere prevails. Benito Mussolini stands down right, facing the audience, his hands in his pockets. Ernest Just, an African-American biologist, has out of desperation come to seek funding for his research as he is unable to obtain it in the racism of 1930s America. Just is middle-aged and dressed in a standard 1930s business suit. He is first seen up stage left rear. He is holding a folder under his right arm—a nervous salesman about to make his pitch.)

ERNEST: It is a great honor.

MUSSOLINI: Signore….

ERNEST: I've always admired you. I've always wanted to meet you. I am grateful that you allow me to have an audience with you.

MUSSOLINI: One does not "have an audience" with me—I am not the Pope.

ERNEST: My mistake.

MUSSOLINI *(coldly-matter-of-fact):* That idiot in the Vatican—let him have his "audience." An audience of beggars—people who come to kiss his ring.

ERNEST: Maybe they like to kiss his ring...Uh, we have a mutual friend: Mrs. Astor.

(Mussolini turns toward Just.)

MUSSOLINI: You know her? You? American Negro?

ERNEST: Yes.

MUSSOLINI: I never meet American Negro. I meet Abyssinian Negro…*(Off-handedly.)* They smell….

(Ernest reaches into his folder, pulls out an envelope.)

ERNEST: My letter of introduction will clarify things. It's from Mrs. Astor.

(He displays the letter to Mussolini, who still refuses to face him.)

MUSSOLINI: I don't read English good.

ERNEST: It's in Italian—

105 Five-Minute Plays

MUSSOLINI: Keep the letter.

ERNEST: I'll leave it with the secretary…in case you change your mind—

MUSSOLINI: Signore, keep the letter.

>   *(Just places the envelope back in the folder.)*

ERNEST *(discouraged)*: It was thoughtful of her to write it.

MUSSOLINI: I no like Mrs. Astor…A big fat cow.

ERNEST: I'd like to be there when you tell her that.

MUSSOLINI: I don't tell her. I am polite man. *(Beat; Darkly.)* But there is only so much I will tolerate.

ERNEST *(Trying to maintain the conversation)*: She's highly intelligent.

MUSSOLINI *(Turns toward Just)*: You, too…And you don't smell.

ERNEST: No, I don't.

MUSSOLINI *(showing more interest)*: I never heard of Negro scientist. I never thought it possible.

ERNEST: There'll be many more someday.

>   *(pause; Mussolini crosses to stage right, passing in front of Ernest.)*

MUSSOLINI: You want money.

ERNEST *(Correcting him)*: I seek funding.

MUSSOLINI: Is the same thing.

ERNEST: Funding is more accurate.

MUSSOLINI: Why come to me?

ERNEST: It was Mrs. Astor's her suggestion.

MUSSOLINI: She American. You American. But she tell you to ask Italia for money. It make no sense.

ERNEST: I tried America. I was not successful.

MUSSOLINI: You try some more—

ERNEST: I tried very hard.

MUSSOLINI: But America so rich.

ERNEST: They hate Negroes in America.

(Mussolini indicates Ernest's folder.)

MUSSOLINI: What is that?

ERNEST: My research results.

MUSSOLINI: What do you do?

ERNEST: I'm a biologist.

MUSSOLINI *(disdainful):* Biologist.

ERNEST: Embryology.

MUSSOLINI: I need new tanks…new bombs…new planes to drop the new bombs—

ERNEST: Please, sir, don't make up your mind so soon.

MUSSOLINI *(testily)*: Signore, I say what I need: Tanks and guns.

(ERNEST hurriedly goes to him.)

ERNEST: What I do have can help you immensely. It's of great practical value, if you'll let me explain.

MUSSOLINI: …Go ahead.

(Just opens his folder.)

ERNEST *(eagerly)*: I've been conducting a series of experiments on a type of worm.

MUSSOLINI: You say *worm*?

ERNEST: A parasitic worm.

MUSSOLINI: Para…SIT-ic?

ERNEST: Worms that are harmful.

MUSSOLINI: You want me to be scared of worms.

ERNEST: The worm eats through wood, makes it rot. The timber industry in your country is losing millions of lire in rotting wood.

(ERNEST removes a sheet of paper from his folder; upon it is written several columns of numbers and a couple of paragraphs of prose.)

ERNEST: I've developed a way to treat wood so that it becomes resistant to the worm.

There are millions of them crawling about; and they can reach into very small spaces and hide there. *(He shows MUSSOLINI the paper.)* My method will eradicate the parasitic worm without harming the wood.

(MUSSOLINI looks at the paper.)

MUSSOLINI: How do you do this?

ERNEST: I make the worms sterile; they can't reproduce anymore.

MUSSOLINI: Does it work on…people?

ERNEST *(frowning)*: …No.

MUSSOLINI: I know somebody I like to give it to. Make good joke, no?

ERNEST: No.

MUSSOLINI: How much money you want?

ERNEST: One hundred thousand pounds.

(MUSSOLINI notices a name at the top of the paper; he points to it.)

MUSSOLINI: Who is this?

ERNEST: My collaborator—also my fiancée. *(He takes the paper from MUSSOLINI and returns it to his folder.)*

MUSSOLINI: That is German name.

ERNEST: Austrian. As I was saying, a commercial product could be available within a year—

MUSSOLINI: You marry Austrian woman?

ERNEST: Yes.

MUSSOLINI *(confrontational):* You…marry her?

ERNEST: Yes.

MUSSOLINI *(indignant)*: I am to pay for this…pollution?

(Pause.)

ERNEST *(mortified expression; still calm):* You are speaking about my future wife—

MUSSOLINI *(supreme loathing)*: You…BLACK ANIMAL!

> *(Pause.)*

> *(Maintaining his dignity, ERNEST removes a business card from his jacket breast pocket and crosses to MUSSO-LINI and offers it to him.)*

ERNEST: I am Dr. Ernest Just, scientist.

> *(MUSSOLINI takes the card and tears it to pieces, then stuffs them into ERNEST'S breast pocket)*

MUSSOLINI *(ranting)*: Black dog!

> *(Long pause.)*

ERNEST *(seething):* And you, sir…are…a…sonofabitch!

> *(LIGHTS SLOWLY FADE TO BLACK)*

Characters:

JOSH: thirteen

GRANDMA: seventy-something

Setting: Today. Josh and Grandma's House.

TOM SMITH is a playwright and director. His plays are published by Samuel French, Playscripts, and Youth-PLAYS, among others. Monologues from his plays appear in five collections of works, and his short plays have been produced internationally. His work has been enjoyed by audiences in cities across the U.S., including Seattle, Kansas City, San Francisco, and Chicago, as well as in Australia, Belgium, Canada, Germany, Ireland, Latvia, Netherlands, New Zealand, Romania, Sweden, Switzerland, and the United Kingdom. Tom is also the author of *The Other Blocking: Teaching and Performing Improvisation* (Kendall Hunt) and articles and reviews for *Theatre Journal, Theatre Topics, The Players Journal,* and several resource books. Tom graduated from Whitman College with a BA in Dramatic Arts and Secondary Education certification, and earned his MFA in Directing from University of Missouri-Kansas City. He is a proud member of the Dramatist's Guild and Stage Directors and Choreographers Society. tomsmithplaywright.com

GRANDMA: You're late.

JOSH: I know, Grams. It was the Sunday edition. They're heavier so I can't ride my bike as fast, remember?

GRANDMA: It's Sunday?

JOSH: Yes.

GRANDMA: But yesterday was…

JOSH: Saturday.

GRANDMA: I know that. Today's Sunday. Sunday. I can't keep track of anything since I retired. Days don't mean what they used to.

JOSH: I brought you an extra copy.

GRANDMA: The print is too small.

JOSH: I can read it to you.

GRANDMA: Fine.

JOSH: Did you eat this morning, Grandma?

GRANDMA: Yes.

JOSH: What did you have?

GRANDMA: Oatmeal.

JOSH: We're out of oatmeal. You ate the last of it on Friday.

GRANDMA: I had oatmeal.

JOSH: Did you have toast? The bread is out.

GRANDMA: No. Yes. I had toast.

JOSH: *(Counting the slices.)* You did. You had two pieces. Let me get you more coffee.

That's my grandma. She's 70-something. I don't really know her exact age. She's taken care of me since my ma went to prison. She'll be out sometime in the next two years. I haven't seen her for a while now. Grams and I used to visit, but three years ago they took away her license so we don't have any way to get to the prison anymore. I get my driver's permit in two years, and I hope that I'll be able to pick my mom up when she gets released.

GRANDMA: I have an empty cup, Toby.

JOSH: I know, Grams. *(hands her coffee)* I'm Josh. Toby is my uncle. Grams confuses me with him sometimes. She's got dementia. It's a condition where you forget stuff and you get confused. Sometimes it's scary. Like last week, when she left the stove burner on. Sometimes it's funny. *(she farts)* See? She doesn't even care that she farted! I take care of her. It takes a lot of focus. I have to count things constantly. The money in her wallet. The slices of bread in the bag. The number of oranges and apples and bananas.

GRANDMA: This print is too small!

JOSH: I'll read it to you, Grams!

Since she can't remember things too well, I need to know everything about everything so I can tell if she's eaten or not. Or paid the electric bill. Or taken too many vitamins. I've become really good at just scanning things and knowing how many there are. And my math grades have improved a lot. My days are filled with numbers.

GRANDMA: Josh!

JOSH: All right, all right. What do you want to start out with? The front page? Arts and Entertainment?

GRANDMA: The puzzle page.

JOSH: All right. *(he opens the paper)*. What do you want first? Trivia? Crossword? Sudoku?

GRANDMA: Trivia.

JOSH: The topic today is world history. There are five questions. Here's the easy level. How many states are there in the United States of America?

GRANDMA: 50.

JOSH: Correct. Level two: How many countries make up the United Kingdom?

GRANDMA: 4: Scotland, England, Wales and Northern Ireland.

JOSH: Correct. Level three: What country lies between Malaysia and Indonesia?

GRANDMA: Singapore.

JOSH: Level four: What Asian country has the same name as a state in the United States?

GRANDMA: Georgia.

JOSH: Good job, Grams. Only one left. What country's name is derived from the Latin word meaning "Southern?"

GRANDMA: I was very good in Latin. I took it for five years in high school.

JOSH: I know, Grams.

GRANDMA: I came in second place for most accomplished in Latin. I was the first girl to ever get that highly ranked. Latin was considered a language better suited for boys. But I always believed that there should never be a difference between what boys could do and what girls could do. My brothers studied Latin, so I did too. It's a shame you kids grow up today without learning it. It's so helpful.

JOSH: Do you want me to read the question again?

GRANDMA: Australia, deriving from the Latin word, Australis.

JOSH: Does this make any sense to you? She can't remember what she had for breakfast ten minutes ago, but she remembers what rank she got in Latin, like, 60 years ago!?!

Perfect score, Grams. Except for Tuesday, it was a clean sweep this week. Do you want to move onto the crossword?

GRANDMA: No, you do that one that you like. I'm going to go shower. Then I'll make a grocery list so we can go out shopping. We need more eggs.

JOSH: We're fine with eggs, Gram.

GRANDMA: I think we're running out.

JOSH: We have 7 left.

GRANDMA: And we're out of oranges.

JOSH: That's true. But we have a lot of tangerines. Twenty two to be exact. And 4 green apples, 5 red apples, 4 bananas, 1 lime, 1 lemon, and 64 grapes. That's the fruit bin. In the veggie drawer we have 5 green onions, 6 carrots, 1 red pepper, 14 mushrooms, and ½ of a head of lettuce.

You'd think that it would all be confusing for me. I mean,

sometimes I'm wrong on the numbers, like if Grams eats something and I'm not here to see it. But usually I'm pretty spot on.

It's comforting in a way, having all these numbers in my head. It reminds me to think about all the things we do have rather than the things we don't have: like, we have 7 eggs, not we've eaten five eggs.

This is Sudoku. I'm addicted to it. I have books and books and books of these puzzles. Have you seen them? You fill in missing numbers in the boxes. You can't repeat a number either this way or this way or in one of these boxes. I play every single day.

I think I like it so much because I can get the numbers out of my head and do something with them. Like, *(filling in a number)* 7 eggs, 5 red apples, this one could be either 6 carrots or 1 red pepper. But I think it's 1 red pepper, and this one is 6 carrots. *(he quickly finishes the puzzle).*

Someday, I'm going to find out if there's a world championship of Sudoku. I know I could win it. Then I could take that money and hire someone to count everything for me. 2 years until my driver's permit. 738 days until my mom gets out of prison. 4 more weeks of school before vacation.

GRANDMA: *(off)* Toby?

JOSH: 1 grandma. 1 Josh.

GRANDMA: *(off)* Toby?

JOSH: 1 day at a time.

Characters:
PEGGY, eighteen.

VOICE

KATI FRAZIER is a playwright, dramaturg, and theater administrator from North Carolina, now based in New York City. She has a deep artistic interest in magical realism, non-linear timelines, and queerness in every sense of the word. Her plays include: *Virtue Of Fools*, *The Last Year*, *15 Feet: A Story Told From A Distance*, *The Couch*, *a sex thing (or, a bunch of liberals getting uptight about the sociopolitical implications of their desires)*, and *Patronage*. Her plays have been produced at Brooklyn's The Brick, Random Access Theatre, Rabbithole Studios, City Arts, Open Space Cafe Theatre, Winston Salem Theatre Alliance, and The Greensboro Fringe Festival. katifrazier.alturl.com

AT RISE: Bare stage, white walls. PEGGY stands center stage, rather goofily. VOICE is only heard, not seen. Think campy but official, sort of like Mr. Movie Phone or an educational film from the 50s.

VOICE: This is Peggy.

PEGGY: *(chirpily)* Hello!

VOICE: Today is her eighteenth birthday

PEGGY: Oh, goody!

VOICE: Peggy's emotions are big.

PEGGY: Are they?

VOICE: Very big.

> *(PEGGY sucks in her stomach.)*

PEGGY: *(whispers)* Are they really that big?

VOICE: They are too big for this room.

> *(The walls and ceiling suddenly move in. CLUNK.)*

PEGGY: Uh-oh

VOICE: It is a rare affliction, and the doctors still don't know what causes it.

PEGGY: Affliction?! I just thought—

VOICE: Her condition has been kept a secret from her for her entire life.

PEGGY: WHAT?!

VOICE: The knowledge of her condition is more than her delicate frame could bear. Knowing her fate would give her emotions—

PEGGY: *(pissed)* I'll say!

VOICE: And her emotions are too big for this room.

> *(CLUNK. The walls and ceiling move in again)*

PEGGY: This is bullshit.

VOICE: Given Peggy's current rate of emotional engorgement and the volume of this room: she has approximately 4 minutes and 37 seconds left to live.

(PEGGY is suddenly stricken with overwhelming fear, wide eyes. CLUNK. The walls move in again.)

PEGGY: Get me out!!! I have to get out!! I DON'T WANT TO DIIIIEEEEEEEEE!

(PEGGY scrambles, clawing desperately at the walls. CLUNK. They move in again. She shrieks!)

VOICE: Medical professionals have advised Peggy's family to keep her docile with the use of treats and positive reinforcement.

(A candy bar lowers from the ceiling. PEGGY suddenly stops her panic.)

PEGGY: Oo! Chocolate!

(CLINK. the walls and ceiling move out a foot. PEGGY munches blissfully on the candy. CLINK. CLINK.)

VOICE: They have also been warned that they must be exceedingly careful with what they chose to placate her with, as any disappointment would give Peggy emotions—

(PEGGY reaches the end of the candy bar. She looks at her hands, covered in chocolate, the empty wrapper, and begins to cry.)

PEGGY: WAAAAAAAAAHHHHHH—

VOICE: And her emotions are too big for this room.

(the walls and ceiling move in again, CLUNK. Twice CLUNK.)

PEGGY: AAAAHHHH!

(CLUNK.)

PEGGY: AH!

(CLUNK.)

PEGGY: AH— *(She stops herself, puts her hands over her mouth, breathes heavily.)*

VOICE: Keeping Peggy's emotions as small as possible has become a full time job. Her stimuli is kept to a minimum. She has been left uneducated as the stimulation to her fragile female brain—

PEGGY: Hey!

VOICE: Would result in frustrations that are...too big for this room.

> *(CLUNK.)*

PEGGY: Fragile female brain?!

VOICE: While her condition is not technically considered contagious, her state is highly influential upon the emotions of others. The release of such an emotional woman on the outside world—

PEGGY: Outside world?!

VOICE: Would result in a societal collapse.

PEGGY: Outside?

VOICE: The leading psychiatrists suggest not informing her of the existence of any world outside of this room.

PEGGY: Let me see it!

VOICE: The feelings of rejection—

PEGGY: I SAID LET ME SEE IT!

VOICE: And rage—

PEGGY: LET ME OUT. NOW!

VOICE: Would rapidly become too big for this room.

> *(CLUNK CLUNK the walls come in again. The ceiling hits PEGGY in the head.)*

PEGGY: Motherfucker!

VOICE: Peggy is currently the oldest living case of oversized emotions.

PEGGY: You have to let me out! I'll die in here.

VOICE: The careful system that has been used to keep her emotions in check is the subject of Dr. Swarofski's new book:

PEGGY: *(desperate, crying)* Please, please, let me out. I can't...I can't ...

> *(CLUNK. The walls move in again, PEGGY is on her knees.)*

VOICE: "The Joy of the Emotionless State" has become an international bestseller almost overnight.

PEGGY: I can't . . I can't move. *(She sobs, almost uncontrollably.)* Please!

> *(CLUNK, CLUNK, the walls move in again. Peggy is barely fitting in the room.)*

VOICE: When asked about the eminent demise of his prized patient Dr. Swarofski said: I consider it a triumph that we have managed to keep a female's emotions contained for 18 years. It is my hope that the work we have done with Peggy will lead to a future where the emotions of all women can be contained for the duration of their natural lives.

PEGGY: Just let me in the open air! I'll fit! I promise!

> *(CLUNK, CLUNK, all that can be seen now is PEGGY's head and arms, crammed into the square of the room.)*

PEGGY: *(a growing panic)* I promise. I'll never feel anything again.

> *(a tiny CLUNK, the walls and ceiling inch in)*

PEGGY: OK, after that I'll never feel anything again.

> *(CLUNK)*

PEGGY: That...that was the last feeling ever. I promise.

VOICE: Peggy's family is planning a small service. Those interested in paying their respects are asked to keep the emotions and flowers to a minimum. Her body will be donated to science.

> *(CLUNK)*

PEGGY:...Family?

> *(CLUNK)*

PEGGY: *(through sobs)* Please.

> *(CLUNK. CRUNCH. The room disappears.)*

VOICE: It is her family's hope that scientific research of Peggy's remains will save other women from such a fate.

Characters:
STEVE

3 ADDITIONAL CAST MEMBERS

Setting: A game show set.

STEVEN MOSQUEDA is a native of Los Angeles and considers Chicago to be his home sweet home. He began performing and taking classes at iO Chicago in the early 90's taught by Charna Halpern, Steven Colbert and Del Close. He became an ensemble member of the Neo-Futurists in 1996 where he wrote and performed in *Too Much Light Makes The Baby Go Blind, 30 plays in 60 minutes,* until 2010. He began his own theater company, The Drinking & Writing Theater in 2002 where he continues to write and perform short and full-length original plays.

Name That Minority Silence!!!! is one of the thousands of plays written and performed by cast members of the experimental theatre company, The Neo-Futurists, in their show, *Too Much Light Makes The Baby Go Blind*, an "ever-changing attempt to perform 30 plays in 60 minutes." www.drinkingandwriting.com

(Perhaps the play begins with some cheesy game show music and recorded applause. Contestants are confused from the beginning and continue to be throughout the game... until the very end. The stage picture is a basic game show setup.)

STEVE: *(Fast paced, loud and very obnoxious)* Hello and welcome to NAME THAT MINORITY SILENCE! First let's meet the contestants... Playing tonight are Number One and next to Number One is Number Two and next to Number Two is Number Three. Welcome. Each contestant will hear a brief moment of silence. The first contestant to raise their hand will have a chance to correctly guess what that silence is from and receive valuable points. There are no other rules to the game, but if we need more I'll make them up as we go along. Now... Let's play NAME THAT MINORITY SILENCE!

(A short burst of fate recorded applause.)

And here's your first moment of silence...

(Nothing happens... Silence... then one of them raises their hand.)

STEVE: Anyone? Oh, I'm sorry. The correct response was... The shocked silence a person of color experienced after first hearing of the white supremacist who randomly shot at and killed two minorities on the streets of Chicago and Indiana during 4th of July weekend, 1999. *(Fake applause.)* I'm sorry, no one got that right. OK, let's move on to our next moment of silence... Contestants, name that minority silence.

(Nothing happens... Someone raises their hand.)

STEVE: No...I'm sorry, time is up. The correct answer is, the awkward silence a person of color experiences when he first enters the elevator of the building he works in when just one Caucasian woman stands inside. *(Fake applause.)* I'm sorry, no one got that one either!

MARJORIE: But...wait...how...

STEVE: I'm sorry, we have to move on to the next round. *(Fake applause.)* Contestants, here comes round number two...

105 Five-Minute Plays

name that minority silence.

(Another moment of silence…someone raises their hand.)

STEVE: Number Two?

MARJORIE: The silence of racism?

STEVE: No, I'm sorry…Number One?

NOELLE: The silence of the majority?

STEVE: Nope…Number Three?

SEAN: How are we supposed to win the game?

STEVE: That is incorrect…the correct response was…that stunned, short moment of silence a person of color experienced when, after exchanging some playful teasing with a rival fan of a local sports team, the only response she had was to call me a minority piece of shit. I'm sorry, no one got that one right either. *(Fake applause.)* Now let's take a look at the point totals. I see that Number One has zero, Number Two has zero, and Number Three has zero. I'd say we have a tie with zero points. *(Fake applause.)* So, let's move on to our final and decisive round.

(Noelle raises her hand.)

STEVE: Number One!

NOELLE: I have a question.

STEVE: I'm sorry, contestants are not allowed to ask questions. Remember, I make up the rules. *(Fake applause.)*

NOELLE: No! Wait a minute! The moments of silence are too subjective. They're moments from your own life.

MARJORIE: Yeah. How are we supposed to know what each one means? We don't know your entire life's journey.

SEAN: So, none of us can really win?

STEVE: Oh…that's where you're wrong! Hopefully by sharing with you and the audiences some of the unpleasant and continuing difficulties of my life as a person of color, we all win! *(Fake applause.)*

SEAN: But I wanted to win the game.

STEVE: I told you, we all win…now shut up and look like

you've won something. (*Music and applause.*) Well, that's all the time we have for *Name That Minority Silence*, thanks to all our contestants for participating, and thanks to the audience for listening. And remember, Hispanics are the fastest growing minority in the United States! Good night!

105 Five-Minute Plays

Characters:

A MAN

A WOMAN

Setting: A bar. Evening.

> RICH ORLOFF is the one of the most popular unknown playwrights in the country. His 18 full-length plays (mostly comedies, mostly award-winning) have been presented at such theaters as Arkansas Repertory Theatre, Dayton Playhouse, Detroit Rep, Florida Studio Theatre and around the world. Rich's 80 short plays have received over 1400 productions on six continents (and a staged reading in Antarctica). His short comedies have been published seven times in the annual *Best American Short Plays* anthology series and three times in the annual *Best Ten-Minute Plays* anthology. Playscripts has published 61 of his short plays in eight collections.
>
> richorloff.com playscripts.com/playwrights/bios/195

As the play begins, the woman nurses a drink. The man walks up to the bar.

MAN: Bartender...

(noticing her)

Hello.

WOMAN: Hi... Nice tie.

MAN: Thanks. Nice outfit.

WOMAN: Thank you.

MAN: Can I get you a drink?

WOMAN: Oh, I don't know. First you buy me a drink, and then we get to chatting, and if we're not too bored with each other, you ask for my phone number, and I figure what the hell, so I give it to you. If you don't call me, I'm disappointed. If you do call me, we go out, and either I don't like you, or I like you and you don't like me. And I'm disappointed. Or we do like each other, and we go out some more, and things become pretty wonderful –great sex, revealing conversations, compatible neuroses – but I discover I want more than you can give. And I'm disappointed.

MAN: But –

WOMAN: Or we stay with it, and we get closer and closer and more in love and more dependent on each other, which gives us the strength to go through periods of emotional turmoil, mutual doubts, and things said in anger that we'll pretend to forget but which will come up again during the post-natal depression I'll have after the birth of our first child. *If* we get married, that is, and Lord knows how many friends I'll lose because they like me but they're just not comfortable around you.

MAN: Yes, but –

WOMAN: After our second child, the unresolved conflicts we buried for the sake of our marriage will propel you into a torrid affair, either with someone you work with or, God forbid, one of my few friends who *is* comfortable around you. I'll try to forgive you, eventually, and either you'll resent the obligation of a monogamous relationship, or you'll try to become philosophical about it, by which point both our children will be in intensive therapy. The divorce will be ugly, expensive, and years later than it should've been. I'll never be able to trust men again, those who aren't frightened off by my sagging features and two sadomasochistic children. The kids'll blame me, of course, and I'll die all alone. I think I'll pass on the drink. It's a nice offer, but the pain just isn't worth it.

MAN: Maybe next time.

WOMAN: Nice tie, though.

> *The man starts to go. The lights dim, as if the scene is over.*
>
> *Then the man turns and speaks, and the lights fade up.*

MAN: Did – did it ever occur to you that *you* might be the one to have the affair? That while my belief in the sanctity of the family unit successfully inhibits me from any extramarital prospects, your ever-increasing sexual confidence *and* capacity will make you irresistible to ever-increasing numbers of men. Your solid moral posture will wither in the face of lavish offers from men who are as attractive as they are rich, including one multinational multimedia multimillionaire who is forced to keep meeting you in exotic places because his wife, a former *Playboy* playmate of the year, would kill you if she found out you made him happier than she could.

WOMAN: But –

MAN: If and when I discover your hedonistic indulgences, we *will* have serious problems. But my love for you and my respect for you as the mother of our two National Merit semi-finalists will inspire me to forgive and forget. And we'll spend our twilight years blissfully exploring new sexual possibilities on Golden Pond.

WOMAN: I'll buy the drink.

MAN: Fine by me.

WOMAN: My name's Lori.

MAN: My name's Andrew.

MAN and WOMAN: *(simultaneously, as they shake hands:)*

> Pleased to meet you.

(to us)

Hmm.

> *They look back to each other.*
> *The lights fade.*

No Way Out

Claire Ann Rice

Characters:
DANNY

ERIC

CLINT

CLAIRE ANN RICE is a San Francisco-based playwright. She has worked with Thunderbird Theatre Company, No Nude Men, Three Wise Monkeys, PianoFight, AtmosTheatre, Wiley West Productions, San Francisco Theater Pub, San Francisco Olympians Theatre Festival, Custom Made Theatre Company, DIVAFest and is a co-founder of Ann Marie Productions and of Loud and Unladylike. She directed *Why Torture is Wrong, and the People Who Love Them* by Christopher Durang for Custom Made Theatre, *You're Going to Bleed* by M.R. Fall, *Kristin Hersh's Rat Girl* adapted for the stage by Stuart Bousel and *Hilarity* by Allison Page for DIVAfest. Her plays include *Sex in the Next Room, Woman Come Down, The Carmine Lie, It Ain't Me, Water Line, Demeter's Daughter, Pride and Succubus, Ares and Eris,* and *The Effects of Ultraviolet Light.* Her most recent works are commissioned one acts: *Purity,* produced by Awesome Theatre for Terror-Rama2, and *Choose Your Own Apocalypse,* produced by ShotzSF for Long Shots: Collateral Damage.

No Way Out is one of the hundreds of plays written and performed as part of SHOTZ, a "theatrical pressure cooker" that presents all-new short plays each month. claireannrice.blogspot.com

---

(Black out. A loud alarm sounds and then the lights come up suddenly. Three men stand in a circle with their backs to each other. Guns drawn. They are all carrying empty duffle bags. They all breathe heavily, their bodies tense. They are all in black with balaclavas covering their faces. Fear and adrenalin are high.)

(Suddenly.)

DANNY: FUCK!!!!

(DANNY pulls away from the circle, throws the bag away and pulls off the mask.)

(CLINT, ERIC and DANNY. DANNY comes in a (Beat.) later.)

CLINT: What the fuck, man? You shouldn't take off your mask, man, you shouldn't take off your mask. I mean, right? I mean…holy shit what are we going to do? Eric? Should we all take our masks off? Eric? What's the plan now? Is there a way out? Eric? Danny? I can't go to jail man. That wasn't part of the plan. I'm not a criminal. We gotta get out of here, man! We gotta –

ERIC: Get your fucking mask back on! There are cameras in here! This thing isn't over! We can still make it out and if you think you are going to puss out on us now you've got another thing coming. I said get your mask back on! Seth is out there, maybe dying, and for what? So you can give the fuck up now! Get your fucking mask back the FUCK ON! I said –

DANNY: …Don't start with me because I don't want to hear it. I don't want to hear it. It's hot and I can't breathe and – you do what you want Clint. Do whatever the hell you want but get the hell off my back. Oh fuck you, Eric. You worry about yourself. It doesn't matter anyway because we are in a locked room with no fucking way out and it doesn't fucking matter anymore and I FUCKING HEARD YOU!

(They stand there for a moment looking at each other. ERIC takes off his mask.)

ERIC: Fuck!

(CLINT raises his hands up as if he will also take off his mask, but he just puts his hands on his head and starts to

105 Five-Minute Plays

*freak out. He goes to a far corner, hands over his face,
silently crying.)*

ERIC: Good. Great.

DANNY: There isn't a way out.

ERIC: There's a way out.

DANNY: The alarm tripped the door. There isn't a way out.

ERIC: There's always a fucking way out.

CLINT: There's no way out, man, no way out. We're going to
run out of air and I'm going to die and there's no way out,
man, no way out!

(He starts to hyperventilate.)

DANNY: He's gonna pass out.

ERIC: He's not –

(CLINT passes out.)

ERIC: Fuck.

DANNY: At least he'll be quiet.

*(Pause. DANNY goes to CLINT and pulls off his mask to
make sure he's ok. As he talks he bunches up one of the
bags and puts it under CLINT's head.)*

ERIC: We should start looking for a weakness.

DANNY: It's a vault.

ERIC: Yeah. I know. But, I mean…how much money do you
think they spent on this really? How much of this do you
think is for show?

DANNY: None of it. I think none of it is for show. They're so-
phisticated enough to have a vault that locks when the alarm
is tripped.

(CLINT starts waking up.)

ERIC: Maybe there's a loose panel somewhere.

CLINT: Hey, what about Seth?

*(ERIC is on the floor, butt in the air, looking for cracks
along the wall.)*

DANNY: You look like an idiot.

John Capecci and Irene Ziegler

ERIC: At least I'm doing something. You're just standing there saying over and over again there's no way out!

CLINT: Maybe he'll get us out. Maybe he's trying to open the door.

DANNY: He's not trying to help us.

CLINT: Is he dead? Did the police kill him?

DANNY: I don't know.

CLINT: But, what about Seth?

ERIC: For fuck's sake! It's Seth's fault we're in here. "Let's knock over the savings and loan! It'll be fun!" FUN? WHAT KIND OF FREAK GETS HIS KICKS THIS WAY? Jesus. At what point did any of us think this was a good idea? I'm not a fucking bank robber! Seth was supposed to get the tellers away from the alarm buttons, but I bet you anything he let that fat guy at the end decide to play the hero and now we are locked in a fucking vault while Seth is hightailing it out of here in the getaway car!

DANNY: We should shoot our way out.

ERIC: Right. Perfect plan. What's the worst that could happen?

DANNY: Is there a weakness?

ERIC: No.

(Pause.)

CLINT: No way out, man. No way out.

DANNY: We didn't do this for the money. We aren't doing this because Seth talked us into it. We're doing it because your best plan was to be a dental hygienist. Clint is going to his seventh year of undergrad with no plans to actually major in anything. Seth's a Lyft driver. And until three days ago I was really excited about opening a yogurt shop. A fucking yogurt shop!

> *(The lights suddenly go out. From the other side of the door. "We have the place surrounded. We will open the door. Put your hands up." The lights come back up, but in a different color. All three are in the positions they were in at the beginning, except with their masks off and bags on the floor.)*

(CLINT and ERIC talk at the same time.)

CLINT: I don't wanna die, man, I wanna be a psychologist or a lawyer or an actor or a caterer or I wanna fuck that guy in my astronomy class I don't know, man. But I don't wanna die, man. I don't wanna die…

ERIC: I don't want to live out some kind of Butch Cassidy fantasy of a suicide. I want to know what it feels like to hold hundreds of thousands of dollars in my hand. I want to live on a beach in Mexico!

(Pause.)

DANNY: I don't want to be normal.

(Pause.)

ERIC: You know, this is a small town. It's not like they have a SWAT team.

CLINT: There's no way out, man.

DANNY: No way but one.

(They stiffen with resolve.)

Characters:

A

B

Setting: Two chairs in an otherwise empty space.
NOTE: Pronouns should be adapted as needed based on the gender of A and B. Because this is a play built on rhythm rather than plot, the dialogue is mapped on the page in a way that should make clear the points of overlap.

JOHN MINIGAN is a playwright, director and teacher whose plays have been produced throughout the US and Canada, Europe, Asia and Australia. He has been in-residence developing new work at the Orlando Shakespeare Theater and the New American Playwrights Project, and his work has been selected three times for the Samuel French Off-Off-Broadway Festival and published in the *Best Ten-Minute Plays* and New England New Play Alliance anthologies. He is a three-time winner of the Firehouse New Works Contest, a winner of the Nantucket Short Play Contest, the Rover Dramawerks Competition, the Longwood 0-60 Contest, New York's 8-Minute Madness Festival, the Nor'Eastern Playwriting Contest, Seoul Players Contest and the KNOCK International Short Play Competition. When not writing, John teaches theater, writing and Shakespeare. He is a member of the Dramatists Guild. johnminigan.com

A and B are seated. A is listening. Nothing happens for fifteen seconds.

A	B
I heard that. I heard It this time.	
	Heard what? I didn't hear a thing.
What do you mean, heard what?	
Not a … what, you didn't hear it?	There wasn't a thing.
	There was nothing.
There was a noise. A definite noise. Some kind of— I don't know — it was — very specific. That's for certain.	What noise? Can you be specific? He doesn't know. Can you tell me, what did it sound like?
I don't know *Silence.*	
	Was it like a bell?
A what?	
	A bell.
No.	
	No.
No. It was nothing like a bell.	
	Well what was it like?
Silence.	
I'd have to hear it again.	
	What if you don't hear it again?
Silence.	

Well, then. I would have
to create, through the
power of my imagination,
some imagistic description
of the noise, wouldn't I?
  Silence.

            Let's hope you hear it
            again.

  Silence.
You heard it, didn't you?

            What?
I said, "You heard it—"   I know what you said.
Then what is your problem, I'm asking you ....
you can't—   The problem is, "What did
            you hear?"

Oh.
Did you hear the noise?

            No.
No?

            I didn't hear the noise.

  Silence.
No. I know that.

            Then why are you ask—
I meant before.

            You meant—
            Oh, before

Yes. When the noise hap-
pened before, you heard it,
I assume.   Did you hear it?
No.

            And was it heard?
            Do we have evidence of its
            existence, the noise?

Yes.
Yes.

  Silence.

Yes, but, if you heard
It, if you heard the
noise the *first time*—

Then why not the second
time?

  Silence.

Yes.
Yes.

  Silence.

The second time—
What?
You.

Okay.
Why didn't you hear it
the second time?

  Silence.

Ah. No, you're right

  Silence.

It sounded like a bell?

You don't know?

Your noise, I'm asking.

Yes.

Then I must have heard it.

Yes, I did. I thought that
was settled.
Yeah?

Why didn't I hear it the
second time?

Why didn't you—
What?

No, you.

Then why didn't you hear
it the first time?

Yes.

It did?

I didn't hear it.

Did it sound like a bell?

Yes.
It sounded like a bell.

Silence.

Well, that's the problem.

Is it?

Yes. Because I don't know
if mine sounded like a bell.

Maybe you didn't hear it.

Of course I heard it.
What are we talking about?
"Distinctly?"

I mean "Distinctly."

Yes. Perhaps—

Perhaps—?

Perhaps you didn't hear it
distinctly.

Perhaps.
But perhaps I, on the other
hand, did.

Yeah?

Perhaps, in fact, there were
two noises.

Two noises?

Yeah.

Silence.

What the hell does that
mean? Two noises. I
don't under—
Yes. First you heard one,
then I—No, first I heard,
then you.

Two noises. It means—

What I mean, supposing it
was two noises ...

Two noises, yes.

... of different types.

Silence.

105 Five-Minute Plays

Not the same noise twice, but two different noises. At two different times.

Two different noises.
Yes.
You think?

I don't know. Maybe.

Maybe I think you're right?

Yes?

Yes.

There's our problem, then.

Yes. Two different noises.

Silence.

Wait, wait—

Ssh!

Did you hear—?

Silence.

No.

No, me neither.

Silence.

Blackout.

Characters:
WOMAN

MAN

YOUNG WOMAN

GIRL

Setting: Adrift on the sea. Barely enough room to stand.

JUNE GURALNICK has created plays, performance projects, and community installations for three decades. A native New Yorker, June's plays have been performed at venues including the Kennedy Center (Washington, D.C.), Abrons Arts Centre/Henry Street Settlement (NY), Southern Appalachian Repertory Theatre (NC), Burning Coal Theatre (NC) and the North Carolina Museum of Art. Works include *Memories of Childhood, The Home Project, In Gold We Trust* (with Guy Nickson), *Women of the Light* (with Cynthia Mitchell), *Space Interlude, Dreams of Flight, Finding Clara, Across the Holy Tell*, and, most recently, *Birds of a Feather: A Comedy About De-Extinction.* Awards include Silver Medal-Pinter Drama Review Prize, North Carolina Arts Council Literature Fellowship, Southern Appalachian Repertory Theatre New Plays winner, Virginia Center for the Creative Arts Writing Fellows, Hambidge Center for the Arts Fellows, and Sewanee Writers' Conference Tennessee Williams Scholar (University of the South). juneguralnick.com

ACT I: REMEMBRANCE GAME

(WOMAN gestures for MAN to begin.)

MAN: Game starting.

WOMAN: Pass the gravy.

YOUNG WOMAN: I'm going out.

MAN: Turn on the TV.

GIRL: Ice cream. I want ice cream.

WOMAN: Where have you been?

YOUNG WOMAN: Running running running but they —

> *(Pause. WOMAN gestures for MAN to continue; he hesitates.)*

WOMAN: Pass the potatoes.

MAN: They're hiring over at—

GIRL: Kitty wants ice cream!

YOUNG WOMAN: Where's my money?

WOMAN: When I was young—

GIRL: Kitty ate my ice cream!

MAN: Where's the aspirin?

YOUNG WOMAN: I hate this house.

WOMAN: What a temper!

GIRL: Gimme, gimme, gimme!

MAN: Lord, give my strength!

> *(The next four lines are spoken simultaneously.)*

GIRL: I wanna go home!

YOUNG WOMAN: Leave me alone!

WOMAN: My mother would have—

MAN: Enough!

WOMAN: Can we please have one quiet minute?

> *(Pause)*

GIRL: I'm scared.

WOMAN: They're coming.

YOUNG WOMAN: You said that three hours ago.

WOMAN: They're coming.

> *(She looks at MAN.)*

MAN: Yes.

> *(Pause)*

> Row, row, row, your boat—

YOUNG WOMAN: Gently down the stream—

GIRL: Merrily, merrily, merrily, merrily—

WOMAN: Life is but a—

> *(Black-out; end of Act I.)*

ACT II: SEARCHING BEYOND THE SEA GAME

> *(WOMAN stands, looks out and hums song like "Beyond the Sea." MAN rises, looks around, glances at WOMAN and starts humming. They switch places. GIRL stands; WOMAN stops humming and sits down. GIRL looks all around, rotating 360 degrees, then nudges YOUNG WOMAN. YOUNG WOMAN hums; MAN stops humming and sits down. YOUNG WOMAN stands and lifts GIRL so she can have a better view. GIRL hums; YOUNG WOMAN stops humming. Changing places, YOUNG WOMAN sits down. GIRL continues humming.)*

> *(Black-out; end of Act II.)*

ACT III: PARADISE LOST GAME

WOMAN: Where will you live? After?

MAN: I can't—

WOMAN: Please. Play the game.

MAN: No.

YOUNG WOMAN: Why do we have to?

WOMAN: *(Pause)*

> Because—

(Pause)

Because. Where will you live?

GIRL: Where bad men won't—

MAN: Where bombs can't—

YOUNG WOMAN: Where soldiers don't—

WOMAN: Stop!

(Pause. MAN weeps; WOMAN touches his face.)

MAN: Begin. Again.

WOMAN: Where will you live?

MAN: A cabin on top of a mountain where I see for five—no, fifty miles. Pine trees and a crystal clear blue lake. Peaceful—just the sound of leaves rustling in the wind and birds fluttering in the trees. Paradise.

GIRL: A castle in Disneyland—alligators live in the moat! A room for Kitty, a room for my rabbits, a room for my horses …

YOUNG WOMAN: High up. On the 20th Floor. The sea of humanity…far, far away. Steel girders gleam outside my window. White walls, cathedral ceiling, chrome furniture. One perfect red rose on a butcher block table and a closet filled with Gucci and Prada. Protected – 24/7; I mean, no one gets in.

MAN AND GIRL: *(To WOMAN)* Your turn.

WOMAN: *(Pause)* Small villa… nothing too ornate. Olive trees…a vineyard…a wrought-iron balcony overlooking the shimmering sea below. Domestic servants answer the phone and I never know who called. A cultured library—leather-bound books, bronze statues, Casablanca fans and Puccini on the stereo. A refined life.

(Sounds of rushing water. Terrified, they rise. MAN looks at WOMAN and continues.)

MAN: I cast a line into the water and bam—I hook a big one!

YOUNG WOMAN: Isn't that DiCaprio at the table next to ours?

GIRL: Come out come out wherever you are…

WOMAN: There'll be eight for lunch on the balcony.

(Sound of torrential water and wood breaking apart. WOMAN screams. Pause.)

WOMAN: They will come.

(She stops.)

GIRL: Merrily—

MAN: Merrily—

YOUNG WOMAN: Merrily—

(They look at WOMAN.)

WOMAN: *(Pause)*

Merrily—

(Pause)

Life is but a dream.

Aaron Adair

Characters:

BARRY: A young man.

MISSY: His very pretty, very pregnant wife.

Setting: The play takes place on the front porch of a suburban home.

> AARON ADAIR is a playwright from the City of Big Shoulders, Chicago, Illinois. He is the author of evening-length, one-act and shorter plays, ranging from 5 to 15 minutes, which have been produced in diverse cities from Chicago to New York, Bangalore and beyond. As one critic noted, "Comedy or drama, Adair's plays consistently demonstrate that thoughtful observation coupled with the right amount of wit can go a very long way." jellobox.com

AT RISE: BARRY is in a bathrobe. A folded newspaper is in his hand. The gazes into the distance.

MISSY enters.

MISSY: What are you doing out here? You left the front door wide open. Are you trying to air condition the entire neighborhood?

BARRY: Dawn.

MISSY: Dawn?

BARRY: There's something unnerving about dawn. Maybe it's the quiet. The stillness. Everything's new. Everything's waiting.

MISSY: Waiting? Waiting for what?

BARRY: The streetlamps to turn off. The paperboy to ride by on his bike.

MISSY: The paperboy comes before dawn.

BARRY: No, he doesn't.

MISSY: Yes, he does.

BARRY: I think you're missing the point.

MISSY: I'm not sure you have one.

BARRY: Haven't you had our baby yet?

MISSY: What does it look like?

BARRY: It's past due.

MISSY: So?

BARRY: *Well* past due.

MISSY: What do you want me to do? Have it right here? Right now?

BARRY: If it's not too much trouble.

MISSY: I think you're being unreasonable.

BARRY: Then, perhaps you should agree with me about the paperboy. I mean, if it's easier.

MISSY: Not while you have today's paper in your hand.

BARRY tosses the paper off stage.

105 Five-Minute Plays

BARRY: Do you think he'll have horns?

MISSY: The paperboy?

BARRY: No. The baby.

MISSY: Are you kidding?

BARRY: Your mother has horns.

MISSY: My mother does not have horns.

BARRY: Anticipation is a funny thing. Your mind wanders through endless scenarios of what will or won't be. And then, one day, standing on your porch, dawn stretching before you: Poof! A baby.

MISSY: With horns?

BARRY: Yes.

MISSY: *(ugh...)* Come inside. Coffee's ready.

BARRY: *(ugh...)* It's decaffeinated.

MISSY: Caffeine isn't good for the baby. If we can't have it, you can't have it.

BARRY: Aha!

MISSY: What!?

BARRY: Did you hear that?

MISSY: Hear what?

BARRY: Dawn. Silent no more. Waiting no more. The streetlamps off. The paperboy has arrived!

MISSY: Good grief.

BARRY: No, just grief.

MISSY: About the baby?

BARRY: Tut-tut. Euphemisms, please. All the best parents use euphemisms.

MISSY: According to who?

BARRY: Whom. According to *whom.*

　　　(with bravura)

Dawn! The sun rises! The silence is broken! Coffee is decaffeinated! Language deteriorates into the who-whom, the goo-goo, the ga-ga—

MISSY: *(hands to belly)* O!

BARRY: What O?

MISSY: The baby! It's coming!

BARRY: Horns and all?

MISSY: Horns and all!

BARRY: Well then, off you go.

MISSY: Indeed!

> *MISSY exits.*

BARRY: Indeed. Indeed-indeed. The fateful day has thus arrived.

> *(calling out)*

I don't hear anything.

MISSY: *(offstage)* Not yet.

BARRY: Now?

MISSY: No. Not yet.

BARRY: *(pacing)* Indeed-indeed... Indeed-indeed...

> *The sound of a baby crying.*

Aha! The silence. Broken.

MISSY: What?

BARRY: I said, "Aha! The silence. Broken."

MISSY: Hey, it's a boy!

BARRY: Does he look like me?

> *MISSY returns to the stage, no longer pregnant. She is holding a baby swaddled in a blanket.*

MISSY: Not really.

BARRY: Horns?

MISSY: What do you think?

> *(MISSY holds the baby forward. BARRY takes him.)*

BARRY: I'd be more excited, if he had horns.

105 Five-Minute Plays

MISSY: I understand.

BARRY: *(gazing into the swaddle)* He does so look like me.

MISSY: Squinty? Red? Dyspeptic?

BARRY: Why isn't he crying?

MISSY: Some newborns are quiet. Still. Like the dawn.

BARRY: Have you decided on a name?

MISSY: I told you: Dawn.

BARRY: Dawn? That's a girl's name.

MISSY: Says who?

BARRY: It's common knowledge. Dawn is a girl's name. (…) Brick. Brick is a boy's name.

MISSY: Brick? That's horrible.

BARRY: He sort of looks like a brick.

MISSY: *(taking the baby back)* Honestly.

BARRY: Are you going to return him?

MISSY: I don't know.

BARRY: You know we can't keep him. Who-whom, goo-goo, ga-ga, decaffeinated coffee and all that. Remember?

MISSY: You aren't ready for a baby, are you?

BARRY: Are you?

MISSY: Fine.

> *(MISSY exits briefly. She returns, pregnant again.)*

MISSY: What are you doing out here? You left the front door wide open. Are you trying to air condition the entire neighborhood?

BARRY: Dawn.

MISSY: Dawn?

BARRY: Dawn is a girl's name.

MISSY: A girl's name?

BARRY: Yes.

MISSY: Don? D-O-N, as in Donald, is a girl's name?

BARRY: Don? D-O-N? Not Dawn, D-A-W-N?

MISSY: Yes. No. Yes, it's Don. D-O-N.

BARRY: You should work on your enunciation.

MISSY: Is that what you've been fretting about all morning?

BARRY: Yes.

MISSY: *(ugh...)* Come inside. Coffee's ready.

BARRY: *(ugh...)* It's decaffeinated.

MISSY: Caffeine isn't good for the baby. If we can't have it, you can't have it.

BARRY: What did you say?

MISSY: I said, you'll survive.

> *MISSY exits.*
> *(A newspaper is tossed onto the stage.)*
> *DIM OUT*

Characters:

MARGARET: twenty-three, a female who takes care of her father.

ED: sixty-six, a man in the later stages of Alzheimer's disease.

Setting: A bathroom. Present.

ERIK CHRISTIAN HANSON earned his Master of Fine Arts degree in Dramatic Writing from NYU's Tisch School of the Arts and was the recipient of an "Outstanding Writing For The Screen" certificate from the Rita & Burton Goldberg Department. Hanson is a published playwright. His plays have been developed and produced in Alaska, California, Connecticut, Massachusetts, Nebraska, New York, and South Carolina. They include: *To Darfur* (The Best Ten-Minute Plays of 2008: 3 actors or more), *Property of Africa* (Boston Theater Marathon), *Same Only Different* (Great Plains Theatre Conference), *The What and Why* (finalist for Lark Playwrights' Week), and *Polish the Turd* (Last Frontier Theatre Conference).

(Lights up. ED, fully dressed, stands in front of the toilet. MARGARET holds his hand.)

MARGARET: You stink, Dad. You know that? You reek, reek, reek. *(Pause)* Ready for your bath?

ED: Bath?

MARGARET: You like baths.

ED: You take one.

MARGARET: I'm clean. I'm not the one who—I smell fabulous.

ED: Your mother should.

MARGARET: Should what?

ED: Take a bath.

MARGARET: She's dead.

ED: Let her have it.

MARGARET: Have the bath?

ED: Let her have it.

MARGARET: I would if cleaning her would do her any good.

ED: Is she dirty?

MARGARET: Very.

ED: Very?

MARGARET: You get very dirty in coffins. *(Pause)* C'mon. Let's clean you up.

ED: I want to go.

MARGARET: Where? Where is it you want to go this time?

ED: Where?

MARGARET: Yes. Where. Any place. You name it. Name it and we'll go.

ED: Pike Place Market.

MARGARET: All right. We can go there again. Let's go to Pike Place Market. *(Pause)* We're at the airport. Walk through security. Come on, Dad. Take a step forward. People are waiting and they're getting impatient.

(ED takes a step forward.)

You are through! My turn. *(Steps forward)* Beep! Uh oh! Didn't think I had any metal on—oops, car keys!

(MARGARET puts the keys aside. Pretends to walk through the detector and flings her hands up in the air.)

No beep! We are good. Got to find our gate so we can board. Let's see…

(MARGARET pretends to take a boarding pass out of her pocket.)

Want window or the aisle?

ED: Window?

MARGARET: You want to look down and see what you're missing? You're a geography nut. Sit near the window. I'll take aisle.

ED: You take it.

MARGARET: Nonsense. Window's yours. *(Pause)* Take off is in about…here comes the captain. *(Impersonating a captain)* "Thank you for choosing United. This is a nonstop flight to Seattle. Weather there is what one would normally expect: wet, rainy and green."

(MARGARET makes an airplane noise.)

Here comes the landing. Hold on, Dad. Hold on.

ED: Hold on?

(MARGARET squeezes her father's hand. She bounces lightly, as if they actually hit a runway.)

MARGARET: It's almost over. Almost! Little bumpy for my taste. Okay, have to wait for the beep before we can take off our seatbelts.

(MARGARET makes a beeping noise.)

There it is! Seatbelt off, Dad. We're here.

ED: Here?

MARGARET: Pike Place Market. You still want to go, right?

ED: Oh yes.

MARGARET: Take a step towards me.

(ED takes a step backward.)

Not backward. Forward. For-ward.

(MARGARET guides him forward.)

Keep coming. One foot in front of the other.

(ED takes two steps forward. MARGARET takes his shirt off for him. Then his socks, pants and underwear.)

Almost there. Al-most. One. Final. Step.

(ED steps into the tub. MARGARET guides him into it.)

And…we…are…here. *(Looking offstage)* Oh my goodness! Look at all the fish on sale, Dad! What are you in the mood for today? They've got Caribbean Rock Lobster Tails, Alaskan Spot Prawns, Smoked Mussels, Live Manila Clams, Live Penn Cove Mussels, Sockeye Salmon, Halibut Cheeks, Black Cod, Chilean Sea Bass, Tilapia Fillet, Tuna Steaks and…Squid Tubes. Lot to choose from, but what'll it be? What do you fancy?

ED: Is that… Is that Margaret?

MARGARET: I'm Margaret. Dad? I'm Margaret. I am. Me. Right behind you.

ED: Is that her? Out there?

MARGARET: Where? Out where? In front of the fish market?

(ED points. MARGARET surrenders.)

Yeah, that's her. That's Margaret.

ED: What is she doing?

MARGARET: Buying fish.

(MARGARET rubs his back with body wash and scrubs it with a poof.)

ED: I want to go see Margaret.

MARGARET: We will. We'll see her. Soon. Just a lot of people at the market today and…

ED: I want to see Margaret!

(ED slams his hand down into the water.)

MARGARET: You can. You will.

ED: I WANT TO SEE HER!

MARGARET: Calm down, Dad. We will. It'll happen. We just need to wait for her to see us. Wait for her to see us and… *(Pointing)* There she is! She's looking at you right now.

ED: She is?

MARGARET: She is. Say, "Hi, Margaret."

(No reply from ED as his attention is offstage.)

Dad? Say, "Hi, Margaret."

ED: "Hi, Margaret."

(MARGARET turns and muffles her speech.)

MARGARET: Hello, Daddy. Hear that? She said, "Hello, Daddy."

ED: She did?

MARGARET: She. Did. Say, "Hello, sweetheart."

(No reply from ED as his attention is offstage.)

Say, "Hello, sweetheart."

ED: Hello?

MARGARET: Say, "Sweetheart."

ED: Sweet?

MARGARET: Heart.

ED: Heart.

(MARGARET cleans her father's back and neck. ED looks for his daughter offstage. Lights dim. Blackout.)

Characters:

GARRY: Stuck in a metaphysical Pity Party.

DAN: Stuck on a metaphysical Soap Box.

Setting: On a sidewalk by a soap box. Present.

> LEEAN KIM TORSKE is a Chicago-based Korean/Norwegian-American playwright, dramaturg, teacher, and performer from the great state of Wyoming. She earned her MFA in Playwriting from Ohio University and her MA in Literary Studies from the University of Wyoming. She has been an Artistic Engagement Associate with Steppenwolf Theatre Company since June 2012. Leean is the co-founder and co-Artistic Director of The Blue Ring in Chicago, IL. TheBlueRing.com

(LIGHTS UP on DAN standing on a box looking trium-phant. GARRY enters, downtrodden and hating himself. GARRY sees DAN and approaches.)

GARRY: Hey Dan.

DAN: Hey Garry!

GARRY: Say, weren't you standing there the last time I saw you, like three weeks ago?

DAN: Yup. I started dating this woman, Jessica, a few months ago. She's great! Really made me aware of things, ya know?

GARRY: Yeah, I wish I were aware of things. I'm not aware of anything.

DAN: Yeah, well Jessica talked me into becoming a vegan, and she took me to a few PETA events, and then next thing I knew—wammo! Here I was on a soap box! Been here ever since.

GARRY: Wow. Soap box, eh? That sounds way better than where I've been. And I'd know. I've been here for months.

DAN: Where's that?

GARRY: Pity Party.

DAN: Ouch. Well, we all gotta be somewhere.

(GARRY sits in front of the box.)

GARRY: I guess. I just wish I could get out of my head, ya know? Say those are some nice shoes. I wish I had some shoes like that. I just have these stupid shoes. Everyday I put them on and I think, man, why did I buy these shoes? These shoes are stupid. Not like your shoes. Your shoes are nice.

DAN: These? Sure they're nice, but I bought them because for every pair of shoes that you purchase of this brand, they donate a pair to a child in need of shoes.

GARRY: Jeez. That's awful nice of you.

DAN: Well, I do what I can. And to think, you could have helped a child in need.

GARRY: Yeah, my shoes aren't helping anybody. Even when I try to help people, I just screw it all up. Like today, I was smoking a cigarette, and I saw this aluminum can right there on the sidewalk. And I was like who just throws their trash on the ground? So I finished my cigarette and I flicked out the cherry and I threw the can and my cigarette butt in this nearby trash can. Then this homeless dude storms over and digs my cigarette butt out of the trash, throws it on sidewalk and bitches me out for throwing it in his trash can.

DAN: What?

GARRY: I know, right? It didn't even occur to me that he *eats* out of that trash can.

DAN: No, back up. You threw an aluminum can in the trash?

GARRY: Yeah.

DAN: You could have recycled that. You know, if everyone just throws their aluminum cans in the trash, we'll never save the planet.

GARRY: *(Punishing himself)* Stupid! Stupid! Stupid!

DAN: You need to lighten up there, buddy. Women are attracted to confidence, not a dude that goes around feeling sorry for himself all the time.

GARRY: I can't help it. I can't seem to do anything right these days. It seems like my life is just one thing after the other, ya know?

DAN: At least you have Candice.

GARRY: She dumped me.

DAN: No wonder you're so down.

    (DAN sits on the box.)

GARRY: Yeah, really messed me up man.

DAN: Real sorry to hear that.

    (DAN gets off the box and hugs GARRY then sits next to him.)

GARRY: I thought she was the one.

DAN: Yeah, I thought that Jessica was the one for me.

GARRY: You're not together anymore?

DAN: No, she dumped me last week for some dude who works for Amnesty International.

GARRY: That's too bad, bro.

DAN: Here we are a couple of great guys—

GARRY: Yeah!

DAN: And what happens?

GARRY: We get dumped.

DAN: And we didn't do anything to deserve it.

GARRY: Oh, I don't know. Candice didn't like that I kept drag-ging her into my pity party. Guess I did have something to do with it.

(GARRY sits on the box.)

DAN: This always happens to me. I change my whole life around for some girl, just to please her. And where does it get me?

(GARRY stands on the box.)

GARRY: You gotta learn to build your self-esteem, bro. You can't base your sense of self worth on another person's opin-ions of you. *(Beat. He is triumphant.)* Hey, the view's not half bad from up here.

DAN: I know, but— wait a minute. You son of a bitch! How did I get down here? You! You did this!

GARRY: You need to take ownership of your actions, Dan.

DAN: I'm so lonely down here.

GARRY: Oh, I'm sure you'll find someone to drag down there with you eventually.

(LIGHTS FADE.)

Characters

CELIA: Late twenties/early thirties.

STEVE: Her husband.

Setting: Dining area of a modest apartment. Small secondhand dinette table with two chairs. A baby's highchair with bibs draped over the back and plastic toys on the tray. Offstage left is the kitchen. Offstage right is the rest of the apartment.

CHARISSA MENEFEE is a playwright, poet, director, and performer. She is on the faculty of the MFA Program in Creative Writing & Environment at Iowa State University, where she teaches scriptwriting, dramatic literature, and performance studies. A recent finalist for the Julie Harris Playwright Award, she has had plays honored by the Utah Shakespeare Festival's New American Playwrights Project, Pandora Festival, American College Theatre Festival, Arizona Theatre Conference, and Tennessee Women's Theatre Project, among others, and she was a Tennessee Williams Scholar in Playwriting at the Sewanee Writers' Conference. Her chapbook, *When I Stopped Counting*, is available from Finishing Line Press. Her poetry is also forthcoming in the 2016 Hippocrates Prize for Poetry and Medicine anthology. After spending many years in the mile-high mountain town of Prescott, Arizona, she now lives in Ames, Iowa. facebook.com/Charissa.Menefee.Author/

(As lights go up, CELIA enters from the kitchen with plates and silverware. She sets the table. Offstage right, a door is unlocked, opened. Keys clatter into a bowl.)

CELIA: That you, Steve?

STEVE: *(offstage)* Yeah.

CELIA: Supper's almost ready.

(She exits back into the kitchen.

STEVE appears in the doorway left. He wears a bowling jacket that is clearly too small for him; in fact, it looks suspiciously like it might be a woman's jacket. The sleeves are too short, the jacket pulls across the shoulders, and there's no chance it would zip in the front. But he beams, absolutely beams.

CELIA enters with glasses of iced tea, napkins, and whatever else she can carry in this trip. She continues to put things on the table and doesn't even look at him.)

CELIA: Did you wash up?

STEVE: Celia.

CELIA: Almost ready. Wash up. And check on the baby, would you? Hoping she'll sleep through supper and we can eat in peace for a change. I need to talk to you about something.

STEVE: Celia.

CELIA: Now?

STEVE: Okay, okay.

(He exits right. CELIA bustles around, back and forth, in and out of the kitchen, bringing food to the table. It's a small apartment, so it's not long before STEVE returns.)

CELIA: Baby okay?

STEVE: Celia, would you look for a second?

CELIA: Baby okay?

STEVE: Sound asleep.

CELIA: Oh, and cute, right?

STEVE: Yeah, cute.

CELIA: Cuter asleep, that's for sure. Hope you don't mind pork chops again. On sale. Probably about to expire. I got them really well done, just in case.

STEVE: That's fine. Celia, look.

CELIA: Be right back.

> *(He catches her by the shoulders before she can get out of the room again. Turns her so she faces him.)*

STEVE: Look at me.

CELIA: What?

STEVE: Just look.

> *(He poses. She laughs.)*

CELIA: *What* are you wearing?

STEVE: Isn't it amazing?

> *(She laughs again. His face falls a bit.)*

No, really.

CELIA: You're so funny. Take if off and sit down. I'll be right back.

> *(She exits to the kitchen. He calls after her.)*

STEVE: No, I can't take it off. It's lucky. A lucky jacket.

> *(CELIA enters, puts the last dish on the table, and sits.)*

CELIA: For a fourteen-year-old girl maybe.

STEVE: *(still standing)* No. Lucky for me. I won it.

CELIA: Won it. You entered a contest to win a too-small jacket for a bowling league you're not in? I don't think that's the exact definition of "lucky." Sit down before it gets cold.

STEVE: You got to hear this. See, Jack comes down the hall right after lunch and says he has tickets to this matinee. Somebody traded with him. You know how he's always doing that weird bartering online. He thought he was trading for tickets to the baseball game. But he's stuck with these, so he says why don't I come with him to see this show.

CELIA: You skipped out at work?

STEVE: That's what I say. I can't skip out this afternoon. He says he's the boss and he doesn't want to go by himself and he'll count it in my hours. So I say okay.

CELIA: Sit down and eat. Before it gets cold. Before the baby wakes up.

STEVE: So we go see these weird plays. Some of them are only a few minutes long. I don't really know what they're about. I'm trying to keep Jack from seeing me yawn. Starting to think about the work I'll have to catch up on tomorrow after wasting the afternoon this way.

(CELIA is halfway through her meal. He still moves around the room, hyper.)

CELIA: Pork chops are a little tough, but they're okay. Better than your mother's at least.

(She expects a reaction, but he is oblivious.)

STEVE: But the funny thing was—after the show, they had a drawing. For things they used in the plays.

CELIA: That's weird. Who does that?

STEVE: I know. But here's the thing. I never win anything. You know that.

CELIA: That's for sure.

STEVE: Never. Never. Doesn't matter what I enter, I don't win. I can't think of anything I ever won in my life. Even when I got Donny Jones to enter that chess club raffle at school— because I felt sorry for my sister—and we were the only two who bought tickets—he won. Right?

CELIA: Yeah, you've told me that story. A few times.

STEVE: So this drawing starts. And I say to Jack, let's go on, get back to the office, go home a little early. He says, no, just wait. No one else is leaving yet. So I'm sitting there, twiddling my thumbs. Then they call out a number. And he says, wait a min- ute, that's your seat number. What, I say, you're kidding. No, it's your number, he says. I'm flabbergasted.

CELIA: Since when do you say flabbergasted?

STEVE: Since I got lucky today, that's when.

CELIA: I'm having your pork chop, too.

STEVE: I was flabbergasted. Flabbergasted. Jack raises his hand and waves. Next thing I know, this pretty girl brings this jacket up the stairs and hands it to me, says congratulations, and I'm saying thanks and I can't believe it. I won.

CELIA: Hmmm.

STEVE: Celia, I won. Me. I won. I'm lucky now.

CELIA: That's great. Can you sit down?

STEVE: I'm never taking this jacket off. It's amazingly lucky. It's going to change everything.

(He finally sits down, looks at his empty plate.)

CELIA: What do you want to change, Steve?

STEVE: Everything. Just think, I might start winning. All the time. It'll all be different.

CELIA: Because of the—

STEVE: Lucky jacket. Yeah.

(Sounds of a baby waking. Not loud yet. The baby is just beginning to stir.)

CELIA: Well, I got to eat in peace. Guess that was pretty lucky.

STEVE: See? It's working already.

CELIA: Oh, your lucky jacket makes me lucky, too, huh?

STEVE: Yeah, of course. If I'm lucky, you're lucky. It's all gonna change. We're gonna have so much more!

(The baby's cries get louder, urgent. CELIA gets up.)

CELIA: *(laughs)* All that's true. It's all gonna change, and we're gonna have so much more.

STEVE: Yeah!

(He starts to put food on his plate. Looks for the pork chops, doesn't see them.)

CELIA: *(over the baby's escalating cries)* I was trying to tell you when it was quiet, but I guess it doesn't matter. More crying, Steve. Lots more crying. More babies. Twins. So much more.

(She exits right.)

(STEVE looks after her. He stands up, tugs at the jacket. Then he takes it off and hangs it on the back of CELIA's chair. Lights down.)

RADIO

Roger Nieboer

Characters:

    CHILD

    WOMAN

    MAN

Setting: A bare stage, set with one chair.

> ROGER NIEBOER is an experimental theatre artist concerned primarily with audience perception. Trained as a playwright, he has utilized a wide range of subjects and styles while exploring anthropological themes related to language, technology and ritual. He has received commissions from Minnesota Opera, Winnipeg Folk Festival, Intersection for the Arts, History Theatre and Northern Spark, as well as grants from East Central Regional Arts Council, California Arts Council, Minnesota State Arts Board and National Endowment for the Arts. Currently he resides on a 99-acre compound in rural Minnesota where he conducts experiments in organic horticulture, avant-garde landscaping and restorative forestry. He also collects cultural artifacts (i.e., junk).

(Lights up slowly. Child enters and addresses the audience.)

CHILD: Though I am just a child, I have seen and heard many things. Some of them are true; they really happened. Others are merely figments of my digitally-saturated imagination, flashing across monitors, reflected in the retinas of concerned observers. *(Pause)* Dreams, nightmares, encrypted mutations. Genetic shards of our shared subconscious. *(Pause)* This one is real because it's happening right now, before our very eyes.

(Exits as lights fade)

(Lights up to reveal man sitting in chair, tinkering with a vintage transistor radio. A woman walks around him

Slowly.)

WOMAN: *(calmly and matter-of-factly)* I want you to do it. *(Pause)* To kill me. *(Pause)* When the time comes, I want you to kill me.

(Man ignores her, continues working on radio)

WOMAN: Did you hear me? *(Pause)* Did you hear what I just said? *(Pause)* You heard me. *(Pause)* Didn't you? You heard what I said.

(Pause)

MAN: Some people are just messed up, you know that?

WOMAN: What?

MAN: People.

WOMAN: What people?

MAN: People who buy stuff on eBay. They're seriously messed up.

WOMAN: What are you talking about?

MAN: This radio... I sold it to a guy on eBay, and he sent it back, said it wasn't what he wanted after all.

WOMAN: Well, people change their minds, I suppose.

MAN: Well of course people change their minds. They have a right to change their minds. That's why I have a very generous return policy.

WOMAN: So what's the problem?

MAN: The problem is when they remove a part, a valuable part, and steal it.

They take the transistor out, and then have the nerve to return the radio, claiming they don't want it because it's missing a transistor.

WOMAN: It all seems kind of sketchy to me. Random people, secret user names, passwords.

(Pause)

MAN:I didn't know what to say. Okay? I never know what to say. *(Pause)* Especially when you... I just don't know what to say.

WOMAN: I want you to assure me that when I start to... when my brain no longer allows me to... function... I want you to... take care of... the situation.

MAN: What am I supposed to do? Go on Craig's List and find a hit-man or something?

WOMAN: I don't want you to tell me how. I just want you to be prepared, so that when the time comes, you'll be ready.

(Pause)

MAN: *(Examines radio)* You ever stop to think about all the sounds that have come out of this thing?

WOMAN: What? Like music?

MAN: Music, yeah. News. Weather. Hockey. I had a clock radio right above my bed. I'd listen to it, late at night, and imagine all the other people who were listening to the very same thing, at the very same time. KAAY, all the way from Little Rock, Arkansas. WGN from Chicago. And I used to lay there in my bed listening to these stations from so far away, and somehow it made me feel really, really small. Just a tiny dot in a massive universe, But at the same time I felt connected, by radio. Waves. To everybody. In the whole world. *(Pause)* You know what I mean?

WOMAN: I guess so. When I was a kid I imagined that tiny, miniaturized versions of the musicians actually came to life right there in the radio, played their songs, and disappeared.

So when I heard Green Day do "Time of Your Life", I envisioned a teeny, tiny Billy Joe Armstrong strumming away on his teeny, tiny guitar and singing his heart out, right there in the radio.

(Pause)

MAN: How about if we fly to Switzerland or something?

WOMAN: Switzerland?

MAN: *60 Minutes* did this thing about euthanasia in Switzerland and how it's becoming like a tourist industry thing where entire families accompany the person who's going to, you know, the one who wants to...

WOMAN: Control the end of their life?

MAN: Yeah, that. They all stay in a nice hotel, go out for a last meal, and check into this special clinic... and that's that.

WOMAN: Sounds kind of creepy to me.

MAN: Well of course it's creepy. Death is creepy! That's what I've been trying to tell you. Death creeps me out.

WOMAN: We're all going to die. *(Pause)* Someday.

MAN: Some day. Sure. *(Pause)* But not right now. Not this very minute.

WOMAN: Not this very minute. No, you're right. *(Pause)* Do you remember Sophie?

MAN: Of course I remember Sophie. Don't bring Sophie into this. This has nothing to do with Sophie.

WOMAN: Remember how she got so bad she couldn't even walk, so we carried her into the clinic?

MAN: Through the side door.

WOMAN: And remember how we we all sat on the floor around Sophie, and the doctor shaved Sophie's arm and inserted that long needle, and we said our good-byes and she took a breath and exhaled a deep sigh and she went to sleep and the doctor gave her another injection, and listened to her heart until it stopped, and then she was dead, but we just sat there on the floor around her and kept petting her, telling her how much we loved her, and we all cried, even the doctor, and then we all hugged each other and went to the Dairy Queen.

MAN: I remember. I had a Blizzard. A Tropical Blizzard.

(Pause)

WOMAN: So... why couldn't I go out like that?

MAN: Because you're a human being. Because veterinarians don't euthanize human beings. Because this isn't Switzerland. Because you are lying on a big, soft bed surrounded by people who love you, with hundreds of radios lined up all around you, thousands of radios from eBay with none of their parts missing, radios with miniature versions of Green Day tucked inside of them. Thousands of Billy Joe Armstrongs pop up out of the thousands of radios and join together in a tender, a cappella chorus of Time of Your Life. And you rise up out of your big, soft bed, and you dance, and dance, and dance until you are tired, so very tired that you want nothing more than to go to sleep. You are very, very sleepy. You have had enough. But your friend, the one who loves you so deeply, he says that the night is young, the party has just started, and it is not yet time to go home. So, you dance... and dance... and dance some more.

(Man sings softly to woman, as they dance)

It's something unpredictable But in the end it's right I hope you had the time of your life

It's something unpredictable

But in the end it's right

I hope you had the time of your life

It's something unpredictable

But in the end it's right

I hope you had the time of your life*

(They embrace)

(Child enters and addresses the audience)

CHILD: Though I am just a child, I have seen and heard many things. Some of them are true; they really happened. Others are merely figments of my digitally-saturated imagination, flashing across monitors, reflected in the retinas of concerned observers. *(Pause)* Dreams, nightmares, encrypted

105 Five-Minute Plays

mutations. Genetic shards of our shared subconscious. *(Pause)* This one is real because it's happening right now, before our very eyes.

(Lights fade)

*Good Riddance (Time of Your Life) c1990 by Billy Joe Armstrong, Mike Dirnt, and Tre Cool, Green Daze Music, Warner/Chappell Music, Inc.

Characters:

SAM: A young black man.

CODY: A young white man.

Both write for a successful fantasy TV show.

Setting: In an alley behind a TV studio. Near a dumpster.

> LIZZIE VIEH is a playwright and actor. Her full-length plays include *The Loneliest Number*, *Backwater Rising*, *Barrier Islands*, and *Wisconsin Death Trip*. Her work has been performed at the Samuel French Off-Off Broadway Festival, The Wild Project, Daryl Roth Theater, MTC Studios, The Kraine and The Brown/Trinity Graduate Program. MFA BrownTrinity, BA Brown University. www.lizzievieh.com

SAM and CODY are smoking cigarettes in an alley by a dumpster behind a TV studio.

SAM: *Rape-happy?*

CODY: I know.

SAM: Me??

CODY: I know.

SAM: I went to Sarah Lawrence! I took a class in feminist performance art!

CODY: It's ridiculous.

SAM: "Rape-happy." They're carrying signs that say "Rape-happy."

CODY: *Protesting.* With all the horrible shit in the world, they're protesting us. What we wrote for a stupid TV show.

SAM: Did we write a lot of rape scenes? Yes. Were they intentionally…I don't know…sensational…titillating…violent?

CODY: Of course they were violent, it's rape.

SAM: But it was part of the story, part of the world. And they didn't even talk to us about it. No discussion. Just —you're demoted.

CODY: How about a friendly, "Guys, lay off the rape scenes…"

SAM: It's not like I *love* writing rape scenes.

CODY: But if we're creating a medieval world, with knights, and warlords, and clashing armies… are we supposed to pretend that's not part of the equation? That women—

SAM: Their bodies were the *site* of conflict—

CODY: They were a commodity, a possession, a tool of warfare—

SAM: Rape was an everyday reality.

> *Pause.*

CODY: From executive story editors to staff writers.

SAM: I haven't been a staff writer in—

CODY: Two and a half years.

SAM: Both of us. "The dynamic duo."

CODY: Replaced by Sasha and Danielle, of all people.

CODY: And you know what just…*gets* me about the whole thing? If *they* write a rape scene…or a scene where a woman is abused…basically anything bad happening to a woman…will there be protests? Will people be *offended*?

SAM: Probably not.

CODY: And why's that?

SAM: 'Cause they're women.

CODY: Exactly! Is that fair? Because they actually *are* women, and because they might actually go *through* some of these types of suffering, hypothetically, that gives them…permission? Ownership? Privilege of speech?

SAM: Privilege of speech?

CODY: They have the privilege to write about certain topics. And we have been denied that privilege.

SAM: You feel…we've been silenced?

CODY: That's a dramatic way of putting it…but yes. I do.

> *Pause. SAM looks at CODY for a moment. He laughs a little.*

SAM: That's kinda funny. Coming from a white American man. Who is straight. And young. And rich. And able-bodied. You feel "silenced?" Welcome to the club. None of us want to be a member, but there's lots of us here.

CODY: Whoa…

SAM: What?

CODY: I don't get what just…A minute ago we were on the same side…

SAM: I guess it just occurred to me that you've never been through this before.

CODY: Through what?

SAM: Being rejected because of who you are.

> *Pause.*

CODY: That might be true. I'd have to think about it.

SAM: If you have to think about it, then it's true.

CODY: We're in the same boat. Audiences were *offended* by what we wrote. And I fear, it's not because of the *content,* but because of the *gender* of who wrote it. Doesn't that make you mad?

SAM: Am I mad I lost my job? Yes. Am I mad at the reasoning behind it? They might have a point…The identity of the writer affects how we feel about the content.

CODY: So we can only write about things we've directly experienced? That doesn't bode well for imagination.

SAM: If someone writes about suffering…a specific kind of suffering…I think it's difficult to accept from someone who has never been through it and never will.

    Pause.

CODY: So…I can't write about, say, American slavery.

SAM: Not from the slave's point of view.

CODY: And you can?

SAM: Yeah.

CODY: You've never been a slave.

SAM: Do you really want to go down that path?

CODY: We can't write about rape cause we're men. What's next? We can't write about war cause we've never fought a battle? Where—

SAM: Cody, just stop…

CODY: This affects you too, their signs out there? They're calling us The Penis Club!

SAM: Yeah, I have a penis. I'm also black and gay. So my club is different than yours. My tiny liberal arts college might have loved my blackness and gayness, but the rest of America? Not so much.

    Pause.

CODY: I better just shut up.

SAM: *(under his breath)* For the first time in history.

CODY: Just because I *am* a straight white guy doesn't mean I *stand* for all straight white guys.

SAM: I know how that feels. Believe me. I know.

> *Pause.*

CODY: I feel left behind.

SAM: *(shrugs)* Changing of the guards.

> *Longish pause. They smoke.*

CODY: I can't believe I'm smoking again.

SAM: It's the stress. With this job, it's eat or smoke. So you're either fat or you're… out here.

> *CODY looks around, peering behind the dumpster.*

CODY: I'm the glad the girls don't smoke out here. I need a place I can vent.

SAM: Don't worry. They smoke by the front door. They call this the rape dumpster.

Characters:

RAY: A god/barista, twenties, male.

THE ALARM CLOCK: A priest, any age, should be able to beatbox.

KATHY: A serpent, thirties, female

BETH: A goddess/librarian, twenties, female

Assorted demons, servants and dream women (can be accomplished by one or two or as many additional actors as needed.)
Setting: The evil darks of 4am/Ray's bedroom.

This five-minute epic uses the format of an ancient Egyptian passion play to tell the tale of Ray's desperate battle to get to sleep. *Materials needed to create this epic: a tambourine, a black sheet, and enthusiasm.*
NB- please feel free to adjust the details of Ray's neighborhood (in consultation with the playwright) so that the audience will recognize their own city.

> REINA HARDY is a playwright from Chicago. Her plays, which usually contain magic and sometimes contain science, have been seen across the country, including at Rorschach Theatre in DC, the Vortex in Austin, and the NNPN National New Play Showcase. She's been a Michener Fellow at UT Austin, winner of the KCACTF TYA Prize, finalist for the Terrence McNally Prize and the recipient of an Interact 20/20 Commission. Reina is the book writer for *Fanatical the Musical* (under development in England with The Stable), and is collaborating with Sky Candy on a devised circus show. She can make things happen with her mind. reinahardy.com

The Alarm Clock, priest-like, begins the play by rattling a tambourine, or crashing symbols.

ALARM CLOCK: The great god Ray's descent into the darkness of four a.m., and his combat with the night serpent. A play in eight acts. Prelude—the Invocation!

Cymbal crash.

Ray enters, raising his arms to the sky.

RAY: Lo, I am Ray, also called he who makes your latte in the morning. Liveth I in Edgewater, in a studio apartment located most convenient to the Starbucks in which I work. Lately I have been having some trouble getting to sleep.

Cymbal crash.

Night is become a dark kingdom through which I battle, tormented by the demon chorus of my own failures, and by the sinuous ghost of Kathy, this married woman I got involved with but am trying not to see anymore. Even the sight of my own bed is terrible to me, as it is a great beast with which I struggle.

Cymbal crash.

Lo, and so my sliding scale therapist hath proscribed that I establish specific bedtime rituals, to prepare me for my nightly battles, and help me to achieve sleep's sweet release.

Cymbal crash.

That helps me not!

ALARM CLOCK: Sorry. Act 1! 10 p.m. The great god Ray refrains from watching the Daily Show, as TV before bed is not conducive to sleep.

RAY: Goddamit. Everyone's going to be talking about it at work tomorrow.

ALARM CLOCK: Act 2! 10:30 p.m. The great god Ray cleans his teeth, in an action which represents the banishment of all ill words that linger in our mouths.

Servants rush on with toothbrush and floss. Brief ritual brushing.

RAY: I hath not dental insurance.

Ray spits.

ALARM CLOCK: Act 3! 10:45 p.m. The great god Ray arrays himself for battle.

Servants rush on with black sheet, covering Ray as he changes into pajamas.

RAY: The problem with trying to sleep is that, per definition, there are no distractions. At work, I achieve a zen busyness. Froth, pull, pour, pour, pump, call smile. After work you can see movies or talk to friends or get drunk. This will help you avoid thinking of how you lost your entire college scholarship and will have to work at a Starbucks for the rest of your life. Lo, the trouble is that eventually you have to try to sleep and between you and the nasty thoughts inside your head there is nothing. Nothing but pajamas.

The servants drop the sheet.

ALARM CLOCK: Act 4. 11p.m. The great God Ray enters the arena.

The servants place the sheet on the floor in front of Ray.

RAY: All right, motherfucker.

He lies down.

RAY: BRING IT!

The sheet (aided by the servants) jumps off the ground and swallows him up.

RAY: AUUUUUUGGGGGHHH!

ALARM CLOCK: Act 5. 1 a.m. The great God Ray lies very still, and counts women.

A series of women line up and jump over Ray, who counts them.

RAY: One, Two, Three.......

KATHY: (*jumping over Ray*) Oh, hi Ray.

RAY: Hi Kathy. I can see up your skirt.

KATHY: Oooohhhh naughty.

She starts to lower herself over him in a pornographic fashion. He sits up.

RAY: Please get off.

KATHY: Gladly.

RAY: No! I won't.

> *He grabs a phone and scares Kathy off with it.*

ALARM CLOCK: Act 6. 2 a.m. The great god Ray calls the wise goddess Beth, she who knows the locations of various books, in hope of counsel.

> *Ray makes the sound of a phone. Beth switches on a lamp, sleepily and answers the phone.*

BETH: Wha? Ray? Why're you calling me, it's like three in the morning.

RAY: It's—

ALARM CLOCK: 2:06 a.m.

RAY: 2:06. I can't sleep. The serpent Kathy invades my thoughts, and will not go away. She bought a caramel frap at my Starbucks this morning and looked like she was going to cry. In truth, I think she loves me. But wherefore can she not leave her husband?

BETH: Ok. Whither your balls, dude?

RAY: I know not.

BETH: Do you realize that you have called me, your ex-girlfriend, three times in this past fortnight, crying about this emotionally manipulative married woman? Lo, that is fucked up. Don't you have some higher power to turn to? Some kind of spiritual teaching?

RAY: I don't know.

BETH: I will say but three things in counsel: One—that girl is poison, and you have got to get her out of your head. Two—thine obsession is merely a marker of the many, many other things thou hast fucked up in your life. Three—don't fucking call me after midnight.

> *She hangs up and switches off her lamp.*

ALARM CLOCK: Act 7. 4 a.m. The Great God Ray battles the demons of insecurities, and the Kathy Serpent of his bed.

> *Cymbal crash. Ray, under the blanket, screams. Demons rush on, saying, variously:*

105 Five-Minute Plays

DEMONS: Diligence escapes you. Adulterer! Adulterer! You have fucked this up irrevocably. You will never be able to afford finishing college. No woman will ever love you fully. You're just a harem boy to her! You'll never be able to support a family. Can't you think of the children? You stupid kid. You can't even get to sleep. You can't solve any of your problems.

> *Hissing, they lift Ray and the sheet up vertically, tearing and tugging. Kathy enters. The demons fall silent, then Kathy and the demons hiss.*

ALARM CLOCK: Act 8! The great God Ray summons his own strength by chanting the names of his spiritual teachers.

RAY: BELL! BIV! DEVOE!

> *The Alarm Clock imitates the distinctive rhythmic hook from Bell Biv Devoe's "Poison," then starts to Beat Box.*

RAY: Girl I must warn you

I sense something strange in my mind

Situation is serious

Let's cure it 'cause we're running out of time

> *The demons, are surprised, intrigued. Then they start to bop their heads, and move, with the blanket, away from Ray.*

It's all so beautiful

Relationships they seem from the start

It's all so deadly

When love is not together from the heart

> *Ray has gained control of the demons and is circling the stage, driving Kathy upstage so that the blanket covers her from the audience's view.*

It's driving me out of my mind

That's why it's hard for me to find

Can't get it outta my head

Miss her, kiss her, love her—

ALARM CLOCK: Wrong move you're dead!

The demons whisk away the blanket. Kathy is gone. The demons dance and sing while covering Ray with the now friendly, pettable blanket.

DEMONS: That girl is poison

ALARM CLOCK: Never trust a big butt and smile.

DEMONS: (*softly*) That girl is poison.

ALARM CLOCK: (*softly, as a lullaby*) That girl is poison. Poison... poison.....

> *Ray sleeps. The demons creep away. After a moment, the Alarm clock makes the noise of static.*

ALARM CLOCK*: (imitating radio announcer.)* Good morning Chicago, it's 6 a.m., and that was Bell Biv Devoe, breaking it down for you early morning commuters. Going to be a beautiful morning out there, high of 75, windy, with clear skies....

> *During the above, Ray yawns, gets up, and shuffles off.*
> *LIGHTS OUT.*

Characters:

PROFESSOR: White male, forties to fifties

HOUSEKEEPER: Latina, twenties

Setting: An office.

DIANA BURBANO is a Colombian immigrant, Equity actress, playwright, and respected teaching artist at South Coast Repertory. She has created notable roles in world premieres at the Laguna Playhouse, South Coast Repertory and Center Theatre/Santa Barbara. Plays include *Picture me Rollin'* (featured at the 35 annual William Inge Festival/2016.) *Fabulous Monsters, Silueta* (about the Cuban artist Ana Mendieta) with Tom and Chris Shelton, and the TYA Shakespeare mash-up, *Caliban's Island. Libertadoras, Vamping* and *Linda* were written for the 365 Women a Year project. She directs, produces, writes and manages Sleep Till Noon Productions and the Gourmet Detective. Diana is one of the original members of the writers circle for Latino Theatre Association/Los Angeles. She is also a member of The Dramatists Guild and The Alliance of Los Angeles Playwrights. 50playwrights.org/2016/03/28/diana-burbano/newplayexchange.org/users/734/diana-burbano

A housekeeper is cleaning the inside of an office. A well-dressed man enters, sits at his desk and buries his face in his hands.

HOUSEKEEPER: Señor? Are you OK? *(She has a thick dialect.)*

PROFESSOR: I'm...I'm...

HOUSEKEEPER: Señor?

PROFESSOR: Yes, Tony?

HOUSEKEEPER: Tonali. Señor. They...they caught the man.

PROFESSOR: They did more than that. They shot him dead. Rounds per second...Per second? How is that possible.

HOUSEKEEPER: Military technology, Señor.

PROFESSOR: He was my student.

HOUSEKEEPER: I know.

PROFESSOR: He...was mentally ill.

HOUSEKEEPER: You would have to be to shoot people.

PROFESSOR: ...

HOUSEKEEPER: So many young people dead. I thought universidades were safe places.

PROFESSOR: They should be.

HOUSEKEEPER: My family was shot in Ciudad Juarez. But that was because of the drug dealers. And my father was the mayor.

PROFESSOR: …

HOUSEKEEPER: They thought they had shot me dead, but my blood mixed with my brothers, and I lay very still. So I lived.

PROFESSOR: Did you...How does it feel knowing you are supposed to be dead?

HOUSEKEEPER: You tell me, señor.

PROFESSOR: I...I don't know. I want to sleep.

HOUSEKEEPER: Thank god they caught him.

PROFESSOR: Macbeth hath murdered sleep.

HOUSEKEEPER: He must've been very rich, that young man, this school is expensive.

PROFESSOR: He was brilliant. He was on scholarship.

HOUSEKEEPER: Money doesn't buy happiness but it buys a lot of guns.

PROFESSOR: Tonali. He shot me. He shot at me, but the, I don't know, I don't know anything about guns, but it kept clicking.

HOUSEKEEPER: He forgot to reload.

PROFESSOR: He had another gun, a bigger one.

HOUSEKEEPER: Assault rifle. Automatic.

PROFESSOR: Yes.

HOUSEKEEPER: But he didn't use it on you?

PROFESSOR: I think he wanted to blow my head off with one shot.

HOUSEKEEPER: It's usually much messier than that. When they executed my father, it took several shots to blow off his head. How does it feel to be alive?

PROFESSOR: Like I want to die.

HOUSEKEEPER: But you lived.

PROFESSOR: A boy, a child, shot 14 people. There was no drug cartel. Nothing. Just the desire to do great, great harm.

HOUSEKEEPER: Then perhaps we should kill ourselves now and save fate the trouble.

PROFESSOR: I feel dead. I think I am dead.

HOUSEKEEPER: You are. The gun was loaded. You just refuse to accept it.

PROFESSOR: Are you dead?

HOUSEKEEPER: I don't know. I think so.

PROFESSOR: Why are you here?

HOUSEKEEPER: I'm cleaning your office.

PROFESSOR: Where are my students?

HOUSEKEEPER: They left.

PROFESSOR: Can you make my phone work?

HOUSEKEEPER: Why?

PROFESSOR: I need to tell my mother.

HOUSEKEEPER: She knows you're dead.

PROFESSOR: Was I arrogant?

HOUSEKEEPER: All North Americans are arrogant.

PROFESSOR: I...I never had children.

HOUSEKEEPER: Good. Then they can't mourn you.

PROFESSOR: Where do I go?

HOUSEKEEPER: I don't know. Do you believe in god?

PROFESSOR: No. Do you?

HOUSEKEEPER: Yes. It doesn't matter. We're stuck here.

PROFESSOR: I don't want to die.

HOUSEKEEPER: Too late. Help me clean the blood off the
    walls. You weren't greatly loved, or particularly admired.
    But you were a nice person. They're leaving teddy bears
    outside the door.

PROFESSOR: I don't deserve to be dead.

HOUSEKEEPER: Professor. None of us deserve to be alive.
    Help me clean.

SCORCHED EARTH TONIGHT

Colin Johnson

Characters:

JESS: Talk-show host in a prime post-apocalyptic time-slot / comes across as Charlie Rose but is, in fact, much closer to an insane rambling person on public access.

JAMIE: Jess' Mother / dressed as a sweet old lady / supportive and enabling of her beloved son / acts as his crowd control, holding up APPLAUSE and LAUGHTER signs.

WEINHARD BAIRDLAW: Talk show guest / target of Jess' aggressive quasi- journalism.

Note On Costumes:This being post-apocalyptic, the more tattered, torn and stained the better. Perhaps clothes that were once fancy.

Note On Audience Interaction: It could be possible for JESS to acknowledge whenever the audience reacts without prompt from JAMIE by appearing confused by the unplanned laughter.

COLIN JOHNSON is a Bay Area-based writer, director and filmmaker. His work has been featured up and down the West Coast and elsewhere by such groups as SF Shotz, SF Olympians, Playground, Theater Pub, Awesome Theatre, Actors Ensemble of Berkeley, Bay One Acts Festival, San Francisco Fringe Festival, Empire Theater Group (Spokane, WA), Wildclaw Theater (Chicago, IL) and numerous film festivals, including the 2014 Comic-Con International Independent Film Festival, with his multi-media production entity BattleStache Studios. Recently, the Bay Area Critics Circle voted his original play, *The Night Before*, Best Script and Best Overall Production at the 2015 TAPAS Short Play Festival. Aside from theater and film, Colin also co-wrote a graphic novel entitled *Daomu* for Image Comics and Magnetic Press. He lives in Berkeley, CA.

Scorched Earth Tonight is one of the hundreds of plays written and performed as part of SHOTZ, a "theatrical pressure cooker" that presents all-new short plays each month.youtube.com/user/BattleStacheStudio/videos

At rise there are 2 chairs CENTER STAGE, facing them-
selves in an interview set-up. JESS enters.

JESS: Hello everyone. Thank you. Tonight's episode is very special, extremely critical. I've been getting an overwhelming push from our viewers to address the immediate concerns facing us and our fair community. And, although certain powers-that-be would prefer I simply gloss over these hot-button issues and continue to focus on the time before and the carefree excess we wallowed in, I feel it is my duty as a journalist and as a sound-minded homosapien to give the people what they want. Thank you, thank you, no need to clap, thank you.

He waits for a non-existent clap – or maybe people do clap, at which point he gets visibly annoyed that it took them so long to clap.

What was that? Oh, yes, I am brave. Okay, then, we have a very special guest tonight. Someone on the cutting edge of secret underground research who may perhaps hold the key to our salvation. Ladies and gentlemen, please welcome—

(he looks offstage, impatiently)

I said – please welcome…

JAMIE comes scurrying onstage, carrying an APPLAUSE SIGN.

JESS: Please welcome … DR. WEINHARD BAIRDLAW!

JAMIE holds up APPLAUSE SIGN. People applaud, maybe.

BAIRDLAW enters, waving at crowd. He shakes hands with JESS, who protects his hand with a LARGE TOWEL, and they sit down.

JAMIE exits.

JESS: Thank you for joining us.

BAIRDLAW: Absolutely, Jess—

JESS: Please, no names. Now, Dr. Weinhard Bairdlaw, to start, why don't you tell us all – who you're wearing.

BAIRDLAW: Well, I found this jacket on the side of the scorched turnpike. It was melted into the asphalt, but I managed to pull it free. The tag on the back says MILLER, O POSITIVE.

JESS: Great designer. What about that hat?

BAIRDLAW: I'm not wearing a hat.

JESS: Oh, I'm sorry. That must be your hair. *(He looks around, waiting for an audience reaction, impatient beat.)* Mom!

JAMIE: *(enters)* Yes, dear?

JESS: I made a joke.

> *JAMIE holds up a sign that reads LAUGH. Laughter, maybe.*

JESS: Yes, thank you, thank you. In all seriousness, though, Doctor, tell me about what secret life-saving items you're keeping from us deep underground. Such as a cure for the deadly Vitamin B12 Famine?

BAIRDLAW: Right. The cure for that would be eating meat.

JESS: Ummm, I'm vegan.

BAIRDLAW: Vegetables don't exist anymore—

JESS: What about protection from the bands of roving feral chihuahuas?

BAIRDLAW: Maybe build a retaining wall, like 3 feet high? That should work.

JESS: WHAT ARE YOU KEEPING FROM US?!

> *JAMIE holds up LAUGHTER SIGN.*

JESS: Mom! No, that wasn't a joke! I was doing guerilla journalism.

JAMIE: I'm sorry, dear, you raised your voice. I got excited.

JESS: Mom, I'm in the middle of the most important interview of my frikkin' life!

JAMIE: You're a tremendous interviewer, booboo. But don't you dare curse upon the cursed earth.

JESS: Mom, I'm 35! I can say frikkin' if I want!

JAMIE: And you could have been anything! You could have been an ash sweeper, you could have been one of those fancy urine-purifiers, they get wonderful benefits, and make terrific, stable breeders!

JESS: I'm a crusader for truth!

JAMIE holds up the LAUGHTER SIGN. Laughter.

JESS: MOM! *(Beat.)* Dr. Bairdlaw, what of the rumblings of an untapped fresh water source underground?

BAIRDLAW: That's just a rumor.

JESS: Reallllllly? Because I mounted an in-depth investigation and discovered such a body of water does, in fact, exist, and it's directly beneath our feet. And it tastes terrible!

BAIRDLAW: I believe you discovered the sewers. And, actually, that would explain the smell.

JESS: Dr. Weinhard Bairdlaw, what can we do to keep alive, and more specifically, what can we do to not give in to the crushing, sun-blasted hopelessness that haunts our every waking moment?

BAIRDLAW: Well, we must work together, we must reproduce at reckless rates, we must limit physical activity and we must regulate misinformation. For instance, the people who attempt to store water in their backs, the factions who have taken to worshipping camels, every single one of them die from cutting a hole in their back. And they're doing it by the hundreds.

JESS: Sometimes faith is unshakable.

BAIRDLAW: So is stupidity.

JAMIE enters with APPLAUSE SIGN. Applause.

JESS: No, do not applaud him! He is the enemy!

JAMIE: No, sugardoodle, he is not the enemy. He's our friend. He wants to help.

JESS: Mom, you don't know what you're talking about—

JAMIE: Excuse me? I raised you all by myself in the wake of a catastrophic solar flare that reset civilization and left us foraging like bloodthirsty Chihuahuas! You show me some respect!

BAIRDLAW: Respect your mother.

JESS: Where is your secret scientific installation, Doctor?!

BAIRDLAW: There isn't one! I'm a general physician! My office is a cardboard box under the bridge!

JESS: Liar! Answer me! My viewers have a right to know!

BAIRDLAW: What viewers? I look into the audience and all I see are charcoal faces drawn on a cement wall.

JESS: They're real! My mom said so! Right, Mom?

JAMIE: Actually, honeyboo, I made it all up. I couldn't stand you being down here by yourself and being so sad—it just broke my heart—so I did what I had to do to keep the spirits up. I even recorded the fake laugh track for you. You had fun, though, didn't you, sweetie?

BAIRDLAW: You, ma'am, are an enabler.

JAMIE: Oh yeah? Then get out of my house! My baby deserves to be happy, apocalypse or no!

BAIRDLAW: Fine. I'm late for distributing sun lotion to the wealthy 1%, anyway. Oh wait—

JESS: I knew it! He was working in secret to maintain the corrupted status-quo! This is discrimination and, if there were laws left, it would be ILLEGAL!

BAIRDLAW: Whatever. This is so beneath me. I don't care if your mom did bribe me with ice cubes. I'm outta here.

She raises APPLAUSE SIGN as DR. BAIRDLAW leaves.

BAIRDLAW: And another thing, you soiled plebians…

The sound of RAVENOUS CHIHUAHUAS cut him off! They grab DR. BAIRDLAW offstage and start dragging him away.

BAIRDLAW: No! The Chihuahuas! They got in! Oh sweet Jesus, they're nibbling me!

He's dragged off.

JAMIE holds up LAUGHTER sign. RECORDING: JAMIE LAUGHING HARD.

JESS: Oh, I hear it now. I love you, Mom. You're the best.

JAMIE: I love you, too, doodypoo. Now finish your program and come upstairs for some canned peaches and tumbleweed.

JESS: My favorite! *(To audience.)* And that concludes our broadcast evening. You came for the truth, you stayed for the

Chihuahua attacks. Until next time, I'm Jess Thomas, telling you: It's not the end, it's only the beginning. Good night, and good luck.

Lights out.

105 Five-Minute Plays

SHE SPIDER

Andrea Lepcio

Characters:

SADA

ROMI

ANDREA LEPCIO is best known for *Looking for the Pony*, a finalist for the Dramatists Guild Hull-Warriner Award and for the NEA Outstanding New American Play Award. It was presented in a "Rolling World Premiere" Off-Broadway at Vital Theatre Company in New York and Synchronicity Performance Group in Atlanta and subsequent productions. She is currently working on a EST/Sloan-commissioned play about climate change, and a new musical, *Somebody Please Tell Me Who I Am* with songwriter Tina DeVaron. Additional Plays and musicals under development include *Strait of Gibraltar* (Geva Theatre Center), *Central Avenue Breakdown* (FwdTheatre), *The Gold* (NYMF) and *Lf&Tms* (Music Theatre Factory). Andrea is a member of the Dramatists Guild, was a Dramatists Guild Fellow and served as the Dramatists Guild Fellows Program Director for ten years. M.F.A. in Dramatic Writing, Carnegie Mellon University. B.A. Human Ecology, College of the Atlantic. She lives in Maine, which means she travels often. lepcio@gmail.com andrealepcio.com

At Rise: SADA sits. ROMI enters. Both have the requisite Starbucks cup. ROMI carries the little bag with some sort of pastry item and an enormous pocket book over her shoulder. SADA is comfortably settled waiting for ROMI. ROMI, despite all she is carrying, is actively adjusting her thong.

ROMI: My thong is driving me nuts.

SADA: Sorry.

ROMI: Help.

SADA: How am I supposed to...?

ROMI: I miss granny panties.

SADA: So wear them. *(enough with the underwear)* If you're uncomfortable.

ROMI: To be female is to be uncomfortable.

SADA: It doesn't have to be.

ROMI: You like high heels.

SADA: I like comfortable high heels.

ROMI: You just have lucky feet. You're just one of those women. Lucky. I have unlucky feet. Horrible. I can barely stand up in most of my shoes never mind walk. Fuck.

ROMI responds to her vibrating Blackberry. She talks as she types her response. This can happen throughout.

ROMI: *(to phone)* Die bitch!

(to SADA)

Fucking endless. This bitch in HR. Edie West. Wait till I tell you. Okay. Remember that guy from the cloud company? Josh Steiger. Kind of chubby, but like with this freakish charisma? Why are you acting like you don't remember?

SADA: I remember.

ROMI: The fattest guy I ever wanted to fuck. My boss, Dick Williams, sent me to that training in Norfolk. Cute sailors. Dismal town. But every time I have to go to get trained, is it ever San Francisco or Monterey or even Austin? Great bars, Austin. Never mind it's like our third cloud. Cumulus—that one was a hit. For like three days. JAG Cloud—Disaster.

105 Five-Minute Plays

And now. File Cloud. So I fly to Norfolk, stay in a second rate Marriott, flirt with sailors. And then I meet Josh Steiger who at first I'm like fat and go back to the sailor bar, but by the third day I'm like take me, I'm yours. Except not really because he didn't have a clue.

Ringing iPhone. ROMI digs in her vast bag. Huge. The phone rings and rings. ROMI digs and digs and talks.

ROMI: Which was cool, because by then, I'm thinking this isn't a one night stand guy, this is a introduce to your parents, do whatever it takes to land guy. Ignore. Mom.

ROMI hits ignore. She's now dealing with two cellphones, the coffee and the pastry. Get the picture. Continue.

ROMI: Want some? Reduced fat banana chocolate chip cake. Kind of delish. Take it!

SADA: I'm good.

ROMI takes a bite.

ROMI: So I come back from the training and I rave to Dick Williams about File Cloud and I rave about Josh Steiger and I get everyone trained. And everyone's happy. And then this bitch from HR. Edie West. Reads some article in Huffington Post and decides HR is vulnerable because File Cloud isn't "secure" enough to hold everyone's social security numbers and addresses and mother's maiden name or whatever and they need to keep everything on their very own server and they are refusing to use File Cloud and Dick Williams is like you go down there and you get them to use the cloud. And I'm like GENIUS. Because this is the perfect excuse to spend more time with Josh Steiger. So I convince Dick Williams to sign up for File Cloud consulting which means Josh Steiger comes to our offices and explains it to HR bitch. I mean I hate HR bitch, but in this moment. Except wait. Wait. Wait. What are you doing?

SADA: Nothing. Waiting.

ROMI: You didn't say anything.

SADA: You were talking.

ROMI: Ohmygod.

SADA: What? What happened next? I'm dying to know.

ROMI: Okay, so. First. Edie West always wears the extremist fuck me pumps. Speaking of heels. So I have to wear my highest when I introduce her to Josh Steiger and she takes one look at him and I'm like holy shit she sees it too. He's like the Ryan Gosling of fat guys and she's working her heels and I'm working my heels and he's totally focused on trying to make a cloud within a cloud to keep her data safe from hackers and I'm trying to figure out how to keep Josh Steiger safe from Edie West. And she's trying to keep him from me. It is on. The two of us eyeball to eyeball over his head. He's short. I told you that. But epic sexy. She's like thanks, Romi, I'm sure you're busy with the big cloud, you can leave Josh and I to figure out HR cloud and I'm like, no, Edie, I'm responsible for all of the clouds and I want to make sure you really get the cloud you need. And Josh goes, done. He is amazingly brilliant. And Edie West is like this is fantastic we should grab a drink and I'm like I need to in-troduce Josh to Dick Williams and he's like great, right, and then he turns to Edie. Josh Steiger turns to Edie and says maybe we could meet up later. Like that. And she's smiling and he's smiling this insipid smile.

SADA: Time's up.

ROMI: Wait. What?

SADA: Just enough, okay?

ROMI: Enough what?

SADA: Of Josh and Edie and you and the cloud.

ROMI: Rude. I'm heartbroken.

SADA: Again.

ROMI: What?

SADA: It's just. I know you are heartbroken, but I just can't. I don't want to talk about what happened and people who aren't here.

ROMI: What else is there to talk about?

SADA: I don't know. Now. Nothing. The sun. An idea. That tree.

ROMI: That tree is sad. That tree is nearly dead.

SADA: I think it's alive.

ROMI: Dead. So Dead. And I want to talk about you and who ever probably didn't break your heart, you broke his. And ohmygod you so hijacked me. I wanted to talk about Josh.

SADA: I need to go.

ROMI: What?

SADA: I'm sorry.

ROMI: You're sorry, you need to go?

SADA: I can't keep doing this.

ROMI: I got Josh fired today. Him. His cloud. The whole thing. Poof.

SADA: I don't want to know. I can't spend my days listening to you talk about everything that happened to you. I don't want to spend my days telling you everything that happened to me. I want to talk about the tree. Or not talk at all. I want to drink coffee and think about the coffee. I want to pay attention to what's around me.

ROMI: Okay, you're like freak show Sada. I want Sada Sada.

SADA: This is me.

ROMI: Go away and come back.

SADA: No. Romi, I love you. I'm sorry. But, I'm going to go away and I'm not going to come back.

> *SADA exits.*

> *ROMI tosses her coffee cup, tosses her crumpled pastry bag. Adjusts her thong. Sits. Blackberry buzzes. IPhone buzzes. ROMI sits.*

Characters:

JEANNE

TANAKA

Setting: A remote, deserted island.

ADAM KRAAR's plays include *Alternating Currents* (The Working Theatre), *Wild Terrain* (EST Marathon of One-Act Plays), *Empire of the Trees* (NY Innovative Theatre Awards nominee, Outstanding New Script), *New World Rhapsody* (Manhattan Theatre Club commission), *The Spirit House* (premiered at Performance Network) and *Freedom High* (Queens Theatre in the Park.)

His work has been produced and/or developed by Primary Stages, N.Y. Stage & Film, Public Theatre, The New Group and many others. His plays appear in five Best American Short Plays anthologies, and his awards include the Bogliasco Fellowship, Sewanee Writers' Conference Fellowship, Inge Center Residency, and Manhattan Theatre Club Fellowship. Member of Ensemble Studio Theatre; Affiliated Writer, The Playwrights' Center.

Adam grew up in India, Thailand, Singapore and the U.S. He earned an M.F.A. at Columbia University, taught playwriting at the University of Rochester and Adelphi University, and lives in Brooklyn with his wife, Karen.
Agent: Elaine Devlin edevlinlit@aol.com adamkraar. com

(The beach, on a remote island. There is no sand, only stones. TANAKA pantomimes building a sandcastle. Then JEANNE enters.)

JEANNE: What do you think you're doing?

TANAKA: I am building a sandcastle.

JEANNE: Have you lost your friggin' mind?

TANAKA: Look. This is the tower where the princess lives. I have built a special balcony, so the princess can watch the rising of the morning star.

JEANNE: Tanaka, for God's sake: for once in your life, could you try to be real?

TANAKA: I know this is very challenging and unpleasant for you.

JEANNE: Why do the sand flies only bite me?

TANAKA: It is better if you try not to scratch.

JEANNE: That's easy for you to say.

TANAKA: I have cooled this bottle in the ocean. Put it on the bites.

JEANNE: *(taking the bottle and putting it on her bites)* You coulda grabbed a roll of toilet paper, but no, you had rescue a bottle of saki.

TANAKA: We will drink it at sunset, no? ...The roar of the ocean will mingle—

JEANNE: Spare me—please.

(Pause. TANAKA goes back to "building" his sandcastle.)

JEANNE: Would you stop that. There's no sand on this whole god-forsaken island!

(TANAKA stops building.)

JEANNE: And that so-called luxury yacht you bought?

TANAKA: I deeply regret certain errors of judgment.

(This strikes JEANNE as so absurd that she laughs, not very kindly.)

TANAKA: They told me it was top of the line. Clipper class, crafted from Portuguese cork, extremely yare.

JEANNE: When you saw that patch, the size of your big head, didn't you think—?

Do you ever think? ..."Yare"!

TANAKA: You will admit, till we passed Easter Island, the vessel was quite yare.

JEANNE: Look: there's part of the deck, sticking out of that reef.

TANAKA: Ah! Perhaps I can use that to support the main tower.

(Referring to his invisible sandcastle.)

JEANNE: We are stuck here, with nothing to eat but coconuts.

TANAKA: If you like, you can nibble on my ear.

JEANNE: *(exasperated:)* Ahhh!

(After a moment, TANAKA resumes shaping the castle.)

JEANNE: You know what my mother told me? If I kept going out with you, I'd lose my way. Ha! – I'm sorry, Mom! ...Coconuts! Coconut milk! Coconut tooth brush! Sick and tired of coo coo coo coo coconuts!

TANAKA: At the masked ball, they will serve us sushi.

(JEANNE stares at him a moment, then for several seconds angrily kicks down the invisible castle.)

TANAKA: Stop! Please! What are you doing?

JEANNE: ...I'm going to the other side, see if I can find some shellfish.

TANAKA: You ruined your tower....The front gate. The ballroom!

(pause)

JEANNE: Come on, Tanaka. Aren't you hungry?

TANAKA: It was so beautiful. The balcony defied gravity! And the ballroom was a circle of dreams. I was going to climb up the tower, on to your balcony, and then, as the sun slipped beneath the waves...

JEANNE: *(in spite of herself; somewhat crankily)* What?

TANAKA: We were going to dance in the ballroom. Spin and spin, like a star slowly rising.

(Admitting that the ballroom is gone.)

...Ha.

JEANNE: ...I'm sorry.

TANAKA: No. You have every right—

JEANNE: It's just, you sometimes drive me nuts. Like these sand flies! Agh!

(TANAKA takes the bottle and puts it on her new itch.)

JEANNE: Jeezus! Agh!...That helps, thanks.....I'm sorry about your "castle."

TANAKA: I have so much to learn. And I don't know if I want to learn it.

JEANNE: Well...

TANAKA: I so wanted to see you in your evening gown, glowing like the morning star.

JEANNE: Tanaka...

TANAKA: It was...so...

JEANNE: Yes, it was.

TANAKA: You mean...you saw it?

JEANNE: No. But, thank you for trying.

TANAKA: Well. It's gone now. I know it was never really there....Let's go to the other side. I will kill the sand flies, and hunt for shellfish. And from the old deck I will build us a real roof. I know what is necessary. And I can do it.

(pause)

JEANNE: First, would you take me to the ballroom?

TANAKA:...Are you sure?

(JEANNE nods. TANAKA leads her into an imaginary ballroom.)

TANAKA: What do you think?

JEANNE: Awesome. The ceiling is big as the sky. And they're playing our song.

(JEANNE lifts one of her arms, inviting him. THEY dance.)

SHOT! in the Name of Love
Carol M. Rice

Characters:

    GERALD: Middle-aged, arm in a sling.

    TOM: Slightly older.

Setting: An office breakroom.

> CAROL M. RICE is a playwright, director, actor, and producer. She has an MA in Drama (Playwriting Emphasis) from Texas Woman's University. Her plays *Murder at the Orient Burlesque* (which received a Column Award Nomination) and *Around the World in 80 Days* have been produced by Rover Dramawerks. Her melodrama, *The Belle of West Texas*, has been presented by McKinney Repertory Theatre and Mesquite Community Theatre, and it is published by Brooklyn Publishers. She has had plays produced in five states, and her most produced 10-minute play, *The Couch*, has been seen in theatres all over Texas. She has several plays published through Next Stage Press, available on Amazon.com. Carol is a proud member of the Dramatists Guild and 365 Women A Year, an international playwriting consortium devoted to writing plays about women from history. Carol has also directed many plays and musicals, including several new works, such as The Cupcake Conspiracy, Written in Time, and Silver Screen Slayer. roverdramawerks.com

At rise: Tom is making himself some coffee. Gerald enters.

TOM: Ah, good morning, Gerald.

GERALD: Morning, Tom.

TOM: How was your weekend? Catch the game?

GERALD: Part of it. The wife shot me during the third quarter.

TOM: That why your arm's in a sling?

GERALD: Yeah.

TOM: Good thing she's not a very good shot.

GERALD: Yeah.

> *(pause)*

So, Tom, should I be worried about this?

TOM: About what?

GERALD: About Gina shooting me on Saturday.

TOM: Oh, I don't think so. Happens in most good marriages.

GERALD: Did...did it happen to you?

TOM: Oh, sure. Linda was just fed up and she went to my closet and got the shotgun....

GERALD: Shotgun? Whoa. Gina just had a pistol.

TOM: Oh, you were lucky. Of course, shooting a shotgun's a little harder for a novice. Linda barely nicked my arm.

> *(showing him his arm)*

You can still make out the scar.

GERALD: Huh. Mine's going to be a bit bigger than that.

TOM: Is it going to affect your golf swing?

GERALD: I don't think so.

TOM: Oh, then you're fine! Nothing to worry about.

GERALD: But...but Gina tried to SHOOT me!

TOM: Yes?

GERALD: And that's not a cause for concern?

TOM: Not at all, my boy. Happens in the best of marriages.

(confidentially)

As a matter of fact, it livened ours right up!

GERALD: What?!

TOM: Face it. All marriages go through a little turmoil now and then, and most wives eventually take a shot at their husbands. There's nothing we can do about it except hope they don't mortally wound us. I feel sorry for those blokes who take their wives hunting or to the shooting range with them. Poor guys don't stand a chance.

GERALD: Do you know anyone who...?

TOM: Who died? Oh, sure. Remember Jeff in Accounting?

GERALD: Yeah, I think so.

TOM: Kenny in Receiving?

GERALD: Um....

TOM: James Dalton, the company's VP of Marketing?

GERALD: What? Really?

TOM: And scads more who were wounded pretty badly. You should be feeling pretty good right about now with just your arm in a sling.

GERALD: I had no idea this was so common!

TOM: Face it, Gerald. Would you want to be married to you?

GERALD: Well...I hadn't really thought of it that way.

TOM: Your wife, like mine—like all wives, really—just needed to blow off some steam. Shootings like yours happen all the time in happy marriages. You just have to get up, brush yourself off, and get on with the next phase of things. If your shooting goes anything like mine did, I can guarantee you, you won't be disappointed.

GERALD: Well, if you say so.

TOM: You don't believe me, do you? Tell me, Gerald. What did your wife do after she shot you?

GERALD: Well, she left the house for a while and came back wearing another blouse.

TOM: Probably went to a friend's and discovered there were

blood splatters. And?

GERALD: And what?

TOM: What happened next?

GERALD: She, uh, brought me a scone and some coffee.

TOM: See? There you go. It's all going to be fine, Gerald. Trust me on this.

GERALD: If you say so.

TOM: *(glancing at his watch)* Oh, hey! We'd better hustle if we're going to make the 10:00 meeting. Got your coffee?

GERALD: Yeah, but...

TOM: But what?

GERALD: What am I supposed to tell people about...

(moving his injured arm up and down)

...YOU know?

TOM: Just tell them your wife shot you. They'll understand.

(They both exit with their coffee.)

BLACKOUT

SISTERS

Maria Filimon, Adam Kraar and Tasnim Mansur

Characters:

RANI: twenty-three

MALLIKA: nineteen

Both characters are immigrants from a South Asian country.
Setting: A subway car in New York City. The present.

MARIA FILIMON is a Romanian passionate for creative art. She studied Advertising in New York and completed various acting classes both in Romania and the USA. Currently, she is putting her experience and passion to work leading one of the departments of a famous book store in Romania. In her spare time she loves to paint, travel, meet new people and learn about other countries' cultures.

ADAM KRAAR's plays include *Alternating Currents* (The Working Theatre), *Wild Terrain* (EST Marathon of One-Act Plays), *Empire of the Trees* (NY Innovative Theatre Awards nominee, Outstanding New Script), *New World Rhapsody* (Manhattan Theatre Club commission), *The Spirit House* (premiered at Performance Network) and *Freedom High* (Queens Theatre in the Park.)

His work has been produced and/or developed by Primary Stages, N.Y. Stage & Film, Public Theatre, The New Group and many others. His plays appear in five Best American Short Plays anthologies, and his awards include the Bogliasco Fellowship, Sewanee Writers' Conference Fellowship, Inge Center Residency, and Manhattan Theatre Club Fellowship. Member of Ensemble Studio Theatre; Affiliated Writer, The Playwrights' Center.

Adam grew up in India, Thailand, Singapore and the U.S. He earned an M.F.A. at Columbia University, taught playwriting at the University of Rochester and Adelphi University, and lives in Brooklyn with his

wife, Karen. Agent:Elaine Devlin edevlinlit@aol.com
adamkraar.com

TASNIM MANSUR was born in Bangladesh and her
parents moved to New York City when she was 6 years
old. She is your average New Yorker at heart: she walks
fast and drives as if in a race. Currently, she is working at American Express as an Analyst. She's somehow
landed in the world of finance, but always had a passion
for literature and arts. She graduated from NYIT in
2009 with a B.A. in Communication Arts. Since gradu-
ation, she's been fortunate enough to travel quite a
bit. She loves traveling to unknown little towns, eating
good food, and meeting people of all sorts of different
backgrounds and cultures.

(Two sisters, RANI and MALLIKA, get on a subway train. RANI sits down, takes out her date book, and tries to re-plan her day. MALLIKA hesitantly sit down near her, but not next to her.)

MALLIKA: Rani—

RANI: I don't want to hear it.

(Pause.)

MALLIKA: I just—

RANI: (*With finality.*) Mallika: you don't want to talk to me right now.

MALLIKA: I just want to say, I'm sorry. Okay?

(RANI shakes her head and goes back to her date book.)

...I'm sorry I messed up your day.

(RANI ignores her.)

...What do you want me to do?

RANI: I want not to hear your voice. If I never have to hear your voice again, that's what I want.

MALLIKA: Could I please just explain—?

RANI: No!

(Long pause. MALLIKA tries to lighten up the situation.)

MALLIKA: (*In a silly voice.*) ...Wazzup?

(RANI, appalled, moves to another seat.)

You almost laughed. Admit it. *Wazzup?!*

RANI: Leave me the hell alone.

MALLIKA: You said hell.

RANI: One more word, Lika, I guarantee you.

(MALLIKA goes to a different part of the train and sits down. She is trying to give her sister space, but she's upset. To take her mind off things, she goes for her cell phone. She can't find it. She gets more upset. She goes back to RANI.)

MALLIKA: We have to go back.

RANI: What?

MALLIKA: The police took my phone….They did! I had it
    when they...and now it's gone. We have to go back.

RANI: You go back. Get used to jail.

MALLIKA: Rani!

RANI: I'm through.

MALLIKA: I was just trying them on—You know I don't like
    sapphires—But these had a great setting, so I wanted to
    see—

RANI: Do you really believe yourself?

MALLIKA: —how that kind of setting would look, 'cause you
    know I have small ears, right?

RANI: And you forgot to take them off?

MALLIKA: Yes.

RANI: Do you know what would happen if you did this back
    home?

MALLIKA: They don't have earrings like that back home.

(RANI, beyond exasperated, says nothing.)

    ...They took my phone.

RANI: The police did not take your phone….You probably left
    it at a club, or some man's apartment. Always leaving things
    behind.

MALLIKA: I swear to you—

RANI: Don't. Save it for the judge….Now would you please
    leave me alone, like for the rest of my life?

*(RANI takes out her date book and tries to organize her
    day.)*

CONDUCTOR'S VOICE: Stop is West 4th Street. Change here
    for the A express and the F and D trains downstairs…. Next
    stop, 14th Street.

(MALLIKA suddenly throws her arms around RANI.)

MALLIKA: ...Rani! It was horrible! They were so mean!

RANI: What do you expect?

MALLIKA: You don't know! This woman, in the jail, tried to

put her hands all over me. And the other ones, did nothing. They just laughed. And the police, the police weren't even there.

RANI: (*Concerned.*) Are you…?

MALLIKA: (*Moves out of the hug.*) It was really, really horrible. I know I'm a pain in your neck, but you have to understand, I'm really …

> (*Beat.*)

I hate this country. I hate my job, I hate the people, I hate our tiny, tiny apartment—

RANI: Then maybe—

MALLIKA: I won't go back! I hate it there, too. Yes! I hate my life. You're the good one and I'm the fucked-up one….I'm sorry. I'm sorry.

> (*MALLIKA cries. Pause.*)

RANI: Mallika...Hey...Do you know how much sleep I lose because of you? Something has to change, radically. Maybe you're better off going home.

MALLIKA: No!

RANI: ...Dad is crazy about you. He doesn't show it, but when he calls, the first thing he always asks me: "How's Mallika?" Of course, he asks me if you're wearing the right clothes and doing your work, but you know the real reason he's crazy about you?... Because you make him laugh.

MALLIKA: He never laughs at me.

RANI: He hides it. But I've seen him. You're the only one.

MALLIKA: …Are you gonna tell him what happened?

RANI: I don't know. I should! Maybe I will.

> (*Pause: MALLIKA looks at RANI. After a while, RANI takes out a cell phone and shows it to MALLIKA.*)

MALLIKA: You…?

RANI: You cannot be taking things, and leaving things behind, and turning my life…

MALLIKA: I swear!

105 Five-Minute Plays

RANI: Don't swear.

> *(RANI gives her the cell phone. MALLIKA impulsively hugs her.)*

RANI: Okay. Okay.

> *(Pries MALLIKA off her.)*

Now, I have to go to work. And you…We'll decide tonight. You'll be there, right?

> *(MALLIKA nods.)*

CONDUCTOR'S VOICE:14th Street. Change here for the L.

> *(RANI looks at MALLIKA for a moment, then gets up.)*

RANI: I'll see you tonight.

> *(RANI exits. MALLIKA looks at her as she leaves. Suddenly, MALLIKA gets up.)*

MALLIKA: Rani! Wait!

> *(Calling after her.)*

Thank you!

> *(MALLIKA, not sure if she heard her, runs off after RANI.)*

Characters:

    WOMAN

    MAN

Setting: The deck of a house in the Hollywood Hills.

> ALEX DREMANN is a playwriting graduate of USC and is the producing artistic director of Secret Room Theatre in Philadelphia. Full-length productions include: *Split Pea Pod* (The Brick Playhouse), *Postcoital Variations* (Philadelphia Theatre Workshop) and *The :nv:s:ble Play* (Madlab Theatre & Theatre of NOTE). Evenings of his collected short plays include: *Slap Happy* (Madlab Theatre, Columbus, OH), *Bipolar by Thursday* (Theatre Neo, Los Angeles, CA) and *B-Sides, Rarities and Unreleased Tracks* (City Theatre, Wilmington, DE). He has had over 300 productions of his short plays including *On the Porch One Crisp Spring Morning* which was produced at City Theatre's Summer Shorts and then went on to be produced as a Heideman finalist at the Actors Theatre of Louisville in the Humana Festival and published both in *The Humana Festival 2009: The Complete Plays* and *Great Short Comedies: Volume 4* from PlayScripts Publishing. alexdremann.com

(MAN is on a deck chair. WOMAN approaches.)

WOMAN: I just cut the demo for "I'm Having an Affair, Do You Care?"

MAN: Do I care you cut a demo, or do I care you're having an affair?

WOMAN: That's the name of the song: "I'm Having an Affair, Do You Care?"

MAN: When did you write that?

WOMAN: Thursday.

MAN: This past Thursday?

WOMAN: Yes, why?

MAN: The night you "slept at the studio?"

WOMAN: Don't say it like that.

MAN: Like what?

WOMAN: Like it's in quotes. I slept at the studio, not "slept at the studio."

MAN: You're awfully defensive.

WOMAN: You're awfully accusatory.

MAN: Do I have reason to be accusatory?

WOMAN: That question is accusatory.

MAN: And that statement is defensive. Do you have reason to be defensive?

WOMAN: Yes, because I'm being accused!

MAN: Are you having an affair?

WOMAN: Yes, but that's not the point. The point is you've unfairly accused me and I don't appreciate it.

MAN: You're having an affair and the *accusation*, the accusation of the *truth*, is unfair?

WOMAN: Exactly.

MAN: But you just stood here and lied to me.

WOMAN: It's that exact tone I'm objecting to.

MAN: You did "sleep at the studio," in quotes, didn't you?

WOMAN: No, I slept at the studio!

MAN: You're sleeping with *another man.*

WOMAN: Yes, but not this past Thursday!

MAN: AH!

WOMAN: I don't feel I deserve this kind of treatment. I think you owe me an apology.

MAN: You *adulterated* ALL OVER me!

WOMAN: It was work. I need inspiration for my music.

MAN: Oh, so now it's my fault "Do Me or Lose Me" only sold half a million copies.

WOMAN: You stopped "doing" me.

MAN: Because you stopped wanting me!

WOMAN: Well, you started *accusing.*

MAN: And you started being defensive all the time.

WOMAN: It was a defense mechanism.

MAN: *(rhetorically)* What do think the accusations were?

WOMAN: You don't love me anymore.

MAN: No, I do, it's you who doesn't love me.

WOMAN: No, I do, but just because I love you doesn't mean I have to take this!

MAN: And just because I love *you* doesn't mean I have to take it either!

WOMAN: Good! Then let's make passionate love *right now* and start again!

MAN: Fine!

(They kiss immediately, violently. End of scene.)

Characters:

CARTER: A boy in his teens.

JESSAMYN: His sister, a few years younger.

Setting: A cabin. Now or then.

> THOMAS W. STEPHENS—playwright, director, educator—founded the Department of Theatre at Randolph-Macon Woman's College (now Randolph College) in Lynchburg, Virginia. His plays have been produced or developed at numerous venues, including the National Playwrights Conference of the Eugene O'Neill Theater Center; Berkeley Stage Co.; Source Theatre; Pittsburgh New Play Festival; D.C.'s Capital Fringe and One-Minute Play Festivals; Dallas Theater Center; American Conservatory Theatre; Audrey Skirball Kennis Theatre; Barter Theatre; the Kennedy Center's Page to Stage Festival; Ashland New Plays Festival; Baltimore Playwrights Festival; and Great Plains Theatre Conference. Honors include Actors Contemporary Ensemble Playwriting Award; Wheaton College Playwriting Competition Award; Doorway Arts Playwriting Award; Carol Weinberg Best Play Award; and the Charles M. Getchell New Play Award of the Southeastern Theatre Conference. A member of The Dramatists Guild, Tom lives and writes in Washington, DC. TomStephensPlaywright.com

Dark. Off, distant guitar music: it is fine and deeply felt. Lights up to reveal a rough interior wall, closed door at center. At one side of the door, back leaning against the wall, sits CARTER, in his teens. JESSAMYN, a year or two younger, enters and stops; she watches CARTER. Music continues softly throughout.

JESSAMYN: He ain't gon' like it—you sittin close like that, list'nin hard.

> *(No response; a pause.)*

You gon' get you a whuppin. Me? I be laughin' out loud at you, fo sho.

> *(No response; a pause.)*

Secret lis'ning's rendered you flat deaf, I reckon.

CARTER: Ain't it...truly, ain't it like angels... ?

JESSAMYN: Door closed, Carter. Man say he never shut that door but when the muse comin on.

CARTER: I know what he tell us.

JESSAMYN: It ain't right—you ear-spyin so.

CARTER: Sweet sound's caught up here in the wall, snared.

JESSAMYN: Like when him an Mama's goin at it? We ain't meant t' be hearin that neither.

CARTER: His music be flutterin my back.

JESSAMYN: Them goin-at-it times—? Even when the two a them get all frisky loud—? We ain't spose t' be awares.

CARTER: Guitar riff's tinglin my spine bones, Jessamyn. Tinglin up, down, tinglin all around.

JESSAMYN: Yo' brain's gone tinglin.

> *(They listen. JESSAMYN drops into a sitting position on the opposite side of the door from CARTER. She leans against the wall. The music comes clearer.)*

CARTER: Daddy's music's got fingers curlin' out t' us, don't it?

JESSAMYN: Got no 'pinion 'bout none a that. But I do know, now I'm fixin t' get me a whuppin too.

CARTER: Here's my figurin: when the muse come on, Daddy's

105 Five-Minute Plays

face—it break open so soft an sweet we couldn't bear witness t' it. It's way too pure fo us. We'd swoon, Jessamyn, we'd pass right on over. So he got him no choice but t' shut that door on you an me. For safety sake.

JESSAMYN: He protecting us?

CARTER: That's what Daddies do. You lis'ning t' him?

JESSAMYN: It's like angels then, you spec'? Real live ones? Hoverin?

CARTER: With spreaded wings.

JESSAMYN: Angels go like that sometime, don't they, Carter? I mean, when they ain't soarin? They spread way out their wings and hold 'em—waitin. Tremblin but still. Why's that?

CARTER: They treadin sky next t' Daddy. Angels ain't content with small like us. They want big an bustin, want it every bit an every way. Spreaded wings—is spreaded hearts.

> *(CARTER turns to the wall and kneels up; he spreads his arms wide and presses himself tight against its surface. The music comes clearer. JESSAMYN turns and kneels up too, also pressing her spread arms tight against the wall. The guitar music grows brilliant. As lights fade down and out, the music swells and soars.)*

Characters:

ARTHUR MORGAN: fifties

MARGARET MORGAN: fifties

JIM MORGAN: thirties

Setting: The Morgan's living room.

> SCOTT GIBSON, a Colorado native, is the author of several novels and plays, and has been fortunate to see some his works produced and performed in Seattle, Dallas, Los Angeles, Denver, Houston, Albuquerque and New York. His play *Someone Else's Life* was co-winner of the Steven Dietz Original Playwriting Competition at the Rocky Mountain Theatre Association in 2005.
> amazon.com/Scott-Gibson/e/B003VZQX3Y/ref=ntt_dp_epwbk_0

Lights up on The Morgans' living room, represented by a couch, center, a coffee table in front of it, and an easy chair SR of the couch. ARTHUR sits at one end of the couch reading the newspaper. MARGARET sits in the easy chair, working on mending a garment with needle and thread.

JIM enters L, holding a slightly creased piece of paper that displays a childishly-crude drawing of a house, tree and stick figures and sun overhead.

JIM: What's this?

(He holds out the drawing for both of them to see. AR-THUR and MARGARET exchange a glance.)

MARGARET: Oh, dear.

ARTHUR: *(to MARGARET)* Told you he'd notice.

JIM: What was this doing in the trash?

MARGARET: Well, it's been on the refrigerator for so long, Sweetheart.

ARTHUR: Thirty years or so.

MARGARET: I was just doing a bit of spring cleaning.

JIM: Well, I'm putting it back!

(JIM exits L in a huff.)

(MARGARET and ARTHUR exchange another look. MAR-GARET sighs. ARTHUR shakes his head. They go back to what they were doing, but JIM is back, just seconds later.)

JIM: So, you decided you didn't like my drawing.

ARTHUR: Son… You did that when you were four.

JIM: Yeah, and back then, you said it was wonderful! You said it deserved a place of honor!

ARTHUR: And it did. When you were four. Five, even. Now…

JIM: Oh, I see. Your tastes have gotten a little more discriminating, is that it? Artwork has an expiration date on it, now?

MARGARET: To be frank, I'd hardly call it artwork, Jimmy. It's three stick figures standing in front of a tree and a house.

JIM: *(wounded)* Oh.

(He sinks down onto the couch.)

I see.

(Considers this for a few seconds.)

So, what else have you lied to me about?

ARTHUR: Oh, for heaven's sake…

JIM: No, I'm serious. I understand now you don't like my picture. You never liked my picture.

MARGARET: Well, it did start to lose some of its charm after about the fourth or fifth year of looking at it while reaching for the milk every morning.

ARTHUR: *(cautioningly)* Dear…

JIM: No, Dad. I appreciate the candor. I think I would like to know just how much of my life has been a sham up until now.

MARGARET: Oh, good heavens, Jimmy, you're a grown man, now. You're married, with children of your own. At some point, you have to take down your own crappy drawings and start putting up your kids' crappy drawings instead. That's how life works.

JIM: Fine. I'll do that.

MARGARET: Good.

JIM: Fine.

(Beat.)

JIM: What else has been a sham? A house of cards?

ARTHUR: Oh, good grief… We're back to that again? Son, give it a rest. We took down your precious chicken scratches after thirty years. Deal with it.

JIM: I am. I have. *(prompting)* So..?

(JIM looks at his parents expectantly. Again, ARTHUR and MARGARET exchange a glance.)

(MARGARET lowers her mending. ARTHUR folds his newspaper and sets it on the coffee table.)

ARTHUR: Well… none of the other children in the neighborhood liked you.

JIM: What? That's ridiculous! Timmy Weederspan and I were best friends!

MARGARET: We paid Timmy.

JIM: You *what?*

ARTHUR: A quarter a week to let you play with him. Until you were both twelve. It was fifty cents after that.

JIM: …I don't believe you.

MARGARET: I had to become The Den Mother before The Cub Scouts would let you in.

ARTHUR: Oh, and you remember Punky?

JIM: Our Beagle who died when I was eleven?

ARTHUR: He didn't die. We just told you that. He went to live on a farm.

JIM: What? Why?

MARGARET: He kept growling at you. We were starting to get a little concerned.

ARTHUR: We figured it was only a matter of time until something happened.

JIM: *(disbelieving)* He… he was my dog! He wouldn't have hurt me!

>*(ARTHUR and MARGARET look at each other skeptically.)*

MARGARET: The principal suggested we home-school you.

>*(JIM gets to his feet. He's reeling from all this. He crosses away a few steps.)*

JIM: And… And I suppose Grandma and Grandpa Morgan didn't really die. They just moved to Florida or someplace to get away from me.

ARTHUR: Oh, no, they died, all right.

MARGARET: They had considered moving to Florida, though.

JIM: To get away from me?

>*(Still another uncomfortable glance between ARTHUR and MARGARET.)*

ARTHUR: They never actually *said* that.

JIM: I… I think I'm going to go home, now.

MARGARET: *(standing)* Well, drive carefully, Sweetheart.

> *(MARGARET crosses to kiss him on the cheek. She turns to go back to her mending, but then she pauses.)*

MARGARET: Oh, and if you go out through the kitchen, would you please take that awful thing down off the refrigerator again?

JIM: *(vaguely)* Sure…

ARTHUR: *(cheerily)* Good night, Son!

JIM: Yeah… 'Night, Dad…

> *(JIM exits.)*

> *(MARGARET picks up her mending. ARTHUR picks up his newspaper, unfolds it and resumes reading. A moment passes.)*

MARGARET: I feel a little bad about all that.

ARTHUR: *(nodding)* Me, too.

MARGARET: But the kitchen does look so much nicer this way.

> *(ARTHUR nods.)*
> *(The lights fade.)*

Characters:

MAN: Age twenties/thirties.

WOMAN: Age twenties/thirties.

Setting: Gramercy Tavern Restaurant in Manhattan. Now.

WILLIAM IVOR FOWKES is an author and playwright based in Manhattan and Connecticut and a member of the Dramatists Guild & the Pulse Ensemble Theatre Playwrights' Lab. His plays include *All in the Faculty* (Dramatists Play Service, Playwrights First Award Semifinalist), *Sunshine Quest* (Fresh Fruit Festival), *The Hudson Family Guide to Table Manners* (Reva Shiner Comedy Award Finalist, W. Keith Hedrick Playwriting Contest Finalist), *The Seeker* (Colonial Players Promising Playwright Award Semifinalist, Princess Grace Playwriting Award Semifinalist), *Private Property* (Penobscot Theatre Company's New Works Festival), *The German Lesson* (Great Plains Theatre Conference Playlabs), *The Brazilian Dilemma* (The Collective NY, McLean Drama Company First Prize Winner), *The Dakota* (Downtown Urban Theater Festival Best Short Play Award), *The Next Move* (Brevard Little Theatre One-Act Play Competition Winner), *The Session* (Strawberry One-Act Festival Finalist), and others. williamivorfowkes.com

A couple is seated at a table.

WOMAN: Gosh, Gramercy Tavern! I've never been here before. I've never even been able to get a reservation.

MAN: I have my ways. And you deserve only the best.

WOMAN: That's so sweet of you!

MAN: Are you sure that seat's okay? I'd be happy to switch. You might like the view better from this side.

WOMAN: I'm fine, thank you.

MAN: *(very solicitously)* Can I get you something to drink?

WOMAN: We already ordered.

MAN: Oh, that's right.

WOMAN: You seem nervous.

MAN: I guess I am. This is important to me. … I wanted to thank you for agreeing to see me.

WOMAN: Why wouldn't I?

MAN: Well, I appreciate it.

WOMAN: No problem.

MAN: Look, how long have we been together, Marni?

WOMAN: I bet it's over ten years now.

MAN: Yes, that's what I thought. And I've gone out of my way to make you happy, haven't I?

WOMAN: I'm sure you think that's true.

MAN: Oh, but it is! I've done everything in my power to give you what you need.

WOMAN: Well, up to a point, maybe. You haven't been perfect.

MAN: Is that what this is all about? You're looking for perfection?

WOMAN: No—I realize there's no such thing. I'm just looking for something better.

MAN: But how do you know things will be any better? Really, Marni—we all dream of something better, but that's all it really is—dreams. We don't know when we have it good. We don't appreciate what we have.

WOMAN: You're saying nothing should ever change? We should just keep doing the same old things, seeing the same old people, going to the same old places…?

MAN: No, of course not. But change for its own sake isn't the answer. What about loyalty? Doesn't that count for something?

WOMAN: I've been loyal. For ten years, I've been loyal! And for what? Look where we are now?

MAN: I think we're in a very good place.

WOMAN: *(getting angry)* You're delusional! I haven't been happy for a long time now, and you've never even noticed! I had to take drastic measures just to get your attention.

MAN: Well, you've certainly got my attention now. I'm here! I'm willing to listen.

WOMAN: No, it's too late. I've made my decision.

MAN: Please, you're breaking my heart!

WOMAN: I can't worry about your heart. I have to think about myself and what I need. I'm going to be happier—and I'm going to come out way ahead financially!

MAN: Money? You're saying it's about money? How mercenary can you be?

WOMAN: I work hard for my money. And no, it's not just about the money. You've made promises over the years that you haven't lived up to. You've disappointed me. You've kept me waiting on the phone every time I've called you. One time you promised to come over, and I waited all day and you never showed up, you bastard!

MAN: I know I'm not always reliable. I'm sorry. But how do you know things will be any better if you dump me?

WOMAN: I don't, but it's a chance I'm willing to take. Besides, if things don't work out for me, I can always come back to you, right?

MAN: Is that what you think?

WOMAN: Am I right?

MAN: Yes, yes, yes—you're right, damn it! But please leave me my dignity!

WOMAN: I really should go.

MAN: Don't! Our drinks haven't arrived. And we haven't even ordered dinner yet.

WOMAN: I'd feel awkward eating at your expense now.

MAN: All right, if you must go. … I'll miss you, you know.

WOMAN: You'll get over me.

MAN: One last question—how much is Verizon FIOS charging you?

WOMAN: 25% less than you guys at Time Warner—and they're giving me more channels.

MAN: What if I throw in three free months of Showtime and HBO?

WOMAN: Sorry, it's too late.

The woman exits.

END OF PLAY

Characters:

ERIN

LAUREL

ANDY

Setting: On the street.

MARK HARVEY LEVINE has had over 1300 productions from New York to Bucharest to Jakarta to London. Thirteen of his plays appear in Smith & Kraus' *Best 10 Minute Play* Collections. Evenings of his short plays, such as *Cabfare For The Common Man* and *Didn't See That Coming*, have been seen in the Edinburgh Fringe Festival, Seoul, Amsterdam, Sydney, New York, LA, Boston and other cities. His work has been translated into over a dozen languages. *Aperitivos*, an evening of his plays in Portuguese, played in Brazil from 2005 to 2010, culminating in a national tour. A Spanish-language movie of his play *The Kiss* (*El Beso*) showed at Cannes and Tribeca and aired on HBO and DTV (Japan). He is the winner of the Alan Minieri Playwriting Award, Best Play at the Annual 15-Minute Play Festival, the Chester Horn Play Festival (twice), the Chameleon Theatre Circle Festival (twice), SlamBoston (twice) and the In A New York Minute Festival (five times!) and many other awards. markharveylevine.com

On the street. ERIN approaches a couple, LAUREL and ANDY. She taps Laurel hard with her hand.

ERIN: Tag! You're it! Ha!

ANDY: Hey!

ERIN: Twenty seven years I've been waiting to do that. Twenty. Seven. Years.

LAUREL: Do I... know you?

ERIN: You don't even remember me?

LAUREL: I'm sorry, I don't. *(to Andy)* Do you...?

ANDY: Who are you?

ERIN: Who am I? I'm it, that's who I am. I'm IT.

LAUREL: I have no idea what you're talking about.

ERIN: Shaffer Elementary School? Pittsburgh?

LAUREL: Oh my God...you're...Erin?

ERIN: Erin Dolan.

LAUREL: Wow! How have you been?

ERIN: How have I been? How have I been?! I've been it, that's how I've been!

LAUREL: You keep saying that, but I don't—

ERIN: Last day of school. Last day of fifth grade. Recess?

ANDY: Are you talking about...tag?

ERIN: Yes! Tag! On the playground! On the last day of school! I can't believe you don't remember this!

LAUREL: Erin that was...a long time ago...

ERIN: Really? I remember it like it was yesterday. We were playing tag. And you tagged me. Like you always did. And I was "it." Again. Like I always was. And the bell rang. Recess was over. And then school was over. And then in middle school I tried to start up the game of tag again. And you said, no, tag was for babies. And I've been "it" for twenty seven years!

ANDY: ...Wow.

ERIN: My whole adult life, I've been "it." It's become the metaphor for my existence. Always reaching out to people, looking for a little touch, a simple connection, chasing after them, and everyone running away from me. Like I'm a pariah. Who has to go to her fifth choice college because all the other ones rejected her? I'm it! Who has her husband leave her for an optometrist with a limp? I'm it! Whose children want nothing to do with her because they find her, and I quote, obsessive and angry? I'm it! Well I'm not it anymore! You're it now! AND I CALL NO BACKSIES!

ANDY: Again...wow.

LAUREL: I know, right?

ANDY: "No backsies?"

LAUREL: Apparently I can't tag her right back.

ANDY: Ah.

ERIN: Who's this? Your boyfriend?

LAUREL: My sweet, loving husband, actually.

ERIN: Of course. Of course. I've bet you've had a perfect, wonderful life. Gorgeous house, beautiful blonde children.

LAUREL: No, Erin, I haven't had a perfect life. I've had troubles, like anyone else. And we've just got a little apartment. But you're right. It is wonderful. We've got one kid — he's brunette, actually if that's okay — and he's great. We've got a happy life. I grew up, Erin. I left the playground a long time ago. I made my own choices. I don't blame anyone for the bad things that happen in my life. But y'know, I do thank someone for the good stuff. Andy, if there's any reason for all the happiness in my life, well you're it.

She touches him gently on the shoulder.

LAUREL *(CONT'D):* You've made my life complete. You're sharing this journey with me. Our little family is what makes my life worthwhile.

ANDY: *(to Erin)* And it's not too late for you. You're still young. Grab the reins of your life. Nothing is holding you back. No school-yard game has cursed you. You're in charge of your own destiny. You can turn your life around at any moment. Starting today. Starting right now. There's only one captain of your ship. And you're it.

He touches Erin gently on the arm.

LAUREL: Good luck, Erin. I really do wish you all the best.

Andy and Laurel walk off. Erin stands there for a moment and then it dawns on her what just happened.

ERIN: NOOOOOO!!!

LAUREL AND ANDY: *(as they run off)* NO BACKSIES!

Characters:
LILY: thirties

HUNTER: thirties

Setting: A one-bedroom apartment in a major city. The present.

CARRIE BOEHM is a Manhattan-based playwright and founding member of PET Productions. Her full-length plays *Knee Deep in Snow*, *Evaporate* and *Blizzard* have been produced in NYC by Coffee Black Productions, along with several commissioned one-acts. Other plays include *bubble*, *Waiting For Kevin* (Actors Studio Drama School), *The Escape Artist* (Theatre at St. Clement's), *The Test* (Secret Theatre, Manhattan Repertory Theatre) and *Think, What Have You Done* (Roy Arias Theatre). She is a 2014 Princess Grace semi-finalist and an associate member of the Dramatists Guild. MFA, The Actors Studio Drama School. carrie-boehm.com

AT RISE: The living room of a one-bedroom apartment, perhaps on the Upper East or West Side. The apartment looks like that of a young, professional couple who's recently graduated from Ikea to West Elm. A couch sits center stage, a coffee table in front of it covered in clutter.

LILY is currently tidying up the living room, her phone to her ear. In her other hand she holds a bottle of beer, making it difficult to clean though she isn't trying particularly hard in the first place.

LILY: Yeah Mom, he actually asked me. …How could it be an April Fool's joke? It's not even April. …I know he has a weird sense of humor but that seems pretty mean even for Hunter, don't you think? …Mom…MOM…would you stop crying for a minute? …Yes Mom, I know I'm your last hope for grandchildren since Rose thinks having a career is more important than having babies… No Mom, I'm just as indignant as you are, honest! …When did he propose? I told you, this morning, over waffles. …What *kind* of waffles? … Engagement waffles, Mom, shaped like a ring. …Of *course* he got me an actual ring!

> *(She collapses onto the couch and sets her beer down. She looks at her hand – there's no ring on it. As her mom chatters on, the sound of footsteps is heard, then keys at the door.)*

Listen Mom, I gotta go, Hunter's back…I don't know, out?

> *(HUNTER enters, hiding a bouquet of calla lilies behind his back, out of breath from walking up stairs.)*

HUNTER: I'm back!

LILY *(to Hunter):* Mom wants to know where you were.

HUNTER: The store?

LILY: He went to the store Mom….Oh my god does it matter what store?! I'm gonna go now okay? …Yes, I'll call you tomorrow, same time as always…Uh-huh…uh-huh. Oh god, I'm sorry Mom I think you're breaking up I can't hear you anymore love you miss you bye!

> *(She drops her phone down on the coffee table as Hunter approaches her with the bouquet, kneeling to present it to her.)*

Lilies?

HUNTER: I just thought, you know, lilies…for *my* Lily.

> *(She carelessly grabs the bouquet and tosses it aside.)*

LILY: You know these are sympathy flowers, right? Like the kind you would send to a funeral.

> *(Hunter stifles a laugh. Lily is unamused.)*

HUNTER: Sorry, I just…I mean, that's kinda funny, don't you think? Considering…

LILY: I told my mom. About the proposal. *Just* the proposal right now, you know how she is. She's ecstatic!

HUNTER: I'm sure she is. That beer for me?

> *(He grabs the beer without waiting for an answer, joining Lily on the couch. He pats his lap, gesturing for Lily to put her feet up. She does.)*

LILY: She started crying when I told her about how you proposed over waffles this morning. How it came out of nowhere. I mean, not nowhere, but…you know. "Took him long enough" she kept saying. Even put Dad on the phone for a second. "Boy finally grew a pair, huh?"

> *(Hunter groans, shifting as Lily's feet fall from his lap. She looks hurt.)*

I mean, they kind of have a point, don't they? Ten years is a long time without any sort of commitment.

HUNTER: Speaking of…

> *(Hunter reaches into his pocket, takes out a ring box and casually extends it to Lily who eagerly snatches it from him. She opens the box and her face falls.)*

Listen sweetheart, it's not like you gave me a lot of time to figure this out.

LILY: So that means you don't even get down on one knee? You don't even *try* sweeping me off my feet anymore?

HUNTER: Now that I know where it gets us? Nah, I think I'm good. And besides, I proposed this morning! Over waffles! When you told me the whole…that was the real proposal, the one that was all romantic and shit. What more do you want?

(Lily takes the ring out of the box and puts it on, her expression changing. She likes how it looks.)

LILY: It fits well, at least.

HUNTER: And now you'll have some decent pictures to go with your new Facebook status.

LILY: …I'm gonna go put these in some water.

(She rises, picking up the flowers. She leans down to Hunter, who practically winces as she kisses him on the cheek.)

I can't wait, you know. You and I…together forever. It's everything I've always wanted.

(Lily exits to the kitchen. Hunter sets his beer down on the coffee table and picks up another object: a pregnancy test. He stares at it.)

HUNTER: You mind getting me another beer babe? I sure could use one.

LILY *(off)* Tell me about it. Not drinking is the worst.

HUNTER: Don't worry, I'm pretty sure I won't have any problem drinking for two.

(Hunter leans back, still fixated on the test. After a moment he realizes exactly what he's holding and drops it on the table in disgust.)

LILY *(off)* Do you want a summer wedding? Or maybe fall, you've always loved it when the leaves change. Mom wants us to get married in the winter, out in the snow. Like a fairytale.

HUNTER: Just pick a season, any season.

LILY *(off)* By then Megan will have already had *her* baby so I won't have to worry about having a fat maid of honor, so that's good, right?

HUNTER: Won't you be fat by then? ...I mean showing, won't you be showing by then?

LILY *(off)* I wasn't even thinking about that! The sooner the better I guess, huh?

(From the table, Lily's phone lights up with a text mes-

sage, catching Hunter's eye. He picks up the phone, reading the message.)

Do you have any idea how long I've been dreaming about this? I bet we could plan something in a week if we wanted. All that matters is that we finally do it, right? That's all I care about at least.

(Hunter looks at the pregnancy test, then back at the phone. He puts two and two together.)

HUNTER: What the—

LILY *(reentering)* What if we just elope? Just get it over with tonight, we could wake up tomorrow morning and already be husband and wife. …what are you doing with my phone?

HUNTER: What did you buy on Craigslist?

LILY: I don't know what you're talking about.

HUNTER *(reading from the phone)* "O-M-G I can't believe he fell for it, too!" "What *can't* you find on Craigslist?!"

(He picks up the test and waves it at her.)

You're obsessed with finding weird shit on there Lily, where did this test come from? Oh god, whose pee is this anyway?!

(Hunter throws the test down.)

LILY: How else was I going to get you to commit?! TEN YEARS, Hunter, ten years! I had to know if this relationship was going anywhere!

HUNTER: So you tricked me into proposing?

LILY: I *persuaded* you. And besides, why wouldn't you want to marry me after all this time? We've been together since *college*, do you know how embarrassing that is? Being the only friend without a husband of my own, a family of my own? It's all I've ever wanted!

HUNTER: What about what I want?

LILY: And besides, you and I are so good together, why shouldn't we be…you know…happy, right? And if it worked for Megan…

HUNTER: Because she's the sharpest tool in your little shed of dumbassery, right?

John Capecci and Irene Ziegler

(Hunter storms out before Lily can respond. She picks up the pregnancy test and returns to the couch. After a moment she realizes what she's holding and drops it in disgust. Her phone begins to buzz. She takes a deep breath and picks it up.)

LILY: Mom, I told you I'd give you a call tomorrow. …Wait, what? Rose is what?! How did that even – of course I'm happy Mom, why wouldn't I be? A wedding and a baby, what more could a girl want?

(Lily stares at the ring on her finger, defeated, as the lights fade...)

105 Five-Minute Plays

Characters:

STORYTELLER

CINDERELLA

FAIRYGOD PRODUCER

PRINCE

FRANCESCA PEPPIATT: writer, performer and producer working in various media. Her television work includes stints with TV icon Dick Clark and "Love Connection;" an Emmy nomination for writing an entertainment news magazine show, "Country Notes;" and segment producer on "The Paula Poundstone Show," which included an appearance with Paula and Lily Tomlin.

Francesca has four published books to her name and an extensive background in theater as a writer, actor and producer. She is the Producing Artistic Director of Stockyards Theatre Project, whose mission statement is "Giving volume to the voices of women.' In 2006, Francesca created Play for Keeps, Stockyards' signature writing workshop.

Francesca's works had been produced on a number of Chicago stages; she writes for Examiner.com about Chicago Theater. Her musical adaptation of *Treasure Island* with composer Elizabeth Doyle, received a staged reading in Chicago and seeks development and production opportunities.

francescapeppiatt.com stockyardstheatreproject.com

(The Storyteller sits alone on stage with a larger than normal book with the title "Fairy Tales." The character speaks as though talking to a nursery school class when telling the story.)

STORYTELLER: Once upon a time there was a beautiful girl.

CINDERELLA *(OS VOICE)*: Woman!

STORYTELLER: Fine! Woman. *(Storyteller voice)* Once upon a time there was a beautiful *woman* named Cinderella. She could sing like an angel.

(Cinderella enters singing beautifully. Or can lip-sync to a song. Cinderella sings quietly while miming gardening left of the Storyteller.)

STORYTELLER: One day Cinderella was working in her garden and singing when a Fairygod Producer walked by.

(Fairygod Producer sticks head out)

FAIRYGOD PRODUCER: Can I be flying?

STORYTELLER: No. You don't need to fly.

FAIRYGOD PRODUCER: But it makes for a better show.

STORYTELLER: No budget. I am sure you get that.

FAIRYGOD PRODUCER: Sure but how about if I drive by in a huge Mercedes?

STORYTELLER: *(quietly to him)* Fine, but you have to mime it.

FAIRYGOD PRODUCER: I do great space work. Can I at least have sound effects and lighting?

STORYTELLER: No, this is Cinderella's story.

CINDERELLA: That's right, this is my story. So can we get on with it, cause I can't do fake gardening work for much longer.

STORYTELLER: *(back to storytelling voice)* One day Cinderella was working in her garden and singing, when a Fairygod Producer was driving by in his huge Mercedes.

(Fairygod Producer enters miming driving a huge car.)

FAIRYGOD PRODUCER: You there!

CINDERELLA: Who, me?

FAIRYGOD PRODUCER: You there! I want to transform you

into a star.

CINDERELLA: Why I am just a humble girl…

STORYTELLER: Woman.

CINDERELLA: Woman… who works as a back-up singer to the true talent in the house.

STORYTELLER: That's right. Cinderella had always lived in the shadow of the lead singer she lived with, who looked just like Taylor Swift.

> *(Both FairyGod Producer and Cinderella look at Storyteller with disdain.)*

STORYTELLER: OK, how about Katy Perry? Miley Cyrus?

> *(Storyteller looks to them for approval, and they reluctantly agree.)*

STORYTELLER: The lead singer that Cinderella worked for looked just like Miley Cyrus.

> *(The Storyteller hands them a photo of Miley.)*

CINDERELLA: Do you really think I could be a star?

FAIRYGOD PRODUCER: You do have a beautiful voice, but you're too gawky and awkward, not like your beautiful lead singer, the Miley wannabe.

> *(The Fairygod Producer looks longingly at the photo.)*

STORYTELLER: Deep inside, Cinderella knew that the Fairygod Producer was right. But she also knew that she had something special deep inside.

FAIRYGOD PRODUCER: There's lots of money in hot vocal chords. But the outside needs to look like the inside sounds. So unless you want to change yourself, I can't help you.

CINDERELLA: But what if I want to stay the way I am?

FAIRYGOD PRODUCER: That's fine, but you can forget about being a singing sensation, so enjoy your gardening. *(quietly to Cinderella)* Great space work by the way.

CINDERELLA: Thanks.

> *(Fairygod Producer mimes driving off with a picture of Miley.)*

STORYTELLER: The Fairygod Producer took the Miley wannabe to the land of success. There, the Fairygod Producer got her a recording contract, a world tour and a fragrance line to sell on QVC.

CINDERELLA: Do I have to keep doing fake gardening?

(Storyteller shakes head 'no.')

STORYTELLER: Once again Cinderella was alone with her beautiful voice.

(Looks to her, but she doesn't sing.)

STORYTELLER: Her beautiful singing voice!!

CINDERELLA: What are we trying to say here?

STORYTELLER: Just keeping up with the story.

CINDERELLA: So I have to either change or die?

STORYTELLER: Well, you don't actually have to die… right now, anyway. But if you want to use that voice of yours on stage, then you better look the part.

CINDERELLA: That sucks.

STORYTELLER: That's life.

CINDERELLA: I thought you said this was a story?

STORYTELLER: It is, and there is a moral at the end. So if you will please let me get back to…*(storyteller voice)* Back to the Tale of Cinderella.

(Prince sticks his head in.)

PRINCE: Hey, when do I come in and save the day?

CINDERELLA: What?! No way. This story better not have some jerky prince saving me from my lowly status.

(Prince enters.)

PRINCE: Look, I don't like that idea either, sister. I was waiting to audition for the bull-headed leader of the Russian Mafia on "Chicago Fire."

CINDERELLA: Really? That's cool. Let's hear it.

PRINCE: *(Russian accent)* I don't care what you tell me to do, I do what I do for me.

(Both Cinderella and Storyteller applaud.)

CINDERELLA: That's good.

PRINCE: Thanks, and so are you. I heard you sing, so just go do it.

STORYTELLER: And she is going to sing some more if we can please get back to the story

(storyteller voice) Back to the Tale of Cinderella.

CINDERELLA: I was going to sing again anyway before either of you said to do it.

PRINCE: You don't need me to tell you how to live your life.

CINDERELLA: See!

PRINCE: You know they're auditioning for "The Voice" just down the hall.

CINDERELLA: I saw that notice about the audition, too. I was going to head down there myself at the end of the story.

PRINCE: Self-directed. I like that.

STORYTELLER: Excuse me. We still have the story to finish.

PRINCE and CINDERELLA: OK.

(Both stand waiting and listen. Storyteller goes back to her book.)

STORYTELLER: So, Cinderella went off with the Prince.

CINDERELLA: Just so we're clear, I did not go with the Prince.

PRINCE: Yeah, we just left together cause we're going the same way.

STORYTELLER: FINE! But Cinderella took her self-directed self to the audition and received huge success. Then she started calling herself Ella Fitzgerald.

PRINCE: That seems a bit contrived.

CINDERELLA: Can we go now?

(Storyteller, who is weary of the two, nods, and they start to leave.)

STORYTELLER: And the moral of the story is … "A bird in the hand is worth two…"

CINDERELLA: No it's not.

STORYTELLER: A fool and his money are soon parted?

> *(Cinderella and Prince shake their heads while Storyteller rapidly goes through morals.)*

STORYTELLER: Haste makes waste? Look before you leap?

PRINCE: Beauty is only skin deep.

CINDERELLA: A bit on the nose don't you think?

PRINCE: You're right.

STORYTELLER: Two wrongs don't make… necessity the mother of invention.

CINDERELLA: You're just rambling.

STORYTELLER: No I'm not. A man is known by the company he keeps

PRINCE: Birds of a feather flock together.

CINDERELLA: Let's go flock off before we hear another ridiculous unfitting moral.

STORYTELLER: Better late than never.

CINDERELLA: OK I'll go with that.

PRINCE: What a scattered fairy tale.

> *(Cinderella exits with the Prince. The Storyteller is glad to reclaim her rightful power.)*

STORYTELLER: And next we'll hear the story of Goldilocks and the Three Bears…better known as a lousy Chicago backfield.

Characters:

HAROLD: fifties or sixties, married to MARJORIE

MARJORIE: fifties or sixties, married to HAROLD

Setting: The play takes place in the home library of Harold and Marjorie.

B. N. REICHENBERGER is a playwright, director, teaching artist, and literary assistant at the Alley Theatre in Houston, TX. Short plays include *Sisterhood* (Mildred's Umbrella), *F*** Kiss Touch* (Cone Man Running), *What The Ladies Do* (Blunt Objects Theater), *Twinings* (Scriptwriters/Houston), *Hey Hey I Wanna Get Married* (Weathervane Playhouse), *And Now, An Education From Our Sponsors!* (American Theatre Company), *The Future* (Chicago Fringe Festival), and *Low-Fat Kosher Recipe Book: An Orthodox Guide To Fitness* (Northlight Theatre), which received an emerging talent award from the Chicago Jewish Historical Society. Full length plays include *Novelty* (Scriptwriters/Houston Reading), and *The Facts, The Truth, And Other Stories* (Loyola University Workshop Production). Reichenberger holds a BA in Theatre and English from Loyola University Chicago. bnreichenberger.com

HAROLD and MARJORIE each sit in a wingback chair, sipping tea in a leisurely fashion from china cups with saucers. They should give the impression of being wealthy and secure. They speak slowly and remain seated for the entirety of the play.

HAROLD: Nothing like it.

MARJORIE: Yes.

HAROLD: Nice cup of tea.

MARJORIE: Oh! Why yes.

HAROLD: Oh?

MARJORIE: I was thinking of something.

HAROLD: Of course.

    Pause.

MARJORIE: Yes, it's very nice.

HAROLD: Hmmm?

MARJORIE: The tea.

HAROLD: Ah! Yes.

MARJORIE: Ah?

HAROLD: Well.

MARJORIE: Hmmm?

HAROLD: Just...

MARJORIE: Really, Harold!

HAROLD: Well, what were you thinking of?

MARJORIE: Oh. Things.

HAROLD: Things.

MARJORIE: This and that.

HAROLD: This and that.

MARJORIE: My list. Must tell Betty to put less salt on the fish, when the Cartwrights come. Gordon is watching his food.

HAROLD: Ah.

MARJORIE: Yes.

Pause.

HAROLD: That list.

MARJORIE: It...insists. Looms.

HAROLD: Indeed?

MARJORIE: A woman's work is never done.

HAROLD: Oh, certainly.

MARJORIE: Well, don't trouble yourself.

HAROLD: Of course I care about your—it's no trouble simply to—hear you.

MARJORIE: Oh, certainly.

Pause.

HAROLD: Well, what else is on it?

MARJORIE: Hmm?

HAROLD: Your list.

MARJORIE: Oh. This and that. *(pause)* A variety of things.

HAROLD: Indeed.

MARJORIE: Well, the Cartwrights.

HAROLD: Yes?

MARJORIE: No carrots in the crudités, when they come. Elise is allergic.

HAROLD: Really? Allergic to carrots.

MARJORIE: Mildly.

HAROLD: Mildly allergic to carrots.

MARJORIE: An itching in the mouth, I'm told. Only when the carrots are raw.

HAROLD: A mildly itchy mouth from only raw carrots.

MARJORIE: I'm told.

HAROLD: How unusual.

MARJORIE: Is it?

HAROLD: I suppose I couldn't say—definitively.

MARJORIE: No.

HAROLD: No. *(pause)* What else?

MARJORIE: Hmm? Just: things.

HAROLD: Things.

MARJORIE: Send your tan suit to be cleaned; write to mother.

HAROLD: Things.

MARJORIE: Yes.

> Pause.

MARJORIE: I don't know why you press me when you aren't really interested.

HAROLD: No?

MARJORIE: No.

HAROLD: It's only...

MARJORIE: Really, Harold.

HAROLD: Well.

MARJORIE: *Well?*

HAROLD: Only these things—your list. A woman's work and so forth—

MARJORIE: Yes?

HAROLD: They don't seem...peculiarly, or...uniquely...looming. Insistent.

MARJORIE: No?

HAROLD: No.

MARJORIE: Hmmm.

HAROLD: And yet—

MARJORIE: Ah. Yes.

> Pause.

MARJORIE: I suppose—the list—is not what I was thinking of, per se. No. I suppose I was thinking of Gordon Cartwright, more specifically.

HAROLD: Oh?

MARJORIE: Of the time he made love to me in this room, while
you played golf with your brother. How attentive he was to
my—femininity—the smell of the books, the polish on the
chairs, my own smell—all together. Combined. Rich. Full.
These things—they insist. Loom. And after, sitting, un-
clothed, in these chairs, drinking tea.

Harold sets down his cup.

MARJORIE: Very nice tea.

Pause.

HAROLD: I think I'll read.

MARJORIE: Yes.

HAROLD: Catch up on my Proust.

MARJORIE: Certainly.

Harold picks up a book. Marjorie sips her tea.

Two Little Sparrows
Joseph Paquette

Characters:

BURGEON: A woman in her twenties.

HENRI: A man in his twenties.

Setting: Burgeon and Henri's bedroom. (Two chairs downstage.) Day, present.

JOSEPH PAQUETTE is a playwright and a visual artist. He has two young grandsons, Nathan and Zachary, whose antics entertain and inspire.joepaquette.com

AT RISE: *BURGEON is seated, staring out the window. HENRI enters, stops and watches her for a moment.*

HENRI: What are you looking at?

(BURGEON stares out.)

HENRI: Burgeon—

BURGEON: What is it, Henri?

HENRI: What's outside that's so interesting?

BURGEON: Nothing.

HENRI: *(moves to her)* I have a hard time believing you're looking at nothing.

BURGEON: Do you believe I'm lying?

HENRI: No, of course I don't think you're lying. When I walked in you were looking at something. Your concentration seemed intense, almost in reverence of something.

BURGEON: My profile amazed you.

HENRI: *(sits)* No, I didn't say that. I'm just curious to know what you were looking at that could be anything new outside our window you haven't seen before.

BURGEON: Two little sparrows.

HENRI: Why couldn't you have said that in the first place?

BURGEON: They were watching me watch them. I didn't want them to know I was talking to you. I didn't want to scare them away. I didn't want to lose the thing we had between us.

HENRI: You had a thing?

BURGEON: Yes, I did.

HENRI: So you had a thing between you and the sparrows. What kind of thing?

BURGEON: No, just her. She's gone now, they're both gone. You ruined it. Talking with you scared them away.

HENRI: It's not like they're gone forever.

BURGEON: Forever is a long time, isn't it.

HENRI: I'm sure they'll be back.

BURGEON: You think she's curious about me as much as I am

curious about her?

HENRI: I think they're afraid you may want to eat them like little roasted chickens from the market.

BURGEON: Perfectly understandable why they would feel that way.

HENRI: *(touches her hand)* They'll be back.

BURGEON: *(stands)* I don't believe you.

HENRI: Why would I lie.

BURGEON: *(sits)* Not telling is the same as lying.

HENRI: See where the two large limbs meet. Follow the limb on the right up to where it branches off. Now continue up and on the left is the sparrows nest.

BURGEON: I see it.

HENRI: There are eggs in that nest.

BURGEON: There are babies involved.

HENRI: You can't see the eggs from here. Soon we'll be able to hear the chicks after they hatch.

BURGEON: Babies do make a family, otherwise they're just two birds with no reason to stay.

HENRI: Tiny eggs the size of a nickel or a quarter. A lot smaller than chicken eggs.

BURGEON: Henri, will you climb the tree for me?

HENRI: What? No absolutely not. I will not climb a tree.

BURGEON: Why not? Climb up and take a picture of the eggs in the nest for me. I'll post it on my Facebook page.

HENRI: Take a picture of the tree from the window. Put that up instead.

BURGEON: I lied to you.

HENRI: You lied to me?

BURGEON Yes, I lied to you. I knew why the sparrows were hanging out in the tree.

HENRI: So you knew all along about the nest?

BURGEON: I actually had you convinced that I had no idea.

HENRI: Yes you did.

BURGEON: I could tell there was something by the way she acted. By the way she jumped from twig to branch and never took her eyes off me. When she thought I wasn't looking she studied and watched me. When I looked back she pretended not to see me.

HENRI: That was very astute of you.

BURGEON: A woman understands about protecting what is hers. Or not hers.

HENRI: I understand that now.

BURGEON: Pretending not to know is a lie. Henri, are you angry that I pretended not to know?

HENRI: It's no big deal. I can live with it.

BURGEON: Admitting is not the same as accepting.

HENRI: I accept some things will take time.

BURGEON: Accepting is hard. It takes longer.

HENRI: *(touches her hand)* In time, the sparrows may trust you...

BURGEON: *(pulls away)* In time they may understand I don't want to eat them. They'll never trust, and shouldn't trust anyone, ever.

HENRI: Everything has limits, boundaries.

BURGEON: Boundaries. That's a funny thing for you to say.

    (stands)

I shouldn't of said that. Forever is a long time, isn't it.

HENRI: *(stands)* I can't imagine forever.

BURGEON: Would you like to go outside? Take a walk.

HENRI: Yes. That would be nice.

BURGEON: Maybe I can convince you to climb the tree for me.

HENRI: You're joking, right?

BURGEON: We'll see how it goes, Henry.

UMBERTON'S UMBRELLA UMPORIUM

Amanda Hill

Characters:

LEO: Male, twenties to thirties. An umbrella salesman.

MERCEDES: Female, ten to fourteen. A customer.

Setting: Umberton's Umbrella Umporium. It is a sunny day. Leo is working behind the counter. No one has come in the store all day. At rise, Mercedes enters.

> AMANDA HILL is an artist, scholar, and educator. Her plays have been read at the Last Frontier Theatre Conference, One Theatre World, the ASSITEJ International Meeting. Other works have premiered at Orlando Repertory Theatre in Florida and Milliebo Art Theatre in Colorado. She has also written short pieces for Write Local Play Global and Assitej France's Play in a Day. amandahill.net

LEO: Welcome to Umberton's Umbrella Umporium. Can I help you find something?

MERCEDES: I need an umbrella.

LEO: Well, you've come to the right place.

MERCEDES: I know. That's why I'm here.

LEO: What kind of umbrella are you looking for?

MERCEDES: I don't know. One that keeps me dry. And is fun.

LEO: Ah, yes. Practical and fun.

MERCEDES: Are you making fun of me?

LEO: No. Sorry.

MERCEDES: It's empty in here. I bet you don't get many customers on sunny days like this.

LEO: Traffic definitely picks up on rainy days.

MERCEDES: Funny. Traffic usually slows down in the rain. This place is small. You should expand your inventory. Maybe like raincoats or boots or something. Luggage, maybe?

LEO: I don't know if that's in line with our mission.

MERCEDES: What's your mission?

LEO: Umbrellas.

MERCEDES: Maybe you should expand your mission.

LEO: Did you want an umbrella?

MERCEDES: Yeah.

LEO: Can I help you find one?

MERCEDES: No. I can pick one out myself.

LEO: Great.

MERCEDES: (*Picking out an umbrella.*) What do you think? These polka dots are a little too little kid-ish, right?

LEO: Too little kid-ish? How old are you?

MERCEDES: I'm not a little kid. I'm short for my age.

LEO: Of course, sorry.

MERCEDES: You say sorry a lot.

LEO: Sor—oh.

MERCEDES: So…the polka dots?

LEO: I think you're right. Maybe too young for you.

MERCEDES: Thank you. That's what I thought. Polka dots are for babies.

LEO: Well, We have a lot of umbrellas. I'm sure there's one that will suit you.

MERCEDES: Yeah. It's just, like, a big decision, you know?

LEO: Sure.

MERCEDES: Like, an umbrella is like, a fashion statement, right? So I can't have polka dots because they're for little kids, and I can't have, like, just green because that's boring, and I can't have black because those are for funerals, you know? Like, in all the movies, how it's always raining at funerals, and everyone has all these black umbrellas, and they're standing there crying with their black umbrellas over the open graves.

LEO: Sure.

MERCEDES: I don't want a black umbrella.

LEO: Of course.

MERCEDES: I don't really know what I want, but I know what I don't want.

LEO: I've got just the thing. (*He pulls out a box from under the counter.*) Here.

MERCEDES: This is a box.

LEO: Yes, but look inside.

MERCEDES: More umbrellas?

LEO: Look closely.

MERCEDES: They're just—eww! Is that one wet?

LEO: Oh yeah, sometimes they don't dry very well in the box.

MERCEDES: Why are they wet?

LEO: Rain.

MERCEDES: Well, duh. I mean, like, why were they out in the rain.

LEO: Ah. See these umbrellas are the most important in the whole store.

MERCEDES: Why?

LEO: Because no one knows where they come from. Lost umbrellas. They just show up here sometimes. So I put them in this box. In case anyone comes for them.

MERCEDES: Has anyone come?

LEO: Not yet.

MERCEDES: Then why keep them?

LEO: Aren't you even a little curious about them? Mysterious umbrellas that just show up out of the blue?

MERCEDES: As opposed to out of the rain?

LEO: Actually you're right. These umbrellas never appear on rainy days. Only bright sunny days like today.

MERCEDES: So you found one today?

LEO: Nope. Nothing's appeared today but you.

MERCEDES: You really should consider expanding your market.

LEO: You talk a lot about markets for a ki – er…young person.

MERCEDES: I'm precocious.

LEO: I can tell.

MERCEDES: If the umbrellas come on sunny days, why is that one wet?

LEO: There's the story, isn't it? I don't know why it's wet. I don't know where it came from. I don't know where it's been. That's the beautiful thing about them. The umbrellas on the racks aren't surprising. We know where they came from. These umbrellas. (*He taps the box.*)These umbrellas tell a story.

MERCEDES: (*Picking up an umbrella.*) You don't have any

orange ones like this in your store.

LEO: That's true.

MERCEDES: It's my favorite color.

LEO: Then it's yours.

MERCEDES: How much?

LEO: On the house.

MERCEDES: You really are bad at business.

(BLACK OUT)

105 Five-Minute Plays

Characters:
    RAY: A young man.

    LUC: A young woman.

Setting: Now. Central Park.
Note: The park setting, brook and arch can be created or left to
the imagination.

> ANDREA LEPCIO is best known for *Looking for the
> Pony*, a finalist for the Dramatists Guild Hull-Warriner
> Award and for the NEA Outstanding New American
> Play Award. It was presented in a "Rolling World Pre-
> miere" Off-Broadway at Vital Theatre Company in New
> York and Synchronicity Performance Group in Atlanta
> and subsequent productions. She is currently work-
> ing on a EST/Sloan-commissioned play about climate
> change, and a new musical, *Somebody Please Tell Me
> Who I Am* with songwriter Tina DeVaron. Additional
> Plays and musicals under development include *Strait
> of Gibraltar* (Geva Theatre Center), *Central Avenue
> Breakdown* (FwdTheatre), *The Gold* (NYMF) and
> *Lf&Tms* (Music Theatre Factory). Andrea is a member
> of the Dramatists Guild, was a Dramatists Guild Fellow
> and served as the Dramatists Guild Fellows Program
> Director for ten years. M.F.A. in Dramatic Writing,
> Carnegie Mellon University. B.A. Human Ecology,
> College of the Atlantic. She lives in Maine, which
> means she travels often. andrealepcio.com

*At Rise: Central Park. The Ravine. The brook under
Huddlestone Arch. A crisp early Spring day. It is just past
dawn. RAY is lying in the brook. Head South, feet North.
Face down. Sneakered footsteps hurry toward him.*

LUC: Ohmygod! Ohmygod!

*LUC runs down the path through the South Portal. She
rushes to RAY, rolls him over. This ain't easy. RAY'S a big
guy and she's a peanut.*

LUC: Are you breathing? How long have you been? Ohmygod!

*She checks his nose/mouth. Kind of sort of knows CPR.
Lip lock. RAY shoots up sending LUC flying into the
brook. He remains sitting in the brook.*

RAY: What the fuck?

LUC: I'm okay.

*LUC is slipping on the wet rocks as she rights herself
squeezing water out of her fleece.*

RAY: What're you doing?

LUC: Lost my balance.

LUC steps out of the brook, on to the path.

RAY: What'd you do to me?

LUC kneels down beside him.

LUC: Are you okay? Do you think? Is your brain? Does it feel
normal? You sound okay. I don't know how long you might
have not had oxygen. It's totally random that I'm even here.
It's not like I get up every morning and go running.

RAY pushes up. LUC jumps up and back.

You shouldn't move! If you have a head inju-

*He pulls himself to the opposite bank. Leans against a 100
ton rock.*

Or neck.

I took CPR once a long time ago. I wasn't very good on the
dummy, but I remember-

RAY: Go away.

LUC: What? Okay.

105 Five-Minute Plays

She doesn't move.

RAY: Now.

LUC: I need to know if you're okay, first. I'm responsible for you. Now.

RAY: I'm fine.

LUC: Are you sure, though? I mean. I still don't think you should get up.

> *RAY's not getting up.*

I didn't see any gashes or anything. Did you fall? Ohmygod. Were you mugged? Do you have your wallet? Did you check? How long have you been here? All night? I thought you were a goner. I almost didn't check. I almost called the cops, and then I thought I should check. That I wouldn't be able to live with myself if I didn't. I could've killed you, being stupid or lazy or insecure or all three. If I'd left you like some people might have. Then you would've been.

RAY: Dead.

> *Cell in hand.*

LUC: I can call an ambulance.

> *RAY lunges up. LUC skitters away. Cellphone flips out of her hand. Bounce, bounces on the path. Only a rock saves it from the brook.*

RAY: No ambulance.

LUC: Okay. I just. I don't think you're all right. I think you should. You don't want to make a mistake. Like Natasha Richardson is probably saving lives now. I know you're young, but you can die really easily.

> *RAY snickers. Sits down in the brook.*

Aren't you cold? It's kind of nippy.

> *RAY lies back in his original position.*

Okay. That's. I know I don't know you. But that seems like a really bad idea.

> *RAY flips so his face is in the water.*

LUC *(cont):* Ohmygod. What're you doing?

I'm not turning you over again.

I almost broke my neck the last time.

I can see your ears. I know you can hear me.

I'm not leaving.

RAY hasn't moved.

What do you have, Moby Dick lungs?

RAY hasn't moved.

LUC steps into the brook. Tentative. Sits. Lies down next to him.

RAY turns his head toward her, face out of the water.

LUC looks straight up.

RAY rolls all the way around. He looks straight up too.

They lie there. LUC wiggles her fingers in the water. Then stops.

RAY: Gravity.

LUC: Not my friend.

RAY: It is at the moment.

LUC: Yea. I don't know.

RAY: What do you see?

LUC points up. RAY nods.

LUC: Uh, the underside of the arch.

RAY: Gravity.

LUC: I don't get it.

RAY: Look at the stones. See how each one fits against the other.

LUC: Kind of.

RAY: That's how the bridge was built.

LUC: Arch. They call it an arch. Huddlestone.

RAY: Arch, okay. They fit each stone. What's their names? I bet you know. The park architects.

LUC: Vaux. Olmstead. Calvert. Frederick.

RAY: They searched the park for uncut stones. Manhattan Schist.

And placed them side by each, the force of one against the other, holding them in place. No mortar. No metal. Just schist.

LUC: What were you doing?

RAY: Dreaming.

LUC: With your face in the water?

RAY: Dying. Trying.

LUC: And I ruined it. Sorry.

RAY: You're wet.

LUC: You're wet.

RAY: I've been wet.

LUC: Me too.

RAY: Life is long.

LUC: It is, kind of.

> *RAY and LUC wiggle their fingers in the brook.*
>
> *Warblers and thrushes warble and thrush.*

RAY: I got nothing to offer.

LUC: Lie. That's a lie.

> *RAY tentatively puts his arm around LUC. She leans in. They walk out the North Portal.*

Inspired by Andrew Wyeth's painting, *Christina's World.*

Characters:

CHRISTINA: Female. fifty-five. Any ethnicity.

ANDREW: Male. thirty-one. Any ethnicity.

Setting: A field between two houses. 1948.

ALLIE COSTA works in film, TV, theatre, and voiceover as a writer, director, actor, and singer. Her original works have been produced internationally, including *Femme Noir* (Best Script, 2015 One-Act Festival), *Who She Could Have Been* (LBDI semi-finalist), *A Taste of the Future* (Lakeshore Players semi-finalist), *Safe Distance, Tofurkey Day, and Can You Keep a Secret?* Her published plays include *Little Swan, a Pas de Deux* and *She Has Seen the Wolf,* both of which were named Best of PlayGround-LA.

Allie is an accomplished stage and screen actor whose credits include *Spring Awakening, Hamlet, 90210, Wake,* and *You Me & Her.* She has lent her voice to video games, appeared in commercials, and narrated audio books. She is a proud member of the Los Angeles Female Playwrights Initiative, the 365 Women a Year Playwriting Project, PlayGround-LA, and SAG-AFTRA. She always has energy to burn and a song to sing. Occasionally, she sleeps. alliecosta.com imdb.me/alliecosta

AT RISE: Lights come up on a field between two houses. CHRISTINA, wearing a modest, peach-colored dress, is sitting on the floor downstage, gazing out. She is leaning her upper body to the side, bracing herself on her arms.

ANDREW, carrying a bag of groceries in one arm and holding an apple in the other hand, enters, crossing through. He sees Christina and stops for a moment, not wanting to disturb her.

CHRISTINA: I can hear you. Waiting is always loud.

ANDREW: *(agreeably)* Is it?

CHRISTINA: Silence accelerates and amplifies your heartbeat until you can feel it in your ears and hear it in your throat.

ANDREW: Rather like a head cold. *(not unkindly)* Why are you staring at my house?

CHRISTINA: I used to live there.

ANDREW: Ah. I was wondering who the previous owners were.

(Bites into the apple.)

CHRISTINA: My parents. Sixty years ago, they built it with their own hands. Can you imagine? Looking at a treeless, tawny field and thinking, "This is where we shall live. This is where my family shall grow." *(after a moment)* Are you using the barn?

ANDREW: Yes, but not for its intended purpose.

CHRISTINA: Oh?

ANDREW: I'm a painter. I've decided to make the barn my studio. Would your parents approve?

CHRISTINA: I'm sure they would. But it must be stuffy in there.

ANDREW: I like to paint with the doors open. Move my easel around with the sun. And I found a lantern up in the hayloft, so I was thinking about giving nighttime painting a try.

CHRISTINA: Oh, you should. The moon makes for a wonderful muse.

ANDREW: That she does.

CHRISTINA: Just don't set the lantern down on any hay bales

unless you want to toast your toes.

> *Christina looks out at the house again and crawls a little further downstage. Realizing Christina is paralyzed from the waist down, Andrew immediately puts down his groceries and moves to help her.*

CHRISTINA *(CONTINUED)*: It's all right. I just wanted to get a little closer.

ANDREW: *(looking around)* Do you have a—a chair or—

CHRISTINA: Yes. My brother took it into town for repairs.

ANDREW: And he left you here alone?

CHRISTINA: I wanted to stay. I needed some time outside.

ANDREW: But what if something happened?

CHRISTINA: It already did, a long time ago.

> *(A thoughtful beat passes.)*

ANDREW: Did you like growing up here?

CHRISTINA: Well enough to come back for my golden years. I traveled a bit when I was in school, studied in some grand cities, but eventually, the quiet pulled me back.

ANDREW: Why don't you still live there, in your old house?

CHRISTINA: *(Small beat.)* Have you ever gone back to your childhood home?

ANDREW: No.

CHRISTINA: It can break your heart. Things aren't exactly as you remember them, and you can't quite reconcile the difference between your memories and reality. The house is – smaller, more fragile. It's better not to get too close. If you keep that distance, you can still hold on to the picture in your mind.

ANDREW: It is a lovely house.

> *(Glances to the other side.)*

And yours looks lovely, too. Quaint.

CHRISTINA: That's a nice way to say "small." But it's big enough for two creaky old siblings to live in. And the ramps are just as creaky as the people who use them.

ANDREW: Do you need them to be oiled or cleaned or—I could
come over some afternoon.

CHRISTINA: That would be nice. Not today, though. I want
to stay out here a while longer. *(Takes a breath.)* Now you
run along, young man. Find your muse and paint something
beautiful tonight.

ANDREW: I will.

> *(Andrew retrieves his groceries and heads off. He stops
> and looks back at Christina for a moment before he exits.
> LIGHTS DIM as Christina continues to look out.)*

Characters:

LAUREN: twenty-nine, a New York professional of Vietnamese decent.

AN: twenty-four, a nail technician and recent Vietnamese
immigrant.

MAN: forty-five.

Setting: A New York City Nail Salon. Present.

CHARLES FORBES' other plays include *Minor Gods*
(Kennedy Center Page-to-Stage Festival, Lincoln
Center developmental grant, performed off-Broadway
at the Summer Play Festival), *Us@80* (Actors Theatre
of Louisville), *Courting Prometheus* (Actors Theatre of
Louisville, Samuel French), *Stirring* (Edinburgh Fringe
Festival) and *The Full Ginsberg*. Charles is a member
of the Dramatists Guild. Charlesforbes@mail.com

(LAUREN, an erudite New Yorker of Vietnamese descent, sits in a pedicure chair, iPhone in hand, suit pants rolled up, cotton balls between her toes. She has requested a specific color of polish...

Below, in a white "nail technician" lab coat, AN, a recent Vietnamese immigrant, prepares to paint LAUREN's toes... if only she can find LAUREN's favorite color. She fumbles through a plastic bin full of different polishes.

AN doesn't speak English—or German for that matter— but keeps presenting a litany of polishes to LAUREN.)

LAUREN: It's called 'Wal-purgis-nacht!' Think: darkest before dawn, winter's night breaking!

AN: *(Incomprehensible, agitated Vietnamese as she searches through the bin.)*

LAUREN: No, no, it's pitch black. With flecks of hope!

AN: *(More incomprehensible Vietnamese as she hold up another incorrect bottle...)*

LAUREN: No, not Wisteria. Walpurgisnacht! It's German.

AN: *(Gesturing towards LAUREN's toes.)* Germs?! Yes, lots! How you say "Mad germs!" I use much alcohol!

LAUREN: Not germs, German. It translates to a caveman's first moment of enlightenment; it's the color of a heathen's first understanding of their humble place in the world.

AN: *(Incomprehensible Vietnamese.)*

LAUREN: *(losing patience)* Can you imagine the color of " being-less-stupid!'?"

AN: *(Incomprehensible Vietnamese, but now louder and angrier.)*

LAUREN: That came out wrong. Okay, settle down! Listen to me: *it's the color of nothing right before there is something.*

(Suddenly, AN stops talking, drops her head and furiously looks through all the colors. LAUREN is surprised at the apparent communication breakthrough.)

LAUREN: (con't) You got *that*? The nothing before the something?

(But it's the presence behind LAUREN that has caused AN's silence A MAN, AN's boss, approaches the women, addressing LAUREN in husky, broken English.)

MAN: Everything okay? There a problem?

LAUREN: No, everything's fine! We are still trying to find my color. But fine. Thanks though!

MAN: An?

(AN looks up at the man and, in her native tongue, launches into a defense that is as angry as it is scared. Although LAUREN (or the audience) can't decipher a word of her manifesto, AN's exaggerated gestures make one thing clear: AN is blaming the delay on LAUREN for being an American princess. Finally, AN ends her tirade by nodding towards LAUREN and making the swirly finger hand-sign for "crazy in the head.'

The MAN sternly taps his watch, then walks away. LAUREN leans down and whispers to AN.)

LAUREN: Did you just make the crazy-in-the-head symbol? That's, like, an international symbol! Did you think I'd miss that? And after I stood up for you? We were in this together, you know? Before you accused me of being a screeching, needy whack-job!

(AN nods politely, not comprehending LAUREN's accusation. She begins to prep LAUREN'S nails with alcohol.)

LAUREN: I'm from Vietnam too. I know struggle. I mean it's a long and complicated story, but I was taken from my orphanage and raised in Macon, Georgia! *(Pause.)* And now that I've said it out loud, my life seems less long and not terribly complicated, but I have worked at shitty places, with shitty bosses, in the exact same skin we share, sister. I mean, no one in Macon wants to spin his or her Camaro around to see my Viet-cong face in the Arby's pick-up window! But I did it. With a smile!

(LAUREN leans back, collects her thoughts.)

LAUREN: *(con't)* This pedicure? It's for an interview. I'm up for a huge promotion. *(Pause.)* A non-salaried lateral-move that *feels* like a promotion. Do you know what I do for a living? Oh, glad you asked! Assistant Director of Chromotism Merchandising for Cosmo Cosmetics. That's right, I name these polishes! I create your colors. Did I just blow you mind?! Hashtag: probably! Without me, you'd be just be digging around in bucket of pinks and blues.

(AN nods again, indicating her process: almost finished cleaning her toes!)

And let's be honest, you're not really good at your job. A ninety-five dollar pedicure isn't supposed to take ninety-five minutes! It's quarter to seven. My job is predicated on me mingling within my industry and it's like you are completely unaware that Happy Hour is over in a few minutes. You don't get it, do you sweetie? Time is running out for you.

Walspurginacht? My idea. What's that? You need "meta" branding for a color that is darker than dark with hints of hope? Well, how about naming it after a female Saint, leading the heathens out of spiritual darkness as the Eastern Europe spring sun dawns on a May morning in 715 A.D.?! Bam! Nailed it! You know now many times you have to Google the word 'black' before you find historical shit like that? And then to present it to a boardroom? It must be nice not to have to look in other people's eyes all day. No forced conversations or brainstorming jam sessions. Just little calcified canvasses all day. What is it like not having to convince others of your creativity? What is it like to have all your thoughts and desires camouflaged by your very existence?

(She looks down at her iPhone.)

LAUREN: Oh, God, it's almost seven! Get up! Get up! Let me try and find it.

(LAUREN crawls down from the pedicure chair, removes AN from her stool, and starts to look for the color herself.

AN looks around, then crawls into the pedicure chair. She surveys the room from the new perspective…and smiles.

As LAUREN searches, AN addresses LAUREN in her native tongue. Although LAUREN assumes AN is directing the search, only the audience can hear her in English.)

AN: Dark before dawn? Winter's night breaking? Please. It's black, bitch! Call it whatever you want: it is tar, it is ink, it is 'eyes-closed,' it is black! AND I've hidden it from you! You will not be finding your flecks of hope in that bucket. And

---

no, I do not speak English, but I understand words. I know that pink is pink and red is red. I know what 'stupid' is. And I am NOT bad at my job.

In fifteen minutes, that man will take your cash, escort you out and pull down the metal gate. Then, he will take me and Han and Linh to the back room. He will order take-out, one dish for three of us. Chinese food, because he thinks he's is being respectful. And then we will wait. And around 7:45 PM, Han will unscrew the only light bulb in the back room, the one over the sink, so only the door cracks glow, and then we will wait some more. At 8:00, a black car will arrive with three older men. They will come into the dark, and my work day will begin.

But, if an irate, crazy customer demands a certain color or screams that we stay open until her nails are perfect, then, that man will place a call to delay the black car. If this happens —sometimes, sometimes— the old men get tired and don't come. That's happened twice in three years. I am not bad at my job.

On Thursdays, I am paired off with a Mexican man from the Bronx who likes to be called, "El Grande." He does not fit this description. In any way. But I am lucky: he is kind and quick. And sometimes calls me by his dead wife's name. And hugs me goodbye. And I find that sweet. Other nights, I get all sorts of demands, but El Grande only asks one thing of me during our time together: keep my eyes open. He keeps his open too. And in that black room, when the door cracks glow, I can see his brown eyes sparkle.

LAUREN: *(lifting up a bottle.)* Oh! I found it! Wait, no! Okay, see this is really close! This is thicker black, with a sticky, gooey after-sheen. I named it… *Valdez Vamp!*

AN: I hate this life, I hate this job, I hate the dark. But to see his eyes? To feel his dead wife's love? *(to LAUREN)* You are not good at your job. It's not even a job. Pushing words around. Looking for hope in jars of black. It's almost 7 on a Thursday night. Time is running out for you.

   (AN reaches into her coat pocket pulls out the Walpurgis-nacht nail polish. In very innocent, broken English…)

AN: Oh? Is this…?

LAUREN: O.M.G! That's it! Where'd you find it? You're gonna love it, especially after it dries!

> (Boldy, AN pulls off one shoe and plops her toes in front of LAUREN. Shocked, LAUREN smiles. Then unscrews the bottle, and wistfully, sloppily, brushes a swath of black on AN's large toe.)

LAUREN: Do you see it now? Dawn breaking?! Heathens humbly accepting their places in life!?

AN: *(in her clearest English yet..)* It's…nothing.

LAUREN: Exactly! Yes!… Before??

> (LAUREN gives her a moment to complete the sentence, as a teacher might a student. But AN is silent. LAUREN gestures to herself and finishes the phrase for her…)

LAUREN: (con't) Something.

> (A Beat.), then a smile breaks across AN's face. A smile breaks across LAUREN's face too. Blackout.)

Characters:

WOMAN: Female, early twenties to thirties.

FAIRY: Male; almost any age can work.

Setting: A child's bedroom in rural Ireland, just before dawn, the present.

JAMES MCLINDON is a member of the Nylon Fusion Theatre Company in New York, and a Next Voices Fellow at the New Rep in Boston. His plays have been produced or developed at theaters across America, including the O'Neill National Playwrights Conference, Lark, PlayPenn, hotINK Festival, Irish Repertory, CAP21, Samuel French Festival, Victory Gardens, Hudson Stage Company, Abingdon, New Repertory, Lyric Stage, Detroit Rep, Great Plains Theatre Conference, Seven Devils, Telluride Playwrights Festival, Ashland New Plays Festival, Boston Playwrights Theatre, Colony Theatre, Theatricum Botanicum, Circus Theatricals, and Arkansas Rep. They have been published by Dramatic Publishing, Smith & Kraus, and Original Works Publishing. jamesmclindon.com

*A distraught WOMAN leans over a crib. She and the
FAIRY speak with Irish accents.*

WOMAN: Dear God, dear God, please: spare my little girl,
spare my baby.

*A FAIRY appears, shabbily dressed. Although he speaks
quietly, he carries a dark menace with him.*

FAIRY: Do you think He'll recognize your voice? So rare it is
that He hears it.

WOMAN: How did you get in? Are you the ambulance service?

FAIRY: The ambulance can't get through. Seems the bridge is
out. Austerity budgets, you know.

WOMAN: Who are you?

FAIRY: One of the good people, I am.

WOMAN: You're, you're a fairy!?

FAIRY: *(Dangerously)* We prefer the good people. You know
why she's sick.

WOMAN: I don't.

FAIRY: Your grandmother's gran would've known. She swung
on the branch of our whitethorn tree. And broke it off, she
did. And now has come the reckoning.

WOMAN: That tree isn't yours. You, you don't own that land.

FAIRY: Ah, well, then, it seems I'm thwarted.

WOMAN: I'm ringing the guards. We'll see if they believe in
fairies.

FAIRY: The telephone's gone out just now, too. And the money
you pay for it, it's a crime.

She is checking the phone. It's true.

WOMAN: Who are you?

FAIRY: I told you. One of God's fallen angels.

WOMAN: What do you want?

FAIRY: How's the child now, missus?

The WOMAN turns to the crib and becomes alarmed.

WOMAN: Ava? Ava!? She's stopped breathing! Please! Good

John Capecci and Irene Ziegler

sir! Help me!

FAIRY: She's young, so we have a bit of time before she's ruined. Or gone.

WOMAN: God and Mary between us and evil!

FAIRY: Ah, you do remember your prayers! But God isn't here. Nor is Mary.

WOMAN: Dear God, please save her!

FAIRY: God's left Ireland, you see. Or is it that Ireland's left Him. I suppose it's much of a muchness.

WOMAN: You must forgive her, good sir, she's hardly three, she didn't know.

FAIRY: You knew. Did you not? You just didn't believe.

WOMAN: Lift this curse and I will, I'll believe. I'll do anything!

The FAIRY begins to slowly circle around her.

FAIRY: But will you also do nothing? For if I cure this wee one, it will be to take her off with me.

The WOMAN begins to circle, too, to stay between him and the child.

WOMAN: No. Never that.

FAIRY: Thwarted again, I am.

The FAIRY continues to circle. The WOMAN stops suddenly. Her right side droops and she crumbles to the floor. She makes odds gurgling sounds. As the scene continues, she struggles to sit up and talk.

FAIRY: Well you've got to speak more clearly, darlin'. But the fairy blast will do that to a girl. They'll just say you've had a stroke, but we'll know, won't we.

The FAIRY approaches the crib and gently strokes the child's forehead with the back of his hand.

FAIRY: Time was when I came for the reckoning, the mothers would say, *(dramatically)* "You can't have her, sir, her soul belongs to God." And I would say, *(calling up to heaven)* "Then let Him send an angel down to claim it." Do you know, sometimes He would and didn't that take the piss out of me.

The FAIRY looks up to heaven. Nothing. The WOMAN tries to crawl towards him, but it's slow progress.

FAIRY: That was long ago, when God still loved the world. Before He abandoned it to us, folk who were here long before Him. Folk who will be here long after. This world may seem to change, but it never does really.

The FAIRY picks up the blanket-wrapped child very gently.

FAIRY: There's a good girl. The cock will be crowing soon so it's good night to you now, missus. The blast will wear off in a bit. Or it won't.

The WOMAN speaks to him out of the side of her mouth. It is a heroic struggle.

WOMAN: Bastard!

FAIRY: What's this then? You can talk.

WOMAN: Take me ... instead!

FAIRY: You'd give me your soul to save your child's?

WOMAN: I would give you ... the souls ... of all the world! Take me!

FAIRY: No love like a mother's. But what need have we of the old? *(Smiling)* None at all, darling.

The smile abruptly changes to a fierce predatory look.

FAIRY: None at all.

He holds the child tight. They disappear.
Blackout.

Characters:

    RICH: A dutiful grown son, twenties to thirties.

    CANDY: A very average Mom, fifties.

    JERRY: Candy's husband, the same age.

Setting: A suburban family's dinner table.

SUSAN GOODELL is author of the full-length plays *Hope Throws her Heart Away* (premiere at Chicago's Genesis Theatrical Productions) and *Heels Over Head* (premiere, Tri-State Actors Theatre; winner, Rover Dramawerk's Seconds Award). These scripts were developed at Virginia Stage Company, The Barrow Group, Provincetown Theatre Company, Tri-State Actors, Festival51 and Atlantic Stage in Myrtle Beach. An evening of her short plays, *One Exit Past Nowhere, Delaware* was presented by AlphaNYC. Individual shorts have been staged at The Abingdon, the Boston Theatre Marathon, NYC's Fresh Produce'd, The Source Festival and Philly's Primary Stages. Other recognition: Steppenwolf Theatre Company commission, Djerassi Resident Artist, Denver Drama Critic's Circle nomination and the Denver Post's 10-best list. newplayexchange.org/users/913/susan-goodell

pdc1.org/memberprofile.php?playwright=339

Band and wife CANDY and JERRY are calmly eating dinner with their grown son RICH.

RICH: These are the best potatoes I've ever eaten mom.

CANDY: You like the chicken this way? I cooked it with lemon.

JERRY: (*Preoccupied.*) It's good. Uh good. I can taste the…uh, uh…

CANDY: What honey.

JERRY: Um. Dear. Something's…(*slowly*) bothering me, and, OK I'll just say it. Here—

RICH: Want me to leave the table?

JERRY: No. Stay. You know when we all ran into your old classmate on our trip last week? What was her name?

CANDY: Nancy, that was Nancy.

RICH: She was very outgoing.

CANDY: She's too old to wear her hair like that.

JERRY: Will you let me say it? What's bothering me about Nancy is the way she kept calling you Mildred. Why did she call you Mildred?

CANDY: Why is that bothering you?

JERRY: Your name is Candy.

CANDY: No dear, it's Mildred.

JERRY: Hon. We've been married 23 years. How can I not know what your name is?

CANDY: Remember the night we met? I saw you, one of the coolest men I've ever seen in my life. I couldn't believe you would even talk to me. So when you seemed interested I told you my name was Candy.

RICH: You told me your name was Candy, too.

CANDY: Naturally if I told your father.

JERRY: So you…All this time you… Gee. But those other things you told me were right? You were really a retired stripper?

CANDY: I almost was.

RICH: You're not a retired stripper? I told everyone in my class…

CANDY: It made you popular, didn't it? (*To JERRY*) You loved that I quit The Life as soon as I met you.

JERRY: So what were you doing when we met?

CANDY: I worked in the handbag department of a department store. I only exaggerated a little.

JERRY: Honey how could you, how could you…

CANDY: When we met that night, I never thought we'd even see each other again, much less get married and have a child. And once we start dating you say how happy you are seeing a retired stripper named Candy when all your friends date boring girls with names like Agatha and Bertha—

JERRY: So all these years you…

CANDY: You're happy aren't you? You love your son.

JERRY: I don't know. I guess it's a good thing. I don't know what to say.

CANDY: So now you know, I hope you can forget and love me for who I am. Mildred Candy.

JERRY: If you thought my name was Alvin, would it have made any difference to you?

CANDY: Alvin? I don't know. Why?

JERRY: Remember the night we met? I'd never picked a girl up before, and I thought if you. *(Winds up courage.)* I'm not Jerry…I'm Alvin. I'm not an environmental lawyer…I'm a textile salesman. I hope it doesn't matter. Tell me it's all right.

CANDY: I…I…

RICH: You're my father. You ever think what it will do to me that…I can't even believe you.

JERRY: I didn't do it on purpose. But once I told your mother, I'm Jerry the environmental lawyer, I started to believe it myself.

RICH: But how did you go to work every day selling textiles?

105 Five-Minute Plays

JERRY: I don't know. I thought I was an environmental lawyer, but just selling textiles that day. I live in the moment.

RICH: I'm trying to understand.

CANDY: Oh, and while we're going over family history, I'm not really you're mother. See, early in our marriage, your father had an affair with a next door neighbor, Mrs. Samuels, and when you were born we all decided you would come over to live with us.

JERRY: Though I eventually discovered Mrs. Samuels had slept with at least seven neighbors, so I'm not sure I'm your father either.

CANDY: She did? Why didn't you tell me?

JERRY: Why complicate things?

RICH: Complicate things. You call this complicating things? Did it ever occur to you this would matter to me a great deal?

CANDY: What does this change? You've always been our little boy, and you wouldn't want to that trampy Mrs. Samuels for your mother.

JERRY: She wore thin very quickly.

RICH: I'm sitting here, and it's almost, like, I don't know who I am anymore.

CANDY: Does anyone know who he really is?

RICH: I thought I did.

JERRY: You're young.

RICH: You know, now that we're revisiting... Remember the day I came home from second grade and you remarked I looked different? Well, that's because, how can I say this... your son, Rich, had got mud on his shirt and he knew he wouldn't get dessert for a week, and since my parents would never notice, and everyone told us how we thought it would be fun to...

CANDY: What!

RICH: It's amazing how much alike Rich and I looked.

JERRY: No. That is wrong, He's has to –

RICH: And then we decided to just stay with—

CANDY: What are you saying, you're not Rich? Yes you are.

RICH: Actually I'm not.

CANDY: Where's Rich? What did you do—

RICH: I don't know. After seventh grade we lost track.

JERRY: You're someone else's son?

RICH: I'm Steve. But I consider you my parents. Actually I liked you better than my parents. I like clean clothes.

JERRY: We did wonder why you've gotten so neat all the sudden.

CANDY: We just assumed something we said finally got through to you.

RICH: That was Rich. You can call me Rich if you like. That's OK.

JERRY: Ah gee.

CANDY: So does anyone have anything else to get off his chest?

RICH: Well actually.

JERRY: Maybe this is enough news for one dinner.

CANDY: Well, I've got dessert in the kitchen, soon as I get some help clearing the table.

> *(Family rises to exit, clearing dishes as they go. Cheerful ad libs as they exit.)*
>
> *BLACKOUT*

Characters:

LARISSA: seventeen to eighteen.

JULIE: early twenties.

They wear winter clothing and boots.

Setting: A changing room in a clothing store in a mall. Evening. It's winter.

It's not necessary to realistically create the changing room. The audience can use their imagination. Maybe use tape to outline the changing room. An acting box is okay. Some women's clothes and plastic hangers scattered around. The mirror can be the fourth wall.

ASHER WYNDHAM is a playwright whose works have been produced across the United States as well as Canada, England, and Australia. His one-act, *Cassius Sargent's Chicken Bones* was awarded the John Cauble Award at the Kennedy Center's American College Theatre Festival, the Holland New Voices Award at the Great Plains Theatre Conference, and a fellowship at the Eugene O'Neill Theater Center. He studied with Lanford Wilson at the Edward Albee New Playwrights Workshop at the University of Houston. His work is published by YouthPlays, Applause, Dramatic Publishing, and Smith & Kraus. newplayexchange.org/users/3039/asher-wyndham

JULIE applies mascara on LARISSA who is seated shivering.

JULIE: Stop moving.

LARISSA: So cold in this changing room. It's like an ice fishing hut.

JULIE: Want your eye poked out? I gotta do the other eye...

LARISSA: It'll seem like forever…

JULIE: I told you: no longer than five minutes. Five minutes means a gift certificate with a big amount. Like fifty dollars....Done.

(LARISSA looks in the "mirror"—the fourth wall.)

LARISSA: What if kids come in?

JULIE: This isn't a toystore. And there's no supervision back here. Just make sure you lock the door before you, y'know. Turn around, lemme do your hair.

(LARISSA doesn't turn around.)

JULIE *(cont.)*: Larissa, turn around.

(JULIE turns LARISSA around and brushes her hair.)

LARISSA: What if he kisses me?

JULIE: I told him not to. Your hair... It's like when you were young... Knots. For real.

LARISSA: Ow… He better not be a smelly fat comic book nerd.

JULIE: Now you're being picky. *(Reveals lipstick.)* Pucker up.

LARISSA: Did you get that on gift certificate?

JULIE: Yep. Luscious Red. Remember, leave a mark.

LARISSA: Like on the stomach, like you. Better not be furry.

JULIE: You choose where you leave yours.

LARISSA: O-kay... Hope he's not old with halitosis.

JULIE: No. He's in his thirties, delivers feed to farms all over the place. I'm not going to be cruel and put you with a geezer for your first time.

LARISSA: Can we just do this another day and get some Taco Bell?

JULIE: You want clown face? Keep your head steady… After you're done, you can get Taco Bell and more—with your mall gift certificate.

LARISSA: …I just want to be Larissa. Don't you just want to be you—Julie—and not some whore!

JULIE: Listen. We can't depend on charity from churches or hand-outs from drivers. We gotta do what we gotta to do to get what we want. Like hygiene products, decent jeans, and good food other than cup noodles. In agreement?

LARISSA: ...I guess so. This sucks. What next? Working at truck stops?

JULIE: No. This is temporary.

LARISSA: We're going to live in your car, forever—with the spiders!

JULIE: No, we're not.

LARISSA: You can't rent an apartment with mall gift certificates.

JULIE: *(reads text message...)* He's in the mall. We gotta hurry. Show me your position. Do it.

(LARISSA reluctantly gets on her knees, head low.)

JULIE (Cont.): You can't give B.J. with your head like that. Head up. Like this.

LARISSA: Like in that porno your ex showed me? No. How do you really know if this guy is clean!? What if he has green dick like Shrek?

JULIE: Duhh: to be safe, you make sure he wears a condom.

(JULIE gives LARISSA a condom.)

LARISSA: Aw, thanks sis. It's flavored.

JULIE: Take your coat off.

LARISSA: *("No")* I'm shivering.

(JULIE quickly unzips LARISSA's winter coat. LARISSA is wearing an ugly Christmas sweater. JULIE laughs.)

JULIE: That's the ugliest sweater on the planet.

LARISSA: Mom gave this to me on our last Christmas as a joke.

JULIE: ...Don't bring up mom. Take it off. And don't smudge your make-up.

(LARISSA takes off her sweater with JULIE's help. And then:)

LARISSA: Mom is looking down at us, crying.

(JULIE breaks away from LARISSA or tries to keep her composure as the big sister. After a moment:)

JULIE: We're on our own, so we gotta get our own stuff. This is the only way, for now!

LARISSA: *(on the verge of tears)* Yeah.

JULIE: *(starts to exit)* I'll be in the shoe section.

LARISSA: *(suddenly)* How do you stop yourself from crying? How?

JULIE: I, I don't cry. Because I close my eyes and think about something else.

LARISSA: Like the way it was when mom was alive? And the house? The fireplace?

(JULIE nods "Yes." The sisters warm up a bit just on the memory of the fireplace and the love of their mother... Then, the cold comes back to the changing room.)

JULIE: Remember, it's temporary. *(fighting back tears)* I promise. See ya, sis.

(JULIE exits with LARISSA's sweater and coat. LARISSA waits, shivering as if she's in an ice fishing hut on the center of a frozen lake at night. She senses the stranger approaching. His footsteps are like cracks on the lake... And then she gets into character. Sexy. It's painful to see.)

LARISSA (Cont.): Heyy. My name is Jenna.

Characters:

BOY

MAN

Setting: Some outlines to suggest the front of a migrant worker's shack. Dustbowl. 1930s.

HOLLY HEPP-GALVAN lives in New York City. Her plays have been presented or developed with Core Artist Ensemble, the cell, The Bechdel Group, Wide-Eyed Productions, The NY International Fringe Festival, The Brick, The Samuel French OOB Festival and more. Full-length plays include *Oddities* (Irv Zarkower Award), *Andrea's Esophagus* (Rita and Burton Goldberg Playwriting Prize), *Cardinia's Calling* (Hunter Playwrights), and *Tamed* (Pioneer Playhouse) Productions for children include *Sprites* (Ballet Austin), *Peter and the Piper, The Big Golt!* and *Trouble on the Double* (Pollyanna Theatre Company). Holly completed her M.F.A. in Playwriting at Hunter College where she studied under Tina Howe. She was a two-time winner of the Irv Zarkower Award and the Rita and Burton Goldberg Playwriting Prize. She was the 2012 Playwright-in-Residence for Voices Inside/Out, a writing program for male inmates, and a finalist for City Theatre's National Short Play Contest. eppgalvan@verizon.net newplayexchange.org

(A shack for migrant workers. A boy peers out the doorway.)

BOY: Mama…?

(He waits and listens. No answer.)

MAMA!

(He comes out and looks around the shack to the left. Nothing there. He runs around to the right – again nothing. Frantically he goes in the house. While he's there, a man walks up. He is wearing striped pants and an old carnival-type jacket. He has only two teeth on his bottom jaw and they stick out of his lips.)

(The boy comes to the doorway and yells in surprise.)

AAAAHH!

MAN: Well that ain't a hello.

BOY: What do you want?

MAN: Well that ain't a hello neither.

BOY: You betta get out of here.

MAN: Now, didn't no one teach you no manners? It's "Hel-lo." Try it, "Hel-lo."

BOY: Hello.

MAN: Ah, now that's better! We're meeting like civilized gentlemen. Now we shake hands.

(He puts out his hand and the boy takes it reluctantly.)

See? That's how you greet someone in polite society.

BOY: My Mama will be back in a minute.

MAN: Well that's fine. But I don't want your Mama. I want you.

BOY: What for?

MAN: Well, I'm looking for a boy to help me with a…an act that I have.

BOY: A what?

MAN: An act. A bit for a show. Have you never seen a show?

BOY: Once. My Mama took me. They had ladies who danced.

MAN: Ah, everybody likes dancing ladies! But my show's different. It has magic.

BOY: Magic?

MAN: Yes. I'm a magician. I make things disappear.

BOY: How do you do that?

MAN: That's a very good question! You're a smart boy, aren't you?

BOY: I guess.

MAN: Oh, I think you are! A very smart boy. And rather than having me explain it to you, why don't I just show you.

BOY: Okay.

MAN: Good. Now watch carefully…

(The Man takes out a shiny ball. He holds it in the air a moment and then tosses it from hand to hand. It is translucent and throws colors all around the front of the shack. The Boy watches intently.)

Isn't this pretty?

BOY: Yes. Can I hold it?

MAN: Sure.

(The Man hands it to him, and the Boy turns it over and over. He holds it up and when it catches the light, it makes his whole body glow.)

BOY: I never seen nothing like this.

MAN: Yes, it's very, very special. And now let me show you something.

(The Man takes the ball back and does some fancy throws up in the air, behind his back and all around the space.)

And….Abra Cadabra!

(With a flourish, he tosses it and it disappears.)

BOY: OH! Where did it go?

MAN: Why it disappeared!

BOY: Can you bring it back?

MAN: Ah…

BOY: Mister, can you bring it back? Please?

MAN: Well…

BOY: Please!

> *(The Man sits down beside the boy.)*

MAN: You see…that's the problem. I can make it disappear, but I can't bring it back.

BOY: Why not?

MAN: Well, magic is a funny thing.

BOY: I don't understand.

MAN: Nobody really does.

BOY: But if you made it disappear, then you can bring it back!

MAN: It doesn't work that way.

> *(The Boy starts to cry.)*

BOY: Bring it back! Bring it back!

MAN: Ssshh.

BOY: I don't like magic!

MAN: Sssh.

BOY: I want Mama!

MAN: When's the last time you saw your Mama?

BOY: Two days ago. She said she was going to get some food. But she didn't come back.

MAN: I bet you're hungry.

BOY: Yes…

MAN: Here.

> *(He reaches into his pocket and brings out a roll in a handkerchief.)*

Would you like this?

BOY: Yes!

> *(He gives it to the Boy and he starts to eat it quickly.)*

MAN: When's the last time you ate?

BOY: *(While chewing)* I don't know. It was back before the men started fighting. And then my brother didn't come back, so my other brother went to go find him. And then *he* didn't come back.

MAN: So it was just you and your mother?

BOY: Yes. And we didn't have no food. So she went to get some.

MAN: And left you here alone.

BOY: She told me to wait.

MAN: You're a good boy.

BOY: Can you bring the ball back, please?

MAN: No, that's not what I do. I can only make things disappear.

BOY: Where did it disappear to?

MAN: Well... a lot of people have theories, but no one really knows.

BOY: Maybe it went to heaven.

MAN: Maybe.

BOY: Do you have any more bread?

MAN: No. I'm afraid not.

BOY: I'm really hungry.

MAN: Ah. You see, YOU'RE like a magician. You had some bread and you made it disappear. Sometimes things are here and sometimes they're gone. *(Beat)* Like your Mama.

BOY: My Mama's coming back!

MAN: I'll tell you what. Would you like to find the ball?

BOY: Yes.

MAN: Well, if I make YOU disappear, then you'll be at the same place that the ball went.

BOY: But if I disappear, then how will Mama find me?

MAN: Well, maybe she'll be at that place, too.

BOY: Really?

MAN: Could be.

BOY: I can find the ball and give it to Mama!

MAN: I bet she'd love that.

BOY: Does it hurt to disappear?

MAN: Sometimes. But usually it's just like going to sleep.

BOY: Okay. Make me disappear, then.

MAN: You're a good boy. Come here.

> *(The Man picks up the Boy. He holds him up and tosses him around just like he did with the ball.)*

And…Abra Cadabra!

> *(The Boy goes limp. The Man lays him gently on the ground and then holds out his hands in a stiff pose.)*

Ta da.

> *(He waits a moment, then bows and straightens.)*

No one ever applauds.

Characters:

SHAWNA

MARIE

Setting: A front porch.

> TALAURA HARMS is a NYC-based playwright and lyricist. Other plays include *Game Night* (for teen actors), *Chrome-Plated Girl*, and the musical *Slaw Slingers!* She also writes for Playbill.com. talauraharms.com

(A front porch. Marie is in a wheelchair with her foot up in a large cast. They are bundled up and Shawna tucks a blanket around Marie.)

SHAWNA: Comfortable?

MARIE: Yeah.

SHAWNA: More cider?

MARIE: My mom—or should I Santa?—always used to put an orange in our stocking. I think it was some weird throwback from the Depression. Not that she was alive in the Depression, but maybe her parents were and so an orange in the stocking was like a real treat or something when they were kids and then they put one in hers and then she put one in ours and out of Depression traditions are born I guess. There was always a full bag of oranges in the refrigerator, too, so it wasn't like OH HOORAY AN ORANGE! More just a shrug and an inventory: candy cane, marshmallow Santa, pencils, orange. I'm still going to put them in my kids' stockings though. Family Christmas will be on Christmas Eve and we will wake up Christmas morning with oranges hung o'er the fireplace with care.

SHAWNA: Cool.

MARIE: Except I'm probably not having kids.

SHAWNA: No?

MARIE: Let's face it. That ship has sailed. That boat has left the dock. That cruise has disembarked. *(Beat.)* That dream has drifted.

SHAWNA: No.

MARIE: It has. I'm too old. And unlovable.

SHAWNA: Not true.

MARIE: Kind of true.

SHAWNA: I love you.

MARIE: I know.

SHAWNA: I do.

MARIE: I'm sorry I don't love you back.

SHAWNA: It's ok. But you aren't unlovable is my point.

MARIE: You don't count.

SHAWNA: That's a terrible thing to say to someone.

MARIE: I really think I'm not a nice person.

SHAWNA: I've seen you be nice.

MARIE: You've seen me be polite.

SHAWNA: No. I'd say nice.

MARIE: Would you say kind?

SHAWNA: They're the same.

MARIE: Not really. Polite: I thank you for bringing me groceries. Nice: You remember that I like Cheez Whiz and Ritz crackers and you throw them in the cart even though they are not on the list. Kind: That you offered to help your broken-footed not-really-very-nice, and certainly not-kind friend.

SHAWNA: How long are you stuck here?

MARIE: I may never walk again.

SHAWNA: So, like what, six weeks then?

MARIE: Yeah, about. It really hurts.

SHAWNA: I'm sure it does.

MARIE: I've never been so still in my life.

SHAWNA: How's that going for you?

MARIE: I like it. I wouldn't have guessed. But I like it. The calm. I used to be so afraid of quiet. I thought that solitude meant loneliness.

SHAWNA: It's only been a week.

MARIE: I can tell though. I can tell.

SHAWNA: So, then the no-kids thing?

MARIE: Might be a choice.

SHAWNA: Because you really aren't too old.

MARIE: A-ha! But I am unlovable!!

SHAWNA: Could you love me back?

MARIE: No.

SHAWNA: Why not?

MARIE: I see. Get me trapped in a chair and ply me with bourbon and Cheez Whiz…

SHAWNA: I'm not going to seduce you.

MARIE: I mean…if you were going to try…bourbon and Cheez Whiz would be the way to go.

SHAWNA: Don't flirt with me. It's not *kind*.

MARIE: And yet, you love.

SHAWNA: And you love that I love.

MARIE: Maybe I do.

> *(Beat.)*

I'm sorry.

SHAWNA: For what?

MARIE: For not being nice. For flirting. For not being able.

SHAWNA: Love-able. *(Long A pronunciation.)*

MARIE: You should go, Shawna.

SHAWNA: Tired?

MARIE: No. I just think you should go now.

SHAWNA: What happened here? Are you mad?

MARIE: No.

> *(Beat.)*

I think you should not come back.

SHAWNA: Wait. What?

MARIE: I will never love you. And I'm being ass to you.

SHAWNA: You're one of my best friends.

MARIE: Except you're in love with me.

SHAWNA: Yeah.

MARIE: So. You should go. And you shouldn't come back.

Because I am not kind and I will keep you around and flirt with you and need you and make you think that maybe one day I'll change my mind. And I won't. But you will stay. And you shouldn't.

SHAWNA: Come on.

MARIE: No.

SHAWNA: Marie.

MARIE: No.

SHAWNA: You're serious.

MARIE: I am.

SHAWNA: You're still going to need help.

MARIE: I can call a nurse for the next week. And then I'll be able to move around here a little better by myself.

SHAWNA: That solitude will turn into loneliness.

MARIE: I'll keep the nurse on an extra week.

SHAWNA: God, you're a bitch sometimes.

MARIE: This is the kindest thing I've ever done.

Death of Comedy, The Copyright by Michelle Hauser. Reprinted by permission of the author. For performance licensing contact mhauser@hotmail.ca

Deep Dish Apocalypse Copyright 2015 by Trey Nichols. Reprinted by permission of the author. For performance licensing contact trey@treynichols.net

Drowning Copyright by Rebecca Robinson. Reprinted by permission of the author. For performance licensing contact rebeccarobinson19@hotmail.com

Each Life Unfulfilled Copyright by Monica Flory. Reprinted by permission of the author. For performance licensing contact monicafloryplaywright@gmail.com

Eight Minutes Copyright by David Lee White. Reprinted by permission of the author. For performance licensing contact davidleewhiteplaywright@gmail.com

Elevator Music Copyright by Kevin Scott Chess. Reprinted by permission of the author. For performance licensing contact swinv@hotmail.com

End of the Line Copyright by Irene Ziegler. Reprinted by permission of the author. For performance licensing contact Iziegler2@gmail.com

End of the Meal Copyright 2004 by Tom Smith. Reprinted by permission of the author. For performance licensing contact tom@tomsmithplaywright.com

Epitaph Copyright by Dana Schwartz. Reprinted by permission of the author. For performance licensing contact danaschwartz29@gmail.com

Favor Copyright by Cristina Luzárraga. Reprinted by permission of the author. For performance licensing contact cristina.luzarraga@gmail.com

Finishing Touches Copyright © 2015 by Michael Frayn, reprinted by permission of Valancourt Books, LLC.

First Song I Learned, The Copyright by Reina Hardy. Reprinted by permission of the author. For performance licensing contact reinahardy@yahoo.com

Fourth Ghost, The Copyright by Arthur M. Jolly. Reprinted by permission of the author. For performance licensing contact info@arthurjolly.com

Friend Copyright by Sara Lyons. Reprinted by permission of the author. For performance licensing contact saralyons1993@gmail.com

105 Five-Minute Plays

COMIC

A Very British Love Scene
All Sales Final
Author Event
Ava Maria
Bad Cop/Worse Cop
Baggage Claim
Bus Stop
Carbon-Based Life Form Seeks Similar
Cess Pool and Lil Tina
Closing Argument, The
Coatroom, The
Cold Calling
Dead Giveaway
Death of Comedy, The
Deep Dish Apocalypse
Eight Minutes
Favor
Finishing Touches
Fourth Ghost, The
Friend
Give Me Back My Scrunchy, Bitch
Interview, The
Just One Time
Last Tree, Easter Island
Look Up
Marriage We Deplore, The
My Emotions are Too Big for This Room
Nice Tie
Noise
Paperboy Comes Before Dawn, The
Pity Party
Pretty Lucky
Ray Play, The
Shipwrecked
SHOT! in the Name of Love
Songwriter, The
Spring Cleaning
Table Manners in Gramercy Park
Tag
True Story of Cinderella, The
Umberton's Umbrella Umporium
Well Really

DRAMATIC

A Gaze Blank and Pitiless
Alone
Anniversary
Christmas in June
Coming Home
Drowning
Elevator Music
End of the Line
End of the Meal
Grey Red Violet
In Transit
Just Before the Drop
Lilies
Mississippi Goddamn
Mussolini and the Negro
My Days are Filled with Numbers
No Way Out
On the Dreamhouse Sea
Pike Market Bathtub
Rounds per Second
Sisters
Spreaded Wings
Twinings
Two Little Sparrows
View From Here, The
Walpurgisnacht!
Watches of the Night
What Some Girls Do for Mall Gift Certificates
Where It Stops, Nobody Knows
With Regards

SERIOCOMIC

410 Days Later
A Joke, Told and Retold
Aboard the Ferry with the Patent Attorney
Andalusia
Bachelor Apartment
Black Press in the White House
Broken Heart Syndrome
Car and Carriage Collide
Clarity of Pizza, The
Cookies
Each Life Unfulfilled
Epitaph

Author	Title
Aaron Adair	*Paperboy Comes Before Dawn, The*
Kimberly Alu	*Alone*
Laura Arwood	*Baggage Claim*
David-Matthew Barnes	*Just Before the Drop*
Andrew Biss	*Carbon-Based Life Form Seeks Similar*
Umberto Boccioni	*Bachelor Apartment*
	Genius and Culture
Carrie Boehm	*Test, The*
Diana Burbano	*Rounds per Second*
Ruben Carbajal	*Car and Carriage Collide*
Kevin Scott Chess	*Elevator Music*
Bruno Corra and Emilio Settimeli	*Grey Red Violet*
Allie Costa	*View From Here, The*
Gabriel Davis	*Anniversary*
Alex Dremann	*Songwriter, The*
Michael Erickson	*Last Tree, Easter Island*
Matthew A. Everett	*Mistletoe #1, Mistletoe #2*
Cheryl Fare	*Bus Stop*
Maria Filimon, Adam Kraar And Tasnim Mansur	*Sisters*
Anne Flanagan	*Ava Maria*
Monica Flory	*Each Life Unfulfilled*
Charles Forbes	*Walpurgisnacht!*
William Ivor Fowkes	*Table Manners in Gramercy Park*
Brynne Frauenhoffer	*Holding*
Michael Frayn	*Cold Calling*
	Finishing Touches
Kati Frazier	*My Emotions are Too Big for This Room*
	Girlfight
Carolyn Gage	*Clarity of Pizza, The*

Scott Gibson	*Spring Cleaning*
Steve Gold	*Mussolini and the Negro*
Susan Goodell	*Well Really*
June Guralnick	*On the Dreamhouse Sea*
Max Gutmann	*Interview, The*
Daniel Guyton	*Dead Giveaway*
Erik Christian Hanson	*Pike Market Bathtub*
Reina Hardy	*Ray Play, The*
	Andalusia
	First Song I Learned, The
Talaura Harms	*With Regards*
Byron Harris	*A Joke, Told and Retold*
Michelle Hauser	*Death of Comedy, The*
Allan Havis	*Aboard the Ferry with the Patent Attorney*
Holly Hepp-Galvan	*Where It Stops, Nobody Knows*
Amanda Hill	*Umberton's Umbrella Umporium*
Tommy Jamerson	*Give Me Back My Scrunchy, Bitch*
Colin Johnson	*Author Event*
	Scorched Earth Tonight
Arthur M. Jolly	*Fourth Ghost, The*
Stephen Kaplan	*Helen Keller Visits Martha Graham's Dance Studio*
David Kodeski	*Christmas in June*
Adam Kraar	*Shipwrecked*
Liam Kuhn	*Bad Cop/Worse Cop*
John Ladd	*Coming Home*
Jennifer LeBlanc	*A Very British Love Scene*
Andrea Lepcio	*She Spider*
	Under Huddlestone
Mark Harvey Levine	*Tag*
Jessica Luck	*Lilies*
Cristina Luzárraga	*Favor*
Sara Lyons	*Friend*
Billy Manton	*Just One Time*
James McLindon	*Watches of the Night*

105 Five-Minute Plays

Charles West	*All Sales Final*
David Lee White	*Eight Minutes*
Thornton Wilder	*Marriage We Deplore, The*
David L. Williams	*A Gaze Blank and Pitiless*
Annie Wood	*Look Up*
Asher Wyndham	*What Some Girls Do for Mall Gift Certificates*
Lior Zalmanson	*Like Friends*
Irene Ziegler	*End of the Line*

JOHN CAPECCI, a former communication and theatre arts professor, owns Capecci Communications (Minneapolis) where he is a consultant, story coach and writer. In addition to editing play and monologue collections, he is co-author of *Living Proof: Telling Your Story to Make a Difference*, a guide to using personal stories to advocate for change (with Tim Cage, Granville Circle Press). He has helped thousands of people from all walks of life use their personal stories and passions to make a difference in the lives of others and better the communities in which they live and work. capeccicom.com livingproofadvocacy.com

IRENE ZIEGLER is an actor, teacher, playwright, and co-editor of seven collections of monologues and plays. She lives in Richmond, VA and participates on many levels in Richmond's diverse theatrical community. She also acts in films and TV, and teaches acting and playwriting. She was the original voice on your smart phone's GPS, and was once yelled at by Anne Bancroft. ireneziegler.com irenezieglervoiceovers.commm